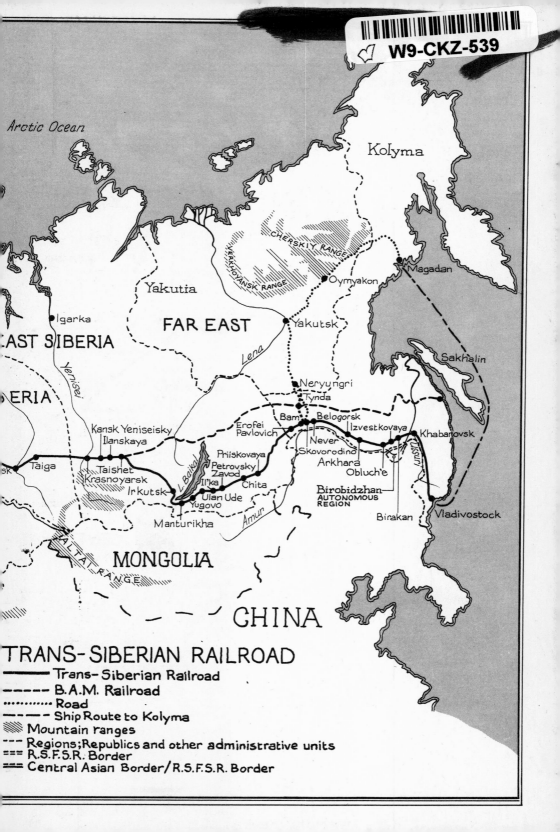

Arctic Ocean

Kolyma

CHERSKIY RANGE

VERKHOYANSK RANGE

Igarka

Yakutia

EAST SIBERIA

FAR EAST

Oymyakon

Magadan

Yenisei

Lena

Yakutsk

Sakhalin

ERIA

Neryungri

Tynda

Kansk Yeniseisky
Ilanskaya

Erofei
Pavlovich

Bam

Belogorsk

Izvestkovaya

Khabarovsk

Taishet

Priiskovaya

Never

Krasnoyarsk

Petrovsky
Zavod

Skovorodino

Arkhara

Obluch'e

sk

Taiga

L. Baikal

Il'ka

Chita

Birobidzhan
AUTONOMOUS
REGION

Ussuri

Irkutsk

Ulan Ude
Yugovo

Manturikha

Amur

Birakan

Vladivostock

ALTAI RANGE

MONGOLIA

CHINA

TRANS-SIBERIAN RAILROAD

—————— Trans-Siberian Railroad
- - - - - - B.A.M. Railroad
·············· Road
- · - · - · - Ship Route to Kolyma
▨▨▨ Mountain ranges
- - Regions;Republics and other administrative units
=== R.S.F.S.R. Border
=== Central Asian Border/R.S.F.S.R. Border

FROM THE YAROSLAVSKY STATION

RUSSIA PERCEIVED

by Elizabeth Pond

UNIVERSE BOOKS

New York

Published in the United States of America in 1981 by Universe Books
381 Park Avenue South, New York, N.Y. 10016

Issued in the United Kingdom as
Russia Perceived: A Trans-Siberian Journey.

81 82 83 84 85/10 9 8 7 6 5 4 3 2 1

Printed in the United States of America.

Library of Congress Cataloging in Publication Data

Pond, Elizabeth.
From the Yaroslavsky station.

Bibliography: p. 278
Includes index.
1. Soviet Union—Social life and customs—
1970– . 2. Soviet Union—Social conditions—
1970– . 3. Soviet Union—Description and
travel—1970– . 4. Pond, Elizabeth. I. Title.
DK276.P64   1981   947.085   81–40497
ISBN 0–87663–368–8   AACR2

This book is dedicated to Petya,
Volodya, Vera Alekseevna,
Vladimir and their
children

CONTENTS

NOTE TO THE READER

You may ask how much of the narrative in this book is "true" and how much invented. My estimate would be 98 per cent for the former, 2 per cent for the latter—a ratio that reflects less on my integrity than on my lack of novelistic imagination. I inserted the more mundane 2 per cent in order to give continuity to fragmentary conversations. The rule of thumb is: the more improbable the anecdote or the remark, the more factual it is.

The rainbows, for example, the exchanges about poetry and God, Petya's escape from the draft, Grandmother's dancing of the Harlequin, and Tanya's spirited defence of Soviet chocolate, glass jars and non-suspiciousness, all happened as here recorded. I have not always followed exact time sequences, however, or attributed the right anecdote to the right person, for reasons that will be obvious to any Westerner with friends in the Soviet Union.

In transliterations I have followed the perhaps unhappy compromise of using the simplest form. Where standard romanizations exist I have employed them (Peking instead of Beijing, Yaroslavl instead of Yaroslavl', Alexander instead of Aleksandr, Gorky instead of Gorkii or Gorkiy). When a word is unfamiliar (*Il'ka, zakonomernost'*) I have transliterated letter by letter. I have dropped diacritical marks in Czech and Slovak names.

E.P.

ACKNOWLEDGEMENTS

My profound thanks go to Henrietta Buckmaster, Agnes and Leo Gruliow, Vladimir Kusin, Melvin Maddocks, Doris Peel, Walter Stoessel, Elisabeth Wendt and Paul Wohl for setting exacting standards of accuracy, perception, and compassion in their review of various chapters or of the entire manuscript. Any failure to meet these standards is, of course, my own responsibility.

I acknowledge the following publishers and authors for material quoted in this book:

To *The Christian Science Monitor* for "Deterring nuclear war" © 1980, "Artists and their inspiration" © 1977, "Soviet Union, a revolution gone conservative" © 1976, "From Russia with Poetry" © 1976, "New Soviet writer" © 1976, "Siberia: song and silence" © 1976, "Grandmother's lib gains in Latvia" © 1975, "Soviets tame 'Tower of Babel'" © 1975, "Soviet secrecy still instinctive" © 1975, reprinted by permission from *The Christian Science Monitor*, The Christian Science Publishing Society.

To William Collins Sons & Co. Ltd, Harvill Press Ltd and Harcourt Brace Jovanovich, Inc., for *Journey into the Whirlwind* by Eugenia Simyonovna Ginzburg translated by Paul Stevenson and Max Hayward (© 1967 by Arnoldo Mondadori Editore—Milano; © 1967 Harcourt Brace Jovanovitch, Inc.); to William Collins Sons & Co. Ltd, Harvill Press Ltd and Harper & Row, Publishers, Inc., for *Gulag Archipelago* by Alexander Solzhenitsyn; to William Collins Sons & Co. Ltd, Harvill Press Ltd and Random House Inc., for *Doctor Zhivago* by Boris Pasternak translated by Max Hayward and Manya Harari, with a revised translation by Bernard Guilbert Guerney; to William Collins Sons & Co. Ltd, Harvill Press Ltd and Atheneum Publishers, for *Hope Against Hope* and *Hope Abandoned* by Nadezhda Mandelstam both translated by Max Hayward; by permission of Oxford University Press for *Memoirs From the House of the Dead* by F. M. Dostoevsky translated by Jessie Coulson, *Notes of a Non-Conspirator* by Efim Etkind translated by Peter France, and *On Stalin and Stalinism* by Roy Medvedev translated by Ellen de Kadt; reprinted with permission of The Bodley Head and Random House Inc., for *The Yawning Heights* by Alexander Zinoviev in the translation by Gordon Clough; Rosemary Edmonds' translation of *Resurrection* by Tolstoy reprinted by permission of Penguin Books Ltd; to William Heinemann Ltd and Coward, McCann &

Geoghegan, Inc., for *A Small Town in Germany* by John Le Carré © Le Carré Productions 1968; to Victor Gollancz Ltd and E. P. Dutton & Co. Inc., for *One Day in the Life of Ivan Denisovich* translated by Ralph Parker © Victor Gollancz Ltd 1963; to the Estate of Avrahm Yarmolinsky for *An Anthology of Russian Verse* edited by Avrahm Yarmolinsky; to Ardis Publishers, for *Snowball Berry Red and Other Stories* by Valery Shukshin, edited by Donald M. Fiene © Ardis 1979, and *Selected Poems* by Anna Akhmatova edited by Arndt © Ardis 1976; to Jonathan Cape Ltd and Holt, Rinehart & Winston CBS Inc., for "Fire and Ice" from *The Poetry of Robert Frost* edited by Edward Connery Lathem © Holt, Rinehart & Winston 1969.

Acknowledgement is also due to Ms. Magazine for a small portion of this work which appeared in that journal.

E.P.

FROM THE
YAROSLAVSKY
STATION

CHAPTER I
MONDAY THE INTRODUCTION

Through our short laughter and cries
I hear a melody blown
By some trumpeter-to-come.
Song by Bulat Okudzhava

Seek the truth
Listen to the truth
Teach the truth
Love the truth
Abide by the truth
And defend the truth
Unto death.
Prayer by Jan Hus

10.00   Moscow's Yaroslavsky Station

SO THIS IS the Trans-Siberian Railroad—that monument, instrument, fable, and epitaph of Russia. This is the carrier of all those Promethean dreams and sacrificial deaths that once spanned the wilderness of the Eurasian continent. This was the defiant *fin-de-siècle* proof that Russia was as civilized as the despised and envied West.

The Trans-Siberian was the thrust of Russian destiny to the East, a quest for the unfettered frontier, for industrial salvation—and for that superior mystic Slavic soul. Or, alternatively, it was the Antichrist of modernization, of man's betrayal of the earth that would eventually damn the betrayer to eternal apocalypse. All of Russia's yearning and suffering poured into this symbol of blessing—or curse.

A few steps from this spot Count Vronsky met and fell in love with the unfortunate Anna Karenina as she arrived on the Petersburg train. From these tracks almost half a century later the colourful Bolshevik propaganda locomotives steamed out to convert the masses to the Communist revolution. From this teeming station Dr Zhivago fled the new utopia, only to be swept up in the chaos of civil war. From here Eugenia Ginzburg left Moscow in the 1930s on her way to spend a quarter of a lifespan in some of the worst camps of the Gulag Archipelago.

For years I have longed to ride these rails, to see for myself the Russia of the early Dostoevsky, the late Tolstoy, and yes, the ripe and raging Solzhenitsyn. My imagination leaps.

But here on a cement train platform, on a Monday morning at ten o'clock, the legend mocks itself. Today's Trans-Siberian is mundane. It eschews all fanfare, pretensions, romance. It's made of no-nonsense East German steel; it bears the prosaic title of "Train No. 2". Existing only in the solid proletarian present, it scorns any ephemeral past. It is ideologically equal, a stubbornly unexceptional train among all its peers in the Soviet Plan. Its colour is red, but this too is functional—a political rather than a festive or regal red.

Even Yaroslavsky Station—belying its nightly entrepôt trade of low-grade prostitutes and sleepy between-train provincials failing the rank to win scarce hotel space in the capital—looks aggressively utilitarian and drab by day. Commuting workers line up at kiosks to buy *Pravda* and lottery tickets. Teary relatives see off more serious travellers with sausages, wild flowers and pickled mushrooms. Train compartments fill with the Moscow-purchased Polish shirts, Czech shoes and other finery of today's prosperity.

The conductor locks the door. We pull out slowly, in the custom of Russian trains. Several friends run alongside the car to wave goodbye until the last moment of parting.

I check out the literature provided gratis in the train's pamphlet library. "Essays in Scientific Communism" and "The Strait of Neo-Colonialism" are the offerings in English, along with "The Liberation Mission of the Soviet Army 1941–1945" in Spanish and "Lenin's Party Congress Speeches" in Japanese and Vietnamese. I learn from a brochure that foreign tourists on the Trans-Siberian must get a veterinary certificate for "animals (dogs, cats, monkeys, etc.) and birds" and that they may carry with them "musical instruments (except pianos and grand pianos), a bicycle, two watches, ten metres of fabric [and] knitted goods (three items per person)". I'm safely within all the quotas.

10.30 Moscow Province

Abruptly, Moscow's concrete-slab apartment buildings fall behind us. We plunge into Russian history. Birch and pine woods predominate, opening up only occasionally into cleared fields and villages of aquamarine- and cyan-painted houses. This is the heartland of Russia, the crude northern forest that supplanted a cultured Kiev in the thirteenth century, was ravaged sporadically by Mongols for the next two centuries, then held itself aloof from all the medieval scholarship and sudden Renaissance of the West. The train cuts through Zagorsk, site of the fourteenth-century St Sergius monastery; Alexandrov, sixteenth-century birthplace, under Ivan the Terrible, of that enduring Russian institution of the secret police; and

Rostov-the-Great, whose splendour outshone Moscow's before Muscovy subordinated the surrounding regions.

As soon as decorum permits, one of my travel mates plucks off her wig of prodigious, cascading, blonde curls and hangs it decisively on a wall peg. Despite her Samsonite loss Tanya retains full authority, and organizes her little band of a high-school daughter and a septuagenarian mother for the fifth time since we boarded the train. They have been vacationing in the Ukraine and are now making the seven-day, 5,800-mile trip home across two continents and seven time zones to the Soviet Far East. Tanya's husband always flies, and from his access to plane tickets I guess (accurately, it turns out later) that he is a military officer.

When daughter, mother and grandmother stand together, the three generations are like stepping stones. Grandmother, her face softened into wrinkles, her white hair pulled back in a bun and secured by a comb, is the shortest. She is officially seventy-three but actually seventy-six; somehow her documents dropped three years when she was evacuated as a girl from the north to the south during World War I. Tanya is taller than her mother, but just as plump. Her own hair is blonde and curly, but not as luxuriant as her wig. Nina, with longer sandy hair, an open face, and a slimmer figure despite her shared big Russian bone-structure, is the tallest. All are pug-nosed.

The three women are travelling on only one paid ticket, since Tanya works for the railroad and is entitled to free fares for herself and one other family member. Workers, she points out, are well taken care of in the Soviet Union.

Tanya grew up in the rich Kuban farmland and has the plainsman's distrust of forests—even the rather domesticated ones we are passing through now—as dark and menacing. She stares out of the window, fretting over black stormclouds and farmers' neglect of fields. She scowls at the tiny groomed private plots and the immorality of tending one's own garden at the expense of collective land. But she rallies to identify the passing flowers for me: colza, St John's wort, blue veronica, cosmos, Queen Anne's lace, camomile, swan flower, purple Ivan's tea.

I exchange my lower bunk for Grandmother's upper bunk so that she won't have to clamber on top whenever she wants to doze. This earns a scolding from the conductor, who checks our tickets and lectures Grandmother that it is forbidden for a Russian to change places with a foreigner. Grandmother snorts at the idiocy of such a rule and lies down assertively on her lower berth as soon as the conductor leaves our compartment. Since Moscow's few hotel rooms are always fully occupied by the top Soviet elite and foreigners, the family did not have a hope of getting beds, and had to spend all last night sitting up in Yaroslavsky Station with hundreds of other travellers. But since the police constantly make vagrants move along in the

stations, the women couldn't catch much sleep there. *Ketch Dvadtsat' dva*—
except that Far Easterners probably haven't yet adopted Moscow's sardonic
plagiarization of "Catch Twenty-two".

It's easy enough to nap in our four-bunk "hard" compartment. It doesn't
quite achieve the elegance of the mirrored, draped and frescoed Empire
sleeping-car displayed as a wishful sample of Trans-Siberian service at the
turn-of-the-century Paris Universal Exposition. But the combination seat-
berths are sufficiently long to stretch out on, and the wide-gauge heavy-steel
ride is smooth. Hard class is friendlier than the elite two-bunk "soft" class and
roomier than "common" class, where more than fifty tiered unpartitioned
bunks are packed into each stuffy car. We pay a little over $100 (£42) for the
week's trip and rental of sheets, blanket, towel and pillow. "Cheaper than
turnips," Tanya notes.

The conductor's wife brings us glasses of steaming tea from the coal-
stoked samovar at the end of the car and tots up a few kopecks on a mental
bill to be paid at the end of the journey. Tanya clucks disapprovingly when I
don't add sugar to my tea and counsels me to "improve myself". Her
admonition is so familiar that I can't suppress a smile. Russians always think
that Westerners aren't chubby enough—and they are still consciously
pleased, after years of deprivation, to have unlimited sweets. They lavish
sugar on a visitor as a sign both of health and hospitality, and the inattentive
guest who fails to guard his glass will find his second sip of tea far sweeter
than his first.

Tanya, I discover in the next few hours, is the real Russia. Provincial.
Suspicious. Proud and defensive simultaneously. Powerful, as an army wife,
and glad of it. Enormously sophisticated in terms of her own peasant past,
naive in any broader European context. If the American housing exhibit had
been shown in Vladivostok, she would surely have been one of those who
waited in line for four hours to see it, then castigated the American guides
for putting so much "non-breathing" plastic in a children's room—and then
immediately boasted that Soviet plastics production will soon catch up with
the US. Tanya is a godsend. I don't meet Russians like her in Moscow. In the
capital all I meet are intellectuals, propagandists and drunks.

Not that I don't like that lot. In my two years as a correspondent in
Moscow some of my best friends have been intellectuals, and some of my
most amusing encounters have been with sloshed proletarians. But as I
make my farewell trip on the Trans-Siberian I still lack a sense of how
ordinary Russians think. For this, Tanya is superb.

In this paranoid country it seems the closest I can get to the man on the
street is the woman on the train. Muscovites—apart from those dissidents,
intellectuals, and starved gum-chewers who actively seek out foreigners—
wear the armour of city-dwellers the world over, as well as the armour of
xenophobia. They shrink from pick-up conversations. Or, more bel-

ligerently, they resent and threaten foreigners photographing Moscow's Sunday pet market or log houses or anything else they believe is backward. Perhaps they feel protective. Perhaps they fear reprisals from the KGB secret police if they fraternize with foreigners. Whatever their motivation, they are as ready to chat as a cub-nursing mother bear.

The situation is even worse on group trips for foreign journalists arranged by the Foreign Ministry. All my visits to collective farms during my term as a reporter have been meticulously organized to exclude any risk of unplanned conversation with plain farmers. Instead, lectures by the kolkhoz chairmen are succeeded by three-hour official banquets, with food and sometimes even cooks imported from a nearby city. At best we are allotted a half hour *al fresco* drive around the actual farm. On these tours ordinary kolkhozniks are conspicuously absent from the clubhouse, store and fields we are shown—and if any maverick journalist takes it into his head to mingle with the natives and walk the two hundred yards to the next destination he is quickly herded back onto the collective bus.

Nor is it just peasants. In this proletarian state foreign correspondents are shielded from any spontaneous contact with proletarians. On one Foreign Ministry trip to show off the second Trans-Siberian Railroad that the Russians are now constructing at breakneck speed, almost all of the workers at Kilometre 13 out of Ust' Kut were conveniently given a holiday on the weekday we dropped in. And when some of us did find a few bridge assemblers to talk to anyway, we were abruptly summoned back to the bus by that vehicle's ineluctable airhorn. "Oops, we almost got to meet a worker," became the standard witticism of the tour—uttered by bemused Polish and East German as well as by American and French correspondents.

The precautions reached their peak on a Foreign Ministry trip to the Autonomous Republic of Dagestan on the Caspian Sea. It wasn't as bad as Stalinist times, when foreign journalists were transported in buses shrouded in black curtains. Nor was it as bad as the sixteenth century, when the monk Maxim the Greek, after journeying to Russia to give liturgical advice at the request of the Muscovy Grand Prince, was detained in Russia for almost forty years because "thou, a man of learning, comest to us and hast seen here of our best and worst, and when thou goest hence thou wilt tell of everything." The aura was the same, however.

Our trip was a special treat, the first time in eight years that Western reporters were allowed to go to Dagestan and to its mountain village of Gunib. Gunib, nestled in crags at 9,500 feet, is where Shamil held out for a quarter of a century against the infidel Russian tsarist occupiers a hundred years ago. Dagestan is the tiny, fiery, dagger-manufacturing land of one million people and three dozen discrete languages that have maintained their stubborn separateness through the ages.

Our non-meeting with the people of Gunib began with a five-hour bus trip from the Dagestani capital—and no, we would not be allowed to stay overnight in the picturesque village. We arrived at Gunib at noon, but the bus, without stopping, continued climbing hairpin turns for another mile to a "tourist base" isolated from the village.

There our schedule was announced: the inevitable banquet with local government and Communist Party officials, followed by talks with these officials. At the end—time unspecified—we would be taken to the village proper just before leaving on the five-hour bus-ride back to our seaside hotel.

As this was by now our fourth day of quarantined banquets in Dagestan we grew restive and managed to break up the feast by 3.15. And this time we even managed to elude the bus and descend the spectacular hairpins on foot. As we walked, our attention was drawn in the treeless panorama to a man in an incongruous black suit preceding us on the road below. The man spoke briefly with all the villagers out on the street, and every one of them vanished into a house, even though the siesta hour was clearly over. By the time we got down to the houses curiosity had again drawn the villagers out to the street. The unidentified stranger in black—whom they assumed to be a KGB agent—had ordered them to stay indoors, they told us, though they couldn't guess why. Who were we anyway? We introduced ourselves—but were always cut off from further conversation by officials who materialized to silence the villagers and tell us themselves what the villagers thought.

We had been promised a 5 p.m. departure time from Gunib. But as punishment for our unruliness we were all suddenly rounded up at 3.50 and deposited on the waiting bus. It was a long trip back, our escorts explained, and the road was dangerous after dark.

Occasionally trains are just as bad. Even in its heyday détente couldn't erase two generations of steady xenophobia. And especially in détente's heyday, party and government officials and Komsomol members were instructed to preserve a proper distance between foreigners and Soviet citizens. In the Ukraine one conscientious conductor evacuated everyone else from my compartment when it became the most popular gathering place in the car. In Lithuania two fellow-passengers in my compartment stepped out into the corridor as soon as they learned I was an American—and returned only in time to retrieve their luggage at our destination six hundred miles later.

But then I've also had more relaxed times on railroads—and I've never had a relaxed time on a Foreign Ministry tour. On trains passengers are thrown together in their compartment cocoons, and it requires superhuman will not to converse when four people must move each other's feet to rummage in suitcases, stand together in the toilet line, compromise on ventilation and an equitable loudspeaker volume, and defer to each other's privacy, in a mixed compartment, for pyjama changes. On trains I have been told people's life histories, pressed to visit their homes, and of course included in communal meals. One neatly combed older collective farmer—from Tanya's black-earth Kuban region in fact—made me celebrate with him his receipt of a mechanics diploma from a correspondence school a few hours before we met. One sanitation worker—whose brother is a high-wire acrobat in a circus, and whose adolescent son is in the stage of infatuation with horses—asked in troubled tones why the US was taking so long to become friendly with the Soviet Union. One state farmer catalogued the entire yield of her kitchen garden and criticized for me all the plots that passed by our window.

After meetings like these, foreign reporters always wonder anew why the authorities make such pariahs of us. When we occasionally evade the restrictions and meet real people with real feelings we always warm to Russia. We grow more tolerant of her foibles, more understanding of her fears. Why not, then, soften us up by letting us meet "the people" instead of alienating us by blocking human contact?

In part, no doubt, the Russians suspect us all of being spies—a flattering Walter Mitty notion once upon a time that has now been inflated to a chronic threat of expulsion. Indeed, given the all-encompassing Soviet definition of secrecy, we are spies. We aren't apt to ferret out missile sites from the villagers of Gunib. Nor, with our Hamlet-like reservations about our own societies, are we likely to prove so eloquent in extolling them as to sow discontent among the almost mystically patriotic masses here. We might, however, hear the humdrum daily complaints about lack of meat, or school uniforms, or motivation. And these dearths are top secret.

For this very reason foreign journalists have acquired a wildly exaggerated popular reputation in the Soviet Union. In a rigid and unresponsive system we have become an appeal of last resort. If Jews, after talking to us, are inexplicably permitted to emigrate, then we must be bureaucrats worth cultivating. If Andrei Sakharov, after constantly prattling his incomprehensible views on "human rights" to us, is still not jailed, then we must possess formidable power. If the local kolkhoz store, in honour of our visitation, is suddenly stocked with consumer goods that have been unavailable for years, then we must be a more effective channel of appeal than the kolkhoz chairman. So we are a fair target for the grumblings of anyone who has collided with the indifference or hostility of Soviet clerks.

The grievances might be political, but they might just as well be personal. An ethnic German who wanted to emigrate insisted that I publish documents she said proved corruption by some district official who had turned her down. A Dagestani cook surreptitiously solicited my help in getting employment in a shashlik restaurant in Moscow. A Byelorussian worker sought redress when he was fired from a job, he claimed, for proposing unwelcome ways to improve efficiency at his place of work. An engineer

accused me of discrimination when I wouldn't hawk some deep-sea inven-
tion of his that no Soviet enterprise would adopt for manufacture. Similarly,
one Moscow woman accosted dissident Vladimir Bukovsky to get the topic
of her leaky roof aired on the BBC as a prod to the delinquent repairman.

In its wisdom, then, the Kremlin is trying to insulate us not only from the
real dissidents, but also from the everyday gripers that lurk everywhere. To
a large extent it is succeeding—at the ironic cost of also insulating us from
the attractive, warm-hearted side of Soviet life.

The best thing, of course, would be to see this country with Petya or
Volodya. But that could hardly be. Neither of them has the right connection
to purchase a scarce Trans-Siberian ticket. And if they did their careers
would be damaged by travel with a foreigner.

Petya is so intellectual he's almost a caricature. He is thin, absent-minded,
careless of nourishment and warmth. His friends constantly have to feed and
clothe him just to insure his physical survival. He has a steady stream of
girlfriends, and is hopelessly in love with each in succession.

He argues that the US should have held fast in Vietnam to resist Communism. He is scandalized when I tell him that religion is not taught in
American public schools. He rejects my advocacy of a better deal for Soviet
women, asking why any woman should want a good position in such an
exploitative society. The shocking poverty and loneliness of elderly people
in the Soviet Union should be tended to first, he insists, and then it will be
time enough to worry about the equality of women.

Petya intended, when he got drafted, to apply to emigrate and thus not
have to serve as a soldier, and he totally dismissed my warnings that he
would never be allowed to leave under such conditions. He is an incurable
dreamer. He adores Solzhenitsyn.

Volodya admires Solzhenitsyn too. If I happen to drop in on him during
the twenty-four hours in which he has a smudged carbon typescript of
Solzhenitsyn's latest novel, I abandon any hope of talking to him. He will
stay up all night and read, then on his way to his job in the morning pass the
precious manuscript on to another friend in the chain.

But Volodya believes in working within the system. He has long since
survived his years of conscription. He has never been in the Gulag, though a
number of his friends have. He is gentle; he bestows peace unselfconsciously
on others. He is a 1980s Prince Myshkin, to whom shopgirls naturally give
saved bits of beef, or perhaps the only umbrella for sale in all Moscow, quite
without expecting any bribe or reciprocal favour. Almost uniquely among
Moscow husbands, he helps with housework and shopping. He comes home
of an evening, opens up his antique briefcase on the kitchen table, and
routinely extracts potatoes, beets or bananas from it.

Photographs attest that Volodya once looked quite dashing in a neatly trimmed beard. The principal at his school made him shave it off, however, under threat of having part of his salary withheld if he didn't. He was only amused by the threat, but for the sake of harmony he complied. I shall miss Volodya.

And, I realize, I shall miss my staff, my own "kollektiv". To be sure, they were all provided by the Diplomatic Corps Administration, the KGB-run organization charged with the quotidien sustenance—and surveillance—of all foreign diplomats, journalists, and businessmen in the Soviet Union. But they too were friends.

My translator, Anatoly Dmitrievich, loved the language of Pushkin. He winced at every desecration of this noble Russian in the popular press— though he would never see in *Pravda*'s cant the inevitable linguistic perversion of propaganda. Surprisingly, given his innate insistence on the precision of words, Anatoly was a magnificent simultaneous interpreter. He once interpreted non-stop for two hours (in Dagestan) at a meeting that had turned into sheer bedlam, with editors, composers, writers and a woman state-farm chairman all speaking at once. In the midst of the commotion he remained, as always, cool and in control.

Anatoly remembered the German occupation well, even though he was only a child at the time. He lost an older brother in the war. His family lost their home as well; before their eyes the Nazi soldiers dynamited it and every other house on their street. Anatoly was sent to live at his uncle's mill, and his uncle uncomplainingly eked out enough flour to feed the young boy as well as his own family.

The son of a shepherd turned steelworker, Anatoly received his education under the Soviet system, and he was grateful. With this education he had risen high, working for foreigners and earning a salary double the average industrial wage.

His role called for it, of course, but he also seemed genuinely affronted by dissenters who criticized Russia. His voice took on a hard edge when he talked about dissidents—and especially when he talked about religious pacifists who refused service in the Red Army. To one growing up under German occupation such people were unforgivable shirkers.

Sasha, my driver, was more withdrawn. My conversations with him centred almost exclusively on our Volvo, which was showing the ill effects of five Moscow winters with no garage. In the best male tradition Sasha was fascinated by engines and motorcars. If he had grown up an American he would have reconstructed his own jalopy by the age of fifteen. As it was, he had to settle for patching up my carburetor when it ailed, or taking the passenger door apart to lock the malfunctioning window shut instead of open. Because of Sasha *glushatel'* and *amortizatory* will forever remain my primary terms for muffler and shock absorbers.

How about getting a new Volvo, Sasha would ask me as often as he dared, or a nice big American car? The average age of Volvos in their fatherland, I would reply sternly, is 16.9 years; and Sasha would continue to yearn silently for a car that might tempt some smitten Georgian millionaire to gesture an offer of 25,000 roubles for it as we cruised the streets of Moscow.

Sasha's other male prerogatives were his weekly visit to the bathhouse to sweat and drink with his buddies in Russia's ancient communal ritual—and a Tyrolean hat with a feather that he once asked me to bring back from Austria. He was immensely pleased with the hat, though he never modelled it for me, and I never could visualize this very specialized headpiece above Sasha's Slavic cheeks and plaid workshirt.

Galya, my maid, was as effervescent as Sasha was literal, and the two were complementary foils in my Russian practice. Galya would reply to my meaning before I had even finished a sentence and force me to follow the flow of a rapid conversation. Sasha, for all his knitted-brow efforts, could never grasp what I was saying if any major word were missing, or if a mistaken case-ending skewed a noun into an impossible relationship with its fellow nouns. Sasha forced me to speak in complete grammatical sentences if the car was to run at all.

Like Anatoly Dmitrievich, Galya remembered her village upbringing. But unlike Anatoly Dmitrievich, she remembered it with nostalgia rather than relief. She had loved dancing in the village square in summer and lying on the warm tile stove in winter. She liked the closeness of knowing everyone and having everyone know her, and with her perpetual cheerfulness she must have had a string of boyfriends.

Galya eventually married a city man, however, and now had seven-year-old twins: a robust, outgoing girl and a fastidious, poetic boy. The boy was saving his money to buy a baby brother or sister; he had campaigned for one, and, sensing some resistance on his parents' part, had decided that cost was the stumbling block. How much would a baby cost? he had asked Galya, and she had given a distracted estimate of a hundred roubles. From then on he had been hoarding his kopecks toward the day when he could walk into a baby store and place his hundred roubles on the counter.

I leave behind other friends in Moscow too. Tamara Nikolaevna, who worries that her nine-year-old son will be smothered by the intolerant Soviet society because he is (as she is not) a believer in God. Alyosha, who lives only for Western jeans and Western rock music, who has every angle figured and always manages to wriggle out of the obligatory "voluntary" potato picking in the autumn and vegetable sorting in the winter. Natasha, who survived twenty minutes of clinical death during her last abortion, and was afterwards advised by her matter-of-fact doctor to go and light a candle in church, just in case.

13.50 Approaching Yaroslavl

We cross the Volga, Russia's "Mother of Rivers", the longest in Europe, the inspirer of countless poems and songs. At Yaroslavl the Volga is less majestic and more personal than in the south, where even far inland it reaches widths of twenty-five miles. The Volga, says a fairytale that surely originated here rather than downstream in Kazan, awakens and flows neither too slowly nor too fast, but just as a river should flow. In the south the Tatars might sing of the Volga's power as they strained against it, beasts of burden pulling their barges. But in the north the Russians spun stories celebrating the river's moderation.

It is high summer now, and the Volga is in constant shimmer. Its pulse is visible. Its procession of steamers and transport boats augurs the unknown around every next bend. Its shady banks and its long northern days invite shashlik picnickers to escape from their cramped apartments.

But this is ephemeral. In this latitude the Volga is rarely warm and hospitable. Its more natural state—the one that has left an indelible mark on Russia—is winter's frost. The frozen river is a friend, making a smooth ice road for horse-cart, train and truck, providing a three- or four-month respite between the perennial autumn and spring "roadlessness" of impassable mud. But the frost is also a recurrent foe, threatening the very life of anyone who loses the protection of fur and fire.

Climate does not invariably predestine national culture. The Scandinavians, who share the harsh Russian winters, fend off the cold with saunas and handsome wooden huts, and metamorphose the ice blues, autumn russets, and spring greens into luminous design. The Japanese of Hokkaido harmonize with nature, venerate any specially felicitous rock or tree—and carve their hard-packed snow into giant sculptures.

In Russia, however, the ravages of winter induced neither a predilection for subtle colours nor yet the American compulsion to conquer nature. They produced instead a fatalism that was only strengthened by the land's constant wars and plagues, lice and rats, and the fires that ignited wooden chimneys and consumed thousands of dwellings every year. Man had no hope of vanquishing fate; his highest goal was simply to persevere, to outlast the cold or famine or terror until the season of the next miraculous spring.

14.00 Yaroslavl

"The painted and gilded bell-towers, almost as numerous as the houses, in Yaroslavl, shine from a distance," wrote the celebrated French traveller, the Marquis de Custine, in the 1830s. In Yaroslavl-the-Great, as in the whole Golden Circle ringing Moscow, the soaring onion domes of sixteenth- and seventeenth-century Russian Orthodox churches defy and at the same time accentuate the monotonous horizontal landscape. Once upon a time they aspired to free the spirit of men trapped in drudgery and mud.

In the latter days the churches' imagery plummeted from spire to dungeon wall. In Joseph Stalin's blasphemy, the emptied monasteries in Yaroslavl and elsewhere were turned into prisons for the overflow of purge victims from the inadequate civil jails. It was here in 1937 that Communist Party activist Eugenia Semyonovna Ginzburg was placed in a solitary cell, wondering why she had been arrested by her own party, straining every effort not to forget how to speak.

"To my dying day I shall not forget the clear, high-vaulted Yaroslavl sky," she wrote after her ultimate release:

No other town has anything to compare with it. And besides, one could sometimes see gulls flying over from the Volga. . . . And the ships' sirens! How can words convey what they meant to a prisoner in solitary confinement, especially to one who, like me, had lived by the Volga?

In those first years of imprisonment Ginzburg had sixteen hours of enforced leisure every day, with ŋo books, exercise, or lying down allowed.

So what was left? Poetry . . . only poetry . . . my own and other people's. . . . After dinner was my time for Pushkin. I gave myself a lecture about him, then recited all I could remember of his poems. Like a chrysalis transformed into a butterfly, my memory, cut off from all outside impressions, suddenly blossomed.

Ginzburg was fortunate, as was a fellow Gulag detainee who occupied her time by recalling and translating the bulk of Byron's "Don Juan", then committing the translation to memory until her release. Others, anticipating arrest, deliberately memorized poetry in preparation, only to have their recollection fail in the shock of the camps.

In 1939, when even the extra monasteries got too crowded with Stalin's endless prisoners, Ginzburg and her sister Yaroslavl convicts were loaded into a wooden freight car marked "special equipment", for delivery to Siberia. After the horrors of solitude, the move was a relief. "Penal servitude—what bliss!" they thought, quoting Boris Pasternak. A labour camp would at least mean "travelling to new lands, rugged ones perhaps, but there would be fresh air, wind, and sometimes even sunshine". On that first communal day they became intoxicated by talking once again with a variety of fellow human beings. And as the train pulled out of Yaroslavl "some began to recite verses, sing, and tell stories even before installing themselves on the wooden bunks. . . . Everyone . . . was rejoicing in the sound of her own voice." One subject alone was banned as too lacerating—any talk of the women's absent children.

In today's less tumultuous times the same train ride is boring to a Russian high-school student. From her perch on the top bunk Tanya's daughter complains, "You just ride and sleep, ride and sleep." She sings along with the tape-recorded pop songs on the train loudspeakers.

Nina's complaint is familiar; I have often encountered it in Western accounts of the Trans-Siberian. The travellers never define their malaise as their own lassitude. But the mattresses are thin. The bunks are uncomfortable. The food is inedible. The scenery is amorphous. The frustrations build up with the relentlessness of the clacking train wheels. There is nothing to do but sleep, fitfully. Nina dozes off again.

Tanya naps a lot too. But she has more awe than her daughter does for the Russian *prostor* or unfettered vastness—actually, the word she uses is the less mystical *gromada*—that the ride displays. She is, after all, one of the rare European Russians who have thrown in their lot with the Soviet campaign to populate Siberia, and after only a few years in the Far East she is already a local fan.

For the moment Grandmother shares neither her granddaughter's ennui nor her daughter's euphoria. She is far too practical for either emotion. Her sleep is no oblivion of escape, but a peasant husbanding of resources against the next harvest time and its twenty-hour day. She no longer lives a rural life. But for her as for all of Russia the peasant cycle of idleness alternating with frenetic activity is still habitual.

18.24   Nikolo Poloma

"But how does Russia feel?" my American friends ask me. "What does it mean? What is it really like?"

It's sputniks and superconductivity. It's Sasha going to the bathhouse every Thursday—and men in black suits ordering villagers off the streets of Gunib until the plague of foreign journalists has passed. It's Anatoly Dmitrievich remembering the wartime deaths of his brother and twenty million others—and Tanya underscoring all the Soviet virtues, lest a foreigner miss them.

It's black bread that smells like a ploughed field after rain—and sour milk, in five varieties, with five distinct names. It's trucks that circle Moscow's ring road loaded with precast concrete building sidings, with bulk flour in cement-mixer drums—or with nothing at all, in order to fulfil monthly mileage plans.

Most of all, the Soviet Union is conservatism incarnate. Six decades ago this country "shook the world" with revolution—in art, foreign policy, social welfare, feminism, penology. But now the habits of an ultra-cautious gerontocracy and its uncertain successors reign. Those dazzling discredited experimenters in modern art have been supplanted by bland socialist realists. Foreign Commissar Leon Trotsky's order to ignore foreign governments and radicalize their proletariats has been forgotten by one of the most protocol-obsessed diplomatic bureaucracies in the world. And the Soviet Union blithely maintains the only major empire left on the globe.

The firebrand feminist Alexandra Kollontai has succumbed to the tired housewife who, in addition to working, spends an extra 4½ hours a day shopping, cleaning and cooking—without even a token woman member of the Politburo to show for it.

Liberal theories of criminal rehabilitation have long since yielded to old-fashioned watchtowers and punitive sweatshops. The guarantee of work to every person has been honoured (except for political mavericks), but the pensions, safety standards, housing, diet, and leisure possibilities of that worker lag far behind those in Western Europe.

Material progress has been enormous, but, in the process, idealism has been bled white. The old moral energy is gone. It is a sluggish society.

Some postulate, therefore, that there must be major changes once the new post-Brezhnev leadership finishes its four- or five-year settling-in period. Modernization, industrialization, the spread of education, normalization of life after decades of catastrophe, and regional stirrings must all force some relaxation of the rigid command economy, centralized politics and directed society of the Soviet Union.

Logically, yes. Practically, I'm sceptical. Whatever Russia is, it isn't Gallic logic or American eclecticism or Japanese curiosity or Teutonic organization. It's a kind of bastard Western state, born without benefit of Renaissance humanism, Reformation individualism, Enlightenment rationalism or counter-Enlightenment empiricism. Its state of mind is moulded by the frozen Volga and peasant suspicion of the outside world.

And yet a bastard is also a brother. Perhaps this is what fascinates us so in Russia—and makes us so uncomfortable. Russia is an *alter ego*, and the cruelty and epiphany we perceive in it, we really perceive in ourselves.

"A riddle wrapped in a mystery inside an enigma," Churchill termed the Soviet Union. Perhaps a week in suspension in Siberia will float the ambiguities and paradoxes into coherence for me.

An arm's length away a westbound freight train hurtles past, impenetrable, mocking, casting our own train's din back upon us.

CHAPTER II
TUESDAY THE INTELLIGENTSIA

I keep telling you: read *Nineteen Eighty-Four*.
*A member of the Soviet scientific
elite, rejecting Western expectations
of Soviet liberalization*

The opposite of love isn't hate; it's apathy. Apathy is our daily bread here.
John Le Carré, 'A Small Town in Germany'

06.30 *Mendelyeevo*

WE WAKE TO the bored cry of the restaurant-car waiter, who is hawking breakfast messplates of goulash and very mashed potato. No one in our compartment responds to his call, and he continues down the corridor.

A few farmers are well into their day's work, scything grass on the railroad verge to feed their private livestock. Settlements are even sparser on this approach to the Urals than they were in the north Russian woods. And one- and two-storey log cabins are more rudimentary now, without the elaborate wainscotting and azure, peacock and pistachio paint of homesteads in the Russian heartland. They lack the characteristic Slavic stamp and could be frontier outposts anywhere in the world.

Only the yellow-vested level-crossing guards verify that this is still Mother Russia. They emerge from their small houses with ancillary flower beds to stand at stiff attention, flags raised, signalling the train on. Most of the Trans-Siberian is on automatic switching by now, so the gesture seems more metaphoric than functional. It's an assertion of communication with the glamorous city perhaps—or some remembrance of the days when the awesome locomotive was invested with the very authority of the tsar.

It must have been near here that Eugenia Ginzburg's wagonload of prisoners became so engrossed in poetry that they inadvertently broke discipline. When each of the Siberia-bound convicts contributed to the common entertainment—and sanity—by lecturing on her own speciality, Ginzburg recited her recollected verse. She narrated Alexander Pushkin, Alexander Griboyedov and, inevitably, Nikolai Nekrasov's "Russian Women", a tribute to the rebel Decembrists' wives who had trekked to their own Siberian exile on this very route a century before.

On that occasion Ginzburg kept on declaiming, without noticing that the train had pulled into a station. Her recitation violated the silence enforced at all stops to prevent local villagers from learning that it was involuntary human cargo that was being transported in the "special equipment" wagons. Angry guards burst through the door, threatening to put everyone in irons unless the culprit with the forbidden book confessed.

Ginzburg had no choice. To prove there was no book present she staged a command performance for the disbelieving guards. And for those few moments there was a transformation. Under the spell of Pushkin's magic verse "Brigand" (as she called one of the guards) and his mate shifted from belligerence to astonishment to curiosity to delight. The flat-nosed guard nodded off under the rhythm. But Brigand turned out to be an ideal listener, "laughing and being moved in all the right places". The chains were averted.

Somewhere near here too another fleeting miracle occurred. The guards forgot to lock the door after one of their prisoner counts. It was still open at the next stop, and Ginzburg and her companions "began to hear sounds of ordinary human life: laughter, children's voices, and the gurgling of water". The village women outside discovered the convicts and spontaneously gave them the milk, eggs and spring onions they had come to sell to passengers on the train. It was, Ginzburg thought, like a scene out of Leo Tolstoy's *Resurrection*.

Today's counterparts of these village women still meet every Trans-Siberian train. At the two-minute stops they sell express items like plums and flowers. At the fifteen-minute stops where the train changes engines or loads supplies, the board expands to include boiled, fried and raw potatoes, carrots, turnips, radishes, onions, raspberries, gooseberries, blueberries, tomatoes, cottage cheese, meat dumplings, gherkins, cucumbers, snow peas, garlic, grapes, melons, plain mushrooms, pickled mushrooms, scrawny boiled chicken. Purchases are wrapped in cornucopias fashioned out of old newspaper.

Raspberries are high-priced and not so good this year, Tanya counsels me, because of excessive rain. A serving of hot potatoes with onions and dill is also expensive at forty kopecks, but a bucketful of raw potatoes is a real bargain at eight roubles. The bucket, of course, is not part of the deal, and the lucky purchaser must skilfully hug all the potatoes to his chest if he has not brought his string bag onto the platform with him.

At each of the longer stops passengers pile out of the train to restock their larder. If necessary—despite numerous posters prohibiting such be-haviour—they crawl under halted neighbouring trains in their haste to get to the station vendors. I flinch, but eventually I do the same.

The dress on these mass outings is informal, running to baggy sweatsuits, pyjamas and dressing gowns. One army officer even mates lumpy sweat-pants to his five-star military blouse, and the incongruity bothers neither him nor others. No Russian would go out onto city streets in such attire, but the train compartments, corridors and, by extension, station platforms, are considered more as one's temporary home than as a public place.

At major stops the trade is two-way. Almost as brisk as the local vendors' sales to passengers are reverse sales from the restaurant car to provincial housewives of foods that local farms don't produce. The most popular items are sausage, fish, and—surprisingly—eggs. Such private commerce "on the left" is illegal in the Soviet Union, and the ban is enforced in railroad stations in the largest cities. But in the smaller towns it thrives and provides diversion as well as profit.

Since it's only our second day out of Moscow, our mini-kollektiv (as we're already calling ourselves) doesn't yet need to replenish our own food supplies. We buy a few blueberries as an excuse for a stroll but otherwise avoid the temptations. As the train pulls out of the station we repeat our mealtime custom of sharing the tomatoes, boiled eggs, cold chicken, sour pickles and cookies we have each brought along. The conductor comes by with the first hot tea of the morning, and Tanya distributes home-made apricot jam to each of us to sweeten it. More basically, she fulfils the rite of Russian hospitality in offering her dark bread and salt.

"Do you have children?" Tanya asks me solicitously. Then, as an after-thought, "Are you married?" I reply in the negative, and Grandmother exclaims, "Good kid!" Tanya is less convinced of the virtues of spinster-hood. You look younger when you aren't married, she acknowledges. But then, who takes care of you? I grope for a way to explain feminism.

Clearly, I fail, for Tanya's train of thought runs to a more romantic byway. "In the West, do you ever go to balls?" she inquires.

Mystified, I search my memory, and eventually come up with debutante cotillions. My confirmation of their existence is a bit abstract, since I've never attended any, but even my vague reply sparks a new animation in Tanya. The army occasionally throws a ball in her town, it seems, and it's always a gala event. Balls are different from ordinary dances in that there are invitations, the guests go back to sit at tables between dance numbers, and those present all know each other, as the gathering is not open to just anybody coming in off the street. It may not be the equivalent of the chandeliered glitter of a Petersburg evening in *War and Peace*, but it suffices. Tanya radiates a recollected flirtatiousness appropriate to a military ball. She wears her good wig to the balls, she confides.

I ask Grandmother if she has seen the life of women change over the years. Emphatically yes. When she was a young mother, there was war. Her husband was off at the front, and whenever there was a bombardment she had to flee to an underground shelter, with her four children holding each other's hands. Often she didn't even know where all the children were. God grant that never happen again. Her voice trails off. Tanya fills the void by asserting that men and women are equal now in the Soviet Union. Husbands and wives both work and get the same pay. Nina can study for any career that boys can study for, even engineering.

Does Tanya's husband help with the cleaning, or buying food? Grandmother and Tanya laugh at such a preposterous idea. In Moscow, I've found that husbands of a certain white-collar level are at least aware of the issue of the "second shift"; even if they don't help their working wives with the extra daily hours of housekeeping and shopping, they feel obliged to pretend to outsiders that they do. Their guilt pangs obviously have not yet spread to the Far East.

"What would Alexandra Kollontai say about that?" I chide Tanya, to no effect. Tanya is shocked by Kollontai's advocacy of free love—she said making love was just like taking a drink of water! The party was right to reprimand her back in the early days.

I protest. I admire her spunk in embarking on a passionate affair when she was no spring chicken (Tanya gives a grudging nod), and besides, free love was hardly the core of Kollontai's theories. She demanded equal rights of feeling and action for men and women, in or out of marriage, in or out of the corridors of power. She abhorred any double standard, sexual, psychic or other. Actually, along with Engels, she abhorred housekeeping tasks, as a distraction from more important revolutionary activity. She wouldn't object to Tanya's husband's not helping around the home so much as to Tanya's still having to do housework at all—and to the survival of the bourgeois individual family sixty years after the revolution. I note that Kollontai is something of a hero in women's liberation circles in the West.

Tanya and Grandmother aren't quite sure what women's lib might mean, and I discuss the issue of women's working outside the home. This is familiar ground to Tanya; she knows about unemployment in the West and how hard it must be for women to find jobs. I mention my sister who, after her seventh child entered school, took up part-time teaching again—and we immediately get sidetracked. With seven children how could my sister afford not to work till then? How did they feed and clothe all the family even with both parents earning an income? Did they all get to take piano lessons? (Yes, except for the youngest, who after her fourth resistant month finally reaped the benefit of the cumulative rebellion of various elder siblings and was allowed to quit.)

When we return to feminism, Tanya speaks with pride of the many women doctors, lawyers and engineers in the Soviet Union. I concur on the lawyers and engineers; on visiting the celebrated Bratsk dam I was very impressed to learn that a third of the chief engineers were women. (The rate isn't so high in the more desirable non-Siberian dams in European Russia.) The Soviet Union now has more women engineers than all the rest of the world combined, and half of the new engineering students are women.

I'm less impressed by women doctors, however, since ordinary Soviet doctors are ill trained and ill paid, and the ranks of surgeons and other higher positions are still overwhelmingly male. The same disparity holds for full professors, enterprise directors, top scientists and politicians. Less than one per cent of Academicians are women; Andrei Sakharov counted his list of members for me once, since I couldn't acquire a list myself.

The insignificance of women is at its starkest in the top echelon of the Communist Party. After Kollontai was removed as commissar in the early 1920s and kicked upstairs to diplomatic service in Scandinavia and Mexico, there was only one woman on the Politburo (in Khrushchev's time). The number of women on the Central Committee has not exceeded three or four per cent since the early days, and even at local level, wherever I have travelled, there has almost always been only one token woman on the executive party bureaus of ten or eleven members. The overall record is a lot better than the West's professionally, but it is still far short of Kollantai's socialist revolutionary ideal of a "new woman".

Tanya frowns disbelievingly. She's sure that more than just four per cent of Central Committee members are women. And anyway, there are lots of women on the soviets. A woman she knows is even on the soviet in her town. Women's liberation may be good in capitalist countries. It's certainly not needed in the Soviet Union.

Feminist aims other than jobs sound downright peculiar to Tanya: establishing a woman's right to work part-time or devote herself fulltime to nurturing her family if she wishes—or establishing a man's right to share in raising children, to be tender, and to cry occasionally. For her, a woman who doesn't work is a slacker—and any normal woman would want to get out from being cooped up in the apartment all day anyway and have girlfriends at work to confide in. But she quickly jumps back to my sister's seven children and still seems stunned at the thought of having to bring up that many herself. She had two abortions, and though they had a big enough apartment for another child, it wasn't worth it. Nina is their only daughter.

I ask Nina if she'll marry and have one child too. She giggles and thinks she will. I imagine her a few years hence at her engineering institute, exasperating Western feminist exchange students with her single focus on snaring a respectable man, preferably a temperate drinker with a Moscow residence permit. I wish her luck.

"But there's one thing," Tanya suddenly blurts out. "I refuse to be a washed up old woman at forty!" Grandmother and Nina both look surprised. "In *War and Peace* the countess was a *starukha* at forty-five. When you were done having children you were finished, pushed out of the picture. We aren't that way any more!" I applaud her vehemence, and so does Grandmother.

Grandmother regards feminism, from what I've told her of it, as pie in the sky—but she certainly thinks men have made a botch of things. I tell her about grandmothers' lib in Latvia, and she chortles her approval.

Latvian grandmothers, I discovered on a trip to that Baltic republic soon after I arrived in the Soviet Union, are tired of being exploited as permanent unpaid babysitters. In a generation gap with a difference they are rebelling against their daughters. And they are no longer bashful about speaking up.

"As soon as mothers become grandmothers they devote themselves to social life—dancing groups, choirs, lectures, different clubs," grumbled one mother who couldn't get either grandmother to tend her child and wrote to the local Riga paper to say so. "Nowadays grandmothers and grandfathers are taking drivers' courses, sitting in cafés and chatting, or raising cactuses!" It's gotten so bad, Mrs B. Rumniece continued, that "the majority of the audience at all the best concerts and poetry evenings are of the age of grandmothers, because they have the time to queue up for tickets, and they have the free evenings."

This slur was too much for Grandmother Anna Brodele. Grandmothers want to live too, she retorted in the same newspaper. They have already denied themselves things in rearing their own children, and they do not understand why the new generation of mothers is unwilling to take this same responsibility. Of course, grandmothers are delighted by the arrival of grandchildren and want to help. But at their age they do not want to be stuck with all the washing, lifting, and running after the children.

Mrs Rumniece's indignation remained unassuaged. Forgetting the grand-children is all right, she allowed, twisting the knife a bit, for those grand-parents who still work after retirement age because they want expensive furniture or TV sets. But it's not fair for a young mother to have to give up her work and career for a whole year just because an idle grandmother "categorically says no" to taking care of the grandchild "because she wants to live". Young twenty-year-old parents are just the age when

> they want to see everything, hear everything, and be everywhere. But a child is not a doll, not a kitten, nor a dog. They cannot leave it at home for several hours. The father and mother would like to see a new play, go to a film, visit an exhibition, hear a concert, or go out of town on Sundays. But when a child is still a toddler, not everybody can find a babysitter, as this job is not popular.

Well, replied Grandmother Brodele tartly, mothers should have thought of that before they begot children.

Grandmother grins. Tanya, half a dozen years past needing a babysitter and another half-dozen years away from being in demand as one, smiles dubiously and broaches another topic.

Outside the Soviet Union, can one travel easily? The word Tanya uses to mean the outside world is simply, in colloquial Russian, "There". The most frequent introductory question I am asked throughout the Soviet Union is: Where is it better, Here or There? Or, as it is bluntly phrased by another Trans-Siberian passenger I chat with in the corridor, "It's better There, isn't it?"

Tanya takes in the information—phenomenal to a Soviet citizen who even inside the Soviet Union must display her internal passport every time she buys a plane ticket—that Westerners travel freely from country to country in Western Europe without needing visas. And she retorts that travel is becoming easy Here too. "You can be an American and nobody will pay any attention to that," she asserts. "We aren't suspicious people. We aren't suspicious of foreigners." She asks who approves the articles I write as a journalist before I send them from Moscow and concludes that I haven't maligned the Soviet Union if I haven't yet been expelled.

Grandmother sends Nina out to fetch a second glass of morning tea for her, and the three of them settle down to a game of cards. Our compartment is beginning to feel cosy, lived in, reminiscent of all my lingering Moscow evenings spent laughing and arguing around some friend's tiny kitchen table.

We would start out as a foursome, perhaps, with Vera Alekseevna making sure that I and her small son, and whichever of her son's friends happened to be on hand, all got plenty of potatoes and cucumbers and garlic mushrooms on our plates. Then the boys would go to study, Mikhail Sergeevich would come home late from the institute as usual, and we would start the meal all over again. Then a neighbour would drop in, and perhaps an old friend from fifteen years ago who was in Moscow for an operation. That would call for more potatoes, sour cream and tea, candies, and perhaps dried vobla fish, in haphazard order.

Conversation would jump from Zhenya's Pioneer concert to Vladimir Soloviev's turn-of-the-century philosophy to cosmic good and evil to renditions of prison camp songs. The exchanges would be sharp and emotional, with everyone passionately committed to a viewpoint.

"Do you like Voltaire?" Vera Alekseevna challenged me once, and my tepid affirmative after failing to think of any particular reason for disliking Voltaire called forth a torrent of rebuttal. He was shallow and cynical, it seems, and he led Catherine the Great in exactly the wrong direction.

Economic determinism and the anti-hero interpretation of history? Nobody disproved it more than the iron-willed Lenin, who single-handedly transformed Russia's bumbling liberalism into streamlined Bolshevism. Tolstoy was wrong, too, to say that individuals don't affect the sweep of history. But then he didn't really believe it anyway—until late in his life, perhaps.

No no no! Russians are not more generous in their friendships than other people. That's a myth. National character doesn't exist, and it's a fraud to claim it does. But Russians' sufferings do give them something to define themselves against. If they are pure under the pressures here then they would be pure anywhere . . .

Russians are congenital liars . . . They are people who want a tsar, a Peter the Great, a Stalin. They don't know how to be free . . .

It's all the fault of swaddling . . . It's all the fault of Russians' natural anarchy . . . It's all the fault of Russians' incredible tolerance of suffering . . . Nonsense! It's the absence of Renaissance or Reformation . . . No, sex is at the heart of it. Children have to sleep in the same room with their parents because of the dreadful housing conditions, and they have to pretend they aren't awake when their parents have sex . . . In Russia children grow up nihilistic from kindergarten on . . .

Don't believe what you hear. Dostoevsky did not undergo a metamorphosis at Omsk. He was always a prober. And besides, the Petrashevsky Circle really was violent . . . Lenin did take money from the Germans . . .

Oh, if only those bored nineteenth-century aristocrats hadn't got drunk on German romanticism! Turgenev was right, but he was too gentle to be appreciated. Herzen was right; there was no escape from man's predicament then, and there's no escape now. Utopias end in the Gulag. But Herzen believed in individuals, while Russians are communal. They have to have their *mir* (the corporate government of peasant villages), their obscurantism, their fatalism, their tsar. Have some more mushrooms. And *Bozhe moi*! You haven't put the tiniest little spoonful of sugar in your tea!

Those evenings were exhilarating, bewildering, exhausting. They taxed my Russian and my stamina. And they seemed altogether typical of the normal intensity of the Russian intelligentsia.

What an overwhelming intelligentsia it is! It's corruscating, comprehensive, morally involved, convinced that truth exists. It's both more and less self-conscious than its blander Western counterparts. It feels its own identity with the acuteness born of siege. Yet it is naive and fresh, with the amazement born of having to discover everything anew.

Intellectuals, of course, play a significant role in any country—generating new ideas, defining goals, distilling self-awareness. But in no nation have they been more important than in Russia.

Giants like Tolstoy and Dostoevsky made Russian novels famous throughout Europe in the nineteenth century. Giants like Igor Stravinsky, Kasimir Malevich, Konstantin Stanislavsky, Sergei Diaghilev and George Balanchine revolutionized music, art, theatre and dance for the entire Western world in the early twentieth century. And a host of lesser-known intellectuals, from the Decembrists on, first made Russia ashamed of its backwardness in the nineteenth century, then spearheaded the demand for radical change that led to the 1917 revolution.

Historically, the Russian-coined word "intelligentsia" had a much broader meaning than the Western category of intellectuals: in a largely peasant society it included not just the leading coteries of academic and artistic thinkers, but also school-teachers, doctors and university students—all those possessing or acquiring a precious higher education.

In its most exact sense, though, the Russian word "intelligentsia" was much narrower than the Western concept: it meant not all intellectuals, but precisely those alienated intellectuals who held up a critical mirror to Russia's passivity and boorishness.

This Russian intelligentsia, in both the narrow and broad sense, was liquidated after the revolution in Joseph Stalin's purges. In an extraordinary act that is sometimes termed Russia's national suicide, the dictator murdered, imprisoned or drove into exile all but a handful of the Soviet Union's poets, artists, engineers, and even the old Bolshevik intellectuals within the ruling Communist Party.

When this class died, the old Western liberalism that originally informed the Russian revolution died with it. What was left was Stalin's modern incarnation of the Tatar-Muscovite despotism of Ivan the Terrible.

The other class on which Stalin declared social war was the peasantry, in the brutal collectivization of the 1930s. But even as he dispossessed the peasants, Stalin replenished the ranks of his secret police and his political and cultural apparat with those uneducated peasants who were willing to administer his terror—until such time as they themselves should fall victim to the bloodletting. This grisly high point in Russian social mobility and nadir in Russian humanity left a raw emerging society bereft of the normal civilizing influence of intellectuals.

It also left considerable semantic confusion about the word "intelligentsia" today.

My friends use the term most often to mean those intellectuals committed to humanist values—a rather small number of people, they regret.

Frequently, however, the term "intelligentsia" expands to encompass all professionals, including even those writers and artists who always hew to the party line, whatever the cost in compassion and integrity. "Careerists", "opportunists" or "pseudo-intellectuals" my friends brand this latter group.

A third meaning, the official Soviet one, expands still more to encompass anyone who is not engaged in manual labour, from professor to laboratory technician, from clerk to censor.

The image of the Soviet intelligentsia so often cherished in the West—that of the Solzhenitsyns and Sakharovs—doesn't accord with any of these three categories. An outsider is wildly misled if he takes the small minority of dissidents as representative of the Soviet intelligentsia. But he can be illumined if he takes them as a touchstone, both to the various kinds of intellectuals and to the Soviet regime.

The human-rights dissidents—who are usually estimated at no more than a thousand activists, excluding nationalists—see themselves as the spiritual descendants of that disaffected nineteenth-century intelligentsia. They feel themselves charged anew with the mission of awakening the conscience of Russia. This is a very special heritage, distinguished by moral fervour, "truth seeking", social commitment, and universal sweep. It is epitomized by the novels of Alexander Solzhenitsyn. The goal is nothing less than the redemption of humanity.

Such a coincidence of moral, social, and artistic concerns seems presumptuous in an America that tends to suspect politically inclined novelists of abandoning art. This Russian preoccupation disconcerts Western readers, but it also excites them. Periodically, they marvel at how passionate and full-bodied Russian literature has been, from Tolstoy through Solzhenitsyn—and, by contrast, how trivial and narcissistic much of Western literature has been.

The epic passions of the Russian intelligentsia have often been warped, in the climate of nineteenth-century autocracy and present-day authoritarianism, into hothouse impracticality. But for the dissenter, practicality is not the point. Rather than arouse a popular following, he hopes to bear witness, to keep alive the vision of justice for those few who have eyes to see. He strives, like Pushkin's Prophet, to have a burning coal as his heart, and to follow the injunction of God:

> Revolt, prophet, and see, and understand,
> Obey my will
> And, travelling by sea and land,
> Burn people's hearts with words.

The burning words of the 1970s (it's not yet clear if they can continue in the 1980s) issued from an astonishing variety of prophets. A newcomer to Moscow's dissident press conferences reeled under the sheer cacophony of intra-dissident disputes—and revelled in the diversity of faces in a society where so many visages are so repetitive.

To begin with, there was Andrei Dmitrievich Sakharov, dean of the dissenters and usual host of the press conferences in his tiny bed-sitting room on Moscow's Inner Ring Road. He has gentle eyes, a receding hairline. He is stooped, measured in his movements. He has the energy of love, and his single-mindedness about fighting persecution has, miraculously, never made him shrill. Andrei Dmitrievich was always ready to take up any cause he was persuaded was legitimate—including the plea of the small dispossessed nationality of Crimean Tatars to return to the Crimea, but excluding any pleas by violent hijackers, no matter what their original grievances.

When he suspected provocation and withheld support for some stranger who claimed to be threatened by the secret police—and when, without

Sakharov's protection, that person subsequently died under mysterious circumstances, Sakharov felt a deep personal guilt.

The other dissidents—in pure Russian the word is *inakomyslyashchie* or "other thinkers"—were equally distinctive: Yury Orlov, the fiery physicist from a working-class family, whose red hair exploded in an unpremeditated Afro; former Major-General and war hero Petro Grigorenko, holder of the Order of Lenin and two orders of the Red Flag and the Red Star, bald as a rock, deceptively robust in appearance despite years of maltreatment in mental hospitals; Alexander Ginzburg, a tough, scrappy veteran of six years in labour camps, a man energized by anger and blazing conviction; Vladimir Slepak, an apocalyptic figure with a wiry, centrifugal beard, the Jew who, as nearly as anyone can remember, has been waiting the longest to emigrate; Anatoly Shcharansky, stocky, blessed with an ageless Yiddish humour, computer scientist and spokesman for the Jewish emigration movement, liaison man between Jews demanding emigration rights and stay-at-home dissidents demanding civil rights.

By now these people belong to the past. Nobel Peace Prize laureate Sakharov is exiled to an apartment with a live-in police informer in Gorky, a city off-limits to foreigners. (He was not dropped from the Academy of Sciences despite an attempted expulsion that ended, according to one account, when someone inquired if there were a precedent for such action. "Yes," replied that grand old man of Soviet science, octogenarian Pyotr Kapitsa, "Einstein." The Soviet Academy thereupon declined to follow the antecedent of Hitler's Prussian Academy.)

Orlov is now spending seven years in a strict regime labour camp to be followed by five years of Siberian exile. Grigorenko is in foreign exile, his Soviet citizenship stripped from him. Ginzburg, as a recidivist, was sentenced to another eight years in the harshest "special regime" labour camps, but was suddenly released to the United States in a dissident/spy swap in 1979. Slepak is in internal exile. An ill Shcharansky is serving a term of three years in prison plus ten years in a strict regime labour camp.

Until Sakharov was exiled in 1980 (administratively, with no court order or hearing) there was a certain dissident momentum. There was a communication network. There was a sense of continuity, however embattled. There were constant newcomers to replace those dissenters who were jailed or exiled.

Sakharov's exile marked the end of an epoch. Communications between dissidents themselves and between dissidents and the West were interrupted. The protection of Sakharov's name and his previous decade of immunity were lost. The dissidents' ranks were decimated in the five months prior to Sakharov's exile by the arrest, imprisonment, or internment in mental hospitals of at least 217 activists—a rate that dissident monitor Peter Reddaway calculates is double the normal one.

The phenomenon of dissent began—and, possibly, ended—under Leonid Brezhnev.

During Stalin's terror there was no dissident movement, much less foreign resonance for dissidence. There were individual martyrs, but their fate was unknown, often even to their own families. On the rare occasions when tales of murders and persecutions did reach the West, they were widely discounted in fashionable intellectual circles as the necessary breaking of eggs on the way to the progressive new Communist omelette.

The situation shifted as Stalinism yielded to Khrushchev's jerky liberalization, but still there was no co-ordinated dissent. In the early 1960s the impetuous leader's loosening of censorship—and especially his personal permission to publish Solzhenitsyn's prison camp novella *One Day in the Life of Ivan Denisovich*—held out the hope that humanists could keep stretching the existing system to greater and greater tolerance. For a decade and a half after 1956—following Khrushchev's electrifying de-Stalinization speech and the Hungarian revolt—an identifiable "counterculture" developed that was not quite allowed but on the other hand was not quite stamped out either.

After his settling-in period as the new Soviet leader, Brezhnev did move to stamp it out, and with this the counterculture went underground.

The new dissidents included Alexander Solzhenitsyn, a neo-Slavophil jeremiah decrying the moral decay of the Russian regime. They included Roy Medvedev, a Marxist idealist writing an extraordinary record of Stalin's purges, urging the Communist Party itself to expiate these sins. They included Andrei Sakharov, a brilliant establishment scientist (co-author of the first Soviet H-bomb, youngest full member ever admitted to the Soviet Academy of Sciences, winner of the Stalin and Lenin Prizes and the Order of Socialist Labour) evolving into a petitioner of his government (for strengthening intellectual education, ending Soviet nuclear testing, and blocking a revival of Stalinism) and emerging finally as full dissenter.

. The counterculture included secret discussion groups at Moscow and Leningrad Universities though not, significantly, at the polytechnical institutes training the new mass intelligentsia. It included scientific studies, poems, novels and literary criticisms once written "for the drawer" and now pulled out to circulate and elicit quasi-public reader reactions for the first time. It included the bimonthly *Chronicle of Current Events* and other *samizdat* ("self-published") typescripts with a content ranging from detailed factual exposure of Soviet human-rights violations to Ukrainian, Lithuanian and other nationalist themes, to Great Russian chauvinism. It revealed a wealth of deviations from the party line, with the most celebrated of the day's heady disputes pitting Medvedev's warning that too much dissent could spoil détente against Sakharov's radical insistence that détente without democracy is inherently unstable.

The dissidents were an infinitesimal number among the Soviet Union's millions, but there were enough of them to alarm the ideological guardians. The authorities, while stopping short of any restoration of Stalin's arbitrary terror, moved to curtail dissent.

They did so with increasing thoroughness after the scare of the 1968 Czech heresy. The few Red Square protesters against the Soviet invasion of Czechoslovakia were summarily arrested, to the cheers of onlookers who loved their motherland and despised its detractors. Thousands of young people who were deemed contaminated by the Czech notion of a humane communism were expelled from the Communist Party and Komsomol youth organization. Artists were dismissed from professional unions, professors from universities. Scientists were squeezed out of research institutes in the regular or special "shrinkages". Protesters were moved from major cities to small towns, denounced by colleagues at "self-criticism" sessions, deprived of their telephones, subjected to illegal home searches and seizures of books and papers. The number of other-thinkers dwindled.

Still, under the broad protection of the long untouchable Sakharov, the Moscow branch of Amnesty International, the human-rights committees to monitor observance of the Helsinki European Security Agreement, the psychiatric abuse documenters, the *Chronicle of Current Events* and the *Chronicle of the Lithuanian Catholic Church* all issued reports and got them to the West. And with the continued filling by new volunteers of the vacancies left by arrests, the dissident numbers stayed fairly constant after the first shakedown.

By the end of the seventies, some twenty-five samizdat periodicals and other publications were appearing. Within one two-year-period— despite the arrest of four out of nine editors and the expulsion from the Soviet Union of a fifth—eight issues came out of an unusually pluralist magazine, *Poiski* (Searchings). In 1979, twenty-three works by famous and less-famous authors that had sat for years in the censors' reject boxes were "published", in an edition of twelve, in the *Metropol'* anthology. (The authorities spurned the authors' contention that *Metropol'* was completely legal and treated it as dissentient; two of the youngest contributors were dropped from the Writers' Union, three of their fellow-writers then quit the union in protest, and one was expelled and emigrated to the United States.)

Most striking of all—and most poignant—was the success of the dissident lobby for Jewish emigration. The exodus the Jews accomplished sealed their evolution from vanguard to victims of the Russian revolution.

Jews were prominent among the zealous early Bolsheviks. For them, the revolution would mean a liberation from the pogroms, ghettos and discrimination of tsarist times, as well as liberation from exploitation for all mankind. At first their hopes were borne out. The famous Jewish State Theatre was founded in 1919, and employed Marc Chagall as stage designer.

Another 17 permanent Yiddish theatres blossomed, as did 1,100 Jewish schools and 170 periodicals. Moscow, Kharkov, Minsk, and Birobidzhan each had a Jewish daily newspaper. For many years the Communists even entertained hopes that the Soviet Birobidzhan Jewish Autonomous Region in the Far East would become the magnet for persecuted and discontented Jews from other lands.

A few rabid anti-Bolshevik Russians took this professed conjunction of interests so seriously that they were prepared to join with Hitler against Communism and "world Jewry". To this day one peculiar form of popular anti-Semitism blames the Jews for the present regime and believes—even after so many years of Jewish troubles—that some of the top Kremlin leaders are secret Jews.

During Stalin's 1920s anti-religion campaigns Jewish synagogues (but not secular cultural activities) were as persecuted as were Orthodox churches. And during the thirties purges many Jewish intellectuals and party members perished. There was not yet any special racial slur in this, however. If the Jews were disproportionately represented in the circles that were prime targets of the purges, then they were disproportionately represented among the victims (as well as among the Chekist implementers) of the terror. It was that simple. Stalin was an equal-opportunity tyrant, at first.

It was only after the Hitler–Stalin Pact (partially) and after World War II (fully) that Stalin demonstrated his own anti-Semitism. Jews returning from the battlefield to civilian life suddenly found their old jobs closed to them. They were excluded from party, state, military, diplomatic and foreign-trade leadership posts. The only elite field that remained open to them was science. By the early 1970s a striking 11 per cent of scientists in Moscow (the home of a quarter of all Soviet scientists) would be Jews. And 14 per cent of all Doctors of Science would come from the Jewish one per cent of the population.

In 1948 the new discrimination was inflated to a Russian chauvinist drive against "rootless cosmopolitanism". The director of the Jewish State Theatre, Solomon Michoels, after giving numerous private performances for Stalin in the Kremlin and being awarded the Order of Lenin and even (in 1946) the Stalin Prize, was murdered by the secret police in an automobile "accident" in 1948. The theatre was closed the next year. Tens of thousands of Jews were sent to the prison camps, and 23 leading Jewish intellectuals were executed in Lubyanka Prison on one day in mid-1952. By the beginning of 1953 Jews were waiting with reawakened dread for the allegation of an anti-Politburo "doctors' plot" by Jewish physicians to ripen into a comprehensive pogrom. This development was averted only by Stalin's death in March of 1953.

The reprieve didn't last long. In the early 1960s Khrushchev mounted his own anti-Semitic campaign. A number of otherwise assimilated Jews concluded that anti-Semitism was endemic in the Soviet system and again began considering themselves Jewish rather than Russian.

Their feelings were strengthened in 1967 when yet another leader, Leonid Brezhnev, broke off relations with the Israel that the Soviet Union had been the first to recognize in 1948, and a new "anti-Zionist" (read anti-Jewish) campaign began. These moves combined with the victory over the Arabs by the greatly outnumbered Israelis in the 1967 war to form a watershed. Many Soviet Jews felt a surge of ethnic pride, and a determination to express their Jewishness by emigrating to Israel.

The Soviet government retaliated with severe restrictions on Jews in the one career left to them, science. Jewish university enrolment dropped by a dramatic 40 per cent from 1968/9 to 1976/7, while Jewish postgraduate enrolment dropped 40 per cent in the shorter period of 1970 to 1975, and the Jewish percentage in the scientific-technological intelligentsia was halved from the early sixties (11 per cent) to the early eighties (5.5 per cent). Not surprisingly, the new discrimination convinced even more Jews that emigration was the only course open to them.

To the Soviet authorities an especially bitter aspect of the new sense of Jewish identity was the strong pull it exerted precisely on those already high-ranking Soviet scientists, mathematicians and scholars who were Jews. And to one Old Bolshevik, Semyon Ignatyevich (formerly Solomon Izrailovich) Slepak, an especially bitter aspect was the pull the Jewish revival exerted on his own son, Vladimir (named after Lenin). Slepak Senior, an old Civil War partisan and Comintern Presidium member, disowned his son and branded him an "enemy of the people" for this betrayal of his father's lifelong ideal. Vladimir Slepak went to his Siberian exile in 1978 unreconciled with his father.

The Jewish renaissance of the late 1960s began with a drive to learn and teach Hebrew (the only language outlawed in the Soviet Union, Jews note sarcastically), and to attend the synagogues that remained open. It ran into the expected KGB harassment and worse, but it coincided with the development of détente and it had a readymade worldwide audience. By 1971 the Jewish movement won a phenomenal victory: for the first time in its five-and-a-half decades of existence the Soviet Union relaxed its equation of emigration with treason to let a sizeable ethnic group leave the country. Despite various policy zigzags and fluctuations of numbers in succeeding years the Soviet Union continued to let thousands of Jews emigrate—for a total by 1980 of more than 200,000. Most of the Baltic and Georgian Jews have left by now, along with significant numbers of Western Ukrainian, Moldavian, Dagestani and Bukharan Jews.

The *coup de grâce* to all the Jewish and other dissident experimentation was effected with Sakharov's banishment to Gorky in 1980. This nose-thumbing at world opinion marked the end of the golden age of Soviet dissent. The political police were well launched in their new silver age, with the KGB's Fifth Section having expanded greatly through its decade of orchestrating the various interrogations, beatings and physical threats directed at dissenters and select members of the humanist intelligentsia.

Beyond the emigration of the Jews and, in their wake, some thousands of ethnic Germans, what has the dissidents' bitter "bearing witness" accomplished inside Soviet society?

Above all, it has established a certain standard of conscience, which the humanist intelligentsia can no longer ignore. Writers, artists and scientists may choose to disregard this standard, but they can no longer pretend to know nothing of it. Nor can they plead that overwhelming force prevents them from living their ideals. The other-thinkers have shown that the Stalinist era is past. The man of integrity no longer forfeits his life (usually) or even twenty-five years, renewable, in prison camp. Today's sentences run to seven years, or three years. And the penalties for mere silence (as distinct from requested denunciation of others) are even less: loss of a trip abroad, perhaps, or demotion. "And who would want to sell his soul," asks one friend scornfully, "for such a cheap price?!"

The dissidents may have lost every single battle that the government has joined. But in the process they have altered the moral scale. On the continuum of conscience and expedience the norm has edged a bit toward conscience.

From the record of repression it is clear that the Soviet Government recognizes this shift and shares the dissenters' high evaluation of their own importance. Westerners often puzzle over the lengths to which the Soviet control apparat goes to curb the relatively few dissidents. The answer lies in that memory of those alienated nineteenth-century intellectuals—and how this minority finally turned the entire educated class against the regime.

Fear of a repetition of this feat in the 1980s seems far fetched. It is true that Sakharov and Grigorenko came out of today's mainstream elite of scientists and military officers. And Sakharov claims to find widespread surreptitious sympathy for his cause among other intellectuals—a claim that is perhaps confirmed by the failure to drum him out of the Academy. Still, these men are exceptions, not models. The vast majority of the intelligentsia emphatically does not endorse the dissidents.

The reasons and implications of this non-support differ for the three categories of the humanists, the careerists and the technocrats. But they all work together to isolate the dissenters.

Many of the humanists do admire the courage and envy the honesty of the other-thinkers. They appreciate the added elbow-room they themselves enjoy through sporadic Kremlin sensitivity to Western criticism of Soviet repression. Others, however, scorn the dissidents, either out of defensiveness or out of genuine misgivings about the dissidents' motives and tactics.

The humanists are perhaps more a moral than a functional category. Their definition depends not on their employment in education, literature, the arts, or other professions in the field of "humanities", but rather on acknowledgment of such principles as truth, free inquiry, and non-injury to one's fellow man. The humanists are exercised by those same cosmic "accursed questions" that haunted the nineteenth-century intelligentsia: problems of virtue, justice, existence. Their vision—and, where possible, their code of conduct—includes intellectual integrity, compassion, an absolute prohibition on denouncing others, and Solzhenitsyn's first commandment of never again telling a lie.

Typically, members of this category might be poets, philologists, sociologists, artists. They might also be the rare Artists' Union bureaucrats who shelter good painters in their seasons of disfavour by slipping them commissions for book illustrations. Or bartenders at the Writers' Union who steer soulmates toward each other, and keep clean clothes ever ready to restore the novelist whose unpublishable prison-camp memories drive him to periodic drunken binges.

Often, the humanists are physicists. Many a Soviet student with liberal leanings chooses the sanctuary of a scientific or technical career just because in this field there are fewer political and personal demands. The hard sciences of chemistry, physics and mathematics (though not genetics in the days of Trofim Lysenko) are relatively unaffected by ideological swings, and their practitioners do not have to berate heretical colleagues with the same frequency that members of the Writers' Union or Artists' Union do.

The humanists maintain their private integrity by wangling Western literature in their fields to check their own professional standards; by setting up networks of forbidden or hard-to-get literature (Solzhenitsyn novels in the former, Mandelstam poetry in the latter class); by selecting more remote specialities (such as early-nineteenth-century rather than twentieth-century literary criticism) in which one can pursue ideas relatively unencumbered by ideology—and often, by avoiding promotion up to a level that would require public political statements.

The humanists maintain their morale, sometimes by collecting modern art, always by keeping a close circle of like-minded friends with whom they can drink and ventilate sensitive subjects. The circle of friends is easier to keep up here than in the West—given the Russian tradition of spontaneous hospitality, the proximity of apartment houses and dachas assigned according to professional employment, and the village atmosphere that pervades even Moscow and throws professors, scientists, writers and artists together in everyday shopping and entertainment. The circle of friends is also more necessary than in the West, both as carrier of the intellectual excitement missing in published Soviet journals, and as assurance that the terrible

Stalinist atomization through universal suspicion is a thing of the past.

All of this might well predispose the humanists to seek out the stimulation and human-rights concerns of the dissidents. But it does not, for mixed reasons. The extent of the humanists' politics, by and large, is to avoid politics—including the politics of dissent.

Honourable reasons for this aloofness can include both an aversion to intellectual or emotional distortion, and a tactical judgment that the intelligentsia can more effectively humanize society by working within the system than by declaring war on it. Relative quiet, in this view, is more conducive to a liberal evolution than is constant public confrontation with the authorities.

Volodya, my gentle teacher friend, speaks regretfully of the obsession of many dissidents with their fight. "They savour each succulent detail of every battle," he notes. They talk about nothing else. They substitute breast-beating for programmes. Volodya grants that Soviet repression demands obsession—the acceptance of dissent as a profession in itself—if the human rights activists are to make any headway at all. But he thinks that the activists sometimes lose sight of the goal of the greatest possible self-realization for each individual. The dissidents' own writings, and sometimes their lives, all too often turn into one-dimensional political harangues. Solzhenitsyn is perhaps an exception, one whose pen manages to coexist with his knife. For most writers, though, Volodya considers it an axiom that polemics warp rather than sharpen artistry.

Seeing the world in black and white can become an easy way out of professional struggle with complexity and the ambiguity of ideas. It can become a mask for lack of talent, or a quick boost to one's self-importance. And opposition can quickly become as tyrannical a definition of oneself as conformity. If a person consents to delineate himself only in hostility to the hated barbarian, then he has already conceded defeat to that barbarian.

Joseph Brodsky, considered by many the greatest living Russian poet, agrees with this sentiment. As the beneficiary of one of the earliest international campaigns on behalf of a Russian writer—after the outcry he was released early from a five-year Arctic labour camp sentence for "parasitism", then banished from the Soviet Union—Brodsky is grateful for the "political" campaign waged in his defence. He pays his debt by helping Amnesty International drives to save others. But both in the Soviet Union and in exile he has always put poetry first, resistance second.

He speaks feelingly of the need to prevent creative energies from being detoured into the struggle against official barriers. A real poet, he contends, is fully occupied in listening to the inner hum of his poems and responding to it. If he gets sucked into fighting, this is a diversion that squanders time and runs the risk of self-aggrandizement as well as of bad poetry. He insists, "A writer has only one responsibility to society: just to write well."

In the view of my Moscow friends, it is Brodsky's victory of artistic accomplishment that will endure, and outlive the manifestos to inspire future generations. Unusually, they say, Brodsky has not only survived exile and forestalled the petrifaction of language common to that state; he is now writing even better poetry than when he lived in Leningrad. This they regard as the highest possible triumph over the censors and literary police.

Volodya's reservations about dissent are not quite the fastidious artistic ones of Brodsky. Volodya is a teacher, not a poet. His concern is that the kind of enmity some dissidents thrive on hinders rather than advances evolution within the present system. He thinks that Pushkin accomplished more by playing the tsar and censor against each other than he would have by Solzhenitsyn's righteous rejection of all manoeuvre and compromise. He thinks that Voltaire accomplished more by getting his play about Christian fanaticism past the censors disguised as an anti-Muslim piece than he would have by refusing to deal with the censors at all. He thinks that even half-light enlightens.

Uniquely, Volodya's own dream of serving enlightenment is to give up his Moscow job and go and teach in a country school. He is appalled by the lack of education, books or any diversion that might expand peasant children's narrow vistas. He echoes those nineteenth-century narodniks (populists) who fanned out to the villages to enlighten the *narod* (common people), to show the suspicious peasants the way out of their squalor and exploitation.

Unlike the disappointed narodniks, Volodya doesn't expect that his action would really change much. But in the long run he thinks that only this kind of slow spreading of the concepts of tolerance and compassion among the peasants could ever achieve any lasting progress toward the kind of Soviet society he longs to see. He describes his notion as one of contributing what he can to improve society, if only "drop by drop". In Volodya's view, if he became a public dissident he would be betraying his own personal goal, sacrificing any reform effect he might have through education.

Another friend of mine, a member of the scientific elite who identifies himself as a humanist but also a realist, makes a somewhat more cynical case for not supporting the dissidents. He regards life in the post-Stalin era as tolerable, even if irritating. Stalin's arbitrary terror has already been renounced as a control technique, after all. If a person does not dabble in forbidden politics, he is not bothered by the police. And a certain minimal area of private autonomy has even been restored. In Moscow, Leningrad, and Novosibirsk one can possess books by Alexander Solzhenitsyn or, among friends, criticize political favouritism without fear of retaliation. Why then be a fanatic and invite trouble as the dissidents do?

The important thing, he says, is to refuse to inform on colleagues to the KGB. If a person holds to this, he can live with his conscience. Anything beyond that is futile grand-standing that may be a psychic salve, but has no impact at all on daily conditions.

Besides, continues this friend, becoming a dissident means forfeiting one's professional life, letting one's mental faculties atrophy, giving up any further chance to do pioneer work in quantum particles or earth structure or hydraulics. He notes the attempt by Jewish "refuseniks", who have been fired from their posts, to fill the intellectual vacuum with weekly science seminars. But he dismisses this as an ineffectual gesture. And he considers Sakharov not saintly but daft, for having sacrificed his career to join the unreal world of dissenters and try to change the immutable Big Brother. "Read *Nineteen Eighty-Four*," he admonishes me again and again, in order to see the definitive description of Soviet society.

For this scientist, the real world that any sane Soviet intellectual must acknowledge and operate in is indeed that of *Nineteen Eighty-Four*. It is the everyday world of his own institute, where he never knows who makes decisions, on what basis. He recoils from George Orwell's main character, who ends up loving Big Brother. But he is reconciled to Big Brother as inevitable.

Big Brother is in fact loved as well as despised by the second category of intellectuals, the careerists. Or, as Solzhenitsyn so delicately calls them, the "contemptible horde of pseudo-intellectuals", "semi-ignoramuses", "abject browbeaten characters" made "pliant" by "devious calculations of vanity, self-interest, personal welfare and tranquillity", "lackeys" marked by cowardice, servility, hypocrisy and toadying.

Typically, members of this category might be poets, philologists, sociologists, artists, or journalists—all those in any field who want the prestige of a non-manual job but not the pain of real intellectual independence.

The careerists deliberately compromise conscience. They voice required political slogans that they themselves are cynical about. They write or paint in the style of idealized "socialist realism" that they privately mock. They exercise self-censorship, avoiding forbidden topics before they need to be instructed to do so. They inform on others as occasion arises.

For their ordinary services the careerists receive promotions and the intellectuals' perquisites of bigger apartments, dachas, resort passes, special import shops, closed showings of Western movies, better education for their children, and access to books that are usually impossible to obtain. So common is this mentality that the secretary of the Writers' Union once seriously suggested to Nadezhda Mandelstam that if only Pasternak had been given more living space at the right time, he probably could have been deflected from writing that troublesome *Dr Zhivago*.

The perquisites of the opportunists extend well beyond roomier apartments if they provide extra services—denouncing prickly associates on order of the party perhaps, or acquainting the KGB with a friend's unguarded oath about the party leadership. For such favours informers receive additional promises and sometimes delivery of trips abroad, where they can indulge all their fantasies of jeans and tennis rackets and plumbing fixtures.

With these privileges the careerists live far better than the average Soviet citizen, and for this they are grateful to Big Brother. Axiomatically, they are hostile to the dissident, afraid that he will expose their mediocrity and threaten their privilege and power.

The conscious cynicism and humiliation of such a position is hard to grasp for someone brought up in a Western pluralist democracy. Sellouts exist there too, but they tend to be less crude and all-encompassing. A Madison Avenue executive may not believe in the product he is pushing, but at least he doesn't have to denounce Saul Bellow to sell his deodorant. Nor does he have to praise the incumbent American president so sycophantically that he compares him to the sun that lights all dawns (as one enthusiast gushed about Brezhnev). The American's or Frenchman's compromise is confined to his particular job; outside of that narrow focus his life is basically his own.

Furthermore, the Westerner's choice of employers gives him a choice of concessions too: if he can't avoid compromises altogether, he can at least avoid the heinous ones by substituting the lesser ones. In the Soviet Union there is no alternative employer to the state, and no alternative compromise (except withdrawal) to that comprehensive one demanded by the party.

In addition, the consequences of being denounced by colleagues are incomparably more severe in the Soviet Union than in the West. Even in the worst periods of McCarthyism in the USA "the blacklist was not the deathlist"—and the blacklist was later repudiated as abhorrent by the same society that perpetrated it.

In the Soviet Union, by contrast, pressure to conform to a narrow ideology and to collaborate with the secret police for material reward and safety is a daily way of life. So is yielding to this pressure. Significantly, ballet star Mikhail Baryshnikov once told an interviewer that he cherishes his new home in the USA as much for giving him the possibility of being honest as for giving him artistic freedom.

George Feifer, observer of the Moscow scene as student and journalist, summed up the self-disgust of many sellout intellectuals by quoting the bitter words of one tipsy Russian friend at a late-night party:

Everyone's having a grand time, yes—but don't let that fool you. Inside we're all sick, full of hate and disgust. We hate those bastards at the top . . . and hate ourselves too. A handful of martyrs are brave enough to protest openly—and we don't even lift a finger for them, we have parties like this to try to *forget* them. . . . We stand by while they're sent to the camps. That's what's inside us, behind the merry façade; pain and disgust, guilt and hate. . . . I drink to the real heroes of this country, the people in the camps—but that's all I do about it: drink.

Émigré writer Anatoly Kuznetsov also conveyed something of the degradation of the sellout intellectual in the Soviet Union when he spoke of the "dangers involved in prostituting yourself, or bartering away your conscience in that strange world of perpetual intrigues and constant self-censorship". Referring especially to the betrayal of one's own standards that this entails he continued:

It is the road to destruction, because the official, external censorship, by engendering self-censorship and compromise, destroys the soul, destroys the artist, and destroys the human being. I, personally, have gone down the road of surrender to the very brink of destruction, where I felt like either committing suicide or going out of my mind.

He spoke literally, not figuratively.

The real careerists are more cheerful than Kuznetsov about their compromises. The real-life protagonist of Vladimir Voinovich's *Ivankiad* had no qualms about manoeuvring to get an extra room for his American-acquired toilet by publishing the hack verse of the ageing poetaster who happened to be chairman of the housing co-operative. And numerous Writers' Union members obediently signed scurrilous statements during the official campaign to accuse Solzhenitsyn of treason.

The Writers' Union, in fact, is one of the most notorious homes of hacks and sycophants in the USSR. When he finally left the union in 1977 after not being allowed abroad (and after watching the expulsion from the union of several colleagues), Georgy Vladimov retaliated with a blistering attack. His breakaway was telling, as he had long tried to work within the system—and the authorities, worried about the brain drain, had long tried to accommodate him.

"Our mighty Writers' Union," railed Vladimov in his resignation letter, "invariably prefers to hinder rather than help writers." He accused the union of condoning the "sufferings, death, and extinction" of more than six hundred of its members imprisoned under Stalin, and of being a "most faithful companion of the evil will of the all-powerful". By hounding Pasternak, Brodsky, and Solzhenitsyn, Vladimov continued,

by persecuting and banishing everything that is rebellious, "mistaken", contrary to socialist realist literature, indeed all which formed the power and prime of our literature, you have destroyed in your own Union any individual undertaking. . . . We have reached the limit of irreversibility, when writers whose books are neither sold nor read dictate to those whose books are sold and read. Your governing bodies, your secretariats, your commissions are flooded with this dismal mediocrity. . . .

Carry on the burden of mediocrity, do what you are fit for and called upon to perform—crush, persecute, detain. But leave me out.

Vladimov's indictment could also be directed at the Journalists' Union—except that the indignation would be less, since this hack occupation is held in general contempt. Outside of the party apparat and the secret police, journalism is probably the most highly politicized professional field in the Soviet Union. One Moscow joke, describing the journalist type, has an ideological cross-examiner ask his subject if he is always straight in following the party line. "Of course not," replies this paragon. "Whenever the party line zigs I zig too, and whenever it zags I zag right with it." That the zigzags require appropriate fabrications by journalists is taken for granted.

All the careerists, in fact, seem to lie routinely—a reflex that repeatedly astounds Westerners. Western journalists are conditioned to expect a certain number of falsehoods in government, of course, and, nowadays, even juggling of experiment results by some Western scientists. But we always assume that any prevarication in the West has a reason, that irrelevant lies are avoided, if only because they generate too many complications. We just do not believe that our interlocutors will compose bald, improvised fibs as their natural first response. We do not credit Dostoevsky's blanket accusation that "among our Russian intellectual classes the very existence of a non-liar is an impossibility".

In the Soviet Union, however, the frugal peasant predisposition to hide everything until the angle of the questioner is deduced has proved to be culturally stronger than "truth seeking", even among today's (careerist) intelligentsia. The congenital lie has become a bureaucratic and pseudo-intellectual habit. As Solzhenitsyn has it, "in our country the lie is not the whim of corrupt natures but a mode of existence, a condition of the daily welfare of every man. In our country the lie has been incorporated into the state system as the vital link holding everything together."

At the most elementary level, an official will tell a visitor quite shamelessly that the sought-after person she is obviously talking to at that moment on the telephone cannot be found anywhere. A concierge will automatically assert that Ivan Ivanovich has gone out of the dormitory for the whole evening—and be quite unembarrassed when Ivan Ivanovich strolls by on his way to the shower as she finishes her sentence. A Foreign Ministry bureaucrat will blandly declare that the city of Vitebsk has no municipal museum then, when the inquirer points out that the *Bolshaya Encyclopedia* mentions a museum, will shift without flinching to say that the museum, alas, burned to the ground, very sad for Vitebsk. (I actually believed that one, and was quite surprised when I chanced by the site to discover that not even the smell of fire had passed over it.)

Something of my own cultural credulity in this area seems to colour other Westerners' observations about the Soviet Union as well. Harvard professor Robert Coles related in some detail in the *New York Review of Books* his conversations with Soviet psychiatrists at an international gathering and their persuasive denials of the charge that normal dissidents are committed to mental hospitals in the Soviet Union. "The two doctors I talked with were not schemers, nor mere cynical opportunists," concluded Coles. "They believed what they said. . . ."

In rebuttal, the authors of the standard English-language compilation of cases of Soviet psychiatric abuse, psychiatrist Sidney Bloch and political scientist Peter Reddaway, drew attention to a long tradition of lying convincingly for a higher cause, and persuading oneself of the truth of the lie in the process. They then quoted the private confession of a top Soviet official writer, a man of equal stature and prestige to the Soviet psychiatrists Coles spoke with. "This person," the author wrote over his own photograph in a book owned by a close Western friend, "is the biggest bastard in the whole of Soviet literature."

Most intellectuals, of course, are neither humanist saints nor opportunist bastards. They fall somewhere in between—and their fiercest arguments about conscience and expediency often rage within themselves. They operate in the interstices. They try to maintain self-respect along with the perquisites of, say, Writers' Union membership. They limit their wheeling and dealing to the minimum necessary to get a marginal satire published. When they get trapped, they give information to the KGB, but they try to pass on only innocuous information, and they count it a victory if they manage to stretch out the reporting sessions from once a month, perhaps, to once every six weeks.

It's a slippery slope. The young rebel poet easily turns into the token rebel, and the token rebel into the suave host who steers visiting foreign writers away from problematical Soviet authors.

But there are intriguing journeys in the opposite direction as well. Novelist Georgy Vladimov's hegira eventually carried him from stubbornly writing his own view of a disapproved truth to making the ultimate break with the official intelligentsia. In 1975 Vladimov was the harbinger of a tentative new wind in literature. After years of waiting for a fresh thaw in the Soviet Union he had finally given up and published abroad his chilling metaphorical tale about a guard dog for a forced labour camp that was turned loose after the mass release of prisoners in 1956. For a season the animal wandered aimlessly around the village, until the day it discovered a procession of Communist Youth League volunteers who had come to build the new Siberia. With this jog to its memory, the masterless dog resumed its duty; it herded the column toward the old camp, attacking and disciplining any who tried to escape.

Notably, Vladimov was not expelled from the Writers' Union for this provocative fiction; instead, he was given a long, friendly interview in the *Literary Gazette*. The reason, according to a friend of the author, was that the government was worried about losing its best writers abroad and was trying to pacify those who did not themselves renounce Soviet society.

By 1977, however, when it became clear that his was an isolated case, Vladimov made his irreversible break with the establishment, sent his bitter resignation to the Writers' Union, and assumed the leadership of the Moscow branch of Amnesty International.

What accounts for such metamorphoses among the minuscule number who slide up instead of down the slippery slope?

For some intellectuals who experience these transformations it's a strong emotional jolt—such as the death of a beloved wife—that makes them reconsider their lives and works. For some it's the maturing of their children into adults that leaves them free to take risks without destroying their children's lives. For others it's the realization that they have got as high in their careers as they are going to get, and that continued compromise will no longer bring any rewards.

For still others, the increment of lies suddenly reaches critical mass and triggers a rebellion. Sasha Sokolov—the son of a general in military intelligence—who is being acclaimed as a possible new Gogol or Nabokov after the American publication of his first novel, attributes his own explosion into a writer of fiercely individualistic prose to being fed up with all the lies.

This burning question of honesty or betrayal, while it is central to the self-definition of the humanists and their reverse-image careerists, hardly matters at all to the third category among the intelligentsia, the technocrats. These "mental workers", or all the skilled, non-manual manpower needed for a complex economy, are so far removed from the moral notions of the humanists that *Nineteen Eighty-Four*'s telescreen, Thought Police, and other control paraphernalia would seem superfluous.

In the official Soviet classification these people comprise the real intelligentsia. They are the proud result of the diffusion of literacy and education throughout the country since 1917. They include all white-collar employees, and they are the rough equivalent of the West's upper-middle class in social status if not in attitude. They consist of technicians and engineers, military officers and party bureaucrats.

This new intelligentsia—which far outnumbers the humanists—is discontinuous with the past. It does not think of itself as a coherent group with a shared outlook. Above all, it is not a hothouse species like the aristocratic nineteenth-century intellectuals.

Solzhenitsyn highlights the distinction in describing a Gulag cellmate, one of the new engineers who had turned cocky and refused to supply some building materials "for a certain prosecutor's dacha", and had ended up in gaol. This engineer, whom Solzhenitsyn identified only as Z-v, felt very sorry for himself, especially because his arrest had prematurely terminated at 290 his meticulous count of women he had "uncorked", and had thus prevented him from reaching his goal of three hundred.

Until the late 1920s engineers were more in the mould of the old-style intellectuals, Solzhenitsyn observes:

> I had grown up among engineers, and I could remember the engineers of the twenties very well indeed: their open, shining intellects, their free and gentle humour, their agility and breadth of thought, the ease with which they shifted from one engineering field to another, and, for that matter, from technology to social concerns and art. Then, too, they personified good manners and delicacy of taste; well-bred speech that flowed evenly and was free of uncultured words; one of them might play a musical instrument, another dabble in painting; and their faces always bore a spiritual imprint.

Z-v, by contrast, "had been one of those dishevelled, unenlightened peasant boys whose wasted talents so distressed Belinsky and Tolstoy". He joined the Komsomol, and his work there

> shot him like a rocket through the Workers' School right into the Industrial Academy. He arrived there in 1929—at the very moment when *those other* engineers were being driven in whole herds into Gulag. It was urgently necessary for those in power to produce their own engineers—politically conscious, loyal, one-hundred percenters, who were to become bigwigs of production . . .

Today's new technocrats may not be as crude as Solzhenitsyn's cellmate. But they certainly do have pragmatic rather than visionary goals: how to swap apartments to finesse more living space, how to wangle a decent piece of red meat from the butcher, how to get a mechanic to fix the new Fiat—these are the important issues.

With his own history, the Westerner considers freedom of expression, association, and travel to be universal human urges. He sees the Soviet dissident as the obvious champion of Everyman's cause.

But their history has given Russians precious little experience with these exotic precepts. For centuries the leisure for expression and travel has belonged by definition to the elite. It has been a byproduct of the nobleman's freedom to own more property and money than his inferiors.

In a peasant society there is only a finite sum of wealth and privilege; any individual portion of this sum must be wheedled out of the ruler in competition with all other claimants. In a hierarchical order one man's freedom necessarily implies another man's unfreedom; anything else would be chaos.

Today's technocrats, then, having so recently gained the freedom to escape physical drudgery and to acquire co-operative apartments, are much more interested in guarding these tangible liberties than in reaching for some nebulous "freedom of speech" that would never put beef and oranges on the table. "Freedom of speech", in fact, sounds like a trick of the hat-and-tie-wearing crowd to appropriate more than its share of the dachas. Nor do those wily ones who manage to get out of Marx's vaunted working class and perhaps rise high enough to travel abroad gain any concept of liberty from exposure to Western Europe or America. They come back from America far more impressed by the toilets than by casual personal initiative.

This means that today's technical intelligentsia—which would include the party's administrative technicians or, in more proper ideological terms, the implementers of the Marxist science of society—are unlikely transmission belts for bringing more individual initiative into Soviet society. Today's narrow technical and ideological education, plus habitual conformity on the job, do not induce broader intellectual or social curiosity among this technical and political intelligentsia.

Nor, apparently, do the technical demands of their jobs inculcate much desire on the part of the new managers to take more responsibility in cutting through the rigidities and inefficiencies of a command economy. There seems to be little push for any decentralization of decision-making in the economic sphere that might eventually spill over into the political sphere. Such expansion of their powers on the job would be a nightmare rather than a luxury—a push out of cosy security into unpredictable trouble.

Even more discouraging for dissidents than any of the intellectuals, though, is the man in the street—the worker-peasant who constitutes the bulk of the Soviet population. The gap between the dissenter and the "masses"—and even between the humanist intellectual and the masses—is as central a fact of Soviet society today as was the gap between the *narodnik* intellectuals and the *narod* in the nineteenth century. The suspicious "dark people" turned the *narodnik* reformers who came to enlighten them over to the police—and things aren't all that different today.

Virtually no workers joined in the Soviet human-rights petitions of the late 1960s—in stark contrast to Czechoslovakia in 1968 and especially Poland in 1980. And when recidivist dissident Ginzburg was convicted in Kaluga, 100 miles southwest of Moscow, local proletarian citizens chanted "Not enough!" and "Shoot them all!" No activist labours under the delusion that all of those public cries come from paid KGB agitators.

Some of this primordial hostility toward dissent arises from what

Alexander Herzen diagnosed in the nineteenth century as Russian "patriotic syphilis"; more of it arises from class antagonism. The dissenters are seen as traitors for criticizing their own country in the area of civil rights, and for scandalously siding with the Czechs against the Russians in 1968. And both the dissidents and the humanist intellectuals are resented as aristocrats by the average citizen.

Ironically, in this society that was founded to eliminate classes, animosity toward the atavistic "upper class" by workers far surpasses class feeling in Western capitalist societies.

The aversion is mutual. Bosses would consider it beneath them to lend a hand in any physical exertion required of their underlings. Mavericks in the various professions are punished by demotion to factory work (even though modestly skilled factory workers earn more than teachers or doctors). City parents go to extraordinary lengths to shield their children from the shame of a vocational education. Party and government bureaucrats are sticklers for gradations of protocol and jealously enforce every iota of deference due them from subordinates.

The privileged Moscow and Leningrad university students catch on quickly and adopt the common disdain for physical labour. They feel crowded by the crude *gegemon* ("hegemon", the pejorative slang word for worker, from the Marxist phrase "hegemony of the proletariat"). They are appalled when they are sent on potato-picking brigades and have to mix with peasants even a short hundred kilometres outside Moscow. They learn then how the "dark people" live—apathetically, in mud, with no entertainment except television, and nothing to buy in the collective farm shop except vodka. The students recoil too from the lice and absence of baths in the melting-pot army (as well as from being beaten up by peasant-worker non-commissioned officers, and from having their few books stolen or destroyed in the barracks).

A few humanists and even dissidents come from worker or peasant backgrounds: Alexander Zinoviev, author of the savage satire, *The Yawning Heights*, for example, and General Grigorenko, the son of a peasant. But most of the *narod* are recognizable successors to the plebs who in the 1930s satirized the effete upper class with such uproarious gestures as threatening to roast live mice in the intellectuals' hifalutin' toasters.

So vast a gap can create problems even when both sides are striving to bridge it. When a group of aggrieved Soviet workers did try to join forces with human-rights dissidents in the autumn of 1977, the attempt led to bruised feelings all around. Vladimir Klebanov, a Donbas mine foreman, appeared in Moscow one day and announced that he had been confined to a psychiatric hospital for four-and-a-half years after he complained that unrealistically high production quotas forced his men to work twelve hours a day in unsafe conditions. Twelve to fifteen miners had been killed and between six and seven hundred a year were injured in accidents in his mine alone, he said.

Klebanov—along with a waitress, a locksmith, a housing maintenance man and various other workers he met in party and government office waiting rooms while they were all seeking redress for grievances—approached the Moscow human-rights dissidents for support in publicizing their complaints to Western journalists. Sakharov first turned them down, thinking, as he told reporters, that the workers didn't know what they were letting themselves in for. Presumably Sakharov also thought—since the timing coincided with a crackdown on the Helsinki Agreement monitors—that however repugnant the firing of a waitress who reported petty embezzlement in her restaurant, this injustice was a less than monumental issue to pick yet another fight with the government on. For their part, the workers insisted on their "right to complain" and told Western journalists bitterly that Sakharov and the rest "consider themselves above us".

Subsequently, with the Helsinki monitoring group's belated blessing, the workers did form two unofficial trade unions, claiming two hundred adherents. The leaders suffered the expected arrests, exiles and committals to mental hospitals. Their only victory was a moral one, outside the country. Their repression by the Soviet Union induced the French Communists—whose nominee had held the post of Secretary-General in the Soviet-dominated World Federation of Trade Unions for thirty-one years—to resign from this position. And it spurred the International Labour Organization to issue a report charging the Soviet Union (and other Communist countries) with violating ILO conventions in not allowing independent trade unions. The reprimand was at least a pinprick to the proletarian Soviet state—and it played a role in the US decision to rejoin the ILO.

The shared baptism of fire gave Klebanov, in his insane asylum, and his fellow trade union organizers, in prison and out, a common understanding with the intellectual dissidents. But the intellectual dissenters' demands for freedom and democracy are less comprehensible to the vast majority of workers who have not themselves tried persistently to exercise a "right to complain" or had such personal collisions with the KGB. To the Soviet masses, freedom and democracy remain class demands that the intellectuals are making to get more of the pie than the workers. They are of no general advantage.

The *narod* know what it's like to compete for one's own share of the limited harvest on the land, or one's own share in a continuing scarcity economy in the city. They are determined not to let those soft-living *ochkariki* ("spectacle-wearers" or eggheads) pull a fast one and muscle them out of that share.

Dissident (now émigré) historian Andrei Amalrik summarized this attitude in observing that the Russian peasants are afraid of freedom. They are afraid someone else can use it better than they can, and they consider that unjust. Therefore they prefer that nobody acquire such unequal freedom.

Again, it was that supremely reasonable and moderate Westernizer, Alexander Herzen, who deplored this phenomenon a century ago as surely as he deplored "patriotic syphilis". Referring directly to Western Europeans of the time but alluding broadly to his fellow Russians, Herzen wrote,

> [The people] are indifferent to individual freedom, [to] liberty of speech; the masses love authority. They are still blinded by the arrogant glitter of power, they are offended by those who stand alone. By equality they understand equality of oppression. . . . But to govern themselves doesn't enter their heads.

While some in the upper class seek liberty, then, the peasants seek its opposite, equality—an equality of result, not of opportunity.

"Be like everyone else" could thus be termed the consummate Soviet virtue, concludes Alexander Zinoviev, novelist, one-time Moscow University logic professor, and now exile, stripped of his Soviet citizenship. What bothers him in this is less the element of compulsion than the element of voluntary conformity. In the dystopian society portrayed in *The Yawning Heights*, the central feature is not that things are forbidden but that "the number of those who want permission to do anything is pitifully small". Anyone who is different is suspect. "A remarkable mind is seen as an abnormality, and remarkable ignorance—as a remarkable mind."

In Soviet society, Zinoviev explained to a British interviewer,

> So far as the average citizen is concerned, he has his bread and his vodka, he need not pay doctors' bills, he is told that housing is virtually free (which it isn't), work is guaranteed, he is not expected to work too hard, and he has learned to live without freedom. If elections were held tomorrow, he'd no doubt vote to keep the present regime in power.

Zinoviev's final damning judgment is that "the Soviet system is eminently suitable for the Soviet people."

08.15 *Perm Province*

We do not see it from the Trans-Siberian Railroad of course. But somewhere out there in the forest is one of the two main penal colonies to which political prisoners are sent. Perm's most renowned inmate (before his exchange for Chilean Communist Luis Corvalan) was Vladimir Bukovsky, convicted for documenting Soviet committal of sane dissidents to insane asylums.

Conditions in the Perm camp, according to prisoners who staged hunger and work strikes in the mid- and late seventies typically include winter cold, hard labour in severely polluted workshops, and malnutrition and hunger on diets well below international standards for minimal calorie rations.

"We are served rotten potatoes and cabbage," reported one Perm convict in a communication smuggled to the outside world in 1973. "Maggots and cockroaches are often found in the food, and the mess hall is frequently permeated by the stench of rotten fish. Despite chronic hunger, the inmates refuse their supper whenever rotten fish is served; this, however, does not improve conditions at all."

Another Perm prisoner named Opanasenko despaired after having served twenty-two years of a twenty-five-year sentence and hanged himself, leaving behind the note: "No more strength to hold out. Curse you, monsters!"

Bukovsky arrived here in 1973, a year after the Perm series of camps was inaugurated. Before, politicals had generally been sent to Mordovia, but Mordovia had become porous: prisoners were successfully bribing camp guards to smuggle protests, announcements of hunger strikes and even one tape of dissident Alexander Ginzburg, to the outside world. Perm would be more isolated. It would not have a couple of generations of hereditary guards who had become slack. It would have a sufficiently harsh winter to give pause to even the worst offenders who would populate the camp. It would not coddle convicts with medical frills.

In accord with this philosophy, all incoming Perm prisoners were automatically classified as fit for work, even one-legged men, even invalids from birth. One such twenty-five-year-term prisoner died of a perforated ulcer a few weeks after being made to perform heavy labour; others seemed likely to follow. Bukovsky somehow got word of the situation to Moscow and thus to the West, and began a campaign of protests inside the camp. As a result of the unwelcome international publicity the camp was inspected daily by a parade of generals, colonels and mysterious civilians, until a surgeon was finally assigned to Perm, invalid status was restored, and the authorities actually began allowing medical treatment for the very sick.

Subsequently, Bukovsky was placed in the "penal isolator", more familiarly known as the "box", for three and a half months. This meant a daily diet of 13.5 oz. of bread, salt, and hot water, supplemented every other day, in theory, by 1.8 oz. of fish, 7.5 oz. of potatoes, 6 oz. of vegetables, 1.5 oz. of groats, 0.3 oz. of flour, 0.18 oz. of fat. On such a regimen, Bukovsky has explained, "after a month the skin begins to peel from your arms and legs. After two months you find it impossible to read; you just can't take anything in."

Bukovsky was finally let out of the box lest he die under the glare of international publicity. Three days later, he and thirty-nine other convicts went on a month-long hunger strike, and those who were too weak went on a normal work strike, to protest coercion. The neighbouring labour camp joined in. The authorities threw the strikers into the box—so their comrades refused to go out to rollcall. In the showdown, remarkably, the non-striking half of the camp, including even the stoolpigeons, broke ranks against orders instead of waiting out the hours-long rollcall. The by now excellent communications again carried the saga to Western correspondents in Moscow, then back on Western radio to Soviet audiences, then back to the Perm strikers in the whispers of the camp guards. Such is the stuff of victory in the labour camps.

The continuity of Russian history is eerie. In Tolstoy's *Resurrection*, it was at Perm that the prostitute Katerina was at last shifted in her Siberian convoy from the group of common criminals to travel with the less harshly treated political prisoners. Tolstoy wrote this late novel to protest inhumane penal conditions; his wrath informed even his descriptive passages:

> There was no wind, and the cloud of dust raised by thousands of feet hovered all the time above the prisoners as they moved down the centre of the road. . . . Line after line they advanced, strange fearful creatures dressed alike, thousands of feet shod alike, all in step, swinging their arms as though to keep up their spirits. There were so many of them, they looked exactly alike and their circumstances were so extraordinarily odd that to Nekhlyudov [Katerina's first lover] they no longer seemed to be men, but peculiar and dreadful creatures of some sort.
>
> The din of voices mingled with the clattering of chains and the horrible smell—always merged for Nekhlyudov into one agonizing sensation of moral nausea which soon turned to a physical feeling of sickness, the one combined with and intensifying the other.

From May to October, in those days before the Trans-Siberian Railroad, such convoys travelled the thousands of miles to exile by foot and river barge, trudging fifteen to twenty miles a day, resting every third day. Prisoners walked with ankles manacled by 5–8 lb. fetters—and went barefoot once they had worn through their flimsy slippers. Their entertainment consisted of gambling over louse races and flea jumps. Disease was rife. Death was a commonplace.

That was in the 1890s. But in the 1930s Eugenia Ginzburg's own experience as a convict immediately evoked for her memories of Tolstoy's *Resurrection* and of the earlier Decembrists' wives. In his Gulag Archipelago Stalin was starting nothing new, only expanding a cruel tradition on a scale that even Russians who lived through it can hardly grasp.

Between those first political prisoners, the Decembrists, and imprisoned Communist Party members like Ginzburg, however, there was one conspicuous disjunction. Even in Siberian mines the Decembrists still clung to the ideals they had gleaned from the French Revolution—and to their faith in the future. On finally meeting her husband again in Siberia, Maria Volkonskaya first fell on her knees to kiss her husband's shackles, embracing the martyrdom that would speed the coming revolution of justice and equality.

The Ginzburgs, on the contrary, had seen all hope betrayed. They had actually created the revolution the Decembrists dreamed about—and they found they had fathered a monster.

Today, three decades after Stalin, the vast majority of those purge victims who survived have been released. Random terror has all but ceased. But directed persecution of political, religious, and cultural dissidents continues. Amnesty International calculates a current minimum of 10,000 prisoners of conscience in the country out of a high total prison population reaching one million in Western estimates, 1.7 million in the estimate of Jewish emigrant Mikhail Agursky, five million, or an astonishing 2 per cent of the population, in the smuggled estimate of inmate Yury Orlov. It's the highest proportion of prisoners to free citizens of any country in the world, greater even than the runner-up South Africa, two or three times greater, even at the most conservative estimate, than the third-place offender, the United States.

The Soviet regime has powerful control tools indeed to persuade any mavericks to join the passive consensus. For the dissident it has labour camps and other violence. For the intellectual it has censorship as well as perquisites. For the man in the street it has *meshchanstvo*, or "philistinism". Classless ideology notwithstanding, it uses all of these tools to maintain gulfs as wide as possible between the three groups. *Divide et impera.*

Arrests, beatings, imprisonment, and confinement in insane asylums of those harbouring democratic delusions form the basic repertoire of violence for dissenters. With an avenging scream Solzhenitsyn has described the horror of Stalin's Gulag Archipelago. With dispassion Amnesty International has catalogued the present-day incarceration of prisoners of conscience in gaols and camps with deliberately inadequate food and health care, while Reddaway and Bloch have documented 210 case histories of dissenters who are held in madhouses in their book *Russia's Political Hospitals.*

The less institutionalized street beatings, nobody has bothered to compile. It is only by talking to Sakharov and others that one learns—or learned—about these, piecemeal. About Russia's outstanding Rilke scholar, for example, who in 1976 was attacked by thugs outside his apartment and fatally beaten, to teach others to toe the line, according to Sakharov. Or about the ill parents of the brilliant but bedridden mathematician Grigory Chudnovsky, who for years was denied permission to emigrate to Israel for medical treatment. In 1977 this couple was similarly beaten, though not fatally, by street thugs. Sakharov regarded this act too as KGB intimidation.

Today's isolation of dissenters in psychiatric hospitals is more of an innovation than the labour camps. To be sure, Nicholas I locked philosopher Pyotr Chaadaev out of the way in a mental hospital in 1836 after Chaadaev returned from a European trip criticizing tyranny at home. But the systematic use of asylums as a memory hole for other-thinkers began only in the post-World War II era.

The present-day practice turns on its ear Lenin's thesis that mental illness has social causes (and therefore would disappear in a reformed society led by the Communist Party). Now mental illness is itself held to be the cause of all anti-social activity. Therefore drunks, murderers, and dissidents, by definition, are schizophrenic and may be treated as such.

From this it is but a short logical step to collective mental hospitalization, and thence to the various diagnoses and descriptions of dissenter symptoms that have been recorded in the Soviet Union: "paranoid reform ideas", "deficient capacity to adjust to his social surroundings", "overestimation of his own person", "political delusions", "sluggish schizophrenia", "grandiose ideas of reforming the world", "an obsessive mania for truth-seeking", "extolling the Western way of life", "considers the entry of Soviet troops into Czechoslovakia to have been aggression", "thinks that he must devote his life to the ideal of communism", "reformist delusions", "wears a beard". Or, "to put up an icon and photographs of people like Academician Sakharov and General Grigorenko goes against our generally accepted norm of behaviour and therefore indicates mental deviance." Or, "meticulousness of thought and insufficiently critical attitude toward the existing situation" (meaning the patient refuses to recant).

Even the absence of any symptoms of mental disturbance during an examination can be taken as a sign of imbalance. One chairman of a psychiatric diagnosis commission investigating a teenaged girl caught distributing samizdat cited as proof of derangement the fact that the girl showed no emotion at all when taken to Moscow's infamous Serbsky Institute for Forensic Psychiatry.

In international circles Soviet officials stoutly deny that any sane person has ever been confined to a mental hospital—a breathtaking claim for any country. In domestic practice, however, it is often made quite clear to the person being committed that his illness is political rather than mental. In 1972 the director of one mental hospital told Yury Belov, "We aren't treating you for illness but for your opinions." In 1974 Viktor Fainberg was informed, "Your disease is dissent. As soon as you renounce your opinions and adopt the correct point of view, we will let you out."

In the one case in which an exhaustive psychiatric examination of a Soviet dissident was conducted in the West—with the concurrence both of the émigré patient and of the Soviet psychiatrists who had pronounced him insane—General Grigorenko was given a totally clean bill of health. Indeed, Washington and Yale University psychiatrist Walter Reich, who participated in the American examination, concluded that where the Soviet doctors "claimed obsessions, we found perseverance; where they cited delusions, we found rationality; where they identified psychotic recklessness, we found committed devotion, and where they diagnosed pathology, we found health."

Committals to mental hospitals are frequently approved by courts without any lawyer's defence of the accused, and also without testimony by doctors chosen by the accused. There have been repeated cases of witnesses perjuring themselves, and of defendants having been drugged before their trials.

Diagnosis on which committal is based is at best casual. The Serbsky Institute's head, Dr Georgy Morozov, one of the most notorious of those Soviet psychiatrists who hospitalize dissenters, once boasted that he took only twenty-five seconds to examine Vladimir Bukovsky, according to Yury Novikov, a division chief at Serbsky and Executive Secretary of the Soviet Society of Psychiatrists who later defected to the West. And Dr Novikov, who was called upon to translate Grigorenko's dossier to West German journalists in Moscow, describes Grigorenko's "symptoms" as plagiarized wholesale from the standard Soviet psychiatric textbook.

Such diagnosis is sufficient to declare dissidents mentally incompetent and relegate them to the harshest special clinics for the incurably insane—even without any previous history of insanity or violence.

These practices do not in any way violate the Soviet psychiatrists' oath. On assuming his healing profession the Soviet doctor does not swear to maintain professional ethics or to keep the confidences of patients. Chillingly, he pledges instead: "I will in all my actions be guided by the principles of communist morality, ever to bear in mind the high calling of the Soviet physician and my responsibility to the people and the Soviet state." Such an oath hardly induces restraint among young psychiatrists eager to exercise their diagnostic powers—or among senior psychiatrists eager to follow KGB directives to find mental illness in specified patients.

That such KGB direction is an integral part of the system is attested to by both patients and doctors. General Grigorenko saw his psychiatric examiner, a head of division in his clinic, coming to work in the uniform of a KGB colonel. Dr Novikov writes that psychiatrists seldom refuse the "recommendations" of the party or KGB, even in cases where they labour under the handicap of having to certify the condition of patients they have never met personally. In Serbsky at least three psychiatrists have direct links to the KGB, and one of them holds as high a post in the parent KGB as he does in Serbsky. The Fourth Division in Serbsky concerns itself exclusively

with dissenters, Novikov continues, and the Soviet Union's twelve special
clinics for incurably insane and political dissidents (in a ratio of nine to one,
Novikov estimates) are the only Soviet hospitals under the direction, not of
the Health Ministry, but of the Interior Ministry.

A psychiatrist who refuses to play along with KGB orders may himself be
sentenced to prison camp. This was the way Dr Semyon Gluzman landed in
the Perm camp with Bukovsky—and the way these two came to co-author a
secret handbook of advice for dissenters undergoing mental examination.
(Typical advice: Say that everything in your life was normal.

> The pregnancy of your mother and your birth ran according to plan. You
> learned at the right time to sit up, walk, and talk. . . . You never liked to
> play alone, . . . were never a sleepwalker, . . . and liked or disliked going
> to school just as much as everyone else. . . . You became interested in the
> opposite sex in puberty, and [later] your sexuality never went beyond the
> bounds of decency.

Furthermore, don't ever get drawn into a discussion of how surrealistic art
can show flying horses or why modern poetry doesn't rhyme.)

When a dissident has been ordered to a mental hospital he stays there until
world public opinion pries him out (biologist Zhores Medvedev, General
Grigorenko, mathematician Leonid Plyushch, psychiatric hospital chronicler Bukovsky), or until the KGB judges that he has been rendered
harmless. Committal to a mental hospital is not subject even to the formal
legal checks of criminal sentences. It continues "pending recovery", that is,
indefinitely.

An ordinary inmate can bribe his way out of a mental institution for a
handful of roubles, Bukovsky recounts; even a legless man in one of his
wards was able to buy enough time to hobble to the nearest bus-stop before the guards sounded the alarm. But for the dissidents there is no such
escape.

These men and women—some 350 in Novikov's, some 700 in Reddaway
and Bloch's estimates—are in for long years of caroming between the mad
world of their genuinely insane asylum mates and the mad world of their
often sadistic warders. The orderlies, common criminals most of them, are
given their crazy fiefdoms to rule over as petty tyrants, and they exercise
their authority with a vengeance. Inside the mental hospitals the common
indignities range from theft of the patients' personal possessions to forbidding patients to go to the toilet without a bribe of tobacco, from sexual
assault to painful forced drugging, from electric shocks to the excruciating
"wet pack", in which a recalcitrant subject is rolled in wet canvas that
gradually binds the encased body more and more tightly as it dries, some-

times causing unconsciousness. Beatings are a routine punishment, a diversion even, and if their beatings happen to cause death, warders are not held responsible.

Apart from such personal maltreatment, the general hospital conditions include overcrowding and underfeeding. The typical day's rations in the Minsk special clinic, according to Dr Novikov, fall far short of the prescribed 1,300 calories per day; they consist of a main noon meal of cabbage soup, a spoonful of porridge in the mornings and evenings plus, now and then, a small potato with vegetables.

Pen and paper are not allowed inside the hospitals, of course. When General Grigorenko protested against this restriction the retort was, "What do you need a pen for? You'll start getting ideas and writing them down, which is not permitted in your case."

Soviet officials have derided Western criticism as "anti-Soviet slander". But they have never denied the specific charges about individual case treatment made in the Bloch–Reddaway book and Dr Novikov's articles in the West. In the absence of such rebuttal the World Psychiatric Association in 1977 condemned Soviet practices, citing "the extensive evidence of the systematic abuse of psychiatry for political purposes in the Union of Soviet Socialist Republics".

For the intellectual who is not a dissident the extreme sanction of prison or mental hospital is not generally needed. The stick of censorship, along with the carrot of dachas, is usually adequate to preserve the party's monopoly on truth, wisdom, morality, and history.

My own brushes with censorship have been slight. Foreign journalists were finally exempted from prior censorship by Khrushchev in 1961, and no longer have to pass multiple copies of stories through a surrealistic post office window large enough to admit the corpus delicti but small enough to shield the receiving clerk from ever being seen. These days resident foreigners are also, in theory, allowed to receive general foreign periodicals without hindrance.

There is, however, one American magazine that reached me only half the time: the *New Yorker*. Its sin, I suspect, was less ideological perversion than irresistible attractiveness to the postal monitors. Basically, I made this small involuntary contribution to cultural exchange cheerfully rather than grudgingly—though I often wondered if the censors who lifted my *New Yorker*s had as much trouble deciphering Edward Koren cartoons as I had appreciating *Krokodil* jokes.

My second touch of censorship was no more serious. It involved the old newspapers that accumulated at a rapid rate next to the claw-footed tub in my office bathroom. I turned them in for recycling and thus gained the right to buy certain books (of the ilk of *The Three Musketeers*) that are available only

to those who help conserve paper. Since the censors' long arm extends
to anything that might slip into public circulation, I had to ensure that even
my waste appeared pure, by binding my discarded Paris *Herald Tribune*s on
the inside, my *Komsomolskaya Pravda*s on the outside. Otherwise, my trash
bundles would have been rejected.

For the Soviet journalist it's rather different. A censor with absolute
powers (one of an estimated 70,000 nation-wide) sits at his own desk in each
newspaper office. (Soviet journalists at least get to associate a real face and
not just the anonymous blue pencil with their ultimate editor.)

Generally speaking, the Soviet newspaper censor exists only to catch
oversights; Soviet journalists can usually be relied on to exercise their own
prior self-censorship. Thus, when the World War II battle site of Stalingrad
(Stalin City) had its name changed overnight to Volgograd in Khrushchev's
1961 de-Stalinization, the morning's *Volgogradskaya Pravda* (which
adroitly changed its masthead overnight too) had the inherent good sense to
report this earthquake in only four lines on page four. Volgograders had to
visit the central square for themselves to see that the city's sixty-foot high
statue had been dismantled sometime between 1 a.m. and 7 a.m., and that
the former Hotel Stalingrad's marque suddenly read only HOTEL ——GRAD.

In more modern times, when a fire swept Moscow's showpiece Hotel
Rossiya in 1977 and an unknown number of guests were incinerated, the
Moscow newspapers were discreet enough to give the item only seventeen
lines, with no mention of fatalities. When two domestic airliners collided in
1979, killing 150 people, Aeroflot told telephone callers for days that it had
no information on the flights concerned—and Tass waited four days before
carrying a skimpy report. When one sex study showed a high rate of frigidity in
the Soviet Union—but no, here the censor reportedly had to intervene to
prevent publication until the numbers were lowered.

Other prohibitions from the serially numbered annual List of Materials
and Information Forbidden for Open Publication in the press include
slander of the state, military secrets, pornography, religious propaganda,
and novels by Soviet authors published abroad. According to mid-seventies
émigré Lev Lifshitz-Losev, they include as well: geographic location of
Soviet deep-sea fish catches; the rouble figure for Soviet investment in the
second Trans-Siberian Railroad; the history of the Sino-Soviet border (and
especially any discussion of the Cossack Far East settlers of bygone
centuries, who might be viewed shallowly as aggressors); the numerical
output of any tractor factory; the number of those who died in the World
War II siege of Leningrad that resulted from Stalin's wartime tactical errors
(the prettified figure of 641,803 may be cited, but not the real figure of over a
million); incidents of cholera and bubonic plague in the Soviet Union after
1937; reference to the special extermination of Jews in German-occupied
Soviet territories in World War II; recognizable photographs of crosses even

on churches that are tourist attractions; and graphics about the various cities' crests, which are showing an unhealthy tendency to imitate heraldic symbols. Nor, of course (unlike Poland), may any publication mention that censorship exists.

The century-and-a-half old list of rapes, murders, floods and disasters that the Marquis de Custine was so astonished to find barred from the pages of the Russian press in the 1830s still applies. Banned too are references to Stalin's pre-war purge of Red Army officers, the secret Soviet–Nazi pact of 1939 partitioning Poland between Germany and Russia, the Soviet World War II massacre in Katyn Wood of 15,000 Polish officers who had been German prisoners of war, and maps showing Soviet post-war territorial gains. Che Guevara's manual, *Tactics of Guerrilla Warfare*, is also off-bounds for being too explicit.

Beyond these specifics anything that "distorts Soviet reality" or "gives rise to uncontrolled associations" is taboo, according to Lifshitz-Losev. The concept would be quite familiar to those Russian censors who have plied their trade ever since before Tsar Nicholas I personally took on the responsibility of expurgating Russia's greatest poet, Alexander Pushkin. Lifshitz-Losev cites the prevailing tone in quoting a Leningrad deputy party secretary's admonition at a meeting of editors: "You, Party editors, ought to be an iron sieve, through which the author must crawl to press."

To illustrate, Lifshitz-Losev's careless reference to "gods" in a children's play about ancient Greece was strained out by the iron sieve of one vigilant censor. Science fiction, that hotbed of quirky dystopias in the West, is kept innocent of any implication that a scientifically perfect society—or technology wedded to repression—might be a nightmare.

Radio, television, and movies are especially sensitive. Live broadcasting is banned, except in the most extraordinary instances (such as the mid-seventies joint US–Soviet space flight). Vodka and prostitution are also banned from public presentation: Beethoven's "Polish drinking song" has gone unperformed in the media for two decades; the drunk scene in Gogol's *Inspector-General* was fudged in the film of this classic; and in the dubbing for the Italian movie *Automobile* the lead prostitute explains unconvincingly that she bought her car with a legacy from her aunt.

Films about the eighteenth-century peasant uprisings (which are otherwise eulogized as forerunners of the 1917 revolution) are barred as too suggestive. Eisenstein's famous *Ivan the Terrible*, Part Two, was banned in the 1930s for its possible allusions to Stalin, and the projected shooting of Part Three was blocked altogether. Then in the 1970s in the film honouring the 150th anniversary of the Decembrists, censors required replacement of the original black-haired lead by a blond actor so as not to remind viewers of the role of Jews in Russian revolutionary movements.

A good rule of thumb in all this is that anything not expressly allowed is forbidden to the screen and to the published word. And the published word, notes Lifshitz-Losev, embraces everything from a sweets wrapper to a wedding announcement. One young professor of his acquaintance was fired because he printed two dozen unauthorized cards adorned with a naked Cupid inviting friends to his nuptial dinner.

To prevent any spread of such abuse, even office photocopy machines must be kept in a separate room with a double- or triple-locked door and barred window. Written permission must be gained to make every reproduction. And in 1977 even more stringent restrictions were placed on the country's eight thousand-odd printing presses and copying centres.

In literature and in the theatre most Russian classics are allowed, so long as they are not perceptibly reinterpreted to criticize the present. Tolstoy is taught in the schools. Dostoevsky has been rehabilitated after his Stalinist blacklisting—though *The Possessed*, Dostoevsky's devastating portrayal of soulless revolutionaries, remains in an indefinite sort of purgatory. Chekhov is still performed movingly by the Moscow Arts Theatre, and excruciatingly by drama school graduating classes.

Modern Western classics are allowed if they are interpreted as critical of the West exclusively. They are barred, however (Samuel Beckett's *Waiting for Godot*, Eugene Ionesco's *Rhinoceros*, Peter Weiss's *Marat/Sade*) if they satirize Eastern as well as Western conformity and alienation.

For a Moscow theatre the formidable array of censors who do not officially exist includes not only Glavlit, or the Main Directorate for the Safeguarding of State Secrets in the Press (formerly the Main Directorate for Matters of Literature and Art) but also the Moscow City Council, the Ministry of Culture of the Russian Republic, and the federal Ministry of Culture.

Foreign books too fall under Soviet censorship regulations on such occasions as Moscow's international book fairs. At the first one, in 1977, *Animal Farm* and *Nineteen Eighty-Four* could not be displayed, of course. Nor could one book on the secret police under Lenin, another on the Chinese–Soviet conflict and Eastern Europe, and a third featuring the American poster from 1945 to 1975. Similarly, before it could open its doors to a clientele of more than one and a quarter million Soviet viewers, the 1977 American photographic exhibition had to pull out of its racks Alistair Cooke's *America*, a National Geographic book on Alaska, and 80 per cent of the photomagazines and yearbooks earmarked for distribution at the exhibition. The 1979 Moscow Book Fair had to go on without several cartoon books, studies of Hitler by John Toland and Joachim Fest, and *Modern Jewish History* by Chazen Chechen.

In art, censorship is no less strict. Here too the norm is socialist realism's rapturous idealization of the Communist utopia as if it were present day truth. Negative views of Soviet life ("distortions of Soviet reality") must not be propagated. In art schools the most talented students must often be rejected, just because these are the ones who are prone to respond to some unpredictable inner voice rather than the voice of prescribed ideology. And those artists who dabble in abstraction may be threatened with incarceration in insane asylums and risk having any open-air exhibit broken up (as one was in 1974) by plainclothesmen-driven bulldozers and water-hose trucks run amok.

Even those seminal modern painters of the early revolutionary years in the Soviet Union must therefore be hidden in cellars. Marc Chagall is an unperson in his hometown of Vitebsk, a town that is now a household name in London and Paris only because of Chagall's whimsical depictions of it. For a major retrospective Russian exhibition shown in America in 1977, Soviet officials released only a few scant works by Kasimir Malevich, Vasili Kandinsky, and Liubov Popova—and exacted as their price "an over-representation of contemporary paintings", in the dry words of the director of the host New York Metropolitan Museum.

And in one attempted dialogue over more than a decade, the Greek citizen and lifelong Moscow resident George Costakis finally found he could not donate his world-famous collection of revolutionary Soviet art to the Tretiakov Gallery with any assurance that it would be displayed. For decades it was his dream to make this unique cultural heritage available to the Russian public, but the Ministry of Culture would never promise that the pictures would in fact be displayed and not just dumped with all the other abstracts in the basement. After some thousand of his lesser-known watercolours and gouaches were stolen under mysterious circumstances, even the optimistic Costakis gave up and agreed in 1977 to give the Soviet government 80 per cent of the collection unconditionally. The remaining 20 per cent he was allowed to take with him on leaving the Soviet Union.

In their efforts the ideological censors have been far more effective in suppressing art than in suppressing literature in the Soviet Union. One of the biggest disappointments of Westerners breaking into the rebel art world in Moscow is the mediocrity even of those painters who defy the official guidelines. Perhaps this results simply from a quirky distribution of talents in our decade. Perhaps in the modern idiom visual stimulation is more crucial than literary stimulation. Whatever the cause, Soviet artists, both official and unofficial, have done far less well under the constraints of censorship than have their poetic and novelistic counterparts. This is one of the great letdowns of a society that inaugurated itself with the inventive, boisterous happenings of that early art commissar, Chagall.

Modern music and ballet exhibit similar trends. Soviet performers of traditional music and dance rank with the best in the world. But even here the most gifted individuals often think they can achieve their greatest artistic fulfilment only in the West—cellist and conductor Mstislav Rostropovich, for example, ballet dancers Rudolf Nureyev, Natalia Makarova, Mikhail Baryshnikov, and Alexander Godunov, conductors Rudolf Barshai and Kirill Kondrashin.

As for creative composers, these have all but atrophied in the Soviet Union. Prokofiev and Shostakovich were good, but they never matched the daring and breadth of early Soviet émigré Igor Stravinsky. Nor is there any contemporary Soviet composer who could compare with Poland's inventive Krzysztof Penderecki.

In the area of popular music the Western fads are anathema to the censors. But a gradual relaxation is setting in. Soviet jazz combos are tolerated in the larger cities and even staged an unprecedented festival in 1979. (The festival shared its debut year with the first performance of Handel's *Messiah* since the revolution.) A few American and European rock groups have toured the Soviet Union too. And in 1977 a Western style hit parade of the top ten Soviet and foreign songs was instituted; Elton John, Uriah Heep, and Abba ranked high. Nonetheless, police still felt obliged after John Lennon's murder in 1980 to break up a meeting of a few hundred young Muscovites who gathered spontaneously to honour their beloved Beatle.

In the field of science, censorship and ideological demands on scholarship are less aggressive. Trofim Lysenko and his dubious claims of turning pines into spruces, wheat into barley, and tropical into Arctic plants (along with his skill at manoeuvring his main rival geneticist into purge and death in a Siberian camp) could tyrannize agriculture and biology in Stalin's and even Khrushchev's time. But following Khrushchev's fall there has been no equivalent ideological enthronement of some sweeping scientific theory at the expense of all contrary experimentation and hypotheses.

Even outside purely academic affairs scientists are granted a little more scope for individuality than are most writers or artists in such matters as wearing beards, or collecting abstract art. And the general awe for science allows a bit more leeway for scientists than for ordinary mortals in the arena of political demands.

Even so, the intellectual restrictions chafe, especially in the periodic "shrinkages" at scientific institutes. Under this system no scientist has tenure in his position. Instead, report cards on the political behaviour of staff scientists are drawn up by an institute's Party and KGB representatives every few years, and those with unsatisfactory records are fired. The liberality or intolerance with which these accounts are rendered varies widely from one place to the next. But often "shrinkages" provide occasions for ideological hardliners and ambitious careerists to rein in the more independent-minded scientists. In the words of Yury Mnyukh, a pioneer in phased transformations in crystals and a 1977 émigré to the West, the person who is weeded out in these reviews is someone who didn't want to include the chief as co-author of his scientific work. Someone who has advanced so much that his work begins to over-shadow the chief's. Someone who has not been good at demonstrating his loyalty by attending political speeches or indoctrinating subordinates.

Mnyukh didn't start out as a dissident—but he did skip political lectures and party activities that stole time from his research, and he did discuss privately with his wife his various discontents at the Pushchino Institute of Biological Physics. These aberrations were enough to get him dropped by the Academy of Sciences in 1973, and to block his desired emigration thereafter. For four years Mnyukh lived in this limbo. Then, deciding he had nothing to lose, he joined the unofficial group monitoring Soviet compliance with the human-rights provisions in the 1975 Helsinki Agreement.

Mnyukh's transformation into a dissident illustrates the constant risk of self-fulfilling prophecy in the regime's anxious censorship. The aim is to maintain a sharp borderline that intellectuals can cross only at the cost of declaring themselves heretics. But in a number of cases the petty surveil-lance has precisely the opposite effect of that intended. Rostropovich, Nureyev, Mnyukh and Vladimov were all, in different ways, driven into exile or dissidence by restrictions at home. More fancifully, one Viktor Bublik, who dreamed of sailing the Atlantic solo, felt compelled to walk for two weeks across Karelia and Finland to Swedish exile, guided by nothing more than a tourist map and a compass, sustained by little more than tea leaves and the lure of the sea.

It's a vicious circle, for the physical or mental flight of such artists provokes the ideological watchdogs to establish even greater safeguards against future defections. And the greater safeguards make artists all the more determined to escape the bounds.

The regime's instrument of control for the masses is both cruder and more sophisticated than the simple prohibitions of censoring the intelligentsia. It is summed up in one word: *meshchanstvo*.

The word *meshchanstvo* is untranslatable into English. The meaning covers the passive traits of complacency, conformity, Babbitry, bourgeois bad taste, vulgarity and anti-intellectualism as well as the meaner traits of careerism, greed, vanity, dishonesty, intellectual pretensions and betrayal of others.

Meshchanstvo is definitely a pejorative. An American philistine might be proud of his anti-intellectual bias, but a Russian *meshchanin* would never admit to his *meshchanstvo*. To some humanists *meshchanstvo*—even more than freedom—is the key issue that must be confronted if Russians are ever to emancipate themselves.

A few examples give the flavour. In Solzhenitsyn's "Matryona's House" each of the three sisters who came to mourn Matryona's death manages in

70 RUSSIA PERCEIVED

her keening to lay claim to precedence in inheriting Matryona's goat and the two hundred roubles she had saved towards her funeral. That's *meshchanstvo*.

Or the youth newspaper *Komsomolskaya Pravda* frowns on the uppitiness of young women who refuse to marry any man except one loaded with a dacha, car and diamond ring. Here the official line is to stamp out *meshchanstvo*. The regime gladly caters to anti-intellectual *meshchanstvo*, however, in nurturing its alliance with the masses (and with the opportunist intellectuals) against the humanist intelligentsia.

American literary critic Vera Dunham calls this alliance "the Big Deal" of Stalin's truce with the new middle class after the devastation of World War II. Stalin gave the new class upward mobility over the corpses he and the Germans had disposed of. In turn, the new class gave its loyalty and conformity to Stalin. It was a modification of Stalin's nationalist wartime treaty with all of the people to a philistine treaty with some of the people, Dunham contends. Stalin asked of the peasant parvenus only a simple indifference to truth and justice. In return, he gave them their Victorian rewards of the scalloped, fringed pink lampshade, lace curtains, the canary in the cage, the grand piano, lessons in dancing and manners, and what Dunham calls "the primordial rubber plant".

These remain the symbols of middle-class Soviet affluence even today, along with 1960s' beehive coiffures and henna-dyed hair. A Western newcomer to Soviet society thinks he is hallucinating when he sees his first lampshade. But after a while it dawns on him that the have-nots of 1917 are finally getting the baubles they were deprived of in their 1890s' childhood.

For these baubles the new middle class gladly pays the price of suspicion of those intellectual nonconformists who champion upper-class notions of freedom and justice. Hatred of the real intelligentsia is as central a feature of Soviet society as is the corruption of power, argues Zinoviev in *The Yawning Heights*:

One need not even attack it. It is enough to leave it unprotected. And society itself will destroy it. The milieu. Colleagues. Friends. Especially the pseudo intellectual milieu. It hates the genuine intelligentsia because it has pretensions to be viewed as such itself. It has power and therefore is merciless. Do you think it takes much to kill the intelligentsia? Nonsense.

Not for nothing did Zinoviev name his fictional society "Ibansk" ("Fucktown").

And yet, and yet . . . This vast gap between the sensibilities of a Zinoviev and the *meshchanstvo* of the Soviet *narod* is spanned by a few overarching bridges. By human kindness and poetry. By religion and nationalism.

The renowned Mstislav Rostropovich recounts that his parents brought him as a boy prodigy to pre-war Moscow to enrol him in the conservatory there. When the senior Rostropovich could find no job and had not a kopeck left, the Muscovite who had rented the family a corner of his room threw the Rostropoviches out, confiscating the family's few belongings. As they stood on the street weeping they were discovered by a total stranger, a woman who lived in a communal apartment with seven other families. That woman took in the four Rostropoviches, feeding and housing them for two years in her own small room—and she even rescued the family's beloved Persian rug and ivory carving from the former landlord.

Dissident Vladimir Bukovsky, on entering a new mental hospital he was to be confined to in the 1970s, met a shoemaker, a returning veteran of the clinic, who immediately took the neophyte under his wing. The shoemaker carried Bukovsky's ten roubles into the hospital himself so it would not be stolen by the guards. Then, when the nurses happily recognized the cobbler, assigned him to the best ward, and began placing orders for heels and soles, he insisted that his new friend Bukovsky be assigned there with him.

In the Gulag as well, Bukovsky found a camaraderie with criminals once he established his own toughness and adherence to underworld ethics. He began writing complaints for the criminals, and they looked to him as an educated man to resolve all their disputes about how many generalissimos there had ever been in the world, how many kilometres it is from Tula to Tambov, or whether Kiev or New York lies farther south.

Nadezhda Mandelstam, widow of Russia's foremost twentieth-century poet, relates how simple villagers banded together to protect her in the textile factory she worked in after her husband was arrested in the purges of the Thirties. They shared with her their meagre milk soup, apples, and bread soaked in kvass. And when the night came that the secret police shut off Nadezhda Mandelstam's spinning machine and took her to the personnel office—a frequent prelude to arrest—her fellow nightshift workers shut off their machines as well, and mounted vigil in the yard outside the office until the plainclothesmen released her temporarily. Then, as soon as the villagers finished their shifts, they filed by her lodging, packed her things, left money on the windowsill for her, and put her on an early morning train to escape.

Nadezhda Mandelstam's last image of her husband before his death in the camps testifies too to the extraordinary affection of the common man for poetry in Russia. Osip Mandelstam's verse was repeated all over the Gulag Archipelago, mostly from memory, occasionally from snatches of lines written down on some contraband scrap of paper. And "L.", a fellow-prisoner in the Gulag, told Nadezhda Mandelstam that in the Vladivostok transit camp he made friends—exceptionally, given the usual civil war between the criminal and political prisoners—with the leader of a gang of thieves. On one occasion the gang boss invited L. up to the loft the criminals had appropriated for their bunks, to hear some poetry. L. accepted—and to his surprise found Mandelstam reciting his own verse. By candlelight the thieves fed Mandelstam white bread and tinned food—unheard-of delicacies in this starvation-rife camp—and listened to his difficult, allusive poetry in attentive silence. From time to time they asked to have a poem repeated; that was the only interruption.

Poet Anna Akhmatova, Mandelstam's great contemporary and friend, understood that scene. She herself spent seventeen months during the purges waiting in line for word of her arrested son. One frozen winter day a woman in the crowd recognized her, Akhmatova explains in the preface to her ten-cycle tribute to Stalin's victims.

> [The woman] emerged from that state of torpor common to us all and, putting her lips close to my ear (there, everyone spoke in whispers), asked me:
> —Could you describe *this*?
> And I answered her:
> —I can.
> Then something vaguely like a smile flashed across what once had been her face.

"Requiem", perhaps the most famous of Akhmatova's poems despite its never having been published in full in the Soviet Union, was the result.

"Russia," Osip Mandelstam once said, "is the only place where poetry is really important. They'll kill people for it here."

Perhaps because poetry strips away non-essentials, and exposes naked truth. Perhaps because poetry is easy to memorize and non-incriminating when not written down. Perhaps because, as Akhmatova's protégé Joseph Brodsky says, a poem is "the closest possible interplay between ethics and aesthetics". Perhaps because poetry is that dangerous communion between the humanist intelligentsia and the masses that rationality is not.

That other deep communion between the humanist and the man in the street is religion. Paradoxically, Lenin's militantly atheist revolution transpired among a Russian people imbued with an innate religiosity. Joseph Brodsky describes it as a female quality, a synthetic rather than an analytical faculty, an intimation of spiritual life. It is a strong and enduring element in Russia.

Often the religious feeling may be little more than superstition. ("Do not go into the garden on St Ivan's Day, or the harvest will be bad.") Or lighting the icon lamps on saints' days may serve as a useful reminder of practical information. ("The early spring sowing is from Yury's Day [April 23] to the middle of St Nikolai's [May 9], the late sowing from St Ivan's [May 15] to St Tikhon's [June 16].") Or there may be a thirst in otherwise drab

lives for the rich pageantry of liturgy, incense, chanting, and candles reflect-
ing off the gilt iconostasis. Or churchgoing may represent less a spiritual
striving than a longing for the communality of belonging to the *sobor* (the
word meaning both "cathedral" and "gathering together").

Whatever the roots, the Russian peasants—those in the factory as well as
those still in the fields—possess an intuitive awareness of spiritual dimension
that the official society fails to satisfy.

Ideologically, the Bolshevik policy of stamping out rather than exploiting
these abundant religious yearnings is understandable. Politically, however,
this decision had distinct drawbacks. An attempt to harness the existing
authority of the Orthodox church (as Stalin finally did in reviving the
destroyed church during the crisis of the Second World War) would have
been far more clever. The church, after all, was no stranger to the halls of
power, to censorship, to Byzantine factionalism, or to other important
features of Communist Party governance. And the church easily out-
performs the party in mobilizing the masses.

The church's success in filling its adherents' lives with mystery and awe has
been so great that the Communist Party has eventually imitated, rather
clumsily, most of the Orthodox rituals. Its parades on the anniversary of
the revolution and on May Day repeat Easter processions in having
crowds as participants rather than audience—and in having the marchers
carry placard drawings of Lenin and Brezhnev that mirror the flat non-
perspective representations of saints on icons. And the bleak secular wedding ceremonies and bizarre ersatz baptisms attempt to invest life's passages
with some of the solemnity conferred on them by church sacraments.

For all this sincere flattery, however, the power structure still finds
religion intolerable. The church challenges the single, revealed truth of
party ideology with its own single, revealed truth. It claims a core of privacy
in individuals that the state cannot reach. It contests the basic Communist
hypothesis that man is solely a creature of matter, mechanistic in his
reflexes, therefore subject to programming and predetermined laws of
history.

To the party, all of these presumptions are heresy.

Some ten million official atheist agitators are therefore employed to
campaign against "the opiate of the masses". Those who resist such
indoctrination are persecuted—despite the Soviet constitution's guarantee
of freedom of worship, and despite official Soviet denials that the practice of
religion is hindered in the Soviet Union.

The persecution has ebbed and flowed over the years. In Lenin's time 28
bishops and more than a thousand priests were killed by the Bolsheviks
before the remaining churchmen agreed to endorse Soviet policies. (Today,
the Russian Orthodox Church can always be counted on for statements of
solidarity not only with various Soviet disarmament appeals but also with

such Soviet military interventions as occurred in Hungary in 1956 and Czechoslovakia in 1968.)

Stalin continued the religious purges but then made a truce with the Orthodox church long enough to fight off the occupying Germans. His successor Khrushchev—an erratic liberalizer politically and culturally, but not religiously—mounted a major new repression that closed 10,000 churches, a good half of those still operating when he came to power.

Since the mid-sixties the situation of the established churches has eased somewhat, partly because of Khrushchev's departure, partly because of the emergence of dissident Orthodox, Baptist, and Evangelical Christian movements. These religious nonconformists charged the central church hierarchies with the complicity of commission or omission in Soviet suppression of religious life. In response, the regime has gaoled religious dissidents while making more concessions to the "loyal" churches—both to discredit the dissenters' allegations abroad, and also to strengthen the more quiescent churches against the vigorous new unofficial congregations.

The improved situation still leaves believers with only a seventh of the Orthodox churches that existed in tsarist times, however, and less than a twenty-fifth of the synagogues and mosques.

Today only 7,500 Orthodox churches are registered. Of these 1,000 are not functioning, and the rest have only 6,000 priests among them. Monasteries and convents—which still numbered 90 in the late 1950s—are now down to "about twenty". Youths who want to enter the three remaining Orthodox seminaries are regularly harassed, conscripted into the army, or co-opted. Parents who have their children baptized may be penalized in their careers or even fired from jobs altogether.

At Easter a high-decibel jazz band will perhaps play just outside the walls of the holy Zagorsk monastery to drown out the shouts of "Christ is risen!" "Truly he is risen!" A special television programme of rock-music—a genre that is otherwise frowned on—will be scheduled for Easter midnight as a counter-attraction for youths who might seek the entertainment of the church. More crudely, young toughs have so often been given licence to break up the congregation's traditional walk around the church that most churches have by now abandoned the procession.

Non-Orthodox Christian churches have suffered equal persecution. The Ukrainian Catholic Church was forcibly merged with the Russian Orthodox Church in 1946. In the Baltic states the pre-war 4,200 Catholic churches are down to 1,000. Only 50 per cent of all Lutheran prayer houses have pastors. Some 1,200 sectarian groups exist only illegally, including the Reform Baptists, Seventh Day Adventists and Pentecostals.

Many sectarian adherents have been imprisoned; the best known of them, the Reform Baptist pastor Georgy Vins, was finally expelled to the West after serving two sentences in a strict-regime labour camp for the offence of giving religious instruction to children. According to Vins, some fifty preachers and about two hundred lay members of the Reform Baptist Church alone are currently in gaol in the Soviet Union on such charges as preaching in parishes other than their own or encouraging children under eighteen to sing in church choirs. Some 20,000 Evangelicals (including Pentecostals, Seventh Day Adventists, and Jehovah's Witnesses as well as Baptists) were arrested between 1945 and 1973.

For all Christians, Bibles are kept in such short supply that some churches have only one copy of the Scriptures for the entire congregation. A very limited importation of Russian-language Bibles from abroad has been permitted occasionally, some clandestine printings have been made, and small legal printings have been allowed once a decade since the 1950s. These, however, are altogether inadequate to meet the demand.

Jews are even worse off than Christians. Out of today's remaining two hundred synagogues, only 91 are officially registered, only 62 are actually open, and these must get by with only fifty rabbis. A 1980 graduate of the Budapest Rabbinical Seminary was the first new Russian rabbi in years. Furthermore, kosher food and matzos, whether domestic or imported, are often hard to obtain.

In Muslim areas of the Soviet Union, the pre-revolution figure of 25,000 mosques has been reduced to 200 or so. The former 35,000 clerics have dwindled to 1,000. The former 14,500 religious schools are down to two, which graduate a paltry sixty students each year (with a few more young clerics now studying Islam in Cairo). Only 25–30 men a year are allowed to make the pilgrimage to Mecca. Copies of the Koran are so scarce that a high-quality edition is said to sell for $2,000 on the black market. To fill the spiritual void Muslims have turned more and more to following underground Sufi adepts who conduct prayers in cemeteries and other mosque substitutes.

The vast majority of churches, synagogues and mosques have thus been closed, then turned into aquariums, theatres, vegetable cellars, warehouses, secret police archives, factories or anti-religious museums. Congregations are barred from building new churches, and if they do so with their own labour (as the Roman Catholics in Rashkovo and the Baptists in Bryansk found out), the new churches are demolished by the police.

Denominations that are less dependent on a church edifice do better than the Russian Orthodox Church in improvising services (and the Baptists are the one Christian group that has grown, from their pre-revolutionary 100,000 to their present official 550,000). But they can be fined 50 roubles, or almost a third of an industrial worker's monthly wage, for holding "unauthorized" services in private homes. The real intent of the mulct is clearly indicated in one official receipt reproduced in samizdat of a "fine for belief in God, 50 roubles".

Religious "propaganda" and any teaching of religious dogma is still forbidden—as are "poisoning the minds" of children and "opposing education and culture". Under these regulations children have sometimes been confiscated from parents who have insisted on teaching their offspring to believe in God.

Healing through prayer is similarly outlawed. So is any threat to internal security by "preaching disobedience to Soviet authorities" (i.e., pacifism) or by "espionage". So is bothering the public in the name of celebrating religious rites—an elastic prohibition that can arbitrarily exact a penalty for anything from loud hymn-singing to holding a prayer meeting in a private apartment. Besides these restrictions there are a host of secret legal bans that have never been published and come to light only as believers are punished for their violation.

Despite the control measures by the authorities, however, the number of active believers still runs to some 20 per cent or even 30 per cent of the population, according to sociological studies published officially in the Soviet Union and regarded as roughly correct in the West. This, some Western European churchmen note, compares favourably with the number of active adherents they can claim in their own free societies.

Such stubborn faith is the heart and soul of Russia, some of the greatest Russian writers have thought. Tolstoy and Dostoevsky exalted this spirit a century ago. Solzhenitsyn exalts it today, and in his own Slavophil (and very un-Western) way looks to it for the salvation of Russia. What he hopes for is an alliance of the religious peasant and the dissident intellectual against the corrupt atheistic regime.

Solzhenitsyn is pessimistic about the realistic possibilities right now. His saintly heroine in "Matryona's House" has little effect on her mean and selfish sisters; she had helped others unstintingly with ploughing or spreading manure or loading timber, but in the end her relatives and neighbours connived to appropriate the few roubles she had scraped together for her funeral. Nonetheless, Solzhenitsyn is optimistic about the perseverance of the Russian soul itself: Matryona Vasilievna, cheated in death, was "that one righteous person without whom, as the saying goes, no city can stand".

For my part, I share the pessimistic rather than the optimistic mood. Despite Russians' religiosity I cannot imagine the Matryonas and the Solzhenitsyns coming together in any way that would affect society. The Matryonas are too passive, the Solzhenitsyns too rarefied. The chasm remains.

Nor can I imagine the Soviet intelligentsia as a class leading an evolution to more tolerance and less *meshchanstvo*. Moscow physicists may stay up all night reading samizdat typescripts borrowed for a precious twenty-four hours. Women engineers may develop a taste for the occasional slick magazine that slips in among the Western technical literature. And such irritants as office taboos on beards and periodic "shrinkages" may make "mental workers" grumble about the everyday hassle.

But furtiveness and censorship and hassle are simply the way life is. One cannot change these conditions of life any more than one can change a natural phenomenon like the weather. And the new Soviet intelligentsia is certainly not going to try. For the vast majority the only sensible approach is to beat the system rather than fight it.

13.15 Sverdlovsk, the Urals, and the beginning of Asia

Nothing emphasizes the flatness of Russia more than the Urals, the low mountains demarcating the Soviet Union's two continents. There are spectacular peaks at the southern Soviet fringes, in the Caucasus and Central Asia. But there is little except plain and steppe in Russia proper. The Urals are the exception that proves the rule. The monotonous Trans-Siberian landscape—*prostor* only to those who like it—is the rule.

The Urals, beyond the reach of the German occupiers' guns, were the sanctuary of Soviet industry and science, and of militarily exempt ballet dancers, during World War II. They were, two decades earlier, the interim retreat of the fictional Dr Zhivago in his vain attempt to ignore the civil war.

And earlier still they were the site of a fleeting reprieve for Tsar Nicholas and Tsarina Alexandra. These two remnants of a vanished world were not killed immediately after the 1917 revolution but were held in limbo in this city whose name (Yekaterinburg) so recently honoured their Romanov ancestor, Catherine the Great. When the changing fortunes of civil war threatened to re-enthrone the tsar and his wife as symbols of the counter-revolution, they were presumably killed—according to the best scholarship and despite contrary speculations by each new generation of romantics in the West. Sverdlovsk is one city that touring European monarchs avoid when paying goodwill calls on the Soviet Union.

Sverdlovsk was also the transit station where Eugenia Ginzburg's train-load of prisoners got a mass disinfectant bath and were shocked to see their age in their first glance at a mirror in three years. Sverdlovsk is the spot where American U-2 pilot Francis Gary Powers was shot down in 1960 to spoil the Eisenhower–Khrushchev summit, back in the days when presidents didn't lie, even about spying. And Sverdlovsk borders on the area of lethal radiation in the 1950s after a hushed-up nuclear accident, according to belated information by émigré Soviet scientists (in 1976) and even more belated US Government scientific corroboration (in 1980).

At the time of the accident—which biologist Zhores Medvedev identified as an explosion in storage tanks holding military radioactive waste—an unknown number of persons were apparently killed. Houses were deserted. A wide area was evacuated and not repopulated; some thirty communities disappeared from maps that were published after the accident. Incoming drivers were warned to proceed through the region as fast as possible;

incoming researchers in various fields kept encountering signs that warned them to proceed no further—and some researchers exhibited radiation sickness after their exposure to the region. Local fish and game—long a staple in Sverdlovsk diets—were barred from the markets. Extensive damming and irrigation work was done southeast of the city, with the apparent aim of preventing contaminated water from flowing out of the radiated area.

A generation after the nuclear accident the industrial and military centre of Sverdlovsk—surely one of the unhealthiest habitations in the country— suffered a mysterious epidemic that led the USA to inquire formally about possible Soviet violation of the treaty banning the production and stock-piling of biological warfare agents. In spring of 1979 several hundred Sverdlovsk people died suddenly of anthrax—a periodic plague in rural Russia but also a favourite germ-warfare disease. When the US presented the Soviet Union with evidence of the incident in 1980, the USSR confirmed the epidemic but attributed it to poor food-handling and denounced American suspicions as slander.

A fifteen-minute visit to Sverdlovsk is quite long enough. We leave the city with no regrets.

17.14   Tyumen'

At last we reach Siberia. Six million square miles of it—a tenth of the earth's land surface. A bleak, rich land of Cossack freebooters, religious dissenters, fabulous gold, diamonds, sable, industrially usable mammoth skeletons (whatever that means), and the world's coldest inhabited spot.

Siberia hasn't had a good press. Nicholas I's Foreign Minister Karl Nesselrode considered it "the bottom of a sack, the end of the world". Nineteenth-century Europeans termed it "the cesspool of the tsars". British and American scoffers called the 1890s' Trans-Siberian Railroad "rusty streaks of iron through the vastness of nothing to the extremities of no-where". Solzhenitsyn, in The Gulag Archipelago, made Siberia synonymous with Stalin's dread concentration camps.

Such abuse is justified. But Siberia has been haven as well as hell. The paradox began with the earliest Russian settlement of Siberia here in Tyumen' in 1586. For the Cossack adventurers who were to expand Russia from the Urals to the Pacific in a brief fifty-eight years Siberia was the new world waiting to be conquered. For the native tribes who were to be dispossessed of their furs and eventually of their lands it was the familiar world falling apart.

The Cossacks, and their handful of Lithuanian henchmen, were outlaws and pirates, about eight hundred in all. They had no army, no decent compasses, and certainly no blessing from Ivan the Terrible, who feared debilitating wars with the successors of Genghis Khan. They came to collect the "soft gold" of sable, ermine, and other furs for the Stroganoff-brother traders who sponsored their expeditions. They brought in exchange vodka, syphilis, tuberculosis and outright theft and murder.

The explorers grew rich, some of them; in the seventeenth century one black fox pelt could buy a good cabin, 55 acres of land, 5 horses, 40 head of cattle and sheep, and several dozen fowl. And their uncontested success in the taiga won the explorers even Ivan's belated accolades as heroic empire builders.

By the eighteenth century Slavs would outnumber the Buryats, Yakuts and other Siberian natives; by the eve of the Russian revolution they would gain a four-to-one superiority among Siberia's nine million; by the 1980s they would have a twenty-to-one advantage over the natives among Siberia's twenty-eight million.

From the late seventeenth century on, a sizeable minority of Siberia's Slav population consisted of convicts. Remote Siberia became the site of penal labour, much as the American colonies and later Australia became the dumping grounds for British criminals and debtors. At the time Siberian exile was a humane improvement in the disposition of the assaulters, fortune tellers, vagrants, prize fighters, snuff takers, accidental arsonists and false beggars who previously would have suffered mutilation. And with the late eighteenth-century discovery of Siberian gold and silver lodes that needed miners, the kinds of offenders who could be exiled to hard labour expanded to include usurers, idlers, debtors, inveterate drunkards, wife-beaters, timber poachers, and men who didn't support their families.

In this scheme of things political prisoners were relative latecomers, joining the ranks only after the Napoleonic Wars with the banishment to Nerchinsk of the Paris-infected Decembrists.

To the jumble of nineteenth-century convicts Tyumen' was a way station to limbo, a two-month march from St Petersburg, a three-month march from their ultimate exile. Yet to Dukhobors, Old Believers and Baptists Tyumen' represented the free soil where they could worship as they pleased, outside old Russia, away from the persecution of the authoritarian Russian Orthodox Church.

To turn-of-the-century peasants this was even more a land of promise. With the aid of government grants these muzhiks came by the new Trans-Siberian Railroad and homesteaded so skilfully that Siberia became the nation's most efficient agricultural producer, exporting butter even to such dairy strongholds as Denmark and Britain.

By now, Siberians say, most of this is past history. There is no seasonal procession of convoys to the east, however many dissidents may be exiled here. Religious dissenters (including at this point Orthodox believers themselves) have few more rights in Siberia than in the rest of Russia. And the prosperous Siberian peasants were liquidated in Stalin's collectivization.

21.30   Ishim

For Eugenia Ginzburg, confined in "special equipment" transport to Siberia, the exhilaration of getting out of her Yaroslavl confinement had worn off by this stretch of track. Days had passed in the lumbering train, with seventy-six women crammed together so tightly in their car that they could turn on their sides in sleep only in unison. And now an accident added fifteen more to their number. There was a jolt, another wagon was smashed, and the guards pushed convict women from the wreckage into Ginzburg's car. The shockingly bald strangers were from Suzdal, the second-largest women's prison in the country; they were rivals for already inadequate water and space. Together, Ginzburg's companions radiated hostility toward the intruders—until Polya suddenly gasped, "Oh, you poor dears!"

"The words were like a signal," Ginzburg recalls.

All of a sudden we saw in the newcomers not parasites with whom we had to share our meagre ration of water and air, but our own sisters, humiliated and suffering even more grievously than ourselves. Their hair—fancy shaving off their hair!

"Come over here, comrade. We can move up a bit."

"Put your coat on top of mine."

"Take your boots off and put your feet up here. We can manage, there's not so far to go now—we're in Siberia already."

And suddenly their own thin grey hair seemed a precious possession.

My compartment mate Tanya was two years old when Ginzburg's train crashed, twenty years old when Ginzburg was finally released from the Gulag. Do she and Grandmother too bear scars from Russia's persistent heritage of cruelty?

Possibly not. In their own lifetime Tanya has shot up socially, from the peasant stratum to top military elite. Personally, she has benefited rather than suffered from Stalin's genocide of the intelligentsia and decimation of the first generation of Soviet generals. And in the present era, no doubt, she would consider dissidents as totally unrelated to her family, as self-seekers at best, traitors at worst.

Yet the very enormity and arbitrary nature of Stalin's terror of the 1930s left few lives untouched. If sober Western and Soviet estimates of twenty-million victims are correct—a figure three times the number of Jews Adolf Hitler exterminated—then an average one in three Soviet citizens lost an immediate family member to the collectivization or purges.

I stifle the obvious question. My instinct stems partly from political prudence, partly from common decency in the wake of disaster. Some of my intimate Russian friends do talk of the pain of the Stalin years and of the abnormality that has perverted their lives, from the civil war's devastation, through collectivization, famine, purges, paranoia, atomization, and betrayal of friends, to a wartime occupation that took another twenty million Soviet lives. But most Russians would rather just forget. I do not open old wounds gratuitously.

01.54 Omsk

I prod myself to stay awake until this late hour for sentimental reasons. As a reader of Dostoevsky I owe a wry debt to Omsk; it was forced labour here which transformed that master from a light novelist to a prober of the dark recesses of evil. Or so the traditionalists believe, and a Trans-Siberian traveller sides viscerally with this analysis and against the gradualist Dostoevsky revisionists.

> In the remoter parts of Siberia, in the midst of the steppes, the mountains, or the pathless forests [wrote Dostoevsky in his thinly disguised description of the Omsk outpost in *Memoirs from the House of the Dead*], lie scattered a few small towns of one, or at most two, thousand inhabitants, plain little towns built of wood, with two churches—one in the town, the other in the cemetery—which are more like the prosperous villages of the Moscow region than real towns. . . . The people there are simple, untouched by liberal ideas; their ways are old and fixed, hallowed by the centuries.

More bitterly, and prophetically, Dostoevsky concluded from his term in Omsk,

> Any man who has once tasted this dominion [of flogging a victim], this unlimited power, over the body, blood, and spirit of a human creature like himself, subject like himself to the law of Christ, any man who has tasted this power, this boundless opportunity to humiliate with the deepest degradation another being made in the image of God, becomes despite himself the servant instead of the master of his own emotions. Tyranny is a habit, it has the capacity to develop and it does develop, in the end, into a disease. I maintain that the best of men may become coarsened and degraded, by force of habit, to the level of a beast. Blood and power are intoxicants; callousness and perversity develop and grow; the greatest perversions become acceptable and finally sweet to the mind and heart. The man and the citizen perish eternally in the tyrant, and a return to human dignity, to remorse and regeneration, becomes almost completely impossible to him. Besides this, example and the possibility of such arbitrary power act like a contagion on the whole of society; such despotism is a temptation. A society which contemplates such manifestations calmly is already corrupted in its roots.

CHAPTER III
WEDNESDAY THE ECONOMY

Communism is soviet power plus electrification of the whole country.

V. I. Lenin

And what sort of a communist society is it that has no sausage?

N. S. Khrushchev

07.30   The West Siberian Plain

A SUNNY DAY dawns, and Grandmother wakes up early to revel in it. As usual, she is cheery from the moment she opens her eyes. She tucks in her sleeping granddaughter's dishevelled blanket, hugs me, and whispers conspiratorially that she is going to go and wash before she has to compete with everyone else for the lavatory at the end of the car. She comes back scrubbed, flings open the corridor window, and bathes in the stream of air that flows over her.

"There's not much woods here," she laments, shaking her head. "Just steppe, steppe, steppe." She grimaces, then grins so I won't take her complaint too seriously.

Custine was more acerbic in his response to the same phenomenon: "The complete absence of picturesque irregularities in the eternal plains . . . from one end of the empire to the other—in short, all that God has failed to do for this country contributes to the impenetrable uniformity of the political and social life of the people," he wrote in the nineteenth century.

Indeed, one might suspect the Trans-Siberian Railroad of being expressly designed to exaggerate the sprawling nature of Russia, to confound any outsider who tries to wrestle meaning or definition out of its formlessness. We are now crossing the largest area of unbroken flatland in the world. The Siberian Lowland extends 900 miles west to east, and it runs a relentless 1,200 miles to the north of us before dipping into the Arctic Ocean.

It was steppe like this that replaced Moscow's forest as the nation's dominant image a century and a half ago, suggests historian James H. Billington. To the Russian imagination of Custine's time the steppe carried its own depressing symbolism, especially in its two degraded life forms of the passive vegetable and the all-too-active predator.

The brutalized peasant, bound to his tiny patch of dirt, emulated the first to avoid the ravages of the second. He buried his meagre treasure like roots hidden away from the intruding locusts, rats, and landlords. But if, through some miraculous transformation—as in those supernatural fairytales or embellished legends of Cossack uprisings—the peasant could turn into a landlord and grain collector himself, why then he was only too happy to join the predators and lay bare the secret caches of his neighbours that he knew so well. In the exposed steppe there was no moderate neutral way between exploiting and being exploited. The uncompromising landscape offered no diversion of tree or shade, suggested no tempering of raw strength with mercy.

Custine's eighteenth-century predecessor, the Abbé Chappe d'Auteroche, drew different, but equally uncomplimentary, geopsychic conclusions from the snowy, swampy steppe he traversed on his way to watch "the Transit of Venus over the Sun" in Tobol'sk in 1761. This avid geologist, botanist, zoologist, ichthyologist, experimenter with electricity, and observer of native customs meticulously recorded his findings on the West Siberian Plain, as well as on his commissioned astronomical rarity, for the king of France. As the 1770 London translation of his *A Journey into Siberia* recounts:

The slope of the rivers in the immense plains of Russia is but small; the rain waters, and those which proceed from melting of the snows, do not easily run off. These waters generally make the country very marshy: the earth, whose surface is almost entirely covered with wood, still contributes to make the atmosphere more moist; and the summer season does not last long enough, to admit of the soil being dried up by the sun. Hence the number of marshes met with in Russia, even in the middle of the continent, and at the distance of three or four hundred leagues from the sea.

The winter appears to be the only season in which the Russians can enjoy the benefits of a pure atmosphere; and then the cold is so intense, that all nature seems to be lifeless and totally inactive. All the inhabitants, shut up and confined within their stoves, breathe an air infected by exhalations and vapours proceeding from perspiration. They pass their time in these stoves wholly given up to indolence, sleeping almost all day in a suffocating heat, and taking hardly any exercise. This manner of living, and the climate, produces such a degree of dissolution in the blood of these people, that they are under a necessity of bathing twice a week all the year round, in order to get rid of the watery disposition prevalent in their constitutions, by raising an artificial perspiration.

Therefore, deduced Chappe, who loathed the steam-and-snow sauna as a barbaric torture,

We may readily conclude from what has been said, that the nervous juice in the Russians is inspissated and sluggish, more adapted to form strong constitutions than men of genius: their internal organs have lost their elasticity and vibratory powers; the flogging they constantly undergo in the baths, and the heat they experience there, blunts the sensibility of the external organs. The nerves being no longer capable of receiving impressions, cannot transmit them to the internal organs; and indeed M. de Montesquieu observes, that, to make a Russian feel, one must flay him. The want of genius therefore among the Russians, appears to be an effect of the soil and of the climate.

Outside our train, a farmer belies such cosmic metaphors of steppe and character, and sets out tranquilly in a horse-cart, his mare's foal trotting behind. Inside the train, a new restaurant-car vendor whose tattoo conspicuously promises "I will never forget my native mother", lurches along the corridor selling breakfast schnitzel with his ineluctable mashed potato.

We don't patronize him, but again spread out our own provisions. This time I supply the bread, and we sprinkle Tanya's salt onto it liberally with our fingers. My remaining chicken, it turns out, has not withstood the heat, but Tanya's milk is still sweet. Soviet dairies, Tanya explains, process milk specially so it can last for a long time without refrigeration.

As a treat I break out some Swiss chocolate. Nina, whose eyes are more or less open by now, savours it sleepily. Tanya checks the brand first to see if it is "ours" or "yours", tastes a piece dubiously, then pronounces her judgement: the Soviet Union has "extra-grade" chocolate too, and it's better than the Swiss. The only Western food that surpasses Soviet food is sausage, and Western sausage is just like Russian "tightly packed" sausage anyway. The one drawback, of course, is that just now it's impossible to find tightly packed sausage in any shop. But the "Baikal" soft drink is also far superior to Pepsi Cola, because Pepsi tastes like soap. And the Russian language is also prettier than English.

Grandmother, mellowed by age, is less obsessed with comparisons. "There's good and bad everywhere," she observes—and reaches the contrary conclusion: "Things always appear better wherever you aren't."

Tanya is not to be deflected by her mother's conciliatory remarks. "How much does an American reporter earn?" she asks me. I divulge my salary—an astronomical income by Soviet standards—and Tanya takes a few moments to digest the information.

"But money goes further in the Soviet Union," she counters finally, "because there isn't capitalist inflation here." She verifies her thesis by comparing the cost of bread in our two countries. I add that Soviet rent and public transportation are also very cheap, but that clothes and refrigerators are expensive.

Tanya pursues the advantages of socialist life and points out that there is no unemployment in the Soviet Union. Cleaning women can get jobs anywhere, for example; there are wanted ads posted all over for char-women. And unemployment payments in the USA last for only a limited period, don't they? I'm intrigued by her uncommon knowledge about unemployment compensation in the West but don't discover how she learned about it.

"Is it true that Russian export goods are of better quality than foreign goods?" she continues to quiz me. The question startles me; I think of the notorious Soviet neglect of the consumer and the fetish Russian buyers make out of any foreign item. Aloud, I reply that Soviet Lada automobiles and generators have a good reputation in the West, but that most other Soviet manufactures do not. Tanya declares that in her experience Russian things last longer; German shirts or Japanese raincoats always have seams that pull apart or edges that fray.

"The only thing we don't have is fashion," she concedes. "Our goods are very soundly made. But when long skirts are fashionable, we have short skirts; when short skirts are in style, we have long ones. When open necks are in we have high necks; when decorated busts are in we have plain fronts." Nonetheless, she has a chic patterned coat from Moscow carefully hung inside-out in the corner, and red-and-white strappy shoes from Leningrad. And she points out that the Soviet Union is now trying to do more in the way of quality.

"In the Far East we have everything," she remarks—warm sweaters from China, dishes from Japan, plastic picnic sets from the Soviet Union. Her proofs of comfortable living further include vegetables, big cities, multi-storeyed buildings, and apartments that are more spacious than those in European Russia. On moving east, for example, Tanya's family not only got an apartment immediately, but found it bigger than their old one, with 37 square metres of living space for the four of them, not even counting the kitchen, bathroom or corridor. Motor cars, which often require a wait of two to five years in the western part of the Soviet Union, are also attainable at once in the Far East, as long as they are ordered through the military.

As it happens, Tanya and her husband don't yet own a car, but they soon will. Just now all their savings have been loaned to friends in a financing pool; next year the pool will come to them, with more money than they could have set aside on their own. Far Easterners do things like that all the time. Whatever they have, they naturally share with others. They are simpler and less stingy than people in European Russia.

By the way—Tanya returns to the key question of living space—how many square metres are there in American apartments? I explain that a lot of Americans live in houses rather than apartments and describe the suburban home I grew up in. It was a New England saltbox, but it probably classifies me as a member of the capitalist class.

Well, aren't Americans a lot more materialistic than Russians? she asks. This time I disagree, as I've never been in a country where people discuss at greater length than Russians do how much they had to bribe the salesgirl to buy razor blades, or where they managed to find toilet paper, or how long they had to queue for a carpet. Tanya nods at the familiarity of the picture.

She ticks off the comparisons with America, though, and concludes expansively that everything is better in the Soviet Union. In fact, it would be impossible to live better anywhere else in the world.

The argument of "you've never had it so good" is indeed persuasive to Soviet citizens. For the first thirty years of their country's existence they endured a procession of famines, wars, purges, and other natural and unnatural catastrophes. Their food, housing and clothing were no better at Stalin's death in 1953 than they had been in 1928, or even 1913, before the revolution. But in the quarter century since Stalin's death the Russians have had peace. And they have gained a precious prosperity. In one generation the standard of living has taken an enormous leap.

Calorie intake has doubled, and personal consumption of goods and services has increased 2.6 times. Pensions, welfare and student stipends, and other transfer payments have sextupled. Urban families—the majority of them, anyway—have escaped from communal apartments and have acquired flats with bathrooms and kitchens that are theirs alone. By now some 80 per cent of urban housing has running water, sewerage, and central heating. 73 out of a hundred families have refrigerators, 67 have washing machines, 22 vacuum cleaners. Every fifteenth person has a telephone, every fifth person a television set. Industrial take-home pay has risen to an average 161 roubles ($252 or £105) per month, or 40 per cent of British, 30 per cent of American levels. And "shock workers" who exceed the "norms" (and thus pave the way for new, higher norms for everyone later) get pay well above the average and—even more important—privileged access to the still limited accoutrements of gracious living.

In the 1970s alone, total personal consumption grew 25 per cent. The portion of meat in diets jumped 19 per cent in the first half of the decade (before dropping again in the second half), to give Russians a peak annual average of 50.8 kilos per person, three-quarters as much meat as Hungarians and Englishmen eat, half as much as Americans, double what Japanese eat.

Moreover, prices for basics have been kept low by government subsidies. White bread, as Tanya points out, costs only 28 kopecks a kilo (about 19 cents or 8 pence a pound). Beef, when it is available, costs only 2 roubles a kilo ($3 or £1.26 per pound); bus-fares costs 5 kopecks. Rents are less than 12 roubles a month, utilities less than 6 roubles, including telephone, for an average three-room apartment. Medical care is free. Education, including higher education, is also free, and those who get into a university or institute (some 17 per cent of secondary school graduates as compared with 50 per cent in the USA) receive modest living allowances.

This leaves enough in the family budget for splurges like caviar and sturgeon (for anyone who can find the right black market dealers) on the anniversary of the October Revolution. And, for a growing number of Soviet families, it even leaves enough for that ultimate trophy of a motor car.

In the veritable consumer revolution that has swept the Soviet Union in the last decade some seven million—2.7 per cent of the total population— are in the early 1980s proud owners of their own cars. This may be modest by the standards of an America that attained this level in the 1920s and now maintains an excessive one car per every two inhabitants. But it's a phenomenal advance for the Soviet Union. Despite Moscow's hiring of unemployed Detroit auto workers during the depressed thirties to make a few Fords for government and party use, it wasn't until four decades later that the Soviet Union finally entered the automobile age. It took the Brezhnev leadership to make an unprecedented $1.5 billion hard-currency investment—the largest in the Eighth Five-Year Plan—to build a Fiat plant in the USSR.

The factory imported from this paragon of Italian capitalism— constructed in the new town that some droll bureaucrat named after Italian Communist leader Palmiro Togliatti—was soon turning out more cars in its one location on the Volga than the entire Soviet auto production of any previous year.

Total Soviet car output exceeded truck output for the first time in 1972. It jumped to 1.2 million annual vehicles by the mid 1970s, with sales to the public multiplying some twelve-fold over the mid-1960s.

By now output has levelled off. A good portion of it still goes into official vehicles or Western European exports. But private sales are holding their own, with a steady 3 per cent increase every year.

The most visibly satisfied beneficiary of this change of automotive heart was state and party chief Leonid I. Brezhnev, who could himself tool around without blushing in the Mercedes and Cadillacs foreign statesmen were forever presenting to him as token gifts on their visits to the Soviet Union. Georgian tangerine growers and Lithuanian cattle raisers ran Brezhnev a close second, however, in appreciating the new dispensation. And so today do a surprising number of army officers and factory "shock workers", despite prices for the Zhiguli (Fiat) VAZ-2103 that at 8,600 roubles ($13,450 or £5,604) eat up more than four years of an average industrial wage.

The delights of getting away to the dacha for the weekend in one's own Zhiguli are tempered by the accompanying frustrations, of course: a dearth of oil and lubricants; a perpetual shortage of spare parts that makes new cars inviting targets for petty theft, sometimes even before the new owner takes possession; a minuscule number of repair stations (16 in Moscow for the capital's million cars, 350 in all west of the Urals); a shortfall of garages; and execrable roads that are 92 per cent unpaved outside of cities, and 70 per cent unusable during the spring thaw.

Car owners quickly adjust to these irritations of affluence, however. Like Sasha with my Volvo they learn to make their own ingenious patch-ups—or else the nine out of ten who don't master the art simply learn instead to live with defects. They forestall theft by removing their windshield wipers except in the driving rain—or by taking the bus home after parking their cars not on the local street, but in depots twenty or thirty kilometres away from the city centres where they live.

At home the Soviet consumers—even those in a high enough income or influence bracket to own a car—often have more basic things to complain about than the tribulations of motor car husbandry. Some 57 per cent of people interviewed in one recent Soviet survey expressed dissatisfaction with their housing.

It's an old problem: Russia has had a housing shortage ever since the freed serfs began streaming into the cities a hundred years ago. But the tenacity of this problem is small consolation to newlyweds who have to sleep in their in-laws' living room for ten years before they can get an apartment of their own—or to divorced couples who must continue to live together for lack of any alternative shelter.

Yury Trifonov caught the prevailing atmosphere in his mordant play, *The Exchange*: a grandmother who does not know she is dying is asked by her son to join with his family and exchange their separate living quarters for a single larger new apartment. The son's aim is not to give solace to his mother in her final days; rather it is to add her allotted living space to his own before it is too late. If the deal goes through before she dies, then his family will be allowed to keep the larger apartment. If not, her space allowance will revert to the state. The complexities are Byzantine, the venality palpable, as more and more apartments, families and red tape get knotted together in the final deal.

Trifonov was not being melodramatic. Every urban family recognizes *The Exchange* as its own experience. Even Anna Akhmatova encountered similar plotting. In her case the scheming didn't originate with her son—then fresh out of Stalin's camps—but with the unrelated couple who shared Akhmatova's rooms prior to her son's release. The couple, fearing that the son would eventually usurp them if he moved in permanently, pitted him against his mother to safeguard their domain.

In these titanic or petty feuds victory does not always go to the black hats. After his year-long struggle dissident novelist Vladimir Voinovich actually won that second room for himself and his pregnant wife over the rival claims of the KGB-connected neighbour who was seeking a fourth room in which to enthrone his splendid American toilet. With a bow to Greek mythology, Voinovich celebrated his triumph in his epic *The Ivankiad*.

So important is housing that the 1977 Constitution added an article guaranteeing it to all Soviet citizens. And one of the chief incentives to attract settlers to underpopulated Siberia is the availability of apartments that Tanya praises in the Far East.

In putting such emphasis on housing, Brezhnev was following the example of his predecessor Khrushchev, the first Russian leader to give any priority to his people's shelter. After Stalin's indifference to proper housing—and the destruction of six million Soviet buildings in World War II—Khrushchev began a massive programme of apartment construction that by the early 1960s made the Soviet Union second only to Sweden in numbers of new housing units per head of population. Khrushchev's shabby but functional five-storey walk-ups became one of his derided hallmarks, as did the neologism *Khrushchoba*, a pun blending the Soviet premier's name with the word for "slum".

Today three-fifths of new Soviet apartment buildings are still five storeys or less. But the rest are high-rise—and are equipped with elevators. The new skyscrapers ring the outskirts of the old cities, slab promontories that suddenly fall away to old-fashioned countryside. They look exactly alike, from Moscow to Yaroslavl to Samarkand. They are going up relentlessly, 2.2 million apartments every year. And still they lag behind the formation of new Soviet households—and by now behind the ratio of home construction in the US, Japan, and Western Europe. The estimated total deficit of housing units to households was a discouraging 9.6 million units in 1970, and has been growing worse ever since, in what some people have started calling a "permanent housing crisis".

Some 20 per cent of all city dwellers (and perhaps 25 per cent of Muscovites) still live in multiple-family apartments and have to fight over who pays the electricity bill and who gets the bathtub when. They get on long waiting lists for single-family apartments, and in the meantime they vent their spleen (according to Dmitri Shostakovich's posthumous memoirs) by spitting surreptitiously into their apartment-mates' tea water, or salting their food unmercifully.

Average space in urban apartments comes to only 8.1 square metres per capita—almost double the 1950 figure but only half the Western European and a third of the American averages. The "minimum" sanitary norm of nine square metres per capita set by the young Soviet regime in the 1920s— that is, an area slightly larger than two king-size beds—will be achieved only by 1983, according to official projections. And those apartments with shared kitchens and baths will persist until 1990, according to the Plan, and probably into the twenty-first century, in reality.

Since 1962 "co-operative"—in effect, private—apartments have been permitted, and these have helped relieve the congestion somewhat. They now constitute 10 per cent of new urban housing, despite costs that can run to $17,000 or £7,083 per flat—and despite the poorer amenities and poorer-quality materials grudgingly provided for them by the state. Friends of mine who are low on the waiting lists for state housing laud the co-operative apartments even more than Tanya lauds her Far East housing. One young couple whose parents bought them a co-op apartment lavished loving months on finishing the interior themselves, wallpapering, inventing attractive light fixtures, installing brass doorknobs and pre-revolutionary tiles. They feel they can weather any other hardship, now that they have a nest of their own.

Even these friends, though, join in the general griping about poor quality and scarcity of consumer goods. My travelling companion Tanya is either putting a good face on things for a Westerner, or else she is unique in preferring Russian over foreign goods. East European and Western products are so often superior to their shoddy Soviet equivalents that Russian shoppers generally scorn the made-in-USSR stamp.

One newspaper reported in exasperation that the Soviet slide projector certified as the country's best has to be turned off every twenty minutes to cool down—and slides have to be held in place by hand if the machine is not to rip them apart. Women frequently object that they can find only dumpy-looking dresses for sale, or refrigerators with microscopic freezer sections, or washing machines with hand wringers instead of spinners. Only 1.4 per cent of Soviet consumer goods currently meet international standards and receive the official Soviet quality seal certifying this. The remaining 98.6 per cent are the butt of innumerable cartoons—like the one in which the salesman hands a gadget over to the customer along with a 500-page compendium of what to do when various parts fail. An old joke postulates that the proper comparative forms of the adjective "good" run "good—better—import". And one gang denounced by the youth newspaper made a small fortune duping the public by simply purchasing three-rouble Soviet T-shirts, printing a spurious West German name on them, and reselling them for fifteen roubles.

Out-and-out shortages can be even more vexing than poor quality. Stores will have cameras but no film, tape recorders but no tape, spectacle frames but no lenses, or lenses but no frames. Knives will be unavailable because tableware enterprises—working under gross planning quotas from above and no customer feedback from below—turned out 11.2 million stainless steel spoons but only 1.8 million knives in one recent year. By now those of us who frequent the cheaper Soviet cafeterias don't expect to see knives at all and automatically take two forks to tear our cabbage apart.

Any Russian could quickly add a dozen examples to the list of absent commodities—balalaikas, batteries, bathing suits, bicycles, breadboxes, rubber washers, meat grinders, sleeping bags, violins, children's cotton tights, small fans, plastic tablecloths, shoelaces, key chains, enamel saucepans, bookshelves, mascara, eyeshadow, nail polish, New Year's trees.

And blue jeans.

The denim fad took the Soviet bloc by storm two decades ago and shows no sign of abating. Yet Soviet manufacturers still turn out only an estimated tenth of the demand for the sturdy material they have nicknamed "devil's hide". As a result—pending the first production runs of the Italian Jesus Jeans factory contracted for by the Soviet Union in 1980—a genuine American denim pants-and-jacket set sells for 330 roubles ($457 or £190) to any buyer lucky enough to sniff out the right black marketeer. One youth I met travelled two nights and a day to the Arctic Barents Sea port of Murmansk to procure a jeans set at a rendezvous with Polish sailors. Young KGB toughs advertise their elite status by wearing their modish denims to the occasional brawls in which they rough up artists or poets. I even got so influenced by the general awe for jeans that on my last trip to the US I bought myself a pair of Wranglers (along with an enormous size 42 pair after I computed erroneously in converting a Moscow friend's Russian size into its American equivalent).

Given the constant shortages, every Russian woman carries her *avos'ka* (meaning roughly "my darling little on-the-off-chance") string bag with her whenever she goes out, "on the off chance" that she might suddenly spy a rare item. If she sees a line suddenly forming any time, anywhere, the rule is: queue first, query later. And, if the surprise item she has lined up for turns out to be especially desirable, loyalty dictates that she automatically buy double to share her good fortune with her best friend. It's a favour that's never wasted.

The most pervasive shortage of all, of course, is that of spare parts and repairs. The parts frequently are totally unobtainable, with or without a vodka sweetener. Mechanics, plumbers, and electricians—who under the Plan get far more credit for new installations than for old repairs—never have time for the latter. The only reliable way to get anything fixed is through clandestine "on the left" operations.

Other services—their dearth is measured by the fact that they constitute only 20 per cent of gross national product in the Soviet Union, as compared with 47 per cent in the USA—are notoriously inefficient as well. With few general grocery or multipurpose stores, food shopping requires a daily round of the various bakery, fish, dairy-product, and canned-goods outlets. Women manage to stock up the necessary household provisions only by a mutual backscratching system in which one employee covers for another so all can slip away from their jobs during working hours in hopes of finding shorter customer lines.

This system—along with an elaborate web of trading illegal dental service, or appliance repair, or whatever skills one has to offer, in exchange for advance notification of when there will be a shipment of beef at the butcher's, or an edition of Mandelstam at the bookstore—works in the largest cities. But it leaves the much more poorly supplied provinces with no recourse but to send busloads of shoppers into the major metropolises regularly to buy up whatever they can find. Nerekhta residents journey to Yaroslavl; Yaroslavl residents journey to Moscow. And every weekend Muscovites become a minority in their own central department-store district.

Of course man does not live by tangerine shortages alone. If she were pinned down, Tanya would argue that the virtues of the rest of daily life here make up for the shortcomings. And she would have a point.

Surely contemporary Soviet society has bestowed one unparalleled blessing on its citizens: an absence of catastrophe in the past quarter century. It has given Soviet citizens that universal education, free medical care, absolute job security and stable prices for basic necessities. It has even provided some endearing extras, like the hotline veterinary counselling service that cheerfully advised one friend at 2 a.m. on the birth of her cat's first litter.

But the free medical care is often so hastily and carelessly given that the ill gladly pay bribes to get special attention. And medical training is inadequate by Western standards—as émigrés discover when they regularly fail qualifying exams to become physicians in Israel, Western Europe and the US.

After doubling its doctors per capita over the past quarter century the Soviet Union now leads the world in this respect—but it still ranks only twenty-seventh in life expectancy, even after averaging in the long-lived 120- and 130-year-old Abkhazians. And uniquely for a developed country, Soviet life expectancy is now falling—to the point that statistics for males are no longer published. Infant mortality too has risen so high in recent years (22.9 per 1,000 live births in 1971 to 31.1 in 1976, as against equivalent US figures of 17 and 15.1) that the Russians have now taken to omitting this figure as well in their official statistics.

The Soviet health record is also marred by the high rate of what is clearly a social disease: alcoholism. Excessive drinking is the third major cause of death in the Soviet Union, after cancer and heart attacks. Soviet revenues from legal sales of liquor alone reach 18 billion roubles yearly, or the equivalent of the overt military budget.

That free Soviet education is similarly spotty. It has brought literacy to the whole country, even to Central Asia, even to Muslim women. It has raised the general educational level some two years over the last quarter century, so that sixteen-year-olds now have an average 7.7 years of schooling behind them.

The quality of education is uneven, however, and can be abysmally low in the countryside and in the less developed republics of the nation. In the mid-1960s the Kremlin abandoned Khrushchev's anti-intellectual levelling of the universities; ever since, higher education has been an increasingly closed shop, with children of peasants especially shut out for lack of a good primary education—or the money to pay tutors to make up the gap.

Outside of the tangible area of health care and education, the broad quality of life is much more difficult to assess. But what is discernible is a yearning for less meanness and drudgery in the Soviet Union, a longing for more flair and gaiety and meaning in life. The biggest source of pageantry and awe in Russian lives, the Russian Orthodox Church, has been reviled. Youth clubs are carefully guarded from venturing too far into rock music or other Western decadence. Public cafés lack atmosphere—and require long waits in line outside, with no assurance that queuers will get inside the door before the attendant decides to lock up for the evening. Movies are didactic rather than entertaining. Fast food joints don't exist. Happenings are suspect as too spontaneous and unpredictable. The upshot is that a big night out for a city couple lucky enough to get seats usually means dining and dancing in a cavernous restaurant in a local hotel. It's no wonder that Tanya treasures her fancy-dress balls.

The best summation, perhaps, is that Tanya and her fellow consumers are a lot better off than they were a generation ago—but they're still a long way from comfort and delight.

Beyond personal gratification, though, there's another dimension of economic life that is very important to Russians like Tanya: patriotic pride in the USSR's impressive achievement of world superpower status industrially as well as militarily. The equivalent in the US might be pride in the free-enterprise "American way of life". But the emphasis in the free-market system, by definition, is so strongly private and fragmented that those rare appeals to national economic honour are viewed rather cynically in America, as a diversion to prevent the underprivileged from getting a bigger share of the pie. Such cynicism is much less common in the Soviet Union (except when directed against intellectuals). Russian workers may scoff at ideological exhortations to produce more; they do not scoff at the demonstrated industrial might of their country.

By now this power makes the Soviet economy the second largest in the world, on the world's richest resource base. The USSR produces more oil, coal, iron ore, steel, diesel locomotives, fertilizer, cement, titanium—and, surprisingly, wheat—than any other country. At the beginning of the 1980s it was the world's only major industrialized nation other than Britain that was self-sufficient in energy. It remains second only to South Africa in gold production.

In the post-war years it has grown faster than the capitalist USA (though slower than capitalist Japan). It has avoided the disruptive business cycles and inflation of the West. Western economists may question whether Stalin really industrialized Russia any faster than the tsarist regime would have done; Russia had one of the most rapidly expanding economies of any major nation prior to the revolution. But certainly Stalin is credited by Soviet citizens with having modernized this country.

In any event, in the 1980s the USSR can produce whatever it really wants to produce, from assembly-line missiles to magneto-hydrodynamic electricity that is five years ahead of the USA. Its productivity per unit of labour and capital, while only a quarter of America's, is still on a par with Britain's. Its priorities in industrial investment have developed a functioning contemporary economy, even if they have been nowhere near as brilliant as Japan's in the late 1950s and early 1960s (to cite a comparably centralized investment system at a comparable stage of economic development).

In addition, Soviet post-war entry into new industries quite alien to Russian tradition—most notably shipping and pelagic fishing—has been so successful that Western competitors worry about future Soviet domination of these industries world-wide. By the end of 1975 the Soviet fleet—with a third of the world's total tonnage—had come to rival the Japanese in fish catches from the open sea. And Greek shipping heiress Christina Onassis's brief quixotic marriage to a Soviet shipping official in the late 1970s inspired as many Western fears about a Soviet corporate takeover of world sea transport as it did cartoons about flower-laden KGB heavies sallying forth to court jet-set millionairesses.

Most important, no Soviet citizen starves or goes jobless for economic reasons. Recently the country has gone far toward equalizing incomes, especially by raising meagre peasant earnings over the past fifteen years. And, Lenin would be pleased to note, his dream of electric power for the whole Soviet Union has been virtually realized.

All this has been accomplished by a command economy of government ownership of means of production, centralized five-year planning, foreign-trade monopoly, forced savings and deferred consumer gratification, and—until détente—autarchy. The Soviet workers play such a subordinate role in this scheme—strikes are outlawed, and in movies and plays about factories the (party) management always wins—that Western economists regard it as state monopoly capitalism rather than socialism.

This system has generated giant successes. It has also, by now, generated giant problems. In the last fifth of the century the Soviet Union faces entirely new crises in diminishing returns on investment, labour shortage, and even a potential energy shortage. It faces as well the perennial crisis of agriculture.

Furthermore, a long-term economic deceleration makes it harder to remedy the defects and even to maintain the present momentum. Between

1951 and 1960 the economy expanded at an annual rate of 5.8 per cent. Between 1961 and 1970 it dropped to 5.1 per cent growth. In the 1970s it dropped still further, to 3.8 per cent from 1971 to 1975, a projected 3 per cent from 1976 to 1980, and a projected 2 per cent (or virtually no growth, in Western categories) in the early 1980s.

This means that the Soviet economy is at present barely gaining on the US economy. After catching up rapidly in the 1950s and 1960s (Soviet output equalled 33 per cent of America's in 1950, 45 per cent in 1960, 53 per cent in 1970) the Soviet economy only crept up a few percentage points in the 1970s, to 58 per cent of the US economy in 1979.

Until now the Soviet Union has achieved vigorous economic expansion by massive infusions of additional capital and labour. Investment has been running about 30 per cent of GNP, a rate much higher than American and roughly equal to Japanese levels. Labour, which has been treated as a free good in its extravagant use, has been fed by the emigration of rural peasants into the cities and by saturation employment of women. This has followed the classical growth strategy of developing countries.

With a maturing and increasingly complex economy, however, the USSR now faces an altogether new situation. In the usual pattern of both capitalist and state-run economies its investment is giving diminishing returns and would have to be pushed up to even higher rates to maintain its past impetus to growth. But the Soviet Union could not do this without excessive sacrifice, and it has already started moving in the opposite direction. In the Tenth Five-Year Plan (1976–1980) gross investment dropped to an unprecedented 24 per cent of GNP.

The labour shortage is equally intractable. Some 92.4 per cent of the working-age population is in fact working, and this already includes virtually every healthy, sane, and non-pregnant woman and man in the country. The reserves of young peasants in the countryside have been exhausted, except in Central Asia, where the coming generation shows no desire to turn proletarian and be cooped up in cities. Similarly 90 per cent of women in the twenty-to-fifty-year age bracket already hold jobs or study. Meanwhile, more and more pensioners are dropping out of work; with the ageing of the population, the number of retired persons grew from only 10 per cent of the whole in 1950 to 19 per cent in 1977. And the birth-rate in the Russian Republic has fallen to a close-to-American level of 16 per 1,000.

What this all adds up to is a sharp drop in the increase in the working-age population from 2.8 per cent in 1977 to only 0.3 per cent in 1986.

Moreover, those new babies that do come along arrive in the wrong places for the purposes of the economy. There are high birth rates in Central Asia and the Caucasus, where fertility runs 30 to 40 per 1,000 and produces a population increase triple the Soviet average—but these are not the areas of either the old or the planned new industry. The traditional economic

heartland in the European part of the country is barely reproducing its existing population. And Siberia, the region targeted for primary development
and mass immigration in the 1980s, still has only 28 million people. Few
Kazakhs, Kirghiz, and Uzbeks, it seems, want to leave their warm homelands and extended families to fight the permafrost and loneliness of the
north.

Recently, officials have again been trying to stimulate a higher birthrate.
In 1974 they reinstated Stalin's "mother heroine" to the list of Kremlin
honours, and increased child payments to low-income families. Mothers of
ten children now receive a "Glory of Motherhood" order and a "Motherhood Medal". The recipients are still overwhelmingly Central Asian, however; Russian and Ukrainian women prefer abortions to medals. One 1968
survey in the Ukraine produced the alarming statistic that 97 per cent of
mothers with one child terminated any further pregnancies. This gives the
Soviet Union what may be the highest abortion rate in the world: two per
every single live birth.

Beyond the deceleration of labour and capital inputs, a third brake on
economic growth in the eighties is shaping up in the area of fuel resources.
This too is an altogether new prospect for the Russians, who long regarded
their West Siberian oil and gas reserves as inexhaustible—and have long
been consuming two or three times the Western amount of energy per
output. According to CIA estimates that caused a sensation when they were
published in 1977, Soviet oil production should peak in the 1980s and
then—after three decades of high-earning petroleum exports—decline to
the point where the Soviet Union and Eastern Europe will become net
importers. This shift from exporter to importer will result, the CIA
calculates, from the 1970s' combination of detrimental forced-draft extrac-
tion of oil from existing wells and sluggish exploratory drilling for new wells.

Soviet oil reserves remain huge. But barring the discovery and quick
exploitation of major new fields, then, the prospect is a slowing of domestic
energy generation from 5.4 per cent yearly growth in the first half of the
1970s and 4 per cent growth in the second half of the 1970s, to an inhibiting 1
per cent in the first half of the 1980s.

Some economic and oil analysts dispute the CIA finding, and contend that
the Soviet bloc will not become a net oil importer during the eighties. The
reservations by a number of leading American economists specializing in the
Soviet Union caused the CIA to postpone its estimated date of oil shortfalls
in its 1980 follow-up report. Nonetheless, Soviet planning and com-
mentary—and announced ceilings on oil deliveries to Eastern European
allies—all suggest an official concern about a drop in production in the 1980s
that fits the trends if not the exact timing of the CIA predictions.

Natural gas and nuclear power could provide a reprieve by the Nineties.
Soviet proven gas reserves are the largest in the world—West Siberia alone

contains more reserves than all of North America—and Western analysts expect gas production to increase steadily to the year 2000. Nuclear power provided only 4 per cent of Soviet electricity in 1979 but, in the absence of any grass-roots anti-nuclear movement, is scheduled to grow to 10 per cent by 1990 and 20 per cent by the year 2000.

The fourth major problem of the Soviet economy is not a new one. Agriculture has been a burden ever since the Bolsheviks seized power. Tanya's Kuban and the Ukrainian black earth still yield abundantly. "Shove a stick into the ground, and tomorrow it will come up a tree," Kuban natives say. But the best southern Ukrainian soil—at latitudes approximating Canada's wheat belt—doesn't get dependable snow and rainfall. Overall Soviet precipitation is 30 per cent less than American, and is erratic. Every few years droughts can be relied on to produce a disastrous harvest.

As for the rest of the country, only Kazakhstan is a major grain producer. Some 30 per cent of Soviet territory lies in Arctic regions and is just too cold for farming, and another 40 per cent is warm enough only for the hardiest of fast-growing crops. The USSR is much less richly endowed than its rival America.

In some ways the Soviet Union does remarkably well with this base. It now leads the world in production of wheat, all its grain imports from the US and Canada notwithstanding. (The US harvests only half as much wheat as the Soviet Union but leads in total grain production by growing ten times as much corn. Hence Khrushchev's infatuation with corn on his American trip in 1959—and his derogatory nickname of "Corn Hick" among scornful Muscovites and Leningraders.)

Actually the USSR would be self-sufficient in grain today but for a major drive in the 1960s and 1970s to put more meat into the Soviet diet. This catering to consumers, and its corollary solicitude for farmers, was a revolutionary departure from Stalin's original bleeding of the countryside to industrialize the nation.

In Stalin's forced collectivization of the early 1930s some 3.5 million peasants who resisted surrendering their land to the state were imprisoned. At least five million died in the executions and famine. Grain—often including rural families' own food stores and even seed grain—was confiscated at gunpoint. Peasants slaughtered their livestock rather than give it up, and in pastoral Kazakhstan the sheep and goat population fell from 19.2 million in 1928 to 2.6 million in 1935. Mass starvation swept the Ukraine, especially in 1935. Collectivization, along with the purges and the war, wiped out an estimated 40 million in all, according to responsible Western and Soviet estimates. Counting the unborn, this came close to halving today's population. According to demographic projections the 1920s Soviet population should have grown to some 490 million today rather than 262 million.

"Corn Hick" Khrushchev and his successor Brezhnev gave high priority to correcting rural exploitation and raising living standards and agricultural production. For the first time they ploughed enough investment back into agriculture to expand output. Khrushchev also gambled, successfully, with introducing 30 million hectares of semi-arid Kazakhstan to crops in the 1950s, in order to expand food production. There were some initial topsoil losses, as urban neophytes tore into the delicate topography, but the Kazakhstan pioneers quickly learned from their mistakes and went on to perfect model shallow-ploughing techniques.

Khrushchev, himself an unabashed peasant who revelled in prying his farm bureaucrats away from their desks and making them tramp about in pig manure, also set out to redress Stalin's broader abuse of the peasantry. Besides channelling 20 per cent of new investment to the farms, he raised procurement prices the state gave farmers for their crops, monetarized payments to the kolkhozniks, and guaranteed them a steady income even in bad harvest years. In a glaring exception to his benevolence toward the peasants he did not, however, budge from the ideological precept that private plots are evil and must be discouraged.

When Khrushchev was dumped in 1964, his successors disavowed many of his policies. But they continued his priority on agriculture, supplying the undermechanized farms with more than a million harvesters, two million trucks, and 3.5 million tractors in the decade after Khrushchev. They boosted overall farm investment to a record high of 27 per cent of all new investment in the 1976–1980 period. For the first time they distributed the standard Soviet internal passports to kolkhozniks so they could legally move off their farms and no longer be bound to them like serfs.

In consequence, farm incomes increased 13.6 per cent anually over the past quarter century (three times as fast as non-farm incomes), rising from an average 41 per cent of non-farm incomes in 1950 to 64 per cent in 1960 to roughly 80 per cent in the late 1970s.

The whole economy as well as the individual kolkhoznik benefited from this. Grain production doubled from Stalin's time to the present. The "disastrous" 1975 grain harvest of 140 million tons—less than two-thirds of the current Soviet needs—still matched "bumper" years of the 1950s and early 1960s. Today's grain imports—which can run as high as 35 million tons in bad years—now go not to make bread, but to provide fodder and put more pork, beef and chicken on Soviet dinner tables. Until the mid-seventies, milk, eggs and vegetables registered big increases as well.

These very real accomplishments still leave the USSR producing only an inefficient 80 per cent of American harvests, however, while using eight times as many farmers—a third of the entire Soviet work force—on a higher acreage of tilled land. They leave Soviet agriculture growing now at a meagre 1 per cent per year, after 5 per cent growth in the 1950s and 3 per cent growth in the 1960s. And in the late 1970s and early 1980s, after the distress slaughtering in 1975/76 and 1979/80, they left meat virtually unobtainable outside the big cities.

Worse, repeated shortages in the late Seventies grew so bad that even the favoured Moscow stores were sometimes unable to obtain common potatoes, onions, carrots, apples and cooking oil, as well as poultry, butter, cheese, sour milk and, of course, coffee. In the Olympics year of 1980 even the old standby of cabbage was unavailable in the capital and—most unusually—milk was scarce. In the same year, butter was rationed in Kazan (one kilo a month), meat was rationed in Novosibirsk (two kilos a month, distributed only at workplaces, not at stores), several cities in Yakutia were said to have been without meat or butter for a year, and some Russians in the Urals began asking relatives in Moscow to send them food parcels.

It's a disheartening picture. In order to maintain artificially low food prices for the consumer, the USSR now dispenses the highest agricultural subsidies in the world, both absolutely and relatively. In 1978 it devoted 22 billion roubles ($32 billion)—5 per cent of its budget and almost 5 billion roubles more than that touchstone of the overt defence budget—to farm support. And planners are currently putting five times more productive investment into agriculture than the USA. But the rewards of this financial commitment are all but invisible. From 1961 to 1972 each rouble of capital stock added to agriculture yielded only 32 kopecks of additional output. Despite all the outlays it still takes the Russians $15 of grain to produce $1 of beef—double the American cost and double the American weight of feed.

Such a low capital productivity is unusual in Western experience—especially for an agriculture that still remains, by American standards, undercapitalized. It is attributed to the poor education and old age of farmers, the unwieldy size of farms (averaging 29,000 acres, some seventy times larger than American farms), chronic idling of machinery for lack of spare parts and maintenance, absence of wage and price incentives, rigid bureaucratic administration, and poor infrastructure that leaves 90 per cent of agricultural settlements on unpaved roads.

With labour, capital investment, agriculture and, presumably, oil all putting drags on growth, the Soviet economy looks like slowing down even more in the early 1980s. In the worst case, the Soviet Union could even experience (as did the US in 1974 and 1975) an absolute decline in output.

A worried leadership is therefore now looking to productivity to stimulate future growth. "Shock work for the Five-Year Plan of Quality" proclaim the emphatic if not especially catchy banners in factories and train stations.

The summons to productivity poses its own difficulties, though, for it assumes progressive technology, a work ethic on the assembly line, flexibility, and managerial skills—all those things in which the Soviet economy is more deficient.

The crucial failing is in technological change, which Western economists now consider the main engine to economic growth in the West and Japan.

Soviet innovation can be striking in theoretical science, space, energy, weaponry and some other fields. Nobel Prize winner Lev Davidovitch Landau was one of this century's seminal theoretical physicists. Astrophysicist Iosef Shklovsky and biochemist A. I. Oparin are world leaders in hypothesizing a modern concept of the origin of organic life and the extinction of the dinosaur. L. S. Vygotsky in the early Soviet years and his student A. R. Luria in later years were pioneer integrative psychologists. Physician Vladimir Negovsky has an international reputation in "reanimation" of the clinically dead. The first sputnik was Soviet, and until 1967 Soviet rockets packed more thrust than American rockets. The Soviet Union holds the record for duration of manned space flight and leads in the technologies of space shuttles and welding new alloys in weightlessness. A Soviet atomic ice-breaker was the first and so far only one to reach the North Pole. The USSR has been a world leader since the 1950s in high-voltage power transmission. It has begun construction of the world's first industrial magneto-hydro-dynamics power plant, with two and a half times the efficiency of conventional stations. It probably leads in fusion research. Soviet tanks, armoured personnel carriers, and guns are tops in their class.

But—curiously for a society in which science is idolized both as ultimate truth and as social model—the Soviet Union manifests what seems to be a permanent technological lag behind the US in important industrial and even military areas. In the world's new research-intensive growth industries such as computers, electronics and polymer chemistry, the Soviet Union has consistently been the last major country to adopt each technological innovation. Its gap in computers, the brains of future technological change, is especially painful. After a mighty catch-up effort the best Soviet microprocessors are now only three years behind America's. These processors are not widely available, however; those computers that are available are markedly inferior in miniaturization and speed of operations.

More broadly, in industry as a whole, a good 50 per cent of Soviet workers—double the American figure—still perform manual labour. Industrial inefficiency means that 25 per cent of metals are wasted in manufacture (as against 5 per cent in the USA). Soviet machinery averages 25 per cent to 30 per cent heavier than American equivalents—and therefore consumes that much more energy. And, laments Pravda, most Soviet design reproduction, for lack of simple photocopiers, is still being done by means of tracing paper and India ink.

Unfortunately for the Soviet economy, diffusion of technology imported from the West—along with adaptation of technology already possessed by the Soviet Union—is very slow. Western-licensed production often takes twice as long to come on line in the USSR as in Western countries. And—even though Soviet blast and open-hearth furnaces, oxygen steel making and continuous casting are among the most advanced in the world—the USSR cannot itself produce the high-quality steel pipe needed to link Siberian gas and oil to the rest of the country. It has had to import $10 billion worth of pipe, lift technology and compressors from the West.

The causes of this technological sluggishness are easy to diagnose. Research is separated from production. There is no stimulus from market competitiveness, nor are there incentives for firms to modernize their production mix. Antiquated capital stock is worked until it dies of exhaustion. New product pricing is arbitrary, and does not cover research and development costs. Secretiveness, lack of advertising and slowness of communication mean that each enterprise constantly has to invent the wheel anew.

But what, my American friends would ask in that quaint New World phrase, is "the bottom line"? Is the Soviet economy going to adjust and cope with all these difficulties, or is it going to collapse?

That all depends.

The "objective" pressures—to reply in Marxist-Leninist jargon—cry out for radical changes that would reanimate the moribund Soviet economy. But resistance to change is a habit. An irresistible force challenges an immovable object.

Pressures for change include an approaching allocations squeeze, rising consumer expectations and rising professional expectations. Resistance to change arises from the convention of past successes, the inertia inherited from two decades of an elderly bureaucracy, and fear that economic changes could threaten political power.

The allocations squeeze is clearly previewed as competition between the demands of defence, agriculture, investment goods and consumption grows sharper. Already some provincial party secretaries are said to be grumbling that they are getting short-changed in their development money.

In the mid-1970s the GNP pie was cut into 30 per cent gross investment, 11–13 per cent defence, 5–7 per cent government, and 52 per cent consumption. The military sector commandeers a third of the output of the machine-building industry, a fifth of metallurgy, a sixth each of chemicals and energy—and, says seventies émigré Boris Rabbot, production from some 60 per cent of all Soviet factories. Any decision to develop new generations of weapons would inevitably push these figures higher. Moreover, maintenance of the present active force of four million men would require a significant diversion of manpower from industry.

Within the gross non-military investment, agriculture currently takes 27 per cent (34 per cent, counting fertilizer and other farm-support industry), Siberian investment takes 16 per cent, and housing 15 per cent.

In the remaining competition between heavy industry and consumption, industry has won consistently. Planners made one brave attempt from 1971 to 1975 to accelerate consumption faster than producer goods. The experiment was quickly aborted, however, and the consumer sector returned to getting the residuals. According to CIA projections, consumption can now grow only marginally (¼ per cent to ½ per cent annually) through the 1980s, barring improbable success in solving energy problems—and this despite a 1981–85 plan that optimistically calls for a 5 per cent annual rise in consumption, a growth marginally higher than that planned for producer goods.

Several possible solutions to the allocations squeeze suggest themselves. The USSR might boost growth and therefore the total GNP to be shared among competing sectors. It might do this by a liberal economic reform or by a contrary streamlining of centralized planning, by injection of Western technology into the economy, or by importing foreign investment and labour. Alternatively, the Soviet Union could cut military spending drastically and apply the released resources to the other sectors.

Liberal reform would mean loosening up the economy so it could respond to needs more flexibly. It would require correction of the system's present rigid centralization, nonsensical gross production targets, arbitrary pricing, decade-long construction delays, workers' habitual sloth, and the taut resources planning that leaves no slack to smooth out uneven distribution of industrial supplies. It would entail real devolution of decision-making, more leeway and reward for managerial initiative, more play for market forces, less secretiveness and manipulation of statistics, and a better flow of accurate economic information between ministries, plants and planners, as well as better worker motivation and incentives in the form of more attractive consumer goods.

This reform route is being followed by Hungary now, and was begun by Czechoslovakia in the "Prague Spring" of 1968. The USSR itself flirted with reform notions in 1965—and has been retreating from them ever since the Czech example linked economic with political revision. In the decade and a half since 1965, Soviet reform has been compromised away into little more than administrative tinkering.

There is one variant of "liberalization" that is tolerated, by default: illegal and quasi-legal private dealings "on the left". Everyone participates, from the truck driver who syphons off his gas (*Izvestia* estimates that a third of private car-owners buy their gas in this bargain fashion), to physicians who divert scarce medicines, to construction gangs for hire who somehow acquire whole shipments of lumber and cement.

Actually, "on the left" operations perform valuable economic functions. They let the consumer repair his balcony, sometimes buy meat, and receive medical treatment he can't get through official channels. And even the legal economy itself could hardly run without the lubrication of each factory's illegal "pushers", who wheedle, browbeat or bribe their suppliers into actually delivering the nails or cotton batting to meet the state plan. In one sense the "grey market"—which émigrés have estimated accounts for anywhere from 10–25 per cent of GNP—is the free market's clandestine rescue of the command economy.

A systematic policy of economic liberalization going beyond mere acquiescence in private arrangements, however, could have a dramatic impact on the Soviet economy, especially in the countryside. Implicitly, officials have been admitting as much ever since the wake of the bad 1975 harvest. As usual in such emergencies the peasants were suddenly lauded rather than scolded for their private efforts. The *Literary Gazette*, with the romantic haze of an urban bystander, turned from excoriating farmers who illegally feed bread to their cattle, to eulogizing private plots as "a powerful means of struggle against drunkenness, lawbreaking, and an unhealthy, sedentary life".

More practically, in a reversal of previous official invective, the Agriculture Minister has now ordered collective and state farms to provide loans to peasants to purchase their own cattle and chickens; to procure feed for these animals; to allot more land for private use if it will go to fodder crops; and to let peasants construct their own buildings. And, in a gesture that must have dumbfounded peasants who have had trouble getting so much as a simple hoe or rake for their own use, the minister even announced in the late seventies that the appropriate ministries had been instructed to produce small garden machines for use on the nation's fifty million tiny family plots. The machines have yet to appear, of course, but even the prospect is a tantalizing bow in the direction of the recent rototiller revolution in Japanese and Western farming.

Continued official encouragement rather than the suppression of family plots could bring about a rapid increase in the amount of food available to Soviet citizens. In 1978 the 3 per cent of tilled land under private cultivation turned out 23 per cent of the nation's food (as measured in prices), including 29 per cent of the livestock products and vegetables, 34 per cent of eggs, 61 per cent of potatoes.

With the slightest encouragement farmers would spend more than the present third of their work time on subsidiary plots and husbandry, and would enlarge their production accordingly. When restrictions were relaxed after Khrushchev's ouster, private livestock holdings shot up 13 per cent. And in the three years it took pig herds to rebuild after the mid-seventies' slaughtering, family-raised pork accounted for half the recovery.

Private farming would not do much in the way of increasing extensively farmed crops like grain. But at this stage the USSR is striving to improve the quality rather than the quantity of diets, and the private sector excels in turning out the very produce that would give variety and balance to the starchy Soviet fare.

The second possible solution to the allocations squeeze would be the exact opposite of liberalization: a streamlining and rationalizing of the present centralization in economic control. Khrushchev, the original champion of this approach, argued that computers and planning were made for each other, and that once man possessed the technical capacity to harness all the myriad bits of economic information from hither and yon, the visible hand of the computer would render a centralized economy far more efficient than the chaotic, irrational individual decisions of capitalism. Brezhnev sometimes echoes this view without making as extravagant claims as Khrushchev. Practice has so far been disappointing, however, largely because the Russians have been unwilling to make the economy supple enough to respond to computer co-ordination.

The third alternative of injection of Western technology into the Soviet economy was attempted in the seventies détente, and many Westerners consider it to have been a prime motivation for Kremlin interest in détente. The impact of Western technology in some industries is striking. Siberian oil and gas production is heavily dependent on Western equipment. Some 74 per cent of Soviet complex fertilizer and 84 per cent of high-pressure polyethylene is now manufactured in plants imported from the West.

Western studies indicate, however, that while Western technology may spur sizeable productivity increase in the specific industry importing the technology, its general diffusion under the Soviet economic system is too languid to have much influence on overall growth.

Besides, many Soviet party and industry officials apparently oppose any broad opening to the West, for reasons of ideology or power. The general Soviet acceptance of a need for productivity increases in the economy, it seems, does not spill over into acceptance of a need to import technology from the West on a comprehensive scale.

As for the fourth alternative of importing foreign investment and labour, the USSR has turned to this only sparingly. From its East European allies it has elicited investment in Siberian resources development—and 20,000 construction workers for the Orenburg gas pipeline. The Soviet Union also employs some North Korean timber cutters in the Far East, and it has admitted Western contract labour for specialized construction of hotels and imported Western plant. At most these add up to an inconsequential 60–70,000 foreigners in the Soviet labour force, however. The Kremlin apparently fears potential mischief from letting the Soviet populace see foreign lifestyles—even East European ones—on any wide scale. It would never let foreign labourers grow to equal the millions of "guest workers" in West Germany.

Since the seventies the USSR has welcomed Western investment in resource development—often in commodity buy-back deals—and in 1975 the Soviet Union borrowed extensively for the first time on the Euromarket. But this too is limited in future potential. In fields other than energy Western companies are loath to tie up huge sums of money in open-ended projects with the skimpy economic and financial information that the Russians provide—or in production where the investing company has no say in management and quality control. In addition—despite the exemplary Soviet credit rating and the collateral of Siberian gas and gold—the enormous Soviet net hard currency debt of $7 to $10 billion gives some pause to Western investors.

The fifth alternative of cutting defence expenditures could release investment, managerial talent, and manpower for civilian production. Some Western economists estimate that a 25 per cent cut in arms spending would free 3 per cent of the most sophisticated Soviet resources for investment or consumption. Similarly, a release of some of the 3.7 million armed forces personnel into the civilian sector could help alleviate the manpower shortage.

Western models of the Soviet economy also suggest, however, that a more realistic freeze of defence spending at present levels would raise growth rates only a tenth of a percent—a low incentive indeed. In any case, the importance the Kremlin assigns to a powerful military force and pursuit of superpower prestige in foreign affairs probably rules out any defence reductions.

Unfortunately, then, the alternatives for coping with the allocations squeeze all seem impossible, unpalatable, or ineffectual.

And this means that after the dramatic improvements in everyday life over the past quarter century, Soviet citizens will see their living standards stagnate or even drop in this decade. It means that industrial engineers will probably have to put up indefinitely with the old inefficiencies and frustrations.

So will they revolt?

Until now, Soviet consumers have proven to be much more docile than Polish or other Eastern European consumers. To be sure, there were price riots in the Cossack region of Novocherkassk in 1962, consumer riots in Dneprodzerzhinsk and Dnepropetrovsk in 1972, and possibly even wildcat strikes by privileged car and lorry workers on the Volga because of food shortages in 1980. Some hints of public discontent can also be read into the imprecations the Soviet press has begun to hurl on "consumer psychology". And official sensitivity can be inferred from the Soviet retreat from raising domestic prices after the Polish price riots of the seventies; the Soviet revision of the 1981–85 economic plan to give a marginal preference to consumer over producer goods after the 1980 Polish strikes; and the first Soviet jamming since détente of the BBC, Voice of America and Deutsche Welle when these stations reported on the 1980 Polish strikes and formation of independent trade unions.

Nonetheless, the Soviet worker seems to be satisfied with far less than his East European comrades—and by and large he doesn't seem to realize how much better fed, clothed and housed the East Europeans are. What the Soviet worker does know is that he is living better than his parents—and that any foolhardy demonstrations would call forth police repression. Besides, he has his sinecure. "It's fair enough," the old saw runs, "the state pretends to pay us, and we pretend to work." The usual resort is not to demonstrations, but to absenteeism and vodka.

But what happens to the third and fourth generation peasant-worker? Or to those young people now reaching their majority who were born after Stalin and who take a normal life for granted? It was the critical third proletarian generation that founded trade unions and socialist parties in nineteenth-century Germany, after all. Like their German forbears, these new Soviet citizens must long for a less spartan life.

They may come to realize that their modest wage rises are being yanked down again by the hidden 2–3 per cent inflation and by the chronic shortages. And as they learn more about the outside world they may begin to compare the cost of bread not in kopecks, but in work time: eighteen minutes per kilo in Moscow, twelve minutes in London, eight minutes in Washington.

Or, possibly, Soviet workers might simply come to want for themselves the cars, dachas and upward social mobility that are now the privileges of the Soviet elite. Inequality between the richest and poorest 5 per cent in the USSR is not as great as in the US, but it far surpasses Sweden and was about on a par with Britain in the mid-1960s, according to the calculations of economist Peter Wiles. And while the Soviet elite may not display its advantages with the flamboyance of the Western jet set, still, the differences between one who possesses a car and one who does not can sometimes seem more urgent than those between the owner of a Ford and the owner of a Cadillac. 1980, after all, was the target Khrushchev set for the full advent of communism, when economic abundance (defined, apparently, as production equal to America's) would distribute the bounty to each Soviet citizen according to his need.

A Westerner with a middle-class cultural bias can easily exaggerate consumer pressures, of course. There is much more of a communal mentality and much less of individual calculation in the Russian than in the American or Western European. There is, by contrast with the Poles, much less resentment of the economic perquisites of power holders. There is a memory of those all-too-recent catastrophes in the Russian that makes him not want to risk his irritating but secure present by agitating for some unknown and possibly disastrous future.

Much the same could be said about the new breed of Soviet technicians. Western theorists often assume that industrialization makes its own inevitable economic and social demands for efficiency and diversification—and that these are inimical to the present Soviet economic system. They assume further that the logical bearers of these demands for change will be the rising technical intelligentsia.

The logic of economics may support this view. But the reality of politics in the Soviet Union does not. The new managers have shown a distinct aversion to any economic liberalization and the added responsibility—and risk—that would fall on them.

So far the Soviet way of coping with the country's various economic dilemmas has been to muddle through and hope that the sheer volume of production will eventually override current problems. And so far the system has shown remarkable immunity both to any revolt of rising consumer expectations and to those sociological convulsions that accompanied industrialization in the West.

Here is "the bottom line", I think. This command economy could continue indefinitely subordinating butter to guns. Despite Karl Marx, it is politics, not economics, that reigns in the Soviet Union.

10.45   The Ob River

We cross the first of the giant Siberian rivers, on a sturdy hogback bridge that every spring must withstand the crush of hundreds of tons of ice. The Ob is the largest river in Eurasia, the fourth largest in the world. Only the Nile, Amazon, and Mississippi exceed its 3,500 mile stretch. With all deference to Mother Volga, the Siberians call their Ob "the Grandmother of Rivers".

These Siberian rivers are strange and compelling. Against all of an American's instincts they do not flow southward to lush semi-tropics, but northward, into barren tundra. They have their own lore, their own argot, their own atmosphere. They fill an elemental need for communication in ways that American rivers have long since ceased to do. They were the arteries for the first explorations of Siberia. For many isolated wilderness hamlets they are still the sole link with the outside world—by summer ship or ice-road truck. They are now being harnessed for mighty hydroelectric projects and may even send a portion of their waters southward through nuclear-blasted channels to irrigate the desert and sweeten the Caspian Sea.

Yet in the end it is still the rivers that tame the men. They caress and swell and refresh, with the inexorable cycles of nature. A wise man fits himself to the river's moods.

Siberians know this. They hunt and trap and fish to the rhythm of their rivers, and they say they would be smothered if they had to live in the confines of Moscow and the bland European rivers.

A Siberian first taught me this here at the Ob, a mile downstream from this bridge. I never learned the young man's name, nor would I again recognize him. But the song lingers on.

At first I passed him by in the dark, scarcely seeing his still figure holding a guitar and waiting. Then something drew me back up the steep road.

"What do you sing about?" I asked.

"I'm not singing," he replied, testing me.

Siberians are deep, other Russians say. They are honest to the point of rudeness. They show hospitality to a stranger, and when they give their friendship it is total. But they are also at peace with themselves, and they do not hurry.

"Are there good songs about Siberia?" I inquired again.

"There are," he said indifferently. He wore a quilted jacket against the cold. His face was lined prematurely, deeply enough to be visible in the shimmer of light from the log house behind him. His hair was probably sandy and curling over his collar.

The smell of coal smoke was in the air. The street was paved, but it was unimprisoned by cement and sidewalks. Instead, packed dirt—real, fertile earth with careless grasses and bushes springing from it—formed the banks of the road.

"Old or new songs?" I persisted.

"Both." He paused, and yielded slightly. "Where are you from, that you ask?"

"America."

Across the way a man walked by with a yoke, carrying water.

"And Siberia?" the guitarist probed. "Do you like it?"

"Very much."

Then the guitarist began strumming. It was a bit above freezing, so he wore no gloves. His stubby fingers looked competent to wield an axe but not to command the subtleties of seven vibrant strings. Yet the chords flowed, in repetitive cadence.

When at last he joined voice to instrument it was a tenor that sounded out. The song developed slowly, adding layer upon layer. The singer loved Siberia as a mother, and the Ob flowed on to the sea.

The spirit of adventurers who fled civilization for the freedom of the empty taiga four hundred years ago communicated itself in the music. *Prostor* was there. So, too, was the yearning for decency of the later Siberian exile and prisoner.

"An old Russian folk song is like water held back by a dam," Boris Pasternak wrote in *Dr Zhivago*.

It looks as if it were still and were no longer flowing, but in its depths it is ceaselessly rushing through the sluice gates and the stillness of its surface is deceptive. By every possible means, by repetitions and similes, the song slows down the gradual unfolding of its theme. . . . The song is an insane attempt to stop time by means of its words.

The guitarist's song finished its delayed rush through the sluice gates. Time did stop, and the vast Siberian silence rested on the heart. I touched the singer on the arm and descended to the Ob.

10.49 Novosibirsk

Our arrival at Siberia's largest city jars me back to the present. In the station ritual that is repeated ten times a day, the conductress wipes grime off the exit handgrips at the door before letting us dismount. Then we jump down, shake out our disused legs, and watch mechanics go the full length of the train, plocking all the wheels to confirm their soundness.

As this is a long, seventeen-minute stop I stroll up to our engine to see if it was diesel or steam on the last segment. It was diesel. I catch the engineer's eye at the cab window and shout companionably to him, "It's a good train!" He relays my compliment warily to his deputy and adds, "She's not one of us." He doesn't smile. So much for the fellowship of the rails.

The station throbs with all the hurly-burly appropriate to the unofficial capital of Siberia. Novosibirsk is Siberia's busiest river port, the seat of the Siberian branch of the Academy of Sciences, home of the Soviet Union's largest opera house. It is a newcomer to such eminence, for it supplanted Tomsk, some hundred miles to the north, only after the turn-of-the-century advent of the Trans-Siberian. The Tomskians (so one unverified story goes) proudly refused to grease the palms of the railroad builders at a critical stage, calculating instead that the importance of Tomsk was too great for it to be bypassed, even without a bribe. The Tomskians were wrong, of course. Their spurned city declined to a capital manqué, fit for inclusion in Tom Lehrer ditties.

Back in those Roaring Nineties, both Tomsk and Novosibirsk (then Novonikolaevsk) and all the other muddy Siberian towns were raw and untamed. Shooting and murders were everyday occurrences, as were frontier swindle and parvenu ostentation. Here Chinese smugglers would slip gold dust past inspectors by blowing it into the skull of a corpse. There celebrated millionaires and embezzlers would send their laundry to Paris for cleaning, or sport an ebony and Gobelin tapestry bed—then sleep on the floor underneath it so as not to spoil the pretty thing. The Siberian *nouveaux riches*—like their counterparts in America and other adolescent civilizations—threw besotted river parties, and filled their parlours with grand pianos they couldn't play.

In Stalin's time, inevitably, Novosibirsk became the site of an over-crowded transit prison. "About 270 men were kept in a cell 40 square metres in area," remembered one inmate, a former procurator cited in Roy Medvedev's *Let History Judge*. "People squirmed under the bunks, even on the corner of the big *parasha* [prison slang for chamber pot] standing in the corner. . . . There was nowhere to sit down and nowhere to move to. Many, standing on their feet, fainted from exhaustion. . . . The cell was stifling. There was a heavy, noisome stench. It became hard to breathe."

Even tsarist prison conditions weren't that inhumane, thundered Solzhenitsyn in *The Gulag Archipelago*. In Dostoevsky's stockade in Omsk convicts worked only seven hours a day in winter, twelve and a half hours in summer. They had leisure time in the evenings that they didn't know how to fill. If they had a little money they could buy meat from outside. And while Dostoevsky's soup was as rotten as Solzhenitsyn's, Dostoevsky's bread was the envy of Omsk.

In the old days, women were exempt from hard labour. Political prisoners were given less severe treatment than common criminals, not thrown at the mercy of these thugs. And the Decembrists working in the mines had a daily quota of a paltry 118 lb. of ore, not the 28,800 lb. norm of Stalin's Kolyma.

Everything changed for the worse in the modern era, Solzhenitsyn railed; even the life of a nineteenth-century serf was better than that of a twentieth-century prisoner. A serf could at least live with his family, in his own hut, and possess a horse, an axe, a scythe, dishes and a seasonal change of clothing.

11.50   Novosibirsk Province

Our train neatly halves the few villages we pass, slicing through the right-angled streets and displaying their intimate pedestrian traffic like some glassed-in ant-hill. At village outskirts women wash clothes in streams—and, less frequently, men wash motorcycles in streams. Even here along the Trans-Siberian, however, where two-thirds of Siberia's population lives, such signs of human presence are already rarities, aberrations in an otherwise empty timberland.

It was in this forest between the Ob and Yenisei Rivers that the "wild people of the Voguls" set up their small felt tents and performed the stylized deerhunts Tolstoy praised as true theatre after his revulsion against more sophisticated art. One Vogul actor would play the doe, a second her fawn, a third the hunter, a fourth the bird that warns the doe of danger. When the fawn is wounded by an arrow, wrote Tolstoy in his 1897 *What is Art?* "the spectators, so the eye-witness tells, become breathless, and in the audience are heard deep sobs and even weeping. I feel from the description alone that this was a true production of art."

Beethoven, Wagner, Faust, Baudelaire and the French "cult of unintelligibility", the Renaissance, even Pushkin, were all to be deplored. Only a very few works—*Uncle Tom's Cabin*, *A Christmas Carol*, *Notes from the House of the Dead*, the Voguls' deerhunts—met Tolstoy's latter-day criteria of goodness and simplicity.

Looking out on Yasnaya Polyana's groomed lawn, placid lake, and the gateposts that so intimidated the visiting Chekhov, Tolstoy conjured up the woods we see now and the artless art of the Voguls. Four generations later, these real-life larch and firs are enriched by his idiosyncratic vision.

Sporadically we are paralleled by the *trakt*, or old post road that predated the train. And occasionally we see a lone truck bouncing along the *trakt*, churning up billows of dry earth in its wake. In the mirage of dust and deserted landscape the truck seems to shed its ephemeral metal chrysalis to become again the horse cart of a century ago, galloping over makeshift wooden bridges at an accelerated pace so that any collapsing span will give way only after the wagon has crossed it. As the vehicle jolts angrily from side to side, the courier on his unbroken 400-hour run between Peking and St Petersburg tries to snatch some sleep before the next change of thick-coated horses—or before the next attack by runaway convicts, tramps or bears. He chokes in the cloud of dirt, but he restrains his curses, for at least it is summer, and he is not bogged down in axle-deep mud.

14.52   Taiga

Despite the name, we never see the really wild taiga, as the trees have been thinned in a 250-foot wide fire-prevention strip for the Trans-Siberian. We search in vain for that forbidding forest, denser than any other except the Amazon, that is the home of the wolf, boar, ferret, bear and, farther east, the Manchurian tiger. In Taiga Station we have to content ourselves with a hint of the real woods in the local speciality: large cedar cones that vendors sell from buckets. We flake off the outer shingles of the cone, extract the seeds within, and bite open their shells to eat the interior flesh.

Then, for good measure, we finish off the bon-voyage garlic mushrooms that a friend gave me in an old Dutch coffee jar back in Moscow. The bottle with its bubble-top lid takes Grandmother's fancy, and as I start to throw it away, she asks if she might keep it instead. I'm willing, but Tanya is not. She commands Grandmother to return the jar immediately; whatever does she need it for when they have so many perfectly good Russian jars at home! Grandmother retorts, sits tight, and the bubble-top bottle stays squirrelled away in her corner. When Tanya finally abandons the argument and steps out into the corridor for a moment, Grandmother celebrates her victory by dancing a jig to the "Harlequin" song coming over the loudspeaker.

The last log cabin of Taiga falls behind us. A little boy in an enormous cap races our train, and loses. His even littler brother waves to the magic and mystery of a passing train to Elsewhere.

CHAPTER IV

THURSDAY THE NATIONALITIES

In the Soviet Union political and economic inequality of all nations and nationalities was abolished, and relations of a new type, relations of unity and friendship among free nations, took shape and are developing.

Soviet pamphlet on the nationalities question

We are a little colony of Russia—in this day and age! What wouldn't we be today if we weren't a colony of Russia?!

Georgian student

23.12   Krasnoyarsk and the Yenisei River

THE HOUR IS confusing. Our schedule and all station clocks remain loyal to Moscow, even though local time has already skipped ahead several hours. Furthermore, we are running late. I give up trying to adjust and simply accept the fact that day is now dawning over Krasnoyarsk.

For three days we have been riding toward the rising sun. We are east of Calcutta by now, and we have left Western Siberia behind. Yet we have completed less than half our journey; we are just beginning to cross Eastern Siberia, the second of the three regions that make up generic Siberia. Even for an American the vastness is incomprehensible. Western Europe and the contiguous United States could both be tucked into Siberia. This chunk of the globe contains close to a third of the world's timber, two-thirds of its reindeer, four-fifths of the Soviet Union's hydropower potential. Its mile upon mile of trackless taiga and tundra form one of the world's last frontiers.

For Krasnoyarsk, Peking is closer than Moscow. During the anti-Enlightenment reaction after Napoleon's invasion Krasnoyarsk, like Moscow, turned to its eastern roots. A collection of Mongolian proverbs was published here as Krasnoyarsk's share in the Slavic revulsion toward Europe. Curiously, the anti-effete, anti-intellectual tradition summoned forth by the Slavophiles reflected the machismo and savagery of the Asian rimland nomads far more than it reflected the refined cultures of the Asian heartland of China and India. But the "Asian" misnomer for this anti-rationalism stuck, and justified Russia's anti-Western mission in the nine-teenth—and the twentieth—century.

In the first starving winter of the Bolshevik Revolution Alexander Blok shouted out the Russian Asian superiority to Europe in his famous ode, "The Scythians":

> Come, fight! Yea, we are Scythians,
> Yea, Asians, a slant-eyed, greedy brood.
> . . . .
>
> Yea, you have long since ceased to love
> As our hot blood can love; the taste
> You have forgotten of a love
> That burns like fire and like fire lays waste.
> . . . .
>
> To welcome pretty Europe, we shall spread
> And scatter in the tangled space
> Of our broad thickets. We shall turn
> To you our alien Asiatic face.

I try to conjure up intimations of some "Asiatic" Southern Sung land-scape in Krasnoyarsk, and at this sleepy hour I almost succeed. The city's industrial chimneys have not yet begun to belch out the morning's quota of smoke, and cargo cranes lined up on the eastern bank of the Yenisei form a soft abstract design in the mist. In the distance I can discern a hint of mountain for the first time since we left the Urals.

But again it is the river that dominates the scene, and this river does not look at all like Southern Sung. The Yenisei runs in an almost straight line, with no meandering detours, from its source near the Mongolian border along the scarp of the East Siberian uplands all the way to the Arctic Ocean. This single-mindedness reduces it to only the fourth longest river in Siberia (and sixteenth longest in the world), but also makes it the one Siberian river that is navigable by deep-draft ships several hundred miles above its mouth. If I tossed a stick into the Yenisei here it would float a thousand miles due north to the inland sea harbour of Igarka. I think of Slava making a new Arctic home there, and of his beloved Georgia so far to the south.

I first met Slava in his native Leningrad fifteen years ago. He spoke fluent English; he was reading Strindberg in the original after having taught himself Swedish in order to do so; and he was currently immersed in learning Georgian, out of enchantment with the fiery acting of the Georgian theatre troupes he had worked with during summers as a student director.

After graduation from Leningrad University Slava was posted as a drama director to Sakhalin—that foggy, earthquake-prone island north of Japan that has meant the end of the earth to Russians ever since Chekhov described a penal colony there at the turn of the century. Characteristically, Slova loved the island. And that was the last I had heard of him, a decade before I arrived in Moscow as a journalist.

A year after I took up Soviet residence, Slava suddenly wrote me a letter care of the US Embassy in Moscow. It was sure to have been read by the KGB (and the CIA), but that had not deterred him. Was I the person of the same name he had met as a student? he asked in a careful English hand. If not, he was sorry to have troubled me. If so, he wanted to say he enjoyed my reportage. He didn't explain how he knew of my articles; obviously he listened to the Voice of America.

Slava wrote that he had learned Japanese in Sakhalin and had done a bit of translating. He had then gone back to Leningrad for a period, but had felt hemmed in there. So now he had returned to *prostor*, this time to Igarka. In that city above the Arctic Circle he had started out as director of the television station, then found this post too time-consuming and demoted himself to the strictly eight-hour-a-day job of engineer. Now he had time to write—what, he didn't say. He was married and had a young son, as I could see from the enclosed snapshots. He loved Igarka as he had loved Sakhalin, and before that, Georgia. He still got to practise Japanese occasionally, with the Yokohama sailors who traversed the Bering Sea and Arctic Ocean to collect Siberian logs. He sent me a portfolio of Siberian Eskimo prints, and I later sent him a furoshiki batik from the Japan he had been so close to but had never seen.

I was not able to visit Slava in Igarka, as it is off limits to foreigners, like most cities in the Urals and Siberia. Nor was I ever able to visit Georgia with Slava as my guide. Yet I carried Slava's atypical Russian enthusiasm for the extrovert Georgians with me when I finally visited the Transcaucasus on my own. And I found his affectionate descriptions of the theatricality of the Georgians amply confirmed.

Especially by Vakhtang. Vakhtang was handsomely moustached, impulsive in his movements. He personified what Russians think of—half warily, half with that eternal envy of the constipated northerner for the carefree southerner—when they call Georgians "temperamental". He spoke, and sang, with a vibrant baritone. He and his mates had come with a jug of wine to Mtatsminda (Holy Mountain), to the twelfth-century church with graveyard on the slope above Tbilisi that is the pantheon of Georgian poets, actors and educators.

The scene could have been Mediterranean, even Florentine. The late-afternoon sky was pink behind grey clouds. The hills were pinned to earth by black Van Gogh cypresses. As at the Piazzale Michelangelo the view was of tiled roofs and laundry-strung balconies stepping down to an S-curved river. As in Tuscany, a certain nobility of style coexisted with an effervescent *joie de vivre*. In Georgia, it is said, every peasant is a prince.

In Georgia, it might be said further, every peasant becomes that prince at Mtatsminda. In the early morning grandmothers climb the steep road to pray at St David's. In the evening students gather there to sing the haunting folksongs handed down over seventeen centuries in one of the world's oldest unbroken oral traditions. The harmonies are close, with a dissonance that sounds contemporary to a twentieth-century ear.

"How did you learn to sing?" I asked Vakhtang. He was astonished by this odd query about natural bodily function; "I breathe; I eat macaroni; I sing!" he replied. Every Georgian baby, it seems, dances as soon as he walks, sings as soon as he speaks, and improvises on the three-stringed panduri as soon as he can manage a spoon.

Vakhtang turned the jug of wine over to his friends, excused himself from their company, and proceeded to give me a tour of the cemetery.

The first tomb was that of Russian writer and epigrammatist Alexander Griboyedov, an honorary Georgian by virtue of having loved and married the daughter of the great nineteenth-century Georgian poet Ilya Chavchavadze. Griboyedov was exiled to Tbilisi for his sympathies with the Decembrist revolutionaries of 1825, Vakhtang recounted acidly, "because Georgia was barbarian. Georgia, which was Christianized and got an alphabet half a millennium before Russia!" Bitterly, he went on to describe the humiliation of a hundred and fifty years under Russian rule.

Did I know, Vakhtang asked, that Georgian culture was two and a half thousand years old? that Prometheus's defiance was set in Georgia's wild mountains, the highest in Europe? that Jason searched for his golden fleece in these same mountains? To Greek mythmakers, as to later Russian writers, Georgians were romantic heroes, their country the mysterious, vital meeting place of Europe and Asia.

Pushkin and Lermontov were inspired by Georgia. Pasternak eulogized:

> We were in Georgia. You can get this land
> If hell is multipled by paradise,
> Bare indigence by tenderness, and if
> A hothouse serves as pedestal for ice.

By the third century B.C. Georgia had established its capital 25 kilometres from present-day Tbilisi at Mtskheta—had I seen that yet?—a church and fortress at the confluence of the Aragvi and Mtkvari rivers that is like no other place on earth. Georgian churches do not repeat the Russian onion-dome motif that contradicts a featureless forest. Instead, the traditional architecture of the Jvari Church at Mtskheta grows organically out of the mountain that drops precipitously from it on three sides. Neighbouring peaks fade away in receding layers of evanescent blue. It's the soul of Georgia you see there.

By the Mtskheta era, established poetic forms had already taken shape that are still sung by today's storytellers in shepherd villages perched on the Caucasus Mountains. By the fifth century there was a written literary tradition, and in the Middle Ages some Greek classics that survived in no other tongue were preserved in Georgian translations. The language—a linguist's delight and a casual traveller's nightmare—is of unknown origin, bearing no relation to the continent's mainstream Indo-European languages. It has a peculiarly rich vocabulary for poetry, as it never discards old words even as it evolves new ones. And don't believe the charlatans who claim that Georgian is related to Basque, Vakhtang cautioned. There are 300 cognates—including the ancient name for Georgia, Iberia—but there is no grammatical link.

The Georgians were conquered successively by Romans (first century), Persians (sixth century), Arabs (seventh century), Turks (eleventh century), Mongols (thirteenth century), Tamerlane's Tatars (fourteenth and fifteenth centuries, in a wave of eight separate invasions), and, alternately, Turks and Iranians (sixteenth and seventeenth centuries). Finally this Orthodox Christian outpost sought the protection of Orthodox Christian Russia and was annexed by Tsar Paul in 1801.

The Georgians were few in number—never exceeding today's three and a half million—but they clung tenaciously to their individual culture through all of this. And when cultural nationalism swept Europe in the nineteenth century, Georgia was more than ready for it. Galaktion Tabidze—Vakhtang stopped to pay reverence to his memorial—wrote poetry with a "mathematical compression" that turns flabby when translated into other, looser languages. "Akaki", another poet buried here, is so familiar to Georgians that he is universally referred to by his first name only.

Shakespearean actor Akaki Alexeevich Khorava rests under a flat pediment of a stage—and there Vakhtang, like every aspiring Georgian actor, paused to declaim some impassioned lyrics and absorb the spirit of Khorava. At any moment I expected him to shed his sandals and explode into the male dance of leaps on toes protected only by the softest glove leather.

No! Vakhtang said fiercely. No collections of these poets' works—or poems by their heirs executed in the 1930s' purges, Titian Tabidze and Paolo Yashvili—are to be had in bookstores in the Georgian capital of Tbilisi. And the twelfth-century epic poem "Knight in Tiger Skin" is available only in Russian, not in the original Georgian. He deplored the constant attempts to Russify books, schools and customs in Georgia. In universities the USSR Ministry of Education is forcing students to write dissertations in the Russian language, even if the topic is Georgian linguistics, he said. And Moscow's constant campaign against "harmful traditions" tries to curtail the drunken four-day weddings and funerals that are the wellsprings of Georgian life, even if they do hurt production. "If they heard me say this, they'd kill me," Vakhtang added apprehensively.

We left the cemetery. It was long after dark by now, and it had begun to rain. The caretaker, whom Vakhtang had sweet-talked into leaving the grounds open an extra half hour, grumbled and locked the gate behind us with a demonstrative clang. Apart from us, the hillside was deserted. Vakhtang's elation of a few moments before was transported into a rage. He spat out, "We are a little colony of Russia—in this day and age! What wouldn't we be today if we weren't a colony of Russia?!" He steered us away from the road, and we slid down a muddy trail for some minutes in silence. Then, didactically, he asked, "How do Georgians survive?"

Partly by outplaying the Russians at their own games, he suggested. His tone mixed pride and accusation. In the original Russian empire, based as much on medieval religious as on national concepts, such assimilation was natural. And the landowning Georgian nobles, who felt more comfortable with their Russian counterparts than with Georgian serfs, integrated easily into the Russian world. Peter Bagration, famed as a Russian general in the war with Napoleon, was actually a Georgian prince. George Balanchine, ballet's ageless Russian-Parisian-American, started life as a Georgian (né Balanchivadze).

Today, Georgian philosophers, mathematicians, and tennis players operate at the top of their fields, in Moscow as in Tbilisi. (And some of them even find it a positive relief to live in Moscow, away from the oppressive hospitality demanded of Georgians of their status at home.) In films, Otari Ioseliani is one of the two best contemporary Soviet directors. And Georgian moviemakers manage, rather better than their Russian colleagues, to get away with portraying lyrical misfits in society or poking fun at a macho soccer team that loses to foreigners.

In linguistics, the Tsereteli Institute of Oriental Studies has recently made what promises to be the world's first breakthrough in a century and a half in reconstructing that original Indo-European proto-language to which Georgian is unrelated. In chess, the world women's champion is a Georgian who won the title as a teenager, and the sixteen-year-long champion she unseated in 1978, the only woman International Grandmaster in the world, is also Georgian. The Soviet Union's most popular guitar balladeer, Bulat Okudzhava, is half-Georgian as well.

In education, Georgia today boasts the second highest level of any republic in the Soviet Union. (Armenia just edged past it in the 1979 census.) In the Soviet Communist Party, Georgia has the highest proportional representation of any republic. Besides, Vakhtang added slyly, Georgia has the gladioli and tangerines that Muscovites crave.

He checked my reaction, correctly assuming that after living in Moscow I would have a stereotype of Georgians as well-heeled black marketeers offloading produce grown on private plots in the northern farmers' markets. Indeed, Georgian farmers are constantly being chided in the Soviet media for hiding their production from state purchasers, then flying to Moscow with suitcases bulging with oranges—or organizing an entire village to knit woollen garments for mail-order sales or, in one co-operative venture, bulldozing an entire new road over the mountains into Russia to avoid vegetable patrols on the Georgia Military Highway.

But those speculators aren't really Georgians, Vakhtang objected, and laid this canard too on the Russians' doorstep. They may be Abkhazians or, more likely, they are Armenians or Jews who have traditionally monopolized the middleman trade among the non-commercial Georgians.

I objected in turn. There must be some foundation for the Georgian and Russian officials' constant complaints about Georgians' private plots—which account for a full half of the republic's agricultural output—and about those mercenary peasants who turn a handsome profit of 50,000 roubles on ten tons of tangerines. I have met Georgian collective farmers who have organized bootleg fruit and vegetable traffic. And the roubles floating around Georgia must come from somewhere; Georgian personal bank savings are almost double the Soviet average, and Tbilisi competes with Kaunas, Lithuania, for the highest per capita ownership of motor cars in the Soviet Union.

Vakhtang remained unconvinced, as have other Georgian friends. Georgians are not merchants, Vakhtang repeated; they are artists: singers and movie directors and politicians who are so good that they accept the Russian rules and still win. Just look at Yosip Vissarionovich Dzhugashvili.

"Well, what about him?" I challenged Vakhtang. "What about the purges?"

"They were needed to chase out capitalists and kulaks." Vakhtang shot back the rote answer sardonically. But then, solemnly, he added, "Stalin was a great man." Remembering Stalin, he implied, was the second secret of Georgian survival today.

Vakhtang was embracing the violent ambivalence that Stalin inspires in his compatriots. To the Georgian intellectuals—whom Stalin persecuted more ruthlessly than any other Soviet nationality except the Azerbaijanis—Stalin is anathema. But to the Tbilisi cobblers and drivers who rioted against Khrushchev's de-Stalinization in 1956 and who today hang the Georgian leader's icon-like portrait in their shops and buses, Stalin is the folk hero who put minuscule Georgia on the map of the world. It is one of the supreme ironies of history that Stalin—who forcibly ended Georgia's three-year secession from Russia with the intervention of the Eleventh Red Army—should have become the focal point of Georgian nationalism.

The real Stalin, the intellectuals argue, was a reject from Georgian society who wreaked vengeance on that society. He was a shrewd calculator who compensated for his own Georgian minority status in the Russian empire by championing a Slavic chauvinism that even founding father Lenin thought repugnant. In World War II he cynically manipulated Georgian loyalty to him and mounted a special campaign to recruit his countrymen. Georgian youths responded, and this small republic—even though it never had any fighting on its own territory in the war—lost 350,000 killed, a tenth of its population and the highest casualty rate in the whole devastated Soviet Union. Yet the Georgians' reward was the exile to Central Asia in 1952 of a further 100,000 Georgians Stalin didn't trust. Exile was particularly onerous to Georgians who, unlike the neighbouring Armenians, have stuck to their home soil over the centuries and rarely emigrated.

Stalin's animus toward his native land extended to refusing to speak a single word of Georgian in later years. He disowned his former Georgian life—including his very Georgian-looking son by his first marriage. Svetlana Alliluyeva, his daughter by a Russian wife, described her father as "completely Russified" and quoted her brother as saying, "You know, Papa used to be a Georgian once." Did Vakhtang know that? I asked him. But he took such a slur as a personal affront. The mood was broken. At the bottom of the hill we parted company, abruptly and stiffly. I never saw him again.

I couldn't gauge how genuine Vakhtang's shock was at my *lèse majesté*, or how much he was repudiating what he already knew to be true. Some of my other Georgian intellectual friends detest Stalin so totally that they refuse even to talk about him. But for ardent nationalists like Vakhtang, Stalin is far too useful as a popular anti-Russian symbol to be discarded. Continued Georgian adulation of the former supreme leader constitutes defiance of Moscow's current downplaying of him. And it has the virtue of being unassailable; those Russian hardliners who would most like to put the Georgians in their place are the very ones who would have most to gain from any nostalgia for Stalin.

"All the Georgians think he was a hero," marvelled one Russian soldier-sightseer I met outside the reverential marble museum erected at Stalin's birthplace of Gori. And a red-haired Georgian factory worker I also met there confirmed the Russian farmboy's words. When I asked just why his countrymen admire Stalin so much the redhead replied instantly, "Because he was ours."

This ours/yours distinction is a crucial one. Georgians are loath to surrender to Russians anything Georgian, be it the memory of Stalin or a cup of coffee that a Russian soldier tries to buy from a Gori vendor who studiously ignores him.

Americans, of course, are welcomed with open arms just because they are adversaries of the Russians. On my first visit to the Stalin shrine in the 1960s, a guard initially took an American friend and me for Russians and treated us coldly. When we certified our genuine Americanness, however—by giving him the only New England postcard we had left (as I recall, an incongruous colour photo of the Boston expressway) he thawed instantly. Without uttering a word he turned, plucked one red rose and one white rose from Stalin's garden, and gallantly presented us each with one.

Later that same day my friend and I were treated to an even more elaborate demonstration of keeping Russians at arm's length while embracing—sort of—Americans. We were neatly intercepted on a public bus we had boarded in order to ride into the mountains and see something of village life. And to keep us out of further mischief, the Gori hotel director and his assistant hosted us to a lengthy personal banquet that did full justice to the Georgian maxim that for a guest, only too much is ever enough.

Had we seen the statue of the spirit of Georgia on the brow of the hill in Tbilisi? they asked. The woman holds a sword in one hand for enemies, a wine bowl in the other for friends. We were obviously friends (once our unauthorized bus trip had been thwarted), and we were to get the full lavish treatment, at a table burdened with lamb shashlik, chicken tabaki, fried cheese, all the succulent fruits and savoury herbs of Orient and alp, all the sharp and subtle flavours that would content the most finicky French or Chinese palate—and, of course, wine, cognac and vodka.

The toasts matched the hospitality. We were wished not only good fortune and happiness in our careers and eventual husbands, but also the zenith of success, so that no one—however clever and talented she might be, however accomplished and well connected—would ever surpass us in our chosen fields, or in our choice of spouses. And when the toasts got serious, and it came time to hail the then political chiefs of our two great countries, the Georgian eloquence and rhetoric came into full bloom. Back in the old days, our hosts said solemnly, with dewy eyes, we had superlative leaders who were seasoned, tried and true, men who were in the prime of their mental and physical power, men who were senior and experienced, men who had stood fast, men who had inspired their nations to victory in the dark hours of the Great Patriotic War. For such elder statesmen of our respective countries as Stalin and Rrroooosevyelt, the hotel director and assistant director went on, we stand when we make a toast. For today's leaders however, good leaders, to be sure, but young men who are new and have yet to prove their mettle in the difficult testing fields of life, we drink sitting down. A toast, then, at our seats, to Kennedy and Khrushchev!

Other expressions of anti-Russian nationalism can be equally telling. In Tbilisi, students stampede to get into the field of Georgian language and literature. This is true of the native language courses in all of the minority republics, but it reaches an especially high pitch in Georgia. Forty-five applicants compete for each opening in Georgian studies; by contrast, the Western foreign languages that are among the most sought-after specializations in Moscow attract only four applicants per place in Tbilisi. Significantly, those students who are so keen on Georgian studies have all been reared on apparently ineffectual Soviet imprecations against "bourgeois nationalism".

Once they graduate, whatever their field, few Georgians want to leave

Georgia. Despite the successful integration of those Georgians who do assimilate, the usual lodestone of Moscow holds little allure for the young generation. And Tbilisi is the one Soviet city in which a Western exchange student who marries a Soviet student can be sure that the match is not just an exit ticket to the West—but is instead a commitment of the westerner to a lifetime in Georgia.

"Why should I travel?" rhetorically asked one Georgian worker whose curiosity hadn't been whetted even by his military service in other parts of the Soviet Union. "I have everything I need here." He told me he expected to buy a Fiat fairly soon, and he reckoned he could take the train to Moscow periodically to trade in tangerines from his cousin's farm whenever he needed spare parts for his car. Or, if tangerines weren't sufficient, he figured he could wangle something by buying Western jeans on the Moscow black market for 100 roubles, then selling them on the Tbilisi black market for 250 roubles and investing the profits in spare parts.

More artlessly, one Tbilisi hotel concierge also expressed her full satisfaction at being Georgian, in Georgia. A guest asked where another Russian guest on the same floor was, and the concierge thought a moment, then replied that the *natsmen* in question had gone downstairs. The Russian questioner was nonplussed; to him the concierge was a *natsmen*, or member of a "national minority". To the concierge, however, quite logically, any Russian in Georgia was himself a *natsmen*.

The Georgian national consciousness shows up as well in a biting performance of Bertolt Brecht's *Caucasian Chalk Circle* that even outshines the Berliner Ensemble's, according to those aficionados who have seen both companies' stagings. I had been unable to attend the Georgian production when it played in Moscow; it had taken the usually blasé Soviet capital by storm that season, drawing a twenty-five-minute final ovation from those fortunate enough to procure scalpers' tickets. I was not among the select few, and I therefore had to squeeze into the sold-out (but not as thoroughly sold-out as Moscow) Rustaveli Theatre in Tbilisi to experience it.

The production revelled in the joke of presenting Brecht's fairytale in the very never-never land the playwright had chosen as his fanciful princedom. To a Tbilisi audience Abashvili, Vashnadze and Mikadze were hardly the exotic, abstract names that Brecht had intended. They were simply the everyday equivalents of the Schmidts among the play's Berlin viewers or the Joneses in Santa Monica, where the author conceived the script. The company teased the audience with the stylized familiarity of it all. The audience laughed appreciatively at every knowing nudge and gave a hero's welcome especially to Azdak, the "drunken onion" judge played by star Ramaz Chkhlikvadze.

It was superb theatre—and it was time-honoured colonial double entendre as well. The spectators applauded not only the entertainment, but also the wisdom of the fool who outwits authority and slyly perpetrates justice for the underdog, no matter who the pompous politicians are on top. "That's a very Georgian play," a fellow theatregoer remarked to me pointedly, "a very Georgian play."

Less subtle are the chronic Georgian fights over Russification. To a degree these fights characterize all the national republics. But Georgia flaunts them more than most. During my time in the Soviet Union the Georgians have been quarrelling openly about attempts to Russify secondary and university education. In a two-year period in the 1970s there were close to a hundred violent incidents involving bombing and arson, with the bold targets including an army depot and the main Georgian government building. These incidents were usually attributed by officials to disgruntled "speculators" rather than to nationalists. But periodic decrees from the Georgian Party Central Committee suggested a different motivation when they railed not only against "money grubbing" but also against "petty bourgeois thinking . . . manifestations of nationalism, outdated and harmful customs and superstition" (i.e. religion).

And then there was the strange case of Zviad Gamsakhurdia.

Gamsakhurdia, an even more intense nationalist than Vakhtang, used every opportunity to press his indictments of the Russians on Western journalists in Tbilisi and even Moscow. He told American reporters that he wanted US troops to come in to support a Georgian national liberation movement. He charged that secret police agents had infiltrated the Georgian Orthodox Church, manipulated elections in the hierarchy, closed seminaries, kept the clergy below strength, and even stolen from the church—and that an honest prosecutor who investigated these abuses had been fired. He accused the Red Army of deliberately maintaining a firing range too close to one twelfth-century monastery and damaging priceless frescoes with their shells.

Gamsakhurdia was so outspoken that—despite his claim of KGB attempts to poison him—he aroused some Western suspicion that he was an agent provocateur. How else could he still be so free in his speech and movements? In the surrealistic Soviet world only a prison sentence—and sometimes not even that—is proof that a person is not a disinformation agent.

The refutation of this suspicion came in 1977, when Gamsakhurdia was in fact arrested in the countrywide crackdown on dissidents. He apparently held out for a stubborn thirteen months of solitary confinement, then broke and recanted at least some of his activities in a statement that was filmed and played on prime-time Moscow news broadcasts in a heavily edited version. The final twist in the story came in mid-1979, when Gamsakhurdia was pardoned; when last heard from he was doing "cultural and educational work" among Georgian shepherds in Dagestan.

The apparent answer to Gamsakhurdia's original immunity came in close reading of the papers he had distributed to Western journalists. A few years earlier this son of a revered Georgian writer had clearly been courted by the then "out" faction of the Georgian Communist Party as part of its manoeuvring against the "in" leadership. In present-day Georgia's less fatal equivalents of the old mountain blood-feuds, it never hurts to have a nationalist bow in one's quiver, it seems. But once the outsiders finally won power in 1972 in a Moscow-sponsored campaign to clean up Georgia's notorious corruption, Gamsakhurdia was frozen out. Apparently he was still kept around for some years, however, as a latent weapon for intramural skirmishing. While it lasted, this was one of the most public displays of nationalism in the entire USSR.

That very fact, however, suggests both the dynamics and the limits of contemporary nationalism in the Soviet Union.

Of all countries on earth, the USSR should be the most prone to centrifugal nationalist forces. Long after the British left India, the French left Algeria, and the Portuguese left Angola, Russia is the only major imperial power remaining in the world. And the subordinate non-Slav nationalities are increasing their 28 per cent share of the total Soviet population at a rate that alarms Russian demographers.

Russia's empire is contiguous, as it was when the tsars' troops first brought successive border regions under Muscovy's and then Petersburg's suzerainty from the fifteenth century on. The Soviet Union's fourteen non-Russian republics enjoy the same legal status as the giant Russian Soviet Federated Socialist Republic, the one that straddles Eurasia from the Baltic Sea in the west to the Pacific Ocean 6,000 miles to the east. Members of all the country's 140 or 150 nationalities (including 22 groups with populations larger than a million) officially enjoy all the same rights and privileges.

Yet the Russians are more equal than the other 149 nationalities. They constituted only 52.4 per cent of the Soviet Union's 262 million in the 1979 census; other Slavs made up 20 per cent, other Europeans 6 per cent, Islamic peoples 17 per cent, and Armenians and Georgians 3 per cent. But the Russians have monopolized the top leadership post since Stalin's death, and they dominate the governing inner circles of the Soviet Communist Party Politburo (71 per cent Russian), Secretariat (100 per cent Russian), the KGB, and the army (Slavs accounted for 91 per cent of the generals of the army appointed between 1940 and 1976). In the national republics the Russians reserve the key Communist Party position of second secretary for themselves (or, rarely, other Slavs); they sometimes hold the top secret-police job in the republics as well. They are the only nationality that is dispersed throughout the USSR, predominant in all major urban industrial centres.

The Russians have been the ones who decided the country's investment priorities—in earlier decades, in Central Asia's favour, in recent years in their own favour. The Russians liquidated the native elites in the early years of Soviet rule. And throughout their more than sixty years in power they have tried to Russify the minorities in numerous ways, curbing local cultures, histories, and traditions.

Surely, in the post-imperial age of Bengali, Quebecois, Basque and even Flemish separatism, such an empire cannot remain immune to the forces of change. Or so a number of observers, including Alexander Solzhenitsyn, postulate.

To Vakhtang's fellow Georgians and other critics in Trans-Caucasia, the Baltic republics, Central Asia and the Ukraine, Russia's ordering about of the smaller Soviet peoples is indeed an insult to national identity. But to Russians, their superiority is only natural, the cultural and economic equivalent of the old "civilizing mission" or "white man's burden".

Whose truth is perceived as correct by the Soviet Union's 125 million non-Russians will determine the future tranquillity or turbulence of the Soviet state far more than any other domestic issue. Chronic and therefore accustomed meat shortages, an inefficient economy, and the concern of the "one per cent" of intellectuals with freedom—all are trifles in comparison with the potential dynamite of the nationalities' question. In an otherwise politically apathetic population, this is the one issue that could fire the imagination of large masses and focus discontent against the regime.

Over the years the Kremlin has responded variously to the challenge. In common with turn-of-the-century liberals and socialists, the Soviet Communists have always expected nationalism to prove itself a relic of the past and fade away under economic, social, and cultural modernization. (Lenin advocated full national self-determination both before and after the revolution, but he expected that any nation that seceded from the oppressive Russian monarchy would join socialist Russia of its own free will.) As the old tsarist empire dissolved in civil war it was therefore easy for the Bolsheviks to outbid the Whites for non-Russian loyalties by promising independence to the major national groups. And as the Bolsheviks consolidated their power it was equally easy for them to renege on their promise.

Red Army troops ended Transcaspian independence in 1920, Georgian independence in 1921, and guerrilla insurgencies in a number of other regions. Then Stalin cynically executed those native Communist leaders who had voluntarily brought their lands into the Soviet commonwealth, in order to pre-empt any future challenge to his own supremacy. Stalin wiped out the national intelligentsia as well in almost all of the minority regions in his bloody purges in the 1920s and 1930s.

In Central Asia in the Thirties Stalin forcibly settled the several million Kazakh nomads for the first time in the history of this people of the steppe.

Rather than comply, many Kazakhs gathered their herds and fled over the Chinese and Afghan borders.

In 1938 Stalin disbanded national units in the Red Army and scattered their troops in mixed units. Within a week of this move he made the study of Russian compulsory in all non-Russian schools. In 1941 he moved the day of rest and bazaar in Central Asia from the traditional holy day of Friday to Sunday.

Then after the 1939 Hitler–Stalin pact, the Red Army overran the Baltic states that had gained their independence after World War I. Mass deportations and arrests of local populations followed. In Latvia—despite the key role of the Red Latvian Rifles in the civil war—some 15,000 were deported in one night. In Estonia almost 10 per cent of the population was sent into exile in Siberia or Central Asia between 1940 and 1949. In the Gulag Archipelago "Balt" became a slang synonym for "political prisoner".

The backlash from this forcible subjugation of the Soviet borderlands became apparent as soon as Germany attacked Russia. Ukrainian nationalists—who had seen millions of their compatriots die in the 1930s' collectivization, famine and purges—quickly offered to collaborate with the Germans (and were just as quickly arrested by them). Even unoccupied Central Asia spawned a pro-German Turkestan National Committee—and turncoats from among Soviet prisoners of war for the German Turkic Legion.

In reprisal, Stalin deported eight small, mostly Islamic, Caucasus and Crimean nationalities in their entirety to Central Asia and Siberia. As a preventive measure in 1944 he also deported the 200,000 Meskhetians (whom he suspected of Turkish sympathies) from their native Georgia. In all, a million Ingush, Chechens, Crimean Tatars, (Buddhist) Kalmyks, Khemsin, Karachai, Balkars and (Christian) Volga Germans were uprooted in the punitive and prophylactic dispersals. Their names were erased from public records. They were driven out of their ancestral homelands and exiled to inhospitable regions under such harsh conditions that from 15–30 per cent (some specialists say as high as 46 per cent) of each of these nationalities died. Khrushchev said later that Stalin wanted to mete out the same punishment to the traitorous Ukrainians, but there were just too many of them. Stalin also wanted to execute Ukrainian intellectuals wholesale, according to Khrushchev's testimony, but Khrushchev prevented this. Stalin did, however, dissolve the Ukrainians' special Uniate Church, in 1946.

By the war's end the Soviet Union had not only reconquered the borderlands lost from tsarist Russia in the World War I weakness of revolution: Estonia, Latvia, Lithuania, the western Ukraine, Rumania's Bessarabia, and Finnish Karelia. The Red Army had also conquered new territory beyond the pre-1914 boundaries of Russia: eastern Poland, East Prussia, Czechoslovak Carpathia and, in Asia, the southern Sakhalin, Kuril and

Southern Kuril Islands. (Southern Sakhalin and the Kurils had once belonged to tsarist Russia, but the Kurils had been traded to Japan in 1875, while Southern Sakhalin had been lost in the Russo-Japanese War of 1905. The Southern Kurils had belonged to Japan for as long as anyone had bothered to claim them.)

The annexation of new territory was not without bloodshed. In the west, partisan bands that had harassed the Germans during World War II turned to harass the Red Army in the late 1940s. It took the Russians eight years to subdue all the resistance in the western Ukraine, Lithuania and Latvia.

The economic and social consequences of empire were radically different in the European and Central Asian parts of the Soviet Union. Those people—like the Balts—who had been much better off than the Russians prior to their accession to the USSR, saw their standard of living and education fall calamitously close to Russian levels. However, those people—like the Central Asians—who had lived not far above subsistence in tsarist times, with high mortality and widespread illiteracy, were yanked up towards Russian levels.

So successful was Stalin in laying the foundations of economic development, health care, universal education and emancipation of women in Central Asia that this region became a persuasive model for emulation by a host of post-colonial Asian, African and Middle Eastern countries in the 1950s and 1960s. Western analyses of the Central Asian economy have concluded unequivocally that Soviet paternalism under Stalin and Khrushchev aimed at equalization rather that exploitation.

At Stalin's death in 1953 the Russians were no better off economically than before the 1917 revolution. But the Central Asians emerged with an entirely new prosperity, with extensive health care, doubled lifespans, literacy, and a nucleus of native leaders able to run a modern society. They also emerged—given the sharply reduced mortality rates and the traditional prestige of large families—with a population explosion that was the best proof of wellbeing Central Asians could have wished for. The old Central Asian elites may have been brutally crushed, and the general population subjected to far more active domination by the Russians than it had ever experienced before, but the average Central Asian lived far better because of it.

After Stalin died there was some relaxation of the Russians' political and cultural repression of other nationalities. The uncertainty at the centre allowed drift at the edges. And in the Kremlin succession struggle KGB chief Lavrenti Beria (a Georgian, like Stalin) apparently made a deliberate bid for support of non-Russian nationalities through policies favourable to them.

Then when Khrushchev consolidated his power, he too flirted for a time with improving the position of the disadvantaged nationalities as part of his

THURSDAY THE NATIONALITIES

broad equalization drive throughout Soviet society. For a brief period he directed relatively greater investment funds to the non-Russian republics. His levelling in peasant income and in education policies also helped the more deprived non-Russians. And at the Twentieth Communist Party Congress in 1956 Khrushchev "rehabilitated" three of the small nationalities Stalin had condemned to oblivion, along with the memory of some other purged national leaders. Eventually all the Caucasus and Crimean peoples were formally rehabilitated, but to this day the Crimean Tatars, Volga Germans and Meskhetians have not been allowed to return to their homelands.

Khrushchev's liberalization had more far-reaching effects than he intended among nationalities subordinate to the Russians—and not only in Stalin's Georgia. In Eastern Europe it sparked the Hungarian revolt. Within the Soviet Union it sparked simultaneous anti-Russian riots in Kaunas, Lithuania, and a burst of less dramatic nationalist bids for autonomy. The alarmed Khrushchev suppressed both the Hungarian and Lithuanian rebels with Soviet troops—and pulled back on his soft line on nationalism.

By 1958 Khrushchev also shifted economic policy away from regional equalization to concentrate on further development of the European heartland and industrialization of Russian Siberia. At the same time, he instituted a reform in economic administration that bypassed the national republics altogether in the management chain of command. And he accelerated the migration of Slavs to Central Asia to administer the region's economy and government. (Swamped by this influx the Kirgiz lost their majority in their own republic, while the Kazakhs lost even a plurality in theirs.)

All these changes were effected for reasons of security and economic rationality—but this hardly assuaged the bruised feelings of the minorities.

Politically, Khrushchev exacted retribution for the ethnic assertiveness he himself had loosed in non-lethal purges of Latvian, Turkmen and other republican leaders in 1959 for their sins of "nationalist tendencies".

Ideologically, Khrushchev threatened the republics at the 1961 party congress with the dissolution of "obsolete" federal state forms—though he endorsed at the same time a contradictory "flourishing" of the nations. The ideal became an ambiguous "rapprochement" of disparate cultures into an eventual "merger" or "achievement of complete unity" of the undifferentiated Soviet citizen.

The ethnic elites, alarmed by this vague new prospect of oblivion, may have played a role in toppling Khrushchev in 1964. Certainly, as in the previous succession struggle, the new leaders made a quick tactical retreat from a hard line on nationalities. The ominous word "merger" disappeared from the official vocabulary and by 1969 was formally relegated to a visionary future "after the complete victory and consolidation of communism in the entire world". Earlier "exaggeration" of the expected results of "rapprochement" was also officially condemned—though a new hedge appeared with the introduction in the late 1960s of the concept of the "Soviet people" as virtually a national category.

After Khrushchev's fall, economic management was again routed through the republics. The chairmen of republican supreme soviets were made ex officio members of the Presidium of the USSR Supreme Soviet; the chairmen of republican councils of ministers were named ex officio members of the USSR Council of Ministers; and presidents of republican supreme courts and planning commissions also joined the equivalent bodies at the all-Union level. Individual national cultures were again encouraged to "flourish".

Once more the pendulum swung, however, as the new party leader Leonid Brezhnev moved to consolidate his power. In what seemed to be a bid for the support of Russian chauvinists, Brezhnev resurrected the concept of "merging" and again stressed the Russian claims to moral, economic, political and linguistic superiority over the other nationalities. Furthermore, Brezhnev speculated publicly that the "exchange of cadres" across republic boundaries would increase—i.e., that each minority republic's share in its own government would be even more diluted.

In the 1970s the tug of war continued between Brezhnev's exasperated wish that other nationalities would "merge" into Russians, and his realistic resignation to the permanence of ethnic particularism. In discussing the new constitution of 1977, "certain comrades" again called for the liquidation of outdated national republics and revocation of the right of secession from the union, Brezhnev reported to the Supreme Soviet, but this change was rejected. (In practice any advocate of nationalist secession is arrested, but defenders of the present republican structure won a modest victory in not having the new constitution say so formally.)

The republics did lose out slightly in the Brezhnev constitution, however, by surrendering some legislative powers, as well as the right of amnesty and pardon of citizens convicted in republican courts, to all-Union authorities.

A more serious attempt to circumscribe national identity came with the corollary adoption of new republican constitutions in 1978. The Georgian draft became known first—and shocked Vakhtang and some 5,000 fellow students into marching on the Tbilisi government headquarters when they discovered that in the new constitution Georgian would no longer be designated as the official language of the republic. The demonstration was successful. The Georgian language was re-enshrined—and Armenia and Azerbaijan, the only other republics with constitutional recognition of their languages, shortly followed suit. Nonetheless, the Russian language did slip into a better position in the new Georgian constitution: laws and decrees must now be published in Russian as well as Georgian.

When the constitutional skirmishing was finished, the outcome turned out to be something of a stalemate. A fuzzy "rapprochement" was once more the codeword in nationalities policy—and Soviet commentators began acknowledging that the nationalities problem is one of the two or three major issues facing the USSR today.

Just how much of an issue is indicated by the various anti-Russian demonstrations that have persisted into Brezhnev's time: in Dagestan in 1968, in Uzbekistan in 1969, in Kaunas, Lithuania, in 1972, in Tartu, Estonia, in 1976, in Latvia and Lithuania again in 1977, in Tadzhikistan and Georgia in 1978, and in Tallinn, Estonia. According to samizdat, the series of bomb and arson incidents in Georgia in 1975 and 1976 were nationalist inspired too. According to rumours so was the 1980 murder of Kirgizia's Prime Minister.

In a non-violent show of solidarity the Crimean Tatars also began under Brezhnev their series of innumerable petitions to be allowed to return to the Crimea. Many did return without permission—and were deported anew to Central Asia. The leader of the homeland movement, Mustafa Dzhemilev, after eight years of prison and labour camps, finally gave up, renounced his Soviet citizenship in 1979, and declared his wish to emigrate to the USA— only to receive a new sentence of four years of internal exile. But his comrades are continuing their petitions and civil disobedience.

Periodic purges of republican officials also attest to the persistence of "localism" and "nationalist deviation". Brezhnev's most spectacular purge removed Ukrainian First Secretary Pyotr Shelest from his republican leadership and from the Soviet Politburo in 1972/3 for coddling Ukrainian nationalism (as well as opposing détente). At the same time "nationalist excess" was strongly condemned in Armenia, Georgia, and Kirgizistan. And when the Georgians didn't take the reprimand to heart, some 25,000 of them were arrested in 1975 and 1976, according to samizdat. The arrest of civil rights dissidents in the Ukraine, Lithuania, Georgia and Armenia in 1977 was to some extent also connected with suppression of nationalist dissent.

For the most part the nationalist quarrels stop short of such confrontation, of course. They play themselves out in more veiled economic, cultural, and political forms.

Grievances about Moscow's economic policy arise from two opposite extremes: the top and the bottom of the Soviet heap. Those republics at the top—like the Ukraine and Estonia—complain obliquely that their economies are being drained to pay for the development of Russian Siberia. Those republics at the bottom—the Central Asian ones—complain obliquely that they are being kept at a permanent disadvantage and that the gap between their economic level and the Soviet average has in fact widened rather than narrowed in the past two decades.

The most thorough Western economic study of any Soviet republic estimates that some 10 per cent of the Ukraine's national income is "exported" to other regions of the USSR. Coal and electricity are delivered to other republics despite the Ukraine's own energy shortages. Chemical fertilizers, sugar, and processed foods leave the Ukraine in greater volume than some Ukrainians would like to see. The demand for Ukrainian money to invest in Siberian industrialization also blocks modernization of the Ukraine's own obsolete plant, which has not been overhauled since the era of postwar reconstruction.

Not surprisingly, Ukrainian leaders resisted the acceleration of Siberian development in the late sixties and early seventies. And according to Ukrainian samizdat publications, Ukrainian officials speak openly among themselves of being "robbed" of capital investment funds.

It's difficult to know just how extensive the feeling of economic exploitation is in the Ukraine, however. The republic's economic growth and money incomes lag only slightly behind the Soviet average, while the cost of living does too. The balance places urban Ukrainians right on the median point for Soviet citizens.

Among Estonians, the popular perception of economic exploitation is clearly widespread. Allusions to it crop up repeatedly in conversations with visitors to that most liveable of Soviet cities, Tallinn. Scorn is heaped on Russian tourists who come to the Estonian capital just to stock up on sausages and shoes and gape at the clean, cosy cafés.

Estonians know that they lead the Soviet Union in virtually every economic index—national income per capita, productivity and capital stock per worker, standard of living, average non-farm wage, savings accounts, living space, urbanization, mechanization of farms, rural standard of living, and even efficiency of milk collection from private cow-owners. They attribute their success to their non-Slavic and almost Germanic work ethic and efficiency, and they resent having to share the fruits of their hard labour with lazier and more inept folk.

No Western analysis of the Estonian economy has been produced of the thoroughness of the Ukrainian study, but presumably at least an equivalent 10 per cent of Estonian income is "exported" outside the republic. And it takes only a wistful glance at Finnish television broadcasts from Helsinki fifty miles away (the two languages are mutually comprehensible) to see how much better off Estonia would be economically if it were linked to the Western European instead of the Eastern European trading system.

Not surprisingly, Estonian officials joined their Ukrainian colleagues in resisting the Siberian development that they would have to help finance. Not surprisingly, they have opted for a small-is-beautiful strategy in their economic plans, limiting Estonian industrial targets to growth no larger than that spurred by productivity increase. Among other things this approach precludes the necessity for immigration of more Russian engineers to Estonia to make up for the acute labour shortage there.

Estonia's modest success in shielding its own productive economy against the encroachments of its neighbours is the very point that offends Central Asians, however. Looking back over six decades of Soviet rule, they see that every republic has the same relative economic position as when it started. (The single exception is Lithuania, which was deliberately kept as an agricultural backwater by the tsars but has now shot up to third place economically, just behind its fellow Baltic republics of Estonia and Latvia.)

The axis of development still runs from the advanced northwest (with the Balts on top, the Slavs next) to the backward southeast (with the six Islamic republics and Moldavia trailing in almost all economic indicators). At present the Central Asian republics, not counting the special case of Kazakhstan, average only 45 per cent of Soviet industrial productivity per capita—and this production is largely confined to the energy and primary-extraction sectors.

Even worse—despite tax preferences and subsidies from Moscow to Central Asia—the gap between the Central Asian republics and the Soviet average per capita national income has been increasing rather than decreasing since the 1960s. The main cause is the phenomenal growth of the Central Asian population rather than any deliberate deprivation—but this explanation hardly satisfies those Central Asians who then ask why investment has in fact not kept pace with population growth in the labour-short Soviet economy. For these Muslims the most important fact is simply that Central Asians lag well behind other Soviet citizens in wages, housing space, available consumer goods, communal services, health, educational and cultural opportunities, electrification, transport and communications. They fill only a small share of the skilled industrial jobs in their own republics. They are far less urbanized than the Soviet Europeans. In the largest Central Asian republic, Uzbekistan, for example, there were in the mid-1960s only 200,000 native industrial workers out of an Uzbek population of some eight million. And in one new aluminium plant in Tadzhikistan less than 15 per cent of the workers are Tadzhiks.

Moreover, despite its impressive incipient industrialization, Central Asia is still primarily dependent on a monoculture plantation economy of cotton-growing. For the past thirty years this has been a bone of contention, with local officials campaigning to build light industry that would diversify the economy and provide more varied job opportunities. Yet 75 per cent of Central Asians still work the cotton fields. And Uzbekistan, which produces 70 per cent of the Soviet Union's raw cotton, still produces only 2.8 per cent of the country's cotton cloth, the Chairman of the Uzbekistan State Planning Commission has noted bluntly.

In a Marxist society this is not called colonialism. But not all Central Asians understand the distinction.

*

In the cultural field the minorities' grievances are even more obvious. In varying degree Vakhtang's singing of those spine-tingling third-century Georgian songs, his impassioned declamation of Georgian poetry, and his anti-Russian venom are repeated by all the non-Russian nationalities.

The latest surge of cultural nationalism began in the 1960s. In Georgia and Armenia, in the Ukraine, in the Baltic republics, in Central Asia—and even in the otherwise quiescent Byelorussia—there were movements to purify the native languages of Russian borrowings. There were drives—successful in Central Asia in the early sixties—to reduce compulsory Russian schooling. There were campaigns—successful in the Ukraine in 1969—to have university textbooks published in the native tongues in addition to Russian. There were rehabilitations of non-Communist writers (some of whom were still living abroad) in Estonia in the late 1960s. There were popular new clubs to study Estonian, Lithuanian and Georgian ethnography, and to visit Ukrainian historical monuments.

In Estonia too there was a revival of those mammoth songfests that had figured so prominently in the nineteenth-century awakening of Estonian nationalism. Some 10,000 sang in the first mass chorus that assembled, and 250,000—a full quarter of the present Estonian population—attended the revival. In Lithuania, a new opera called *The Rebels* was written in 1957 on the theme of the 1863 uprising against the Russians—and had to wait two decades for its premiere. In Armenia, commemoration of the Turkish massacre of the Armenians took on anti-Russian overtones. Among the Tadzhiks, the only Persian nationality in the USSR, a renaissance of interest in their classical literature sent readers back to Omar Khayyam.

In Central Asia in the sixties there was a renewed pride in the traditional Turkic epics—which glorified heroic resistance to tsarist Russian invaders. In Uzbekistan there was a revelling in the ancient glories of Samarkand and Tashkent. Throughout the Soviet Islamic world there was a more open adherence among villagers to old customs that the Russian Communist reformers had tried to stamp out: bride price, Muslim weddings, circumcision, seclusion of women, fasting, work absenteeism on Muslim holidays, sacrifices of sheep, competitive cattle raiding, the Zakat donation to the poor.

In addition, there was a new focus among historians on the various nationalities' pre-Soviet periods—and a very positive revision of these histories. Kazakh poet Olzhas Suleimenov challenged stereotypes that branded nomadic ways as backward and praised instead the unbounded freedom of this lifestyle. Rather rashly, he even attacked the twelfth-century Russian saga *Host of the Lay of Igor* for maligning the Kazakhs' forebears, the Polovtsy (of "Polovtsian Dances" fame in Borodin's opera *Prince Igor*). Since the official line is that tsarist Russian subjugation of the border-lands was historically progressive, this heresy won Suleimenov a severe reprimand in 1975. Among other sins he was accused of kowtowing out-rageously to Islam and of setting Asia against Europe.

Despite this and other official diatribes against "idealization of the past", the Turkic movement of *mirasism*, or reassessment of the historical heritage, has continued. And it has displayed a disconcerting tendency to praise centuries-old ties between brother Turkic nationalities.

Partly to counter this greater danger of pan-Turkism—and partly to impress visiting Arabs and Turkic peoples across the border in rival China—the Soviet ideologists have been reluctant to suppress individual nationalist stirrings in Central Asia altogether. And even this miserly toleration emboldens the nationalists.

The phenomenon is especially apparent where national and religious feelings converge: in the Muslim faith.

The most striking manifestation of Islamic vitality in the past decade and a half has been the appearance of unauthorized itinerant mullahs to supple-ment the wholly inadequate 300 regular mosques available for today's 44 million Soviet people of Islamic descent. These holy men, despite the obloquy heaped on them by the Soviet media, travel about performing the traditional mullahs' religious duties, officiating at weddings, circumcision rites, funerals, mourning ceremonies and recitations of the Koran. The underground mullahs have even led prayers in the official mosque at Alma Ata, and Soviet writers complain that they now outnumber the registered clerics. Clearly they enjoy vast authority—so much so that in some Uighur communities villagers who do not give them a donation for their services can be ostracized.

In Kirgizistan the "unofficial mosque" of unregistered Muslim con-gregations is said to exist in almost every town and village. And throughout the North Caucasus and in scattered areas in Central Asia, adamantly fundamentalist and nationalist Sufi Brotherhoods have formed for secret worship and the teaching of Arabic—and direction of the various guilds of copper-workers, barbers, taxi drivers and the like. Many of the faithful make religious pilgrimages to tombs of revered Muslim warriors inside the Soviet Union as a substitute for the *hadj* to Mecca that they are not allowed to make.

Despite all the atheistic propaganda, one official questionnaire revealed in 1972 that more than 75 per cent of Central Asians surveyed considered themselves believers. Another questionnaire in Kirgizistan showed that some 68 per cent of students—who ideologically should be the most emancipated from religion—favoured the observance of traditional Islamic burial rites. And much of the vitality of the revived Sufi Brotherhoods has come from lay members among the young Muslim intelligentsia.

Furthermore, even among religiously passive Central Asians there seems to be a growing feeling of Muslim cultural identity. Soviet ideologists regularly berate popular confusion between Islam and nationalist ideas.

At the other end of the Soviet Union, the vigour of the Lithuanian Catholic Church is no less pronounced. Churches in Vilnius hold mass five or six times each Sunday—for standing-room-only congregations that include men in army uniform. Teenaged girls in white dresses flock to every confirmation. Half the republic's children are baptized. One petition in 1972 for an end to persecution of the Catholic church was signed by no fewer than 17,000 Lithuanians. Another appeal, to reopen a church in Klaipeda, was signed by more than 148,000.

The Lithuanian Catholic Church is aided, of course, by the proximity of the strong Polish Catholic Church on its border—and by the current occupancy of St Peter's throne by a Lithuanian-speaking Polish pope. It is aided even more by the stubbornness of Lithuanian Catholics in practising their religion despite all the official barriers.

This determination is attested to by the *Chronicle of the Lithuanian Catholic Church*, a samizdat publication that was born during the Soviet crackdown on dissidents in the early 1970s and continues to provide a steady flow of up-to-date information about Catholics. The range and detail of this periodical—and of the nine other Lithuanian samizdat publications that have spun off from it—are extraordinary.

The *Chronicle* contains the usual news about interrogations, arrests, trials, imprisonments and committals to psychiatric hospitals of Catholic activists. It identifies KGB agents within the church hierarchy and the theological seminary—as well as those "timid" priests who simply don't insist on performing their religious duties to the full when they encounter opposition. It reports, with photographs, on conditions in labour camps where Catholic dissenters are held.

It keeps track of the various parishioner requests for permission to rebuild churches. It records protests against the denial of last rites to patients in hospital. The *Chronicle* and its companion samizdat journals document as well the odd strike in a Kaunas factory, the welcoming party for a returning political prisoner, the appeal of a conscript to do his military service in Lithuania, or the petition to abolish Soviet rocket-launching sites in Lithuania.

They note bookburnings. They announce the formation of study circles on the history of the Soviet pacification of Lithuania. They even carry their own version of society notices, describing the wedding in a Mordovian labour camp of a political prisoner whose bride had travelled from Lithuania with a priest. (Before the bride was sent away the couple were granted two super-vised hours together at separate tables, with no conversation in Lithuanian allowed, and not even a handshake at the end.)

The zeal of the Lithuanian Catholics has won a few grudging concessions from the state. In 1977 the Church of St Peter's and St Paul's in Siauliai was permitted to ring its bells for the first time in twenty years. One exiled bishop was allowed to celebrate a major mass. Enrolment at Lithuania's one theological seminary was increased (though still not sufficiently to replace more than half of the twenty or so priests who die each year). Teaching of catechism is now carried out openly—and priests who do the teaching are fined only and not sentenced, as they were a few years ago, to a year in a strict regime labour camp.

Political manifestations of nationalism are much rarer than cultural ones.

To be sure, republican politicians apparently condone a certain amount of nationalist assertion among intellectuals. There are indications that Georgian factional leaders try to keep lines open to students. The Baltic Janissaries, from the Communist generation that grew up in Soviet exile and returned to their own lands to become leaders at the heels of the Red Army, nonetheless managed to keep their eleven-year school systems intact when Khrushchev reformed all other Soviet schools to ten years' duration.

Estonian First Secretary Ivan Kebin, who ruled his republic virtually from the Soviet takeover until his retirement in the late seventies, obviously looked the other way when his cultural ministers tolerated abstract art and old patriotic songs. And he obviously arbitrated in Estonia's favour for Tallinn to get away with calling major landmarks not Marx Boulevard or Lenin Outlook, but rather such frivolous Hanseatic names as Long Leg and Short Leg Streets and Peep into the Kitchen.

Despite such benevolence toward harmless national manifestations, however, the Communist Party leaders in the republics do not publicly identify themselves with nationalism. They do not harness this force and then lead their compatriots in an autonomous direction, as the Czechoslovak, Polish, and Hungarian Communist Parties have all done. Inside the USSR that sort of politicking has not been practised—with one partial exception: the Ukraine.

The Ukrainians, of course, are in a very special position. Their 42 million people make them the second largest nationality in the USSR after the 137 million Russians. Their shared Slavic blood gives them (along with the nine million Byelorussians) an advantage in a Soviet Union run by Slavs. Kiev's historic role as the cradle of Russian civilization lends the Ukraine some moral authority. And the Ukraine's more recent historic role as the locale of both Khrushchev's and Brezhnev's rise to power makes it sensitive to factional politics.

With this background, it is perhaps not surprising that the Ukraine's nationalism spilled over into the party in the sixties and early seventies. First the republic's well-developed intelligentsia—especially the intelligentsia from the latecomer western part of the Ukraine that did not have the eastern Ukraine's cautionary experience with Stalin's 1930s purges—began exploring nationalist themes in linguistics, historiography and ethnography. Then Ukrainian party First Secretary and Politburo member Pyotr Shelest seconded his intelligentsia.

At the 1966 Writers' Union Congress Shelest supported the calls for "purification" (i.e. de-Russification) of the Ukrainian language. In 1970 Shelest wrote a book (or at least had it credited to himself) entitled *Oh Ukraine, Our Soviet Land* that devoted an inordinate number of pages to the pre-revolutionary Ukraine and the pre-revolutionary Ukrainian Cossacks.

Then, at the very time when Brezhnev was turning to a Russian chauvinist line, Shelest kept stressing the need for equality and reciprocity in cultural exchange among all Soviet nationalities. Furthermore, Shelest was expanding Communist Party membership in the Ukraine to give himself a stronger political base. By 1972 Shelest's factional challenge within the party (as well as his challenge to Brezhnev's détente with the West) had grown too great for Brezhnev to ignore. And Brezhnev's own strength within the Politburo had grown sufficiently for him to risk a showdown.

Brezhnev won. Shelest was purged. And Shelest's successor Vladimir Shcherbitsky has gone out of his way ever since to condemn nationalist tendencies.

Clearly, the early Communists were as wrong in expecting national feelings to vanish under modern proletarian revolution, as even earlier enthusiasts had been in expecting nationalism to end wars. In the Soviet system modernization has turned out to stimulate rather than dissipate nationalism. And the federal state system has provided natural channels for the expression of this nationalism.

The Baltic republics, with their own glorious history (in the case of Lithuania) or just their own full integration into Western European culture and society (in the case of Estonia) possessed from the beginning of their Soviet association a certain disdain for the uncouth Russians. So, with their ancient Mediterranean civilizations, did the Georgians and Armenians. In these countries the liquidation or levelling of the former aristocracies served not to destroy these elitist views, but rather to spread the contempt for Russians throughout the native populations.

The nationalizing impact of political and social mobilization has been even more strikingly proven in Central Asia, a backwater of the Muslim world in which there was virtually no sense of nationhood prior to Soviet rule. The fledgling reforming intelligentsia that developed in some of the Muslim nationalities in the early twentieth century was wiped out altogether by Stalin. And in nationalities like the still nomadic Kazakhs and Kirgiz there was not even an inchoate intelligentsia—nor even a written literature—to begin a common rallying.

The Soviet Central Asian intelligentsia was thus formed from scratch. It came—and continues to come—direct from the village, from a class that in theory should be among the strongest supporters of Communist rule, regardless of what nationality is doing the ruling.

In addition, the Russians have expected the new Central Asians to be grateful to them for the emancipation of their lands from dirt, illiteracy, squalor and sloth. They keep citing the comparative statistics of the much poorer and dirtier neighbouring states of Turkey and Iran (though no longer Afghanistan). In Soviet Central Asia, they point out, there is a higher standard of living, with more doctors and hospital beds, more electrification and industry. Moreover, education is now the rule; enrolment of the Soviet Muslim people in secondary education doubled between the 1960s and 1970s, so that by 1979 almost 800 per 1,000 adults in the Muslim regions had completed a secondary education—a level close to the Russian average.

Despite all of these obvious benefits the Russians are reaping less gratitude than they expected from the Central Asian generations that have grown up under Soviet rule. Young Uzbeks shout anti-Russian slogans at a soccergame riot. Central Asian newspapers and magazines have all but buried the deferential phrase "elder brother" in referring to Russians. And the old tributes to "Soviet patriotism" have been supplanted in Central Asia by a more ambiguous word meaning "patriotism to the motherland".

The young, it seems—including the children of high-level party officials—take their new university education, doubled lifespan, dams and television for granted. And their new sense of politics—even one nurtured on rote Marxism-Leninism—raises their expectations and makes them ask why in their own republics they must so often be subordinate to a Russian engineer or party secretary.

The young do not care much for abstract comparisons with foreign lands they aren't allowed to visit in any case. They do care a great deal about the unfavourable comparisons they see with their own eyes as they move around the Soviet Union as army conscripts.

The generation of Central Asians coming of age do not become assimilated as the Russians had once hoped they would. They do not intermarry extensively with Slavs—and even when they do, their children overwhelmingly consider themselves Central Asian rather than Slav.

Furthermore, some 80–85 per cent of Central Asians never learn to speak Russian very well. This handicap effectively condemns draftees to assignment in low-prestige army units and keeps them out of the officer corps. It cuts off university students from advanced Russian technical education as well, thus increasing the number that choose nationalist-reinforcing studies in literature and the humanities.

Under these circumstances, young Central Asians find in nationalist pride the sense of belonging that they miss in a disorienting industrial world and in dry ideology. They have established communications with one another, through university friendships and through the burgeoning vernacular press that the Russians have encouraged. They are beginning to articulate a new national assertiveness, and they are carrying their close-knit families and rural communities with them beyond a parochial village or clan conscious-ness to what some Western specialists expect will be an unprecedented modern nationalism in Central Asia.

For the new nationalists in Central Asia as for the older ones in Georgia and the Ukraine, the Soviet federal system provides natural foci of percep-tion—and channels for complaint. The founding fathers originally intended the Union of Soviet Socialist Republics, like the United States of America, to be a melting pot. But, unlike America, they initially established the Soviet Union out of distinctive national building blocks. The Irish might eventually cluster in Boston and the Italians in New York City, but in chaotic America there are no separate states where the twenty million Irish-Americans or the ten million Italian-Americans are concentrated. In the USSR there are such national republics, with populations that are much less mobile than the restless Americans—and the Kremlin has never been able to drop what it began as a temporary expedient.

As a result, the fact that Tadzhikistan remains at the bottom of the list of industrialized republics after sixty years of Soviet rule is plain for all Tadzhiks to read in the statistics. Lithuanian officials who condone the persecution of the Lithuanian Catholic Church can more easily be branded as quislings than they could be in an anonymous multinational bureaucracy. The 83,000 feisty inhabitants of the Abkhazian Autonomous Region in Georgia can embarrass Moscow by raising a fuss about "Georgianization" of their culture, ask to secede from Georgia and join the Russian republic— and thus blackmail Moscow into giving them a special $750 million (£312 million) grant of economic aid.

Conversely, Russian hegemony and the crudities of Russian chauvinism are all the more irritating when they are displayed in the forum of a non-Russian republic. Estonians' anger wells up at Russians who come in, pre-empt the best technological jobs and the best housing in Tallinn, declare the finest Baltic beaches off-limits to Estonians, and never even learn to say "thank you" in the Estonian language.

Latvians, Lithuanians, Azerbaijanis, Turkmens, Moldavians, Uzbeks and Tadzhiks all resent being made minorities in their own capitals by Slav immigration. Kazakhs and Kirgiz resent being made minorities not only in their capitals but in their republics as a whole. Other Central Asians resent having a share of elite Communist Party membership that, relative to population, is only about half of the Soviet average.

So will the non-Russians revolt? Probably not, barring some catastrophe like the prolonged, stalemated war of 1914–17 or the German occupation of the Ukraine in 1941. Despite strong nationalist emotions, there are just too many positive incentives to assimilation, negative disincentives to mutiny, and neutral safety valves for venting frustrations.

The very powerful positive incentives to assimilation include opportunities for Russified native leaders to join the governing elite and share in its perquisites: economic integration throughout the entire USSR; access of less advanced regions to the modern technological world through Russian ties; and, for Central Asians, freedom from the old exhausting local warfare.

Today, many Balts, Trans-Caucasians and Central Asians have a strong personal stake in the system. In the 1980s no non-Slav could repeat Stalin's feat of seizing power in the fluid 1920s. But at levels short of the very top, there is little racial discrimination in the Soviet Union. In a system similar to the old French colonial practice and even the old tsarist practice (as it applied to the ethnic nobility), any citizen can advance up the central bureaucratic ladder, regardless of nationality. In tsarist times, non-Russian aristocrats needed only to embrace Orthodoxy to be accepted—and enough did so to constitute two-thirds of the Russian gentry by the end of the seventeenth century. In Soviet times, non-Russian elites need only embrace Marxism-Leninism—and, of course, prove adept at factional infighting—to be accepted into the party hierarchy.

Once inside the hierarchy, the Central Asian now stands a much better chance of getting a high position than was the case in former years. Slav migration into Central Asia has virtually stopped, for one thing—for the first time since the 1897 census. Out-migration of Europeans has begun. And even if the reason for this is only demographic necessity, the result is still the same in opening up more ranking jobs for Central Asians.

Under Stalin an overwhelming three-quarters of party and state posts in the Central Asian republics went to Europeans. Now only one quarter does. Many prestigious posts—including those of party first secretaries, party secretaries for agitation and propaganda, chairmen of republican governments and legislatures, and directors of most enterprises—are already reserved for Muslims, even if their assistants are Slavs.

Thus a Tadzhik can rise from his barefoot boyhood in the poorest Badakhshan mountain to become chairman of his republic's Supreme Soviet. A Dagestani woman—in a land where less than a century ago a predecessor had her mouth sewn shut for trespassing on the male preserve of composing poetry—can become a bestselling poet as well as a member of the republican legislature.

Kazakh Dinmukhamed Akhmedovich Kunayev can become the first Central Asian on the Politburo, gaining an increased claim on economic resources for his republic from this membership. Ukrainian Vladimir Shcherbitsky can be promoted to the Politburo even before he is named Ukrainian First Secretary by virtue of the importance of his republic's

Communist Party—and as a Slav, he can aspire to succeed Brezhnev as the supreme leader of the USSR.

Additional incentives to assimilation also include the general absence of discrimination in everyday life—in housing, for example, or ordinary hiring, or public respect. Even though the economic gap between national republics has been growing in recent years, the gap between Central Asians and Europeans living in Central Asia has been narrowing with regard to health, education, housing, living standards and jobs. The nationally conscious elites may resent the ultimate Russian domination of their republics, but the Central Asian man in the street at least probably has few personal encounters with Russians that would fan his national bitterness.

The penalties for challenging the system are as powerful as the rewards for co-operation. Military suppression of the rather rare nationalist riots and periodic purges of insolent national Communist leaders are only the most extreme sanctions. They are usually made unnecessary by the constant vigilance of Slav second secretaries in the republics. Within the unitary Communist Party of the Soviet Union there is no federalism; on the contrary, the iron rule is "democratic centralism", i.e. unquestioning obedience of orders from above.

Within the republics, the Russians control the all-important appointments decisions. They frequently hold the top KGB post; they always command the local army units, and they do not tempt fate by allowing national units to be formed in any case.

One additional disincentive to minority restiveness lies not in organization but in attitude—in the potential chauvinism of the master Russians. The Russians were not immune to the rising nationalist tide of the sixties; signs of a xenophobic Slavophil renaissance in Russia accompanied all the signs of Lithuanian patriotism and Central Asian *mirasism*. And any crescendo of anti-Russian emotions would be sure to set off a counter-crescendo of both official and popular Russian chauvinism.

In any such showdown the Slav reaction would undoubtedly be the decisive one. The Russians, besides controlling the organs of Soviet power, will continue to have a controlling plurality in the Soviet Union for as long into the future as anyone can project.

Despite the concern of some Russian demographers about the Central Asian baby boom and the mid-seventies fall of the Slav birthrate below population replacement levels, the 137 million Russians (1979 census) are still three times the size of the next largest nationality, the Ukrainians (42 million) or the country's 44 million of Islamic descent. Even if the present disparity in births continues it would not give the Central Asians a politically significant gain on the Russians in this century: the Slavs formed 72 per cent of the population in 1979, and are expected to retain their majority with 65 per cent of the population in the year 2000.

To be sure, the Uzbeks overtook the nine million Byelorussians as the third largest nationality in the 1970 census, and every third draftee in the year 2000 will be a Central Asian or Trans-Caucasian. But even if present birth rates persist it would take the Uzbeks until the mid-twenty-first century to pass the Ukrainians, let alone challenge the Russians. And Central Asian conscripts can still be effectively dispersed among the Russian commanding generals. The "revenge of the cradle" would seem to be a long way off.

In the decades since Stalin, too, the Russians have practised a certain saving tactical flexibility and tolerance of national variation. To some extent these have defused the explosiveness of minority discontents.

The pragmatic Estonians, who are unlikely to get carried away with their emotions, now have their giant songfests and other folklore. The "temperamental" Georgians win an occasional skirmish in the temporary demotion of some education official who is too aggressive in Russifying. The ancient Armenian Church, one of the prime attractions to prospective immigrants to the Soviet Union from the large Armenian diaspora, is allowed to have its own publishing house and operate with fewer restrictions than other Soviet churches.

So far, this sometimes pliable police state has proved effective in holding a nationally complex Soviet Union together, and the prospects are that it will continue to do so. The random nationalist riots by hot-headed youths after soccer games or cancelled pop music concerts demonstrate the bitterness of the minorities toward the Russians. But they also demonstrate the nationalists' weakness.

None of the straw-fire riots, so far as is known, has been sustained or well-organized. None has lasted beyond two nights at most. None has been synchronized, either with consumer demonstrations by compatriots or with nationalist demonstrations in other republics. None has demonstrated a capacity to rouse the man in the street out of his normal political inertia and preference for a quiet life to the fanaticism and sacrifice required for any real uprising. None, apart from the unique case of Georgia, has got very far in engaging the sympathies of the native power elites.

These elites may seek a limited political legitimacy in lobbying for the interests of their own republican bureaucracies. The Central Asian elites will undoubtedly wrest more cultural autonomy and even investment decisions from the Russians as their population growth shifts the balance.

But the nationalist hotbeds of Georgia and Lithuania are too tiny to force a showdown with Moscow. The Ukraine as a whole, in its 325 years of union with Russia, has fought for its independence only when a wider war has created a reasonable chance of success—and it is doubtful in any case that the Ukraine's postwar generations consider independence from Russia a burning issue.

This leaves the question mark of Central Asia. There some observers expect the population explosion, the growing national awareness, the revival of Muslim political fundamentalism south of the Soviet borders—and the new contagion of the Afghans' fierce Holy War against Soviet occupation—to coalesce into a major challenge to Moscow's centralism. Several hundred (or possibly thousand) Soviet Muslims, after all, had their first taste of being assigned abroad to administrative, technical and military posts in Afghanistan in 1979/80. A few deserted. A larger number fraternized with the Afghans, and bought Korans in the Kabul market. In February 1980 the Soviet commanders deemed it best to replace the Central Asian reserve units in Afghanistan with Slav regulars, and the Central Asian administrative cadres with Slavs or even East Germans.

Could a prolonged Afghan resistance, then, reawaken memories of the Uzbekistan Basmachi guerilla movement from 1918 to 1928? Or of the Muslim political ferment in Russia after Japan's 1905 defeat of tsarist troops? Or of the Tatar, Ukrainian and Polish nationalist ferment in response to Shamil's quarter-century defiance of the Cossacks in the crags above Gunib?

Again I conclude: probably not. Under normal conditions, the pressures would seem too weak to displace Soviet police control and the allegiance of native power holders to the system that has advanced their own careers so dramatically. The Uzbeks might just as readily identify with the Soviet overlords as with the Pushtun underdogs in Afghanistan. And the Central Asian record of one known riot in a dozen soccer seasons doesn't really suggest a population waiting to be inflamed.

For Muslin fundamentalism to have a strong impact, or even to become known in Soviet Central Asia, the country's borders would have to become considerably more porous than they are now, Afghanistan or no Afghanistan. For a real crisis of nationalist confrontation to develop, the new Central Asian elite would have to make a quantum leap from the present cultural nationalism to political nationalism. For mass resistance to Russian rule to develop, there would have to be some colossally foolish policy, like an attempt at full suppression of the Muslim religion perhaps, or compulsory settlement of the surplus Central Asian populace in labour-short Soviet Europe and Siberia.

Short of such a contingency—or Soviet involvement in a much wider war than the one in Afghanistan, or an extraordinarily acrimonious and prolonged succession struggle—any real nationalities crisis would seem unlikely in this century.

Vakhtang will no doubt become a famous Georgian actor in cryptic anti-Russian plays—but in the year 2000 his son will still be swearing at the Russian colonialists as he guides visitors around the Mtatsminda cemetery.

03.36 Kansk-Yeniseiskii

Our conductor drops by the compartment to share some gooseberries he purchased at the last stop. I take the offering as a token that he has relaxed from his initial role as disciplinarian following Grandmother's and my bed swap. Soviet bureaucrats can be sticklers for rules, but as the days wear on, the innate Russian anarchy tends to break through. With Russians, time establishes its own camaraderie. A stranger is not engaged in conversation, or an exchange of smiles, as quickly as he would be in America. But neither is he challenged to prove himself charming or witty or dominant. If he endures he is accepted.

The conductor and his conductress wife host our car all the way to Vladivostok, sleeping in their own cubbyhole opposite the samovar, then staying on duty for the return trip to Moscow that begins ten hours later. At home in Moscow they will get equivalent days off before the next round trip. They both wear Komsomol pins, and they are proud to have Moscow residence permits and to be entrusted with the stewardship of the "Rossiya". The good old Trans-Siberian does have a name, after all, it seems. Intourist may call it, impersonally, "Train No. 2". The conductors, with affection and respect, call it "Russia".

Grandmother chaffs with the conductor from her prone position on her now uncontested bunk, and Tanya is scandalized by this impropriety. When the conductor is distracted by another passenger in the corridor Tanya whispers peremptorily to Grandmother to get up, for goodness sake! Grandmother dismisses the order with a wave of her hand and continues her repartee lying down.

Tanya doesn't admit defeat. Instead, with a concentration signalling that there shall be no further encroachment on her consciousness by such mundane affairs, she returns to reading and underlining the book in her lap. The novel, it turns out, is Dostoevsky's *Crime and Punishment*. And Tanya is perusing it, it turns out, not for her own amusement, but for her daughter's edification. Nina is in her last year of secondary school, and the study load is excessive, leaving no time for all the assigned reading, let alone movies or television. Nina likes math and chemistry. But "there is so much homework your head spins, and you can't remember anything." She therefore welcomes assistance in her assignment of listing the novel's positive and negative characters and clearly has no intention of ploughing through the book herself.

Dostoevsky is hard to read, Tanya observes, because he's so psychological. Tolstoy—ah, Tolstoy is easier. She liked him better when she was younger, though. She thought then that everything he wrote was just as it must be. But now that she is more experienced she knows how different real life is from the way he wrote it. For example, Anna Karenina created her own suffering by not marrying Vronsky. Nowadays people just get divorces, and that's that. Things are much simpler than Tolstoy imagined.

In fiction Tanya prefers Jack London and Theodore Dreiser, and so does another army wife in the next compartment who is reading *Sister Carrie*. Dreiser is, in fact, one of the most popular American authors in the Soviet Union. He is perfect ideologically, demonstrating how the capitalist environment degrades, and, as a naturalist, reinforcing the nineteenth-century determinism that underlies Soviet Marxism. Moreover, he is a rollicking good storyteller—which most Soviet socialist realists are not.

Grandmother has read all of Dostoevsky and Tolstoy (I assume she means all of the best-known novels), and she has read *War and Peace*, her very favourite, many times over. She smiles with recollected pleasure, and she doesn't join Tanya in disparaging *Anna Karenina*.

I ask Tanya if she has ever written any stories, and she and Grandmother both hoot at the idea. Who would have time when raising a family? Besides, writing is for specialists. I demur, offering the evidence of a worker-poet I bumped into in Moscow; they speculate that perhaps men have more time than women do for that sort of thing. Their interest is piqued, however, and they inquire further.

My Moscow poet approached me one day as I was seated on a bench in the municipal army park. I had adopted the Russian habit of treating the nearest green space as my living room and went there often to read in the summer or stroll in the winter.

It was a friendly place. Mothers wheeled baby carriages there. Husbands walked the german shepherds and doberman pinschers they otherwise kept in cramped Moscow apartments and loaned out to the police for periodic reserve watchdog training in return for dogfood subsidies. Families boated on the duckpond. Young people danced in the open air enclosure. Fanatics played chess in the official chess pavilion, and bored aunties listened to lectures about the 1980 Olympics in the little theatre. Mercifully, on this occasion, I was in the park before the high season had started, so the ubiquitous loudspeakers had not yet begun their harangue.

I had just opened my book when a male voice blurted out, "I'll read my poetry to you." An unshaven face appeared, topped by a grey-and-white cloth cap. The man had never quite finished tucking his shirt into his belt that morning. His laces ran impatiently through only the bottom and top eyelets of his shoes. His hands were tattooed. And he fully lived up to the Russian reputation of loving poetry with a passion.

Once or twice he interrupted his recitation to inform me that Yelizavieta Ivanovna in the fourth line was his mother or that Krasnaya Presnya, the well known workers' district, was where he lived.

The gist of his "Confession of a Hooligan" (a title borrowed from 1920s proletarian poet Sergei Esenin) was that he scorned the beautiful and admired the unlovely. The language was peasant colloquial.

The full meaning was a bit obscure to me at first hearing, so I asked if I might read the manuscript myself. He started to hand it over, suddenly thought of a better idea, and trotted over to the nearest notice board where the day's *Pravda* was posted for public reading.

Without explaining his actions he stretched to reach the top of the little protective roof over *Pravda*, then jumped three times before successfully retrieving a box that had been cached there. Triumphantly, he returned to my bench with the checkers set that was the communal property of the convocation of men who competed and kibitzed on a neighbouring bench every afternoon.

Having thus devised a lap desk, my new friend borrowed pen and paper from me and proceeded to copy the entire poem as a gift. Neither the glorious spring sun, the dogs scouting for enemies to attack, the small boys on wobbly trainer bikes, nor the older ball-bouncing children disturbed his absorption in his task. Engrossed in his oeuvre, he bobbed his head with fresh satisfaction at the completion of each line. At the end he made a solemn written vow—"Here I decided to surpass Sergei Esenin"—and signed his name with a flourish.

"Where are you from?" he inquired paternally, and when I told him asked which state.

I identified my homeland as Massachusetts and asked in turn if he knew where this was. "But how could I not know?!" he exclaimed reproachfully, "I have a map of the world on my wall. . . . Do you know which is the biggest country in the world?"

"China?" I ventured, never having been too good at geography and not yet having travelled the Trans-Siberian.

"No," he corrected me, "the USSR! My motherland! And do you know which is the second biggest?"

He sensed that I was about to propose China again, so he quickly replied himself: "America! . . . Don't forget Alaska!

"In land the USSR is first. In population it is third; China is first; India is second."

At this point the enormity of superpower responsibility came home to him, and he proclaimed, "America and the Soviet Union must never fight a war. Too many people would perish. Remember that a real Russian muzhik told you that!

"Do you realize that the Russians and Germans fought each other?" he went on. "I was in the army in the Ukraine. He was my commander." He gestured as if firing a machine gun and nodded toward the nearby statue of Marshal Fyodor Tolbukhin and the pot of hydrangeas someone had set at its base. "I fought everywhere—in the Ukraine, Germany, Hungary, Poland. Only I wasn't in Czechoslovakia."

The worker-poet volunteered further that he had a splendid wife and three sons, that he was employed in an enterprise whose name I didn't catch, and that he writes verse when he can't sleep at night. He also gave his date of birth and confided that he was now going to begin writing about "an altogether new theme".

"We are educated now," he concluded. "Everyone is studying. We don't just drink vodka any more."

Then, as abruptly as he had appeared, he departed. "I'll go now," he announced, and said goodbye in Russian. He walked ten paces in the direction of his bronze commander, then turned impulsively and added, "Adieu."

"Hmmph," sniffs Tanya suspiciously. "He was probably drunk."

Grandmother chuckles and nods, either out of agreement with Tanya's judgment or out of sympathy with my worker-poet.

04.10   Ilanskaya

We pass our first mass graveyard of retired steam engines that would gladden the hearts of old train buffs. The locomotives are not streamlined in the contemporary fashion but are downright pudgy, with satisfying geometric volumes stuck together honestly and visibly.

They too have a political past. In Stalin's last paranoiac years it was forbidden even to whisper the possibility of replacing steam engines with diesels as the decadent West was doing. Nor, in an earlier period, could one ask any questions about all those railwaymen who suddenly vanished in the 1930s—a higher percentage of them, perhaps, than of any other profession. Special courts in train sidings like this one sentenced thousands of these members of the pre-Bolshevik intelligentsia to camps or executions as "Trotskyite-Japanese spies". I met one locomotive engineer in Moscow who had survived the camps and showed me a tattered book of the brotherhood from the proud 1920s. He pointed to name after name and shook his head. Dead or disappeared.

Perhaps it was one of these mothballed engines that hauled Eugenia Ginzburg's "special equipment" train back in 1939. The freight trucks would have long since collapsed or been cannibalized for lumber and metal. But her steam locomotive surely survives yet. Something about the Soviet labour theory of value, or perhaps just an instinct for hoarding, blocks the Russians from scrapping any obsolete machine. Every boiler in this graveyard must have its own ghosts of the 1930s.

And what were Ginzburg and her sister convicts thinking about as they passed this spot? One thing, I'm sure: water. After the luxury of getting to wash in Sverdlovsk, their daily mugful of liquid seemed more miserable than ever. It wasn't enough to sluice down the salty herring-tail soup, let alone slake the women's constant thirst in those July days in their baking, sweaty, stinky, dusty, suffocating, overcrowded car. Even the guard dogs got more to drink than they did.

"What a pity one's belly has no memory!" mused Polya reproachfully somewhere along here. "I must have drunk at least a gallon at Sverdlovsk, and now—what a state of affairs!"

Others, less temperately, quarrelled over their rations. The day Sara knocked a tablespoonful of water out of Lena's mug as she extracted a bandage from her pocket for her raw foot, Lena almost struck the miscreant with whom she had to share her bunk. And for all the inmates of Car Number 7, peeking out at one station and seeing a youth let water trickle over his bare sunburnt back was almost as great an agony as glimpsing a mother outside casually holding the hands of her two small sons.

Nothing short of water could have moved the prisoners to their one abortive revolt. Tanya Stankovskaya, so ill she could hardly stand, hammered on the door and cried for water, and the other women called out, "Swine! Torturers! You've no right to do this! You're subject to Soviet law the same as we are! . . . We'll smash up the car! Shoot us and be damned! Wa-ter! . . ."

Brigand came running, ordered Tanya and one other woman to be taken off to the punishment cell, and put everyone on short rations, withholding their soup and halving their bread. The revolt evaporated. Brigand intended to hold Tanya in the punishment cell five days for her mutiny, but brought her back on the third day, apparently to be spared the nuisance of making out a death certificate for the rapidly fading woman. She had had to sit with her knees bent the entire time, in a box even more stifling than the common cell. The prisoners pulled off her boots and dedicated a few drops of precious water to wiping off her face. Chava miraculously produced five lumps of sugar she had hidden away in Yaroslavl, and gave them secretly to Tanya. Tanya's pulse revived, and she vowed not to die before she reached the Vladivostok transit camp and could look for the party district secretary who had defended her after her arrest and for this had himself been arrested. Tanya Stankovskaya did last until Vladivostok, but only until Vladivostok. She was carried off the train, was declared fit for heavy labour in the physical examination, and died a few hours after this report. So emaciated was she that even the hordes of bugs that gorged on the prisoners shunned her body.

By now some things have changed. But not the thirst. It was still as strong when Vladimir Bukovsky rode airless convict trains in the 1970s. You know you will be tortured by thirst the rest of the day, Bukovsky relates, but you still eat your bread and your stinking, rotten regulation herring, because you don't get anything else.

The prison trains themselves haven't changed much either, give or take a few diesel engines. The uninitiated prisoners still look just as confused; the veterans still move just as fast to exploit their superior knowledge. You can pick out the old con instantly when you get thrown in with a new crowd, Bukovsky found: while others hesitate, the "genuine con" immediately occupies the middle shelf on the right, with its glimpse of freedom if the guards can be talked into lowering the corridor window a crack. His small sack contains all the essentials: a shirt to swap for tea at some point, a knife, a clean mug, a bit of frisk-proof hidden cash. He is a virtuoso at swearing, a connoisseur of such black experiences and tales that when his tongue is loosened by a drop of eau de cologne, he turns your prison term into grand theatre.

Bukovsky's own veteran Lower Depths companions ran the gamut. There were the Lithuanians and Ukrainians, men who had been in the slammer ever since they fought the Russians in the national liberation struggles of the 1940s, men who still preserved the old-fashioned accordion melodies and their old-fashioned work ethic that was so out of tune with the contemporary Soviet contempt for work. There were the thieves, with their "tribute", their caste system, their own complicated unwritten code adjudicated by "regulators". There were the homosexual outcasts who had lost at cards, perhaps, and had to pay by being the passive partner forever after one such humiliation, with anyone who wanted to rape them.

There was Bukovsky's cellmate at the Leningrad Special Mental Hospital who had murdered his children, cut off his own ears immediately afterward and eaten them. There was Daniel Romanovich Lunts, chief of the political department of the Serbsky Institute, who could be depended on to produce the politically required diagnosis of any patients' psychiatric condition—and loved to while away the time discussing Bergson, Nietzsche, and Freud with these patients.

There was the petty camp official who, when he visited Moscow, hated the guts of all the smiling, laughing people he saw walking around at liberty and longed to teach them a thing or two, And there was Bukovsky himself, yearning in prison's monotony just to catch a glimpse of the colours of ordinary street crowds going about their random business, then, when he was free, like the camp guard, hating the untroubled, animated faces of those who hadn't done time.

06.52 *Taishet*

Ever since Krasnoyarsk we have been passing freight trains crammed with logs, coal, motorcars, heavy-duty trucks, earthmoving vehicles, cranes, machinery, rails, railroad ties, prefabricated concrete housing sections, Soviet Morflot containers—and also Cti and Mitsubishi containers.

The latter signify success in the recent Trans-Siberian drive to capture the booming Japanese-European trans-shipment trade and earn sorely needed hard currency. By undercutting Western sea charges by as much as 50 per cent, disgruntled Western shippers allege, the Soviet Union has now wrested for itself a good 27 per cent of this container-transport business. The Trans-Siberian has indeed come a long way since its early days of simply deflating gougers' prices for leather and metal in Siberia and finally getting Vladivostok officials to Petersburg faster overland than via a round-the-world voyage across the Pacific Ocean, the American continent, the Atlantic Ocean, and Europe.

All the freight trucks of creosote ties and Japanese construction equipment turn off at Taishet, onto the beginning spur of BAM, the Baikal–Amur Mainline that will become the second Trans-Siberian railroad—planners hope—in 1983. This $15 billion, 2,000-mile long undertaking is probably the largest construction project in the world today. The railway, and the new towns it is begetting at the rate of one every three weeks, are what the Estonians and Ukrainians resisted—unsuccessfully. They are what the Central Asians view as a diversion of investments that could otherwise be coming to them. BAM was begun in the thirties, interrupted by World War II, then revived as a priority project in the mid-seventies. The grandiose construction is to link all the new Siberian extraction and processing industries with their markets—and lure more Russian settlers to fill the empty spaces of a China-bordering Siberia.

For strategic reasons, the new line beginning here in Taishet will run north of the present Trans-Siberian, farther away from the Chinese frontier. And because of this it will require even greater engineering feats than the original Trans-Siberian. It will tunnel through more rugged mountains than our present route; it will penetrate more active seismic areas and longer stretches of permafrost, with subsoil perpetually frozen even in summer temperatures of over 90 degrees F.

Free labour is building this Soviet Trans-Siberian, while prisoner labour built the old tsarist Trans-Siberian, Tanya notes informatively, if not completely accurately. It may be true that today workers on the new line consist primarily of the 100,000 Komsomol volunteers (and Red Army conscripts) who are the Soviet equivalent of a mobile construction force. It is true that free labour is attracted by wages three times the Soviet industrial average for workers who stick it out for three years. And there are some idealists who still share the early revolutionary zeal for communal industrialization.

But the first labourers at Taishet back in the 1930s were convicts, not volunteers. And, unlike the tsarist prisoners who built much of the first Trans-Siberian, they didn't even get reduced sentences for their exceptionally hard labour in installing two hundred-odd miles of track in the taiga. In Stalin's time, railroad construction was just like the land improvement, tunnel digging, state farm and port building, gold mining, copper pulverizing, logging, timbering, or any other ordinary Gulag task.

Such strenuous work on a poor diet in −50 degree winters, of course, meant extermination as surely as if the camps had been equipped with gas chambers. And there was no escape, nowhere to run to in this endless, magnificent, bitter forest. "You come to hate this forest, this beauty of the earth, whose praises have been sung in verse and prose," grieved Solzhenitsyn.

You come to walk beneath the arches of pine and birch with a shudder of revulsion! For decades in the future, you have only to shut your eyes to see those same fir and aspen trunks which you have hauled on your back to the freight car, sinking into the snow and falling down and hugging on to them tight, afraid to let go lest you prove unable to lift them out of the snowy mash.

Even after Khrushchev dismantled much of the Gulag, Taishet continued to serve as one of the large remaining concentration camps. After Pasternak's death his companion Olga Ivanskaya, the model for Lara in *Dr Zhivago*, spent four years imprisoned in this dismal spot.

19.34 *Irkutsk*

As we approach the station I peer out of the window to see if I can catch a glimpse of those renowned log houses that Irkutsk is proudly preserving rather than (like Moscow) condemning. But no. All I can make out in the darkness are some glum exhortations to fulfil the Five-Year Plan and give glory to the Communist Party of the Soviet Union.

It's difficult to imagine Irkutsk as the 1890s "Paris of Siberia", where one goldminer advertised his wealth by lining up champagne bottles in a row and shattering them with stones, another millionaire bought bolts of printed cotton cloth and laid down strips on the muddy streets for his walkway; where fur traders gambled away fortunes in one roll of the dice, and garotte and other murders averaged one a day.

At least one Yankee entrepreneur even showed up here in the boom days at the end of the nineteenth century outfitted with six-shooters, vodka, tea, sugar, salt, spices, hams, sausages, biscuits, cups and eating utensils, a mattress, two pillows, furs, sheepskin coats, a sensational buffalo robe from America, ropes, nails, "Persian powder" for dispatching vermin, and a teaspoonful of red pepper inside his socks to ward off the cold, records Trans-Siberian chronicler Harmon Tupper.

Leo Tolstoy's 1890s connections to Irkutsk were more sombre. On 22 October 1896 he wrote a letter to the Irkutsk commandant:

Into your disciplinary battalion there have entered, or shortly will enter, two men, who by the Brigade Court of Vladivostok were condemned to three years' imprisonment. One of them is Peasant Peter Olkhovik, who refused to do military service, because he considers it contrary to God's law; the other is Kirill Sereda, a common soldier, who made Olkhovik's acquaintance on a boat and, learning from him the cause of his deportation, came to the same conclusion as Olkhovik, and refused to continue in the service. . . .

I will not conceal from you that personally I not only believe that these men are doing what is right, but also, that very soon all men will comprehend that these men are doing a great and holy work.

But it is very likely that such an opinion will appear to you as madness, and that you are convinced of the contrary. I will not permit myself to convince you, knowing that serious people of your age do not arrive at certain convictions through other people's words, but through the inner work of their own thought. There is one thing I implore you to do as a Christian, a good man, and a brother—my brother, Olkhovik's, and Sereda's . . . I implore you not to conceal from yourself the fact that these men (Olkhovik and Sereda) differ from other criminals; not to demand of them the execution of what they have once for all refused to do. . . . Without departing from the law and from a conscientious execution of your duties, you can make the confinement of these men a hell, and ruin them, or considerably lighten their sufferings. It is this I implore you to do, hoping that you will find this request superfluous, and that your inner feeling will even before this have inclined you to do the same. . . .

I shall be thankful to you, if you answer me.

Our train pulls into the platform and the familiar mêlée of too many people trying to find too few free seats. Some argue with the conductor, swearing that they will stand in the corridor for the next three days if necessary. Voices are raised. The conductor prevails. The excess ones are cast back into the lap of Irkutsk. The elect quickly stow their bundles in the overhead baggage holes in the compartments and establish proprietary rights.

Within minutes of our departure all is still. No matter what the clocks say, it's really after midnight. In the corridor the conductor sweeps the white floor runner with a besom, vacuums it, shakes out the wrinkles, and repins it to the Oriental carpeting with huge safety pins. Then he too retires. The wheels clack on. Our train whistle shrieks.

CHAPTER V
FRIDAY THE WORLD

They wish to rule the world by conquest; they mean to seize by armed force the countries accessible to them, and thence to oppress the rest of the world by terror. The extension of power they dream of is in no way either intelligent or moral; and if God grants it to them, it will be for the woe of the world.

Marquis de Custine, 1839

So far from regarding the foreign policy of Russia as consistent, or remorseless, or profound, I believe it to be a hand-to-mouth policy, a policy of waiting upon events, of profiting by the blunders of others, and as often of committing the like herself.

Lord Curzon, 1889

01.10 Manturikha

AGAIN, IT IS a soft, hazy dawn, over what is surely the most enchanted lake in the world. Every fairytale that once upon a time rose out of mysterious forest and luminous shore must first have been enacted at Lake Baikal. We cross streams and rivers that tumble 2,000 metres straight down from the Khamar-Daban ridge towering above us on our right. And where the granite dissolves into a beach of bog, we see scrawny willows poking out of hummocks floating in primeval glue.

Snow has already dusted the highest mountain peaks in these late August days, and frost has begun to translate the summer's green shimmer of aspen into autumn's less volatile gold. Now and again there is a flash of scarlet rowan against the steadfast viridian of fir and larch. Soon the osprey will begin its southward flight; the bear will eat the season's last blueberries and lumber off to its den. The incoming waves will congeal into splinters of ice as they strike coastal rocks and leave behind a foam of brittle shards. The spoken word, the native Buryats say, will freeze in the air.

The Buryat shamans were in awe of Old Man Baikal, whose three hundred and thirty-five obedient river daughters flow ever homeward but whose one wanton daughter, the Angara, runs away, to elope with the dashing Yenisei. In his rage, the Old Man threw a giant stone after his lone rebel offspring, the legend has it, and for millennia to come the rock jutted out of the lake, a monument to the futility of parental wrath.

The scimitar-shaped Lake Baikal is indeed subject to impetuous anger.

Everywhere except at the effluence of the Angara, Baikal's mountain banks are steep and dramatic—and they are liable to the sudden dislocations of earthquakes. The lake's mile-deep trough was formed some thirty million years ago and is still being deepened by subterranean tremors. In this century the southern tip of shore we have been hugging ever since we left Irkutsk has averaged one violent epicentre per decade.

Baikal's weather is equally capricious, conjuring up on the eastern bank a rainy Barguzin forest, the lair of the crown sable and ermine, but casting up a scant twenty miles away a semi-desert mid-lake island. In autumn Baikal's turquoise water can be whipped into five-metre waves by 80 mile per hour hurricanes. In winter the solidly frozen ice on the lake's surface can cleave apart unpredictably, leaving fissures two metres wide and up to 18 miles long. It is a hazard that plunged innumerable sleighs, horses, a train and, on one occasion, 20,000 gold roubles to the bottom of Baikal in the years before the Trans-Siberian tracks were grafted onto the lake cliffs.

Baikal is relatively small in surface. Like its twin, Tanganyika—for long years some amateur geologists hypothesized an underground connection between the two lakes to explain their uncanny similarity—Baikal is long but narrow. Its width never exceeds 50 miles. Its length is 400 miles. Its area cannot match Lake Victoria or Lake Michigan.

However, Baikal and Tanganyika are both more than twice as deep as any other mass of fresh water in the world, and its extraordinary depth gives Baikal by far the largest volume of any lake on earth. Its shoreline is 455 metres above, its bed 1,165 metres below sea level. If all its tributaries were to be dammed off and all of Baikal to be drained dry it would take close to half a millennium to complete the task. Yet this languid circulation is accompanied by a rare purity of water; the mineral content is—or was, before the Russians built pulp mills here in the 1960s—only half or three-quarters as high as in ordinary lakes.

This oldest—and yet seismically youngest—lake in the world casts as strong a spell on limnologists as on Buryat shamans and scribes of fairytales. Its 600 species of plants and 1,200 species of animals contain giant and dwarf and vestigial life forms found nowhere else. Its fresh-water seals—those trusting, gregarious creatures that once upon a time gave it a try on land but then thought better of it and reverted to water—are unique. They may have been pushed here from the Arctic during the Ice Age, but no one knows for sure.

No less strange are the viviparous golomyanka fish that adjust their specific gravity to match the exact water pressure at any depth—and are so transparent that anyone with a notion to do so could read a book through them. The lake's prehistoric shrimp, cycloid fish and living fossils—and of course its living, changing geology—make Baikal a researcher's dream.

The Russian fascination with Baikal started early. As with so many places in Siberia and the Arctic North, the infatuation began with religious or political exiles. These outcasts applied that prickly curiosity that had once alienated them from Moscow and Petersburg society to the exploration of their queer new worlds. Baikal's earliest essayist was the archpriest Avvakum, the fanatic anti-Western fundamentalist who rent the Orthodox Church with his Old Believers' schism. Avvakum, surely one of the most hypnotic figures in Russia's long history of perceived struggle between darkness and light, was finally burned at the stake—and some 20,000 of his followers immolated themselves too, rather than submit to what their prophet branded as the marks of Antichrist: a census, realistic likenesses in art, and making the sign of the cross with two fingers instead of three. Before his martyrdom Avvakum was exiled to Siberia; while here he wrote his autobiography, a masterpiece of seventeenth-century Russian literature that—oddly for a rigid traditionalist—was the first prose work to use demotic Russian instead of archaic Church Slavonic. In this book Avvakum described the wondrous Lake Baikal, which was then so inaccessible.

As late as the early twentieth century, travellers from St Petersburg or Berlin had to be almost as intrepid as Avvakum to venture this far from civilization. After the Irkutsk stretch of the Trans-Siberian, they left behind the gourmet pleasures—as one contemporary recorded—of "excellent cold roast, chickens, partridges, blackcock, and other game" washed down with Crimean claret or French brandy. They were well advised, according to Harmon Tupper, to bring along their own revolvers, candles, heavy woollen underwear, well-lined rubber boots, warm furs, mosquito netting, pillows, sheets, blankets—and portable india-rubber bathtubs, since the train's bath was usually pre-empted for storing meat and ice. (The lounge piano was often similarly commandeered to provide a shelf for dirty dishes, but apparently no passenger was on this account counselled to pack his own keyboard.)

The company too was less elegant east of Irkutsk. One Yankee, a Congregational pastor who rode this stretch in 1900, described his peasant fellow-passengers (relates Tupper) as

filthy with a grime that has accumulated since their birth, and alive with unmentionable parasites. . . . Odours indescribably offensive made the air thick and almost murky. The stench, the dirt, the vermin grew worse the longer the car was inhabited, and one simply resigned himself to the inevitable and lived through each wearisome hour as best he could.

By far the most gruelling of the turn-of-the-century travellers' vicissitudes was the crossing of Lake Baikal, at least in winter. In summer the boat passage was quite comfortable, so long as the ship did not hit one of Baikal's impenetrable fogs. So pleasant was it, in fact, that it became fashionable for couples to marry afloat in the train ferry's chapel. In the cold months, however, the icebreaker piggyback ride had no such romantic attraction.

For several years after the 1898 inauguration of the Krasnoyarsk–Irkutsk line to the west and the 1900 inauguration of the Transbaikal line to the east, engineers postponed joining the two with the final Circumbaikal segment. The granite and diorite lake cliffs were too sheer for railroad construction, the rivers and ravines too numerous, the lakeside shelf too narrow, the seismic uncertainties too great, at least for the allotted budget.

But then in February 1904 Japan attacked Russia. Troops and matériel had to be rushed to the Far East. Baikal was a bottleneck, where soldiers had to dismount from the trains and cross the lake by foot or sledge, following the signposts, oil flares and, during heavy snow, bells. In transit the men stopped only long enough to cook a hot meal and perhaps to wait for a makeshift bridge to be erected over some new crack in the ice; but the passage still took seventeen laborious hours.

The trains rolled across the lake on tracks supported by tree-length timbers placed at 30-foot intervals to distribute the weight. In this stopgap fashion, relates Tupper, some 65 locomotives, 2,400 railroad cars, countless gun batteries and thousands of troops crossed Baikal within five weeks during that crucial winter.

The crisis spurred St Petersburg to a crash effort to lay the last elusive 162 miles of track. Russian, Persian, Turkish and Italian workers dynamited 33 tunnels, constructed more than 200 bridges and trestles, fought off hordes of gnats and, in their off-duty hours, played with their pet bear cubs. By September 1904 they were finished. The steel rails were too soft; the green, untreated railroad ties were often too short; and the ballast bed was only half as thick as it should have been (thus repeating defects of the notoriously unsafe American railroads of the nineteenth century). But the Trans-Siberian was now complete.

I have brought along Tupper's affectionate account of the building of the Trans-Siberian, *To the Great Ocean*, and I show it to Tanya, Grandmother, and Nina. Entranced by the exotic photographs of their own not-so-distant history, they crowd together to search each picture for points of recognition. They waste no time on the unwashed yamshchiki coach drivers or stockades on the Great Siberian Post Road. Nina quickly turns the page on the 1900 picture of booted and capped "fifth-class" passengers sprawled over their bundles; they look too much like the hordes she sees in the Kiev railway station. But the three women all giggle at the lugubrious Bactrian camels pulling military sledges in this region in the old days. They linger over the Fabergé Great Siberian Railway Easter egg; they explore every detail of the elegant Mandarin-decor wagon-salon exhibited at the Paris Universal Exposition of 1900. And Tanya plies me with questions about the tsars and princes portrayed in the photographs. Did Alexander II—here captured on glass at his corner desk, stroking his beard—always wear so much braid? I suppose he did, and my presumption takes on the aura of fact.

When my store of tsarist information and surmise peters out altogether, Tanya moves on to more contemporary royalty. Is the Swedish queen, she inquires, beautiful? I offer assurances that Queen Silvia is indeed beautiful, and add that she was a commoner before she married King Carl Gustav. Tanya sighs with vicarious contentment. "It's just like a fairytale!" she exclaims. "A simple, ordinary girl marrying a king!"

I try to imagine the militantly egalitarian Swedes viewing their nominal sovereigns as fairytale monarchs. But not even the early-morning mists of Lake Baikal can persuade me of that particular transmogrification.

03.00 Yugovo

We have started climbing the valley of the Selenga River, following the route of Avvakum and the seventeenth-century Russian ambassadors to China. Like them, we have no choice. If we want to proceed eastward, this is the sole corridor. Only three tributaries of any length flow into the cleft of Baikal, and the other two lead north. All remaining tributaries are steep and brief, carrying the melted snows of the surrounding rim of mountains to the lake in the most direct line.

Baikal's narrow, self-contained system is emphasized by the proximity, yet inaccessibility, of the Lena. The headwaters of the last of Siberia's mighty Arctic bound rivers gather within some four miles of the western shore of Baikal. So sharp is the divide, however, that these waters are forever repulsed from the lake. They flow west instead, then curve north-east to empty at last into the Arctic Ocean two and a half thousand miles away.

Yugovo is a tiny place. Yet, located as it is on the single eastern exit from Baikal, it has, in the Russian phrase, "perspectives". The Chinese and Siberian passenger trains roar through here every day, and even if they do not stop, they constitute a tangible link with the outside world. Yugovo has a store or two, and perhaps even a cinema. It is incomparably better off than the "non-perspective" villages tucked away obscurely on other Siberian rivers.

I'll never be allowed to visit these other, dying villages, of course. But I know them through one Siberian novelist, Valentin Rasputin. These villages have no store, no cinema, no future prospects. Young people who have the misfortune to grow up in them find them excruciatingly boring and leave as soon as they can. Economic planners welcome their demise—but Rasputin laments their loss.

A husky, cherub-faced man who looks the very antithesis of his dissipated namesake, Rasputin was born in a log cabin in just such a village on the Angara. His mother lives there still. His novels are nostalgic epitaphs for this fast disappearing way of life.

His Atamanovka in *Live and Remember* had only thirty homesteads.

[It] was really a hamlet rather than a village. Despite its resounding name [derived from *ataman* or chieftain] it had been decaying, alone and silently, ever since the prewar period. Already five cottages—and strong ones at that, not dilapidated ones—stood dead, with their windows boarded up. . . . People began to move away from Atamanovka, especially youths, especially those who had not yet nestled themselves into homes. They were drawn away to larger, livelier villages that held the future promise that Atamanovka lacked.

Atamanovka had been built in a remote spot a long time ago. . . . Steamships went right past Atamanovka, carrying news elsewhere; everything passed it by. It stood like a forlorn lighthouse on the bank, dim and orphaned.

Like others in the "countryside" school of writers that sprang up in the 1970s, Rasputin praises the simplicity of the village—to the distress at times of both the Soviet ideologues and the urban humanists. The ideologists say the countryside authors sentimentalize the past. They "sob" over outmoded hamlets, complains the *Literary Gazette*; they advocate "antihistoricism" and serve up "militant apologetics of village patriarchality as opposed to city culture. . . . While one misses the old churches and crosses, another weeps over horses, and a third over roosters." For their part, the urban humanists accuse the countryside writers of being Slavophil, chauvinist, anti-Western, anti-urban, anti-modern, anti-rational and possibly even neo-Stalinist.

Rasputin cheerfully laughs off attacks from both quarters. What he regrets in the passing of the Siberian hamlet, he told me in an interview, is precisely the death of the old humanity, of "the many moral and ethical values such as care of the elderly and respect for work, ancestors, the land, and animals". His moral concern focuses on the individuals who are crushed in the process of modernization.

In the Soviet context, Rasputin's characters are rather daring and picaresque. Andrei in *Live and Remember* is a World War II Red Army deserter who has drifted home after being repeatedly wounded. Nastyona, the wife who harbours and loves this tired, hunted man, is the kind of woman who has unselfconsciously sustained Russia over the centuries, nursing her child and doing the wash under Tatar sword and winter famine alike. Far from condemning the doomed couple, Rasputin exposes the inhumanity of the vigilantes who track down Andrei.

Similarly, Rasputin's latest novel, *Farewell to Matyora*, is a threnody for a hamlet that is flooded out by the reservoir of a new dam. In this book he treats spoliation of nature as the main question of conscience for today's generation, comparable, he told me matter-of-factly, with acquiescence in Nazism and Stalinism by the preceding generation.

Russians who share Rasputin's ecological fears have so far failed to halt the growing pollution in their land. On the upper Ob all of the fifteen fishery collectives have been forced to close because the dumping of agricultural and industrial sewage into the Grandmother of Rivers has produced miles of alkaline suds, shallowed and poisoned spawning sites, and dried up two Ob tributaries altogether. In more thickly populated parts of the Soviet Union—European Russia, Central Asia, Trans-Caucasia and the Ukraine— contamination has been joined by the profligate use and discharge of surface water that has raised water tables in the soil and sometimes undermined the foundations of high-rise buildings and industrial plants.

The one victory of ecologists over the industrial movers and shakers was scored here at Lake Baikal. In the mid-sixties scientists launched a campaign against pollution of the lake and especially against the planned construction of new pulp and cellulose mills in the Baikal basin. At that point the seal population had already dropped to four or five thousand, the omul whitefish was facing extinction, and other plant and animal life was also threatened. In 1971, the Communist Party Central Committee was finally induced to decree industrial sewage standards and curb the wildcat cutting of timber in the Baikal basin. The pulp mills that had been erected in the early sixties were not dismantled, but their discharges were more strictly regulated, and one plant at Selenginsk is still operating at less than full capacity because of failure to meet the new requirements. Baikal limnologists say the clean-up has built the seal herd back up to a good 60,000 and reinstated the omul as a sport and commercial fish.

However, not even the lobby that rallied to protect the lake's ecology seems eager to preserve the human ecology of the Siberian hamlet. Rasputin seems resigned to defeat in his campaign, yet he continues his solitary championing of all the forgotten Atamanovkas.

Rasputin's maverick preference for humanity and environment over industrialization is especially striking, given his origins. He is totally a pro-duct of the Soviet era; he was born a peasant on a collective farm twenty years after the revolution. He is one of the leading young authors (in this gerontocratic society any writer in his forties is still a fledgling) in a country whose votive shrines are the dam and steel mill. He has had no Western-influenced intellectuals to tutor him—but he still arrived at some of the same moral conclusions as the urban humanists. Is he, then, a candidate to bridge the gulf between the humanist intelligentsia and the masses?

I sound out Tanya and Grandmother. They have never even heard of Rasputin. I sketch the plot of *Live and Remember*, and Tanya immediately bridles at Andrei's disloyalty in deserting. I defend him, pointing out that he had been wounded and that he deserted only at the end of the war, when the Russians were already winning. Like numerous angry readers who have written to Rasputin, however, Tanya argues that his wife should have turned

Andrei in to the authorities. Furthermore, she considers Rasputin's reservations about Siberian factories bizarre. In this Trans-Siberian microcosm of public opinion, at least, Rasputin is fighting a losing battle.

Tanya's categorical rejection of Rasputin gnaws at my subconscious until at last I recognize the question. Why is even the tentative individualism of a Rasputin so alien to her? Why did the independence of those turn-of-the-century pioneers have so little impact on the Russian psyche, while the self-reliance of their nineteenth-century American counterparts had such a decisive impact on the American psyche?

The new Siberians had to depend on their own strength and wits in a rich but often hostile land, just as the American settlers did. Both experienced the same wilderness absence of tradition, one would have thought, the same infinite space, the same possibility of running away from a failed farm or career or marriage. They lived with the same transience, crudity, and lack of cultural refinements, the same gregarious disdain for privacy that so appalled European visitors. Both could get rich, or lose their shirts, in the land rush, the gold rush, the drunken brawls. (Desperadoes in Irkutsk were even known to have finished off one worthy by lassoing him in good American fashion, though they completed the job by the very un-American method of tying him to their troika and dragging him at a gallop across the ice.)

Both sets of homesteaders fought off fugitives, cattle rustlers and "savages". Both preened their braggadocio in their own national forms of hyperbole (Paul Bunyanesque "tall talk" in America, Khlestakovite *vran'yo* in Russia). So similar were the lives of both sets of border adventurers that historian Philip Longworth even claims that the unruly Cossacks fit the image of the footloose American cowboy rather better than the cowboy himself did.

Yet in America this frontier experience moulded the national temperament, at least according to historians of the Frederick Jackson Turner school. "The West" became synonymous with unfettered freedom.

In Russia, on the contrary, the frontier left hardly a trace; scholars treat the settlement of Siberia as just one of those discontinuous hiccups of Russian history, no more significant or lasting than ancient Kiev's proto-democracy or Catherine's early embrace of Voltaire. Siberia became synonymous with the Gulag Archipelago and an anachronistic return to Ivan the Terrible's cruel paranoia.

In the end the dissimilarities of the Russian and American wildernesses overpowered the resemblances. In Russia the burden of a scarcely reformed peasant feudalism weighed society down until the turn of this century; in the New World the peculiar American blend of Enlightenment rationalism, eclectic pragmatism, and a chaotic class structure provided no ballast of tradition and encouraged change and experimentation.

Before the emancipation of the Russian serf in 1861 and the American

Negro in 1863, the percentage of bonded labour was far higher in Russia than in the USA. And after emancipation the freed serf remained chained, in a way that even the maltreated freed slave was not, to his inadequate plot of earth and to the comforting yet stifling collective of the village *mir*.

When Nicholas II finally eased the ban on internal emigration and then even promoted Siberian colonization at the turn of the century—in the modern era, the Russian eastward drive was purely a government programme and not a spontaneous movement—it was these former serfs who comprised the vast bulk of the settlers. Very few of the gentry, merchants, artisans or professionals wished to live in the primitive Siberian conditions, and none of the diverse foreign refugees and fortune-seekers who so enriched the USA and Australia were allowed to immigrate to Russia or Siberia.

As a consequence, Siberia developed far more slowly and far more conservatively than did the American West. It simply repeated all the old cultural and social institutions—and administrative corruption—of Mother Russia on a dismal provincial scale.

Nothing could have been further removed from the extreme decentralization and do-it-yourself political organization of every group that ever banded together to cross the Missouri or homestead Nebraska. In the USA, suggests historian Daniel Boorstin, "upstart" communities and governments were no more than a useful but expendable tool. They "had neither the odour of sanctity nor the odium of tyranny". In Russia and in Siberia the musty governing institutions had both.

In one realm only did the 3.5 million Siberian colonists of the early 1900s carve out a distinctive way: agriculture. They exploited well the absence of the restrictive landlordism of European Russia. They purchased their own fields, quickly mechanized their farms beyond the level of Central Russia and the Ukraine, supplied them with more stock, formed co-operatives—and regularly exported butter and cheese.

Their initiative and prosperity were rewarded by Stalin's 1930s collectivization, which wiped out the wealthier kulaks of Western Siberia no less thoroughly than the kulaks of the Ukraine. Whatever influence the enterprising new Siberians might have had on the Russian character died out with these murders.

With a push from the self-reliance of the Western frontier, then, the typical American demeanour became a sometimes cantankerous individualism and a sometimes indiscriminate tolerance for diversity, laced with a contradictory conformity to peer opinion. Regardless of Siberian self-reliance, the instinctive Russian demeanour continued to be imperiousness toward subordinates and servility toward superiors, laced with conformity to tradition. The old predatory steppe prevailed over the new co-operative homestead.

03.55 Ulan Ude

A surprise awaits us in this capital of the Buryat Autonomous Soviet Socialist Republic. The chief adornment at this station is not yet another silver-sprayed statue of Lenin pointing to the future. It is, instead, a bush that has been trimmed into the shape of a mother bear and a baby bear. The baby bear sticks its paw out appealingly, and the mother bear holds a bouquet of what looks like, but surely cannot be, artichokes. I wonder idly how many black marks this lapse into topiary levity will bring the Ulan Ude party secretary, but then I recall that this is the city where a 22-foot-high sculpted head of Lenin dominates the main square. Perhaps the biggest Lenin head in the world sanctions a little subordinate playfulness.

Apart from the bears and Lenin—and a habit of pouring its raw sewage into the river that provides half of Baikal's water supply—Ulan Ude is indistinguishable from every other city in Russia. The cluster of prefabricated apartment buildings on this railroad gateway to Peking could just as well be Yaroslavl or Sverdlovsk or Perm. There is no architectural hint of neighbouring Mongolia, or even of temple influence from the Soviet Union's lone Buddhist monastery twenty-five miles away.

Ulan Ude's inhabitants are distinctive, however. Half of the people milling about on the station platform have the high cheekbones and flat eyelids of Mongolian–Buryat stock. To Slavs, they are exotic reminders of Genghis Khan—or, more recently, General Gregory Semenov.

The Buryat–Russian blackguard Semenov was one of the more colourful—and appalling—figures in early Soviet history. Along with some stranded Czechoslovak legionaries, American, French and British expeditionary troops, and the Japanese occupiers of Chinese Manchuria, he took part in one of the most confused chapters in the entire revolution and civil war.

The two divisions of Czechoslovaks had originally been fighting on the side of the tsarist army against Germany and Austro-Hungary in World War I. The Russian revolution and withdrawal from the war left them in a limbo that they initially proposed to resolve by travelling the thousands of miles east to Vladivostok, sailing around the world, and rejoining the war in Western Europe. Some 15,000 of them made it to Vladivostok on the Trans-Siberian Railroad; the remaining 25,000 were stuck west of the Bolshevik-held Lake Baikal, subject to the anarchic shifts of power between Reds, Whites, splinter factions, partisans, escaped convicts and ordinary brigands—and in the developing British and French intrigues against the new Bolshevik regime.

An attempt by the Bolsheviks to disarm the Czechoslovaks (as required in the separate Soviet–German peace treaty) flared into shooting, the Czechoslovaks seized both Vladivostok and the Trans-Siberian Railroad—and various Whites took the opportunity to overthrow various Reds in Siberia.

The legionaries in Vladivostok then started back on the Trans-Siberian to rescue their stranded comrades and, with the disintegration of the old Russian army, the Czechoslovak Corps suddenly found itself the strongest single military unit in all of Siberia. At this point the Corps joined forces for a time with the Whites, advanced westward to Yekaterinburg (precipitating the assassination of Nicholas and Alexandra) crossed the Urals and were repulsed by War Commissar Leon Trotsky at the Volga.

The Allies, hard pressed by the collapse of their eastern front, initially wanted to restore a second front or at least to bring the tough and disciplined Czechoslovak Legion into the western war as soon as possible. And some Allied officials—most notably British Secretary of State for War Winston Churchill—had the ulterior motive of using the Legion in an Allied intervention to crush the Bolsheviks.

Woodrow Wilson thought (incorrectly) that it was the 1.6 million more-or-less freed German and Austro-Hungarian prisoners of war in Russia who were impeding the Czechoslovaks' departure. The British and French suspected the Bolsheviks (incorrectly) of giving secret help to the Germans. They speculated (incorrectly) that the shaky Bolshevik regime would be easily overthrown with a little extra push—and they were not averse to planning on the Ukraine as a French sphere of interest and Trans-Caucasia, Central Asia and the Cossack lands as a British sphere of interest. They feared that the Russian Bolsheviks, if established in power, would live up to their avowed world revolutionary goals and subvert European societies. So they badgered the reluctant American President into sending an expeditionary force of 7,000 men into Siberia from Vladivostok to join a British battalion and some unattached French officers in (ostensibly) extricating the Czechoslovaks.

Meanwhile the Japanese, who had been competing with the Russians for control of Chinese Manchuria, happily joined in the sport by dispatching their troops into Manchuria and eastern Siberia. And as their agent in the Lake Baikal region the Japanese patronized the Buryat–Russian Semenov and his gang of Buryat, Cossack and Mongol bandits.

This private army terrorized the civilian population. From trains armoured with 18-inch-thick concrete and steel plating, Semenov's men patrolled Transbaikalia, extorting, torturing and murdering. Their idea of amusement consisted of such games as ambushing a Trans-Siberian passenger train, forcing the 350 men, women and children on board to march into the nearby fields, then machine-gunning them down like rabbits. In winter, the gang might kill by chopping a hole in the frozen river, dunking victims until they had several coats of ice, then leaving them to the elements. In any season they enjoyed hanging up men and women by their ears to the fronts of their own houses. Semenov, Tupper quotes the commander of the American forces as noting, "openly boasted that he could not sleep at night when he had not killed someone during the day."

In the midst of such grisly anarchy the Czechoslovaks never got out of Siberia before the end of the European war. The British intervened militarily in Murmansk and Archangel'sk to the north, sent small army contingents to Central Asia and Trans-Caucasia, deployed one naval gun unit from the H.M.S. *Suffolk* in Vladivostok harbour 4,000 miles inland to fight in the Urals, and gave various counter-revolutionary regimes a hefty £100 million of military and economic aid. And Churchill would have poured still more into the anti-Communist cause if his more realistic Prime Minister, David Lloyd George, hadn't quickly realized the impossibility of sending enough outside forces to Russia to decide the outcome.

In the event, Trotsky's army held together, and this sufficed to neutralize the few thousand Western troops (once the Czechoslovaks fell out with the Whites) that were committed to intervention. Lenin was grateful for this much, and left it to later Soviet historians to glorify the exploits of the Red Army in routing the foreigners.

In Siberia the Japanese stayed on until the Reds finally retook Vladivostok and the maritime provinces in 1922. The Americans also lingered for one and a half years after the end of World War I, monitoring the Japanese presence, exchanging shots once with Bolsheviks, and otherwise incurring the hostility of both Reds and Whites for their political passivity in the maelstrom.

Eventually the atrocities of the assorted Whites, including General Semenov, got so bad that the Siberian peasants revolted. The Allied intervention only helped to further compromise the Whites and turn the population toward the Reds, concluded diplomat-historian George Kennan. The whole affair, he wrote, was a "fantastic brew" of misunderstandings, war hysteria, coincidences, and mistakes. In a personal note he added:

> Until I read the accounts of what transpired during these episodes, I never fully realized the reasons for the contempt and resentment borne by the early Bolsheviki toward the Western powers. Never, surely, have countries contrived to show themselves so much at their worst as did the Allies in Russia from 1917 to 1920.

It was an inauspicious beginning to Soviet-Western relations.

For Tanya, the Allied intervention is clear proof of the attempted capitalist encirclement of the infant Soviet Russia. And the stripping of the USSR's rightful possessions of Finland, the Baltic provinces, the western Ukraine and Bessarabia was a humiliation that had to be avenged sooner or later.

She believes further that during World War II the Western Allies deliberately delayed opening a major second European front in order to let the occupying Germans bleed Russia. She knows that the USSR bore the brunt of the Great Patriotic War, turning the tide against the fascists at Stalingrad and sacrificing twenty million lives—fifty times American casualties, half the total casualties of World War II. She isn't old enough to remember personally all the boots and Studebakers and spam that the US shipped to the Soviet Union during World War II or the appreciation of the ordinary Soviet footsoldier for this aid.

For Tanya it was only natural for the USSR, at the end of the war, to retake all the tsarist territory it had lost in its early revolutionary weakness. It was only prudent for the USSR to secure a large buffer zone in Eastern Europe to protect itself against future attacks by those Germans who had already invaded Russia twice in a quarter of a century, or by encircling capitalist enemies.

Tanya does not know that during World War II the USSR completed the extermination of the Polish intelligentsia begun by the Germans. She knows nothing of Stalin's plunder of Eastern European and Manchurian industry or of his mortal purges of Eastern European non-Communist and Communist leaders in the late 1940s and early 1950s. She takes it for granted that East Europeans are grateful to the Russian army for liberating them from the fascist yoke—and even if they aren't, she takes it for granted that they should be compelled to be grateful.

If she were aware of it, she would also find it only just that Russians—who had suffered so grievously in the war—initially demanded cession of Iran's eastern districts and refused to withdraw the Red Army from postwar Iran. Or that the Soviet Union employed military threats in the late 1940s to try to secure free naval passage in the Dardanelles. In none of these actions does a Red Army officer's wife see any Soviet contribution to the hostility of the Cold War.

Thus far, Tanya's world view is mundane and not especially revealing. What catches my ear, however, is the way she opens our discussion of foreign affairs. Significantly, she does not begin with the standard challenge I encountered in the Soviet Union in the 1960s: "Why does America want war?!"

Instead, Tanya begins with a reverse disclaimer: "It's not true when people say the Soviet Union wants to expand. We're such a big country already that it takes seven days to travel across it. We have enough to do to master our own land. We know what war is like; we don't want another one."

Here is something new: a recognition that America has a different point of view from the USSR, that the West worries about Soviet intentions as much as the Soviet Union worries about Western intentions. A small fruit of the 1970s' détente, perhaps, but a welcome fruit.

*

Actually, both the USA and the USSR were surprised to emerge in the aftermath of World War II as the two lone superpowers in the world. Until 1941 the USA had been isolationist, eschewing any prominent role in world order. And in 1945 the Soviet Union was devastated, after a foreign occupation of half a million square miles of its territory and the destruction of 1,700 towns, 70,000 villages, and the homes of some twenty-five million people.

The rest of the world was hardly better off, however. Western Europe was also in ruins; Germany and Japan were defeated nations; a backward China was in the grip of civil war.

The United States demobilized, but still lurched into the gap of Western leadership left by Britain's exhaustion and subsequent loss of empire. Stalin successfully disguised his country's weakness under a cover of truculence. The Cold War began, fanned by Stalin's pathological paranoia and America's unsophisticated inflation of anti-Communism into a doctrine.

In a sense, the world that emerged out of this rigid and potentially unstable bipolarity has proved remarkably durable. The balance of nuclear terror has so far provided a better deterrent to general war than either the expectation of inevitable progress that preceded World War I or the multination balance of power that preceded World War II. The superpowers have exercised relative restraint—despite the Korean War, the nuclear-threshold Cuban missile showdown, American intervention in Vietnam, and Soviet intervention in Africa and Afghanistan. We survived the postwar social dislocations in Western Europe, decolonization in the Third World, the Hungarian revolt against Soviet rule, four passionate Middle East wars, and the 1970s crises in the world trade system—all have passed without either of the two superpowers being incapacitated or blowing up the globe. We even thawed our original Cold War confrontation to some extent by a second-thought détente.

Détente, by another name, began with Khrushchev—and came close to ending with him. In 1956 he broke with his ideological heritage to proclaim that war with capitalist states was no longer inevitable, and that "peaceful coexistence" was now possible. In 1962 he put his novel thesis to a severe test by installing missiles on the United States' doorstep in Cuba. In retrospect, Khrushchev's move seems an attempted shortcut to full superpower military status. Unlike the USA, the Soviet Union did not at the time have the diversified land, sea, air and space forces for any eventuality across the entire spectrum of conflict. Its few intercontinental ballistic missiles and heavy bombers were no real threat to the USA. Its maiden nuclear-missile submarine had been at sea only a year; its navy was still capable only of coastal defence, its tactical air force only of passive interception and battle artillery. Its one glory was its massive army.

Under these circumstances, when the USA and the USSR came "eyeball to eyeball" in the Caribbean it was Khrushchev who "blinked" and withdrew his missiles. The Soviet leadership apparently resolved never again to get caught in a position of inferiority in which it would have to back down from such a test of strength.

This determination meant less "adventurism" of the sort of which Khrushchev was accused by his successors—but it also meant a crash buildup of missiles that within a decade would bring the Soviet Union to the nuclear parity recognized in the Soviet-American strategic arms limitation agreements of 1972 and 1979. It meant a protracted buildup of conventional arms that would give the Soviet navy and air force a global reach in the 1970s. It meant a risky 1980s for both superpowers as the new vulnerability of fixed land-based missiles threatened to undermine the nuclear deterrence of the previous quarter-century.

Just how risky the remainder of this century will be for Russia, as for the rest of the world, is a matter of conjecture. The degree of danger depends on the unknowns of today's revolutionary technology, America's political lurchings, the Soviet Union's sphinx-like strategy, and the particular dynamics of nuclear proliferation, once a Libya-financed Pakistan becomes the ninth possessor of the A-bomb.

What is clear is that the quarter-century Pax Americana is finished. The USA no longer has, nor could it restore, the military superiority it enjoyed in the earlier postwar era.

The Pax Americana, however, has yet to be replaced by any new world security system with understood sources of power and understood restraints on the use of power. It's a volatile period, this decade we live in—and it coincides with a volatile current state of war technology. It's a hazardous new environment for Russians, and for other human beings.

Technologically, both superpowers should be able to shoot down satellites with lasers in the late eighties or early nineties. One side—presumably the USA, given its history of pioneering almost every major innovation in nuclear age weapons and its current lead in every nuclear-related field except side-looking radar—could go on to shoot down missiles with lasers a year or two in advance of the other side. A real missile defence could then overturn the present perversely benign deterrence of mutually vulnerable populations and mutually invulnerable weapons. At best, a new utopian balance of invulnerable populations and vulnerable weapons might arise. At worst, a dicey transition period to the new nuclear regime might induce hairtrigger anxieties.

Even before the laser age supplants the missile age, technology is already eroding the old Western deterrent verities. New fuel-air explosives are giving small 500-lb. non-nuclear bombs as much blast as nuclear weapons, and there are far fewer inhibitions on committing such "conventional" weapons to a confrontation. Mixed-role tactical and strategic vehicles, like Cruise missiles, are becoming indistinguishable from each other

—and in future arms control agreements, counting them will be a nightmare.

Most disturbingly, the marriage of the multiple-warhead missiles of the Seventies with the unexpected pinpoint accuracies of the Eighties has suddenly rendered the fixed-base missile obsolete—and weakened the weapon invulnerability and "assured second strike" that restraint has so far rested upon. The workhorse intercontinental ballistic missile (ICBM)—that most reliable, accurate and flexible missile of the entire arsenal—has suddenly become liable to 90 per cent destruction in any first strike. The previous assurance that the bulk of one's own missiles could ride out any surprise enemy attack and still be available for a calibrated retaliation, after time for a rational damage assessment, is now called into question. And this doubt is inviting panicky instant retaliation even to ambiguous initial indications of attack.

The USA, having prudently (and bureaucratically) spread its eggs in land, sea and air baskets, would lose only a quarter of its total nuclear warheads in absorbing any attack on its ICBM silos; its bomber and submarine missiles would remain to pulverize Moscow and Leningrad, and Kazakhstani launching sites. The USSR, however, having concentrated three-quarters of its warheads in those now vulnerable silos, would lose the bulk of its missiles in absorbing any attack; only a quarter of its nuclear warheads have been diversified to planes or submarines.

American concern therefore focuses on the early 1980s, when any surprise attack by the Soviet Union's much heavier missiles could leave the USA with far less explosive punch than the USSR in the post-attack balance. Soviet concern must focus on the late 1980s, when the USA presumably will have deployed a mobile, land-based missile with its own strong "first strike" potential for leaving an inferior Soviet balance after an attack.

That "post-attack balance" may be only a mathematical abstraction, a theological wrangle about just how many angels of death can dance on the pinhead of prestige. It's doubtful that either superpower could now construct the kind of "disabling" first strike capability that would preclude unacceptable retaliation. It's unlikely that either would be so complacent about even a "minor" retaliation by its rival's surviving missiles as to plot a cold-blooded nuclear attack, or even use blackmail backed up by the threat of attack. Nuclear war does not yet look significantly less horrifying to one side than to the other in any rational analysis.

If push comes to shove in some 1980s' version of the Cuban missile crisis, however, or a Middle Eastern crisis, or a Berlin crisis, the superpowers will find the new balance especially precarious. If a nuclear exchange looks inevitable anyway, then it would be folly to wait for the adversary's attack to wipe out 90 per cent of one's own fixed-base missiles. The less disadvantageous course would be to initiate one's own pre-emptive attack and wipe out 90 per cent of the enemy's fixed-base missiles. Trigger fingers are itchier.

This is the real danger of the new equation. The threat of holocaust by madness, which has haunted mankind ever since that first mushroom cloud at Los Alamos, is once again being joined by the threat of holocaust by miscalculation. We thought we had vanquished that fear when we made the arms race predictable in the 1970s SALT agreements. We were wrong.

How much of a chill does this bring to Soviet hearts? How serious is the USSR—in the pungent phraseology of Western hawks—about nuclear détente? How serious is it—in the rhetorical counterquestion of Western doves—about survival? Why should it—in the Russians' own formulation—conform to Western strategic concepts devised to shore up a world division of power that the Soviet Union does not regard as legitimate?

We'll probably never know for sure. If Washington overexplains, Moscow underexplains. If in America it is difficult to see the pattern in the bedlam, in the Soviet Union it is difficult to see the pattern in the silence. Soviet nuclear strategy is secret, and if outsiders want to pry into it, they can jolly well content themselves with such oblique clues as the ideological mandate of revolution, Khrushchev's thesis about the noninevitability of war, projections of Soviet military doctrine, and inventories of military hardware.

The mandate of the self-proclaimed revolutionary is obvious. The urge to expand the Soviet Union's international influence is untempered by any vigorous domestic political restraints. The drive is strong on triple grounds: history (harking back to the tsars), ideology (heralding the messianic triumph of Communism), and paranoia (involving a definition of Soviet security so total as to demand on occasion the total insecurity of the USSR's neighbours). It is exacerbated on the one hand by an inferiority complex towards the West, and on the other by a pride in the USSR's new global power. It is manifested in the Soviet refusal to endorse anything short of the total world victory of Soviet-led socialism.

The outcome of history may already be determined (Marx shared that blissful nineteenth-century expectation of permanent progress), but the Soviet Union is still tasked with the mission of hastening the advent of the inevitable. In Marxist theory, the dialectical process of struggle between opposing forces will know no lasting stability until that final, all-encompassing socialist triumph. This is a concept vastly different from the West's model of world pluralism, the stability of the status quo, and the imperative of not upsetting the existing international order by force.

It's especially different in the 1980s, according to America's perennial architect of foreign policy, Henry Kissinger. It's a matter of intentions. For a decade, the Soviet Union has had rough strategic parity with America. In the latter half of the seventies it also acquired the capacity to project its conventional military might in far-off Africa and Asia. As a parvenu, a new "imperial" nation with global interests and, suddenly, the wherewithal to pursue them, the USSR is eager to demonstrate its strength to the world. Awkwardly, it doesn't yet have enough self-confidence, or enough middle-aged boredom, to curb its appetite for power. Awkwardly, the only fellow superpower standing in the way of Soviet aggrandizement is an America that was traumatized by its Vietnam misadventure. Hence the Soviet 1979/80 occupation of Afghanistan. Hence the impotence of the West and the Third World in the face of this aggression. Thus spake Kissinger.

Western doves speak differently. They point out that world revolution, while revered rhetorically, ranks low among the Soviet Union's practical priorities. Survival of the Soviet Union and its considerable domestic achievements is the top priority—and ever since Khrushchev this survival has been seen to require deterrence of nuclear war above all else.

To be sure, Khrushchev intended his "peaceful coexistence of states with different social systems" to be only a transitional period. It was not that two antithetical systems could remain forever abroad and tolerated in the world. Rather the world "correlation of forces" could now shift benighted countries to Soviet-style socialism pacifically, without cataclysm. And there was always an implicit hooker that if noninevitable nuclear war should come, why then it would be less devastating for the Soviet side than for the West. Capitalism would be expunged, but the surviving socialists would pick themselves up from the radioactive rubble and build the good society on top of it.

Still, Khrushchev's "peaceful coexistence" began to look suspiciously durable, in sharp contrast to Lenin's fleeting "peaceful cohabitation". The Soviet practitioners of détente came to seem very "realistic"—to borrow their word for American practitioners of détente. And Khrushchev's successors, in the course of a three-year domestic debate from 1974 to 1977, made Soviet policy even more "realistic".

War would be catastrophic for both sides, Brezhnev said, full stop, without the 1960s reservations that it would be more catastrophic for some than for others.

There's more security to be gained through agreed superpower parity than through any Soviet surge for elusive military preponderance, Brezhnev said further.

The Soviet Union does not seek military superiority, Brezhnev concluded explicitly and publicly in 1977.

Various uniformed officers resisted such revisionism by their top marshal and commander-in-chief. Nuclear war wasn't so different from any other war, after all; it was still a Clausewitzian extension of politics, after all, quite thinkable, quite winnable; anything else smacks of defeatism and false equality, and undermines morale.

The resistance was to no avail. Brezhnev won. In 1977 his (civilian) defence minister and the Warsaw Pact commander repeated Brezhnev's renunciation of superiority, word for word. And even military spokesmen who had earlier rejected such heresy now blandly called parity a "reality", and noted that it had been the basis of US-Soviet relations "in recent years".

But, interject Western hawks at this point, below the policy-declaring level some generals and colonels still emphasize the notion of "war fighting" and "war winning" weapons. Operational manuals continue to portray all war as winnable, nuclear war not excepted. Military doctrine continues to glorify surprise and the decisiveness of the first phase in any nuclear exchange—a hint that the military establishment may consider pre-emptive war a real option. And these views represent the genuine uncensored Russia. The civilians' conciliatory words and Soviet acquiescence in détente are only a propaganda ploy to lull the West into forgoing various new weapons while it sells the Soviet Union those crucial computers and ball-bearing grinders.

Not so, retort Western doves in that bewildering crossfire of contradictory interpretations of Soviet capabilities and intentions. Soviet stress on "war winning" weapons doesn't negate deterrence; it is seen rather as giving the most credibility to deterrence. (Similarly, American strategic systems—that is, superpower-to-superpower intercontinental weapons—also have their own "war fighting" rationale, or they would never have been adopted. This was finally made explicit in the 1980 shift of America's declared nuclear strategy away from final-spasm city targeting to graduated weapons targeting.)

Furthermore, the 1960s Soviet emphasis on "war fighting" nuclear capability—along with the reorganization of Soviet civil defence—mirrored the early Kennedy administration's emphasis on very thinkable limited nuclear war. And in any case, concurrent Soviet insistence that "limited" nuclear war would escalate uncontrollably to all-out nuclear war belied any real Soviet "war fighting" intentions with nuclear weapons.

Besides, doves continue, it's bizarre to dismiss Brezhnev's statements as mere propaganda, while regarding less authoritative military statements about battlefield situations as the real key to Soviet strategic thinking. Those military manuals are geared to bolstering troop morale, so don't dare treat nuclear war as unwinnable. And military doctrine consists only of ambiguous and generalized guidelines about the likely nature of future war. The broader strategic analysis of the role of war and the use of nuclear weapons in war, peace and diplomacy remains the prerogative of the top civilian policymakers. These politicians' intentions still incline toward deterrence rather than superiority or blackmail in the strategic balance.

But force postures, the hawks again protest, don't bear out so charitable a view. Military hardware shows a Soviet push for superiority rather than mere equivalence with the United States—an evaluation finally endorsed by the definitive American National Intelligence Estimate of 1979.

The US, for example, reached a high point in defence spending and nuclear and conventional weapons deployment at the end of the 1960s, and reduced its real military spending throughout the decade of the seventies. The Soviet Union, however, did not meet America's unilateral restraint with restraint of its own. On the contrary, for the past decade the Soviet Union has ploughed more than twice as much as the USA into military spending in percentage of gross national product—a steadily rising 15 per cent in 1975 and 18 per cent in 1980 for the USSR, according to the CIA, compared with 8 per cent in 1970 and 5.5 per cent in 1980 for the USA. Since 1971, the USSR's absolute military spending has therefore been substantially higher than America's—some 30 per cent higher at the end of the 1970s, according to the conservative end of CIA estimates, or almost a third of total world military spending.

The Soviet Union also developed seven new ICBM systems between 1965 and 1979, while the USA developed only one. It has deployed a monster SS-18 ICBM that carries ten times the weight of America's Minuteman and gives the Soviet Union twice America's "equivalent mega-tonnage" in weight of total warheads.

Soviet defensive weaponry displays as much disregard for equilibrium as does the offensive missile arsenal, Western hawks continue. There is no indication that the Soviet Union ever accepted the old Western analysis that nuclear stability is based on each side's guaranteed ability to wreak unacceptable damage on the other. In the pre-1980 American theory, this required both sides to abstain from the destabilization of weapons capable of a "disabling first strike" against the opponent—and also to abstain from any defence that would limit unacceptable damage and thus make nuclear war thinkable.

Yet the Soviet constellation of active civil defence, the most extensive conventional air defence in the world, and "counterforce" capability to knock out enemy ICBMs, lacks only an anti-ballistic missile system to constitute a comprehensive "damage limiting"—and therefore destabilizing—defence. And the Soviet Union is working hard to acquire that missing ABM against incoming missile warheads—so hard that the USA challenged it over possible violations of SALT-1 limits on ABM development, and secured an end to the radar tests in question.

There is also evidence that the USSR has breached the spirit if not quite the letter of various treaties by testing anti-satellite systems in space. Furthermore, the Russians are currently experimenting intensively with charged-particle-beam anti-weapon devices that might give Moscow a decisive breakthrough—and administer the *coup de grâce* to mutual vulnerability and, therefore, mutual deterrence.

The USA, by comparison, hawks point out, has virtually no civil or air defence, and has never even deployed the minimal ABM installations permitted under SALT-1. Its declared targeting, until 1980, was primarily "countervalue" rather than "counterforce", aimed at hostage Soviet city populations rather than weapons—and therefore not threatening to Soviet missile survival. (In practice however, whatever its prevailing theory, the USA has consistently targeted Soviet missile silos and command bunkers far more widely than it has publicly admitted.)

In their final riposte, Western doves scorn the hawks' "bean counting" of force postures. They do not regard the development of the Soviet Union's vaunted heavy missiles and counterforce targeting as proof of malevolence. They see it rather as a natural response to the US jump from only 200 silo missiles in 1963 to 1,190 in 1966—and to the US capacity in the 1960s (in contravention of later deterrent theory) to fire off a "disabling first strike". They view the Soviet buildup of missiles and conventional forces since the mid-sixties despite the American spending plateau as a cyclical progression. In a period of US retrenchment and drawing down of excess weapons inventories after the vast Vietnam outlays—and nervousness in Moscow because of the outbreak of Sino-Soviet border hostilities—the Soviet Union began its own reactive cycle of huge military spending and modernization.

Even after the grudging American acceptance of the principle of super-power nuclear parity in the 1972 SALT agreement, the Soviet Union still lagged behind in the strategic balance, doves point out. Even while the USA let the USSR build more missiles, it shot ahead in the new category (and American innovation) of multiple "MIRVed" warheads on single missiles. And these let the USA maintain a substantial lead in the one item that counts most: total warheads. At the beginning of the 1980s, the USA still had some 9,200 to the Soviet Union's 6,000 warheads, though under SALT-2 the numbers would be equalized.

The one area of American superiority that will probably not be equalized in the 1980s is strategic submarine warfare. The USA is well ahead of the Soviet Union in electronics, sonic, signal intercept, wave and other analysis, and in computer processing of these data in order to locate hostile submarines as well as surface ships. According to public statements by Pentagon officials and officers, the USA tracked every single Soviet strategic sub as soon as it left home port from the 1960s to the late 1970s, while in the same period the Soviet Union didn't manage to track even one of America's strategic subs. To be sure, ever since the late seventies the Soviet Union has had the capability of firing missiles at the American heartland from submarines that do not leave their Barents Sea sanctuary. But with the counterforce capability of the accurate new American Trident subs, the underwater balance still shows an American superiority.

Under these circumstances it could well be that the USSR perceives itself, despite its heavier missiles and "throw weight", as still trying to catch up with America rather than trying to surpass it.

Similar observations could be made about Soviet civil defence, anti-ballistic missile, and anti-satellite programmes.

On close scrutiny, Soviet civil defence looks less like a real "damage-limiting" programme than a bureaucratic morale-building exercise, worthy of the irreverent Muscovites' instructions for an alert: "Grab a shovel, walk as far as you can, and dig." A 1977 Congressional study and a 1978 CIA study suggested that with a few hours' warning 110,000 key cadres could in fact be protected—but that they would have little to administer when they emerged from their holes to find 50 million Soviet dead and their very undispersed industry and transport, as well as their too-dispersed agriculture, in shambles.

As for the ABM, Soviet concepts still appear to be centred on radars, and radars remain so vulnerable to any initial attack that they would not constitute a credible missile defence. And Soviet tests of ASAT anti-satellite weapons have so far involved only fairly primitive means for shooting down low-orbiting satellites; they do not approach the range of American navigation, communication and early-warning satellites. Moreover, the American ASAT research programme announced in reaction to the Soviet testing already utilizes much more sophisticated and longer-range devices.

In the more exotic technologies, some (though not all) top American specialists dismiss the Soviet charged-particle-beam programme as a waste of money in a dead end. More importantly, in the area of ASAT laser beams, supersecret American advances already outstrip Soviet experiments.

Doves conclude from all this that the Russians do not by any sensible measure have superiority over the USA (except in the drawing-board "superiority" available to whichever side fires a first nuclear salvo in the 1980s). They further conclude—or at least concluded, up until about 1979—that there was no urgent Soviet threat to the overall superpower nuclear balance.

By 1980, however, the combination of fixed base missile obsolescence, the Soviet nuclear and conventional build-up of the previous decade and a half, and the Soviet occupation of Afghanistan effected some convergence of Western doves toward hawks—and of American nuclear strategy toward inferred Soviet strategy. In Presidential Directive 59 the USA abandoned its twenty-year-long credo of city targeting for a declared weapons targeting that finally aligned its analytical framework with its long-time targeting practice—and clearly anticipated nuclear "war fighting" in any superpower war. *Pravda* immediately denounced the new strategy for raising "the threat of a first strike against military objectives in the Soviet Union". The newest arms race—in mobile missiles and probably also in anti-ballistic missiles and anti-satellite weapons—was formally joined.

In the 1980s the inhibitions of the "balance of terror" still prevail, from a primitive fear of consequences if not from the more sophisticated articulation of restraints worked out by American theorists in the 1970s. Both the Soviet Union and the United States do still adhere to the broad imperatives of deterrence. But in the 1980s the risk of nuclear war by miscalculation has risen greatly.

Even more disturbing in the new era is the question of deterring the superpowers from becoming engaged in third-party wars below the strategic nuclear threshold. This troubles the North Atlantic Treaty Organization and—especially after the Soviet invasion of Afghanistan—it troubles numerous Third World countries. It does not trouble the Soviet Union, which has always explicitly exempted Soviet aid to "national liberation movements" from any link with détente's pledge of non-violence.

So far, Europe's peace has benefited from the superpower nuclear stalemate. The continent has been so important to both the USSR and the USA that neither of them has pressed hard enough for change to risk a war that could go nuclear. Americans gritted their teeth but did nothing about the Soviet invasions of Hungary in 1956 and Czechoslovakia in 1968. Russians got a glint in their eyes but did little to subvert a tempting Portugal after the 1974 coup.

In recent years, however, an impressive Soviet military buildup in the European theatre has combined with the shift in the strategic balance to make Westerners wonder how long Europe can retain its immunity to hard confrontation.

Ever since NATO was founded, the American security guarantee for Western Europe has rested on potential Western escalation of any conventional war to either tactical or strategic nuclear war, in order to offset the Warsaw Pact's perennial conventional superiority. But the Soviet strategic parity of the 1970s and, suddenly, a Soviet theatre nuclear superiority in the early 1980s, now neutralize the former US nuclear advantage. America's ability and will to implement its European guarantee are called into question. This is perhaps the one ramification of silo vulnerability that most worries Western strategists.

The Soviet theatre buildup is most dramatic in the long-range "Eurostrategic" weapons—the mobile MIRVed SS-20 missile and, to a lesser extent, the supersonic Backfire bomber. After two decades of simply letting its intermediate-range nuclear systems depreciate, the USSR began deploying the new 3,000-mile-range SS-20 in 1977. The accuracy, speed and power of the triple SS-20 warheads gave the Soviet Union, for the first time, a potential pre-emptive capacity to wipe out NATO's tactical nuclear weapons. This cancelled NATO's last-resort option of nuclear escalation in case of imminent defeat at the conventional level.

By 1980, a total of some 2,240 Soviet-Warsaw Pact long-range Euro-strategic warheads faced some 1,260 comparable US-NATO warheads, with the numbers scheduled to rise by the mid-eighties to an unknown Warsaw Pact level and a projected NATO level of 1,832. The 1980 figures included, for the Warsaw Pact, 120 Soviet SS-20s and 80 Backfire bombers and, for NATO, four or five American strategic subs (whose use is restricted, since it would imply an escalation not just to tactical nuclear but to strategic nuclear warfare), plus four British and four French missile subs, some ageing British Vulcan bombers, British-based 3,000-mile-range American F-111s, and carrier-based fighter bombers.

The mid-eighties' NATO figure would include, if no arms control agreement is reached in the interim, 572 1,000-mile-range Pershing missiles and 1,500-mile-range Cruise missiles. These NATO weapons would be the first Europe-based weapons since the early sixties capable of reaching targets in the USSR, though they would not match the SS-20s, which could be removed behind the Urals out of the Cruises' range and still retain any target in Europe within their striking range. The aim of the NATO weapons would thus be the minimal one of blocking overwhelming Soviet military preponderance in Europe.

Current Western European concern about the SS-20s is heightened by the rapid expansion in Soviet air power in the 1970s. The change began with the Middle East war of 1967, when the decisiveness of conventionally armed Israeli tactical aircraft in the first few hours of conflict was a revelation to Soviet strategists. The Soviet Air Force budget was dramatically increased in the first half of the seventies. By 1973 Soviet aircraft production surpassed American production and was starting a new series of multi-mission fighters with advanced avionics—the MiG 21 J, K, and L, the MiG 23/27, SU 17/20, and SU 19/24.

The Soviet tactical air force (with numbers that finally stabilized at double America's aircraft) was freed from its former straitjacket of passive interception of enemy aircraft, or support of the army as a kind of extended artillery. In the late seventies, with the aid of new stand-off targeting, the air force took over some conventional and nuclear deep-strike tasks formerly reserved for surface-to-surface missiles. Its new offensive role in Europe came to be the destruction of NATO's theatre nuclear capability and the aggressive reduction of NATO air capability. The Warsaw Pact fighter bomber force was expanded by 1,300 aircraft, with attack helicopters rising from 400 to 600 between 1974 and 1978. By the early eighties, the Soviet fleet of armed helicopters was the largest in the world, and the Soviet MI-24 was considered the best helicopter in the world.

Soviet airlift capability was also strengthened in the 1970s. NATO observers were duly impressed by the rapid initial transport to Afghanistan at

Christmas 1979, of 5,000 soldiers with heavy weapons and equipment in 200 flights over a distance of 3,000 miles—from Black Sea bases that were prepared for Middle Eastern intervention in 1973, and would be used for any future intervention in Yugoslavia or Turkey.

The coming of age of the Soviet Air Force has dealt an especially hard blow to the US because until now, the US Air Force has enjoyed not only superiority, but virtual air supremacy in every combat area it entered from the early 1940s on. The new Soviet capabilities have especially exercised Western Europeans because the new NATO rear targets—nuclear sites, airbases, and command centres—are few and relatively "soft", while the corresponding targets in the Warsaw Pact countries are dispersed and "hard", protected by the densest air defence in the world.

With the enhancement of its air force the USSR has gradually been narrowing its tactical air gap with NATO, but it has not emulated the feat of its SS-20s to achieve air superiority. The West still leads in electronic countermeasures and avionics, as well as airborne radars and missiles, high technology engines, airframes, and weapon aiming systems; its new generation of aircraft now coming on line will outperform the Soviet generation that has just finished deployment. In addition, Western planes are more versatile, Western pilots better trained and more adaptive. With these advantages, NATO commanders still seem confident that their 2,000 combat aircraft on the central front (6,000 after an all-out reinforcement) could take on the Warsaw Pact's 3,400 combat aircraft (7,000 after reinforcement), fly about the same number of total sorties, and hold NATO airspace.

The USSR's comprehensive upgrading of its European forces has included its army as well as its intermediate missiles and air power. The Red Army of 1.8 million men, the largest branch of the 3.7 million-strong Soviet armed forces, is the most powerful army in the world. (China's army of 3.6 million is larger, but is equipped only at primitive 1950s levels.) The Red Army expanded from 140 to 173 divisions between 1965 and 1980—a large but not disproportionate size, since the Soviet Union faces some 4.5 million men under arms, counting both NATO and China.

The total number of Soviet and Eastern European troops assigned to the Warsaw Pact (with an 11:8 numerical advantage over NATO troops) has not increased since the Central European arms control talks opened in the early seventies' heyday of détente. These already heavily mechanized forces have significantly increased their lead in mobility, however—a development that has aroused particular Western concern because of the emphasis on attack and surprise in Soviet military doctrine. Uniquely among major armies today, the Red Army glorifies the blitzkrieg offensive as its central manoeuvre. NATO's defence objectives are limited to repulsing an attacker and, at most, pushing him back beyond threatened border areas. But in

Soviet theory, even defence against enemy aggression calls for a counter-attack. This means, according to military writer V. Ye. Savkin "total defeat of the defending enemy and capture of vital areas of his territory" and "destruction of him piecemeal". Such annihilation of the enemy's armed forces and conquest of his homeland is a chillingly broad definition of "defence".

In quest of this kind of offensive capability, the Warsaw Pact increased its tank superiority in the central front from 2:1 to 3:1 between the mid-sixties and early eighties. It increased its quantitative superiority in artillery from 1.5:1 to 2:1 (and almost 4:1 in North and Central Europe) and enhanced its qualitative artillery superiority (in gun technology if not in propulsion or ammunition) by the introduction of new self-propelled guns. Soviet guns currently outnumber and outrange NATO's and have higher rates of fire. The Warsaw Pact's surface-to-air missiles remain better than NATO's. Its tactical bridging is superior, and its preparation for chemical and biological warfare has no equivalent at all in Western Europe.

As for the new BMP armoured personnel carrier and fighting vehicle—considered by some Western officers the finest in the world—this has worked possibly the greatest military revolution since Genghis Khan. It has converted the infantry into cavalry. In the 1980s all the soldiers in the thirty crack Soviet divisions in Eastern Europe, and many of their Warsaw Pact counterparts, can now ride as they shoot. In operations they are pro-grammed to advance 70 miles per day—a speed unprecedented for populated Europe, one which would have Soviet forces controlling all of West Germany in two days, all of France within a week.

At the same time Soviet logistics have improved so much that they have probably eclipsed the former NATO logistical superiority in standing posi-tions in the forward area. (Once any Warsaw Pact incursion into NATO territory took place, the Red Army could quickly outrun its supply lines, however, because of its dependence on railroads and its shortage of ordinary trucks.)

The Soviet Union does remain inferior to the West in electronic deception and counter-deception measures, computers, integrated circuits, miniaturi-zation of computers and engines, night vision and terrain-following radar, air-to-air missiles, look-down shoot-down systems, precision-guided muni-tions, remotely piloted vehicles and strategic Cruise missiles.

So far, the growing Soviet military might has not been translated into corresponding demands for political concessions from Western Europe. In sharp contrast to its big stick—and to Khrushchev's earlier periodic threats to West Berlin—the USSR has for the most part spoken softly in Western Europe over the past decade. In the early 1970s it forced East Germany into détente with West Germany and itself regularized West Berlin's status in the four-power agreement—and it has not seriously jostled the exposed island of a city since then. For a period in the late seventies and early eighties the USSR even nursed its own détente with West Germany during a troubled period in Soviet-American relations.

By the late 1970s the burgeoning Soviet tanks in Europe—plus the Soviet intrusions in Angola with Cuban proxies—jolted a somnolent Western Europe into a response. France sent paratroopers to several brushfire wars in Africa, developed a neutron warhead that is anathema to the Soviet Union, and returned to a closer association with NATO. NATO jacked up its funding for the first time in a decade, went on to become the first military alliance in history to survive thirty years of peace, and finally agreed on those new long-range theatre nuclear forces procurements for the first time in two decades.

By the 1980s—after the Soviet occupation of Afghanistan—the Western European Union removed the three-decade post-war tonnage ceilings on West German ships, and West Germany extended its area of naval operations northward from Bergen towards the world's most heavily armed naval base on the Soviet Kola Peninsula. NATO fielded new tanks of its own with greater survivability from Chobham super armour (though this advantage was quickly offset by Chobham-armoured Warsaw Pact tanks). It issued its troops new precision-targeted metal-piercing missiles that went far toward neutralizing the Soviet tank superiority. It strengthened its air power and air defence quantitatively and qualitatively—keeping the Warsaw Pact's deficit in air cover as the biggest brake on that alliance's otherwise impressive attack mobility.

In addition, Western Europe—after the 1980s' Soviet threat to invade Poland, to reverse liberalization there—moved closer to America's post-Afghan pessimism about détente. The Kremlin chose to stress its menace to the Poles rather that its peaceableness to Western Europeans, and Western European governments drew the relevant conclusions.

Ironically, one of the strongest checks on the increased Soviet military power in Europe has come not from NATO itself, but from China. The determination of post-Maoist China to build a modern army and economy— and the continuing Sino-Soviet feud—have sharply cut the number of reinforcements Soviet commanders could move to Europe in case of hostilities. A quarter of Soviet ground forces and tactical air forces are currently pinned down on the Chinese border. In 1978/79—the year the Chinese confounded the USSR by attacking the Soviet ally Vietnam—the International Institute for Strategic Studies in London knocked down its estimate of Soviet reinforcements for any European war front from 141 to 99 divisions. In any war lasting long enough for the slower Western mobilization to be implemented, then, NATO would have a slight manpower edge of 2.8 million to the Warsaw Pact's 2.7 million.

The upshot of all this is that the Warsaw Pact, especially by its own qualitative improvements, has challenged NATO's traditional reliance on technology to offset the smaller Western European standing-force strengths. But a Warsaw Pact attack would still run a strong risk of being repulsed, or of unleashing nuclear war. "The overall balance", the Institute of Strategic Studies' Military Balance concludes every year, "is still such as to make military aggression appear unattractive" in Western Europe.

The overall balance in the Third World, however, makes indirect military intervention in these parts seem very attractive. It is here that the Russians are attempting to turn their military growth and new global reach to political advantage. It is here that the sharpest East-West disagreements about détente have arisen.

Much of the new Soviet capacity for power projection outside the Eurasian heartland has come about through the rise of the Soviet Navy.

For centuries—despite a navy that ever since Peter the Great's infatuation with Dutch shipbuilding has been the third or fourth largest in the world—Russia was a typical continental power. Its fleets, isolated in four different seas along the world's longest coastline and frozen in harbour during winter except in Arctic Murmansk, were individually puny. The nation entrusted its defence to its lumbering army. As late as 1965, the missions of the armed forces, including the navy, were still restricted to protecting the Soviet homeland and exercising Soviet power in contiguous areas.

In the sixties, however, the missions were reformulated to include protection of Soviet interests and international socialism worldwide. The ideological foundation was what the West came to call the "Brezhnev Doctrine", asserting—in the wake of the Soviet invasion of Czechoslovakia—a Soviet right to intervene wherever the Russians saw a threat to "international socialism" (irrespective, apparently, of whether the Czechs or other beneficiaries of such intervention also saw a threat).

In 1972 the concept of interventionary war was introduced. In 1974, Defence Minister Marshal A. A. Grechko spoke explicitly for the first time of a commitment to resist "imperialistic aggression" in "whatever distant region of our planet it may occur". Troop training manuals came to emphasize the new international role of the Soviet military. And in 1980—in the wake of the invasion of Afghanistan—S. V. Chervonenko, the Soviet Ambassador to France, expanded the Brezhnev Doctrine well beyond the Soviet Eastern European empire in declaring that any country anywhere on the globe has "the full right to choose its friends and allies, and if it becomes necessary, to repel with them the threat of counter-revolution or a foreign intervention". Similarly, continued Chervonenko, the Soviet Union has a right to be consulted and involved everywhere in the world on all major issues, as an equal of the USA.

In the case of the navy there is some question whether the new political role of power projection was a deliberate aim or a haphazard byproduct of the developing capability. An argument can be made from the evidence of shipbuilding patterns, stationing, and a dearth of propaganda exploitation that the Soviet Navy originally moved out of home waters to "forward deployment" from 1961 on, primarily to counter the new threat of American strategic subs that could attack the USSR from ever greater distances.

By 1964, however, when Soviet ships chose the time of the Cyprus crisis to begin sailing the Mediterranean on a regular basis, the Soviet Navy was clearly taking on a political role. This role increased as the Soviet Union finally succeeded in pressuring Egypt into permitting Soviet access to naval facilities at Alexandria after the 1967 Middle East war. By 1968 Soviet vessels took up steady-state deployment in the Indian Ocean (where no Western strategic strike forces were to be found); by 1969 they began periodic cruises in the Caribbean. By 1970 the Soviet Union conducted its first worldwide naval exercise. Shortly thereafter it began offering logistic support before and during third-party conflicts, along with protection of client states, on the west coast of Africa, where no Western strategic striking forces were to be found.

By the mid-seventies the Soviet Navy—which had already overtaken the USA in numbers of combatants over 1,000 tons, largely because of the obsolescence of American craft—got its first mini-carriers for anti-submarine warfare and for the anti-aircraft protection of the surface fleet. By 1975 it was ready to keep 18 to 20 ships permanently stationed in the Western Pacific and Indian Oceans—and to put in more ship/days there each year than the US.

In 1978 the navy launched a highspeed roll-on/roll-off vehicle and container ship capable of landing large naval supplies in primitive ports, and of accommodating helicopter and hovercraft operations. In the same year, it was ready for the mass transport of military supplies to aid the Ethiopian government and a phalanx of Cuban troops in suppressing the Eritrean rebellion. And on at least one occasion this supply role would expand to the more active function of evacuating Ethiopian troops after a defeat by the rebels.

By 1979, the Soviet Union was testing a light titanium-hulled nuclear-powered attack submarine that moves faster and dives deeper than any US sub. It was also building its first nuclear-powered attack aircraft carrier.

By 1980, the USSR outnumbered the USA (though not the combined NATO and Japanese fleets) in all major warship categories except carriers. For the first time, the Soviet Union anchored warships in Cam Ranh Bay, Vietnam, and stationed nuclear-powered attack submarines in the South China Sea near major world shipping lanes. It began using port facilities on Ethiopian islands in the Red Sea (as a poorer substitute for the more strategically located naval base it forfeited in Somalia in its shift of allies in the region). By the 1980s too the Soviet Union began working on what appeared to be the first Soviet nuclear-powered surface warships—heavy cruisers designed to be the nucleus of long-steaming task forces. It was, noted Captain John Moore in the 1980/81 *Jane's Fighting Ships*, "the largest naval and mercantile peacetime building programme of the century".

The Soviet Navy's potential strength is hard to gauge. Given the asymmetries of vessels, geography and missions, raw numerical comparisons are even more deceptive for the navy than for any other service. The early 1980s statistics of 289 Soviet and 173 American major surface combatants (not counting strategic subs) give quite a false picture. The Soviet fleet is now ageing, while the American fleet is beginning a period of renewal and expansion, with the best new American vessels leapfrogging the best Soviet ships. Those 173 American combatants, with the aid of allied NATO, ANZUS and Japanese ships and subs, still rule the high seas. The Soviet Navy can still be bottled up in the Black Sea, the Sea of Japan, and the Baltic (though perhaps no longer the Barents Sea), the chokepoints that kept Russia land-locked for so many centuries. Soviet ships have only minimal air cover at sea; *Jane's Fighting Ships* sees an "overwhelming superiority" for US naval aviation. The Soviet Navy, lacking general-purpose ships, also has low staying power in blue water, compared with America; both surface ships and subs must return to port much more frequently for refitting and reloading of ammunition and supplies. In addition, Soviet naval firepower is inferior to America's.

Despite these limitations the Soviet Navy would now be a strong challenger to the American and NATO navies in any wartime confrontation. Its mission would be to interdict rather than protect supply lines, a much easier task, made even easier by the current tilt of technology in favour of "sea denial" rather than "sea control". The Soviet Navy could now inflict heavy losses on Western oilers in the eastern Mediterranean and on American transports resupplying Europe across 3,000 North Atlantic miles. It could probably prevent sea reinforcement of Norway's skeletal defence. The Western intelligence consensus seems to be that in any war lasting longer than thirty days NATO would probably be able to assure its sea control and thus its supply lines. But the fact that admirals say "probably" now when they would have said "surely" a decade ago is a measure of their awe at the birth of one of the great navies in history.

Within a meteoric two decades continental Russia has become a major sea power, its merchant fleet rivalling Greece's, its fishing fleet rivalling Japan's, its cruisers playing chicken with American ships from the Atlantic to the Pacific oceans.

With their new naval reach, the Russians were more than ready to pick up Khrushchev's Third World interest of the sixties fifteen years later—and to handle it much more authoritatively than Khrushchev had ever done. They chose as their first major client a nation with a long coastline, one easily supplied by sea—Angola. They acted at a time when their own shift from a continental to a global military power coincided with unexpected opportunity in the breakup of Portuguese empire. They conducted this first foreign adventure after the inauguration of détente in a relatively risk-free period, when the USA appeared to be withdrawing unilaterally from geopolitical competition in the Third World—yet also appeared to be denying Russia the promised fruits of détente in trade and credits. At this juncture, suggests émigré foreign policy scholar Dimitri Simes, the Russians came to view the USA as neither a "formidable rival" nor a "reliable partner". They probably regarded the USA as "demonstrating hostility from a position of weakness" rather than "being generous to the USSR from a position of strength".

In 1975, then, the Russians flew enough Cuban combat troops into Angola to turn the tide among the fairly small numbers of feuding guerilla forces. The MPLA, outnumbered by the rival guerilla factions in the tribal loyalties at its command, would not have won with the 12–15,000 Cuban soldiers (and without the kiss of death South Africa gave the Unita and FNLA factions by its help in the infighting). For the first time ever, it was Soviet and not Western military support that was decisive in Africa.

In Ethiopia—where a Soviet decision to intervene was no doubt made easier by the afterglow of Angolan success—Colonel Mengistu Haile Mariam presumably would have emerged victorious in the post-coup in-fighting with or without Soviet help. The shaky new regime would hardly have routed the turncoat Russian-client Somalia in the Ogaden in 1978, however, without the assistance of three Soviet generals and a massive Soviet airlift of 20,000 Cuban troops and $1 billion worth of tanks, armoured personnel carriers, artillery, and other military equipment (double America's military input in Ethiopia in the previous quarter century).

The Afghan case of 1979/80 was even more dramatic. This time it was not Cuban proxies, but some 80–100,000 Soviet troops, that did the fighting. And this time the Soviet military might was arrayed not behind a national liberation movement but, remarkably, against both the rebels and the Soviet-allied government the rebels were fighting. The Afghan government leader was killed by the Russians, and so little pretence was made that the Afghan government had really invited its Soviet friends in that no Afghan was ever identified as having issued such an invitation. This was the first time that Soviet troops were sent to use force outside the borders of the USSR and the Eastern European empire that the Red Army secured in the after-math of World War II. This was unambiguous aggression: it violated the UN Charter; it violated the tacit understanding of a quarter of a century that, for all their competition, the superpowers do not take over independent states that do not invite intervention.

A shocked United States worried that the Soviet Union was ditching the painstakingly worked-out restraints of détente. Ascendant hawks saw themselves vindicated and warned that this was only the beginning of what the USSR would do with its new global military machine. The doves—who had earlier argued that the USSR's traditional expansionist opportunism had been harnessed by her growing stake in tranquillity and a sophisticated prudence in assessing risks—now feared that the Soviet definition of the threshold of unacceptable risk had risen dangerously. Given the ideological and organizational bias of the Soviet system toward hardline solutions, the doves feared too that the elderly Brezhnev leadership (and its power-struggling succession) no longer had the political perception or will to check a fatal military momentum in decision-making.

In response to Afghanistan the USA jettisoned a number of its post-Vietnam inhibitions, increased its defence budget to over 6 per cent of GNP; arranged to sell China "non-lethal" military equipment and granted her most-favoured-nation trade status (which it still denied the Soviet Union); declared a vague American defence umbrella for the Middle East, with stepped-up Indian Ocean naval patrols and a new quick-reaction force; solicited and acquired the use of several Middle Eastern air and naval bases; curtailed major grain and technology exports to the USSR—and boycotted the 1980 Moscow Olympics.

As a result (or possibly autonomously, given Soviet substitute grain imports from Argentina and elsewhere) Soviet meat consumption was frozen for another year or two at below 1975 levels. 1980 Olympics year food supplies hit a twenty-year low. Soviet drafting of the 1981–85 Five-Year Plan was complicated and delayed. With little to lose in Western public opinion, the Soviet authorities expelled Sakharov from Moscow. Soviet Jewish emigration dropped. SALT-2 looked dead in the US Senate, and both superpowers appeared to be headed for a new, expensive, dangerous arms race. Détente as we knew it in the 1970s was over.

In other parts of the world too the Russians found their invasion costly. India went ahead with a $1.6 billion weapons purchase from the Soviet Union and hedged its criticism of the invasion. But it began a tentative rapprochement with China. China stayed away from the normalization talks with the USSR and let the thirty-year-old Sino-Soviet alliance expire in 1980. Turkey and the USA, after a six-year standoff, signed a new defence agreement. More remarkably, perhaps, Turkey and Greece sought to contain their Cyprus hostility in the face of the greater common Soviet threats. And Greece, which had withdrawn from the NATO military command over the Cyprus issue, returned to the NATO fold.

In the Muslim world an emergency session of thirty-six Islamic Conference nations worried about the porous Iranian and Pakistani borders with Soviet-occupied Afghanistan, and called for the immediate withdrawal of

Soviet troops from their fellow Muslim, nonaligned state. The swearword "colonial" was even applied by some Arabs to the Soviet Union. Their final resolution was the strongest Third World rebuke ever directed at the USSR—and was led by the Soviet Union's treaty ally, Iraq. It was concurred in by the virulently anti-American Ayatollah Ruhollah Khomeini of Iran. It was a complement to the overwhelming Third World vote in favour of a 104:18 (January 1980) and 111:22 (November 1980) UN censure of the Soviet invasion, and it was followed by the partial rapprochement of radical Iraq and conservative Saudi Arabia.

Words are cheap, of course. With time, new power realities tend to dim moral indignation. Syria was not deterred from concluding a new twenty-year friendship treaty with the USSR after the invasion of Afghanistan, and in the Arab world at large anger at the Soviet Union over Afghanistan was attenuated by anger at the USA over the festering Palestinian problem and alarm about the Iran–Iraq war.

Whatever the consequences in world opinion, the remainder of the record shows that Soviet arms (but not Soviet or Cuban troops) aided four other seizures of power or territory by pro-Soviet parties from 1975 on: North Vietnam's final conquest of all of Vietnam and the corollary Pathet Lao victory in Laos in 1975, the South Yemen coup in 1978, and the Vietnamese occupation of Cambodia in 1978/9. At the beginning of the 1980s Soviet military personnel abroad numbered close to 100,000 in Afghanistan, some 2,000 in sub-Sahara Africa, another 2,000 in the major staging area of South Yemen, close to 1,000 in Libya, some in Iraq, 3,500–5,000 in Cuba, 800 in Vietnam. Cuban troops abroad numbered an estimated 19,000 in Angola and 16,500 in Ethiopia. These were supplemented by perhaps 2,000 East German intelligence, communications, and security police advisers, especially in South Yemen, Angola and Ethiopia.

In as yet undecided conflicts, the USSR has long been the main weapons supplier for the SWAPO guerillas in Namibia. Soviet arms also figured in the two invasions of Zaire's Shaba Province by expatriate Katangese from neighbouring Angola, and (in one recent count) in five out of six other armed conflicts in Africa. According to another calculation, the Soviet Union is currently shipping more military hardware to sub-Sahara Africa than the US, France and Britain combined. (The equation changes drastically if northern Africa and the Middle East are included: the $25.5 billion worth of arms supplied to the Middle East by the USA between 1970 and 1976 was more than double the amount of Soviet arms in the region.) In 1979 Soviet sales of weapons to Third World countries reached $8.4 billion, according to the CIA, as against US arms sales to the Third World of $6 billion.

*

Does the Soviet record then constitute what Kissinger complains is impermissible "selective détente?" Does it contravene the 1972 SALT pledge by both the US and the USSR not to seek "unilateral advantage at the expense of the other, directly or indirectly?"

The Russians answer these questions in the negative, arguing that détente never meant freezing the status quo. They have never hidden their intention of supporting national liberation movements, and they are proud that the ardent Cuban revolutionaries are finding new fields of battle. They certainly view the West's dominance in Africa, Asia, and the Middle East as illegitimate, and see their own intervention as modest in comparison with the previous intervention of American troops in Korea, the Lebanon, the Dominican Republic and Vietnam. As a continental power (until now), the Russians have never set up the far-flung network of military and naval bases that the US has maintained since World War II. They have never manipulated a coup or countercoup in a major country bordering on the US (as the US did in 1953 in Iran on the Soviet Union's southern boundary), then poured $12 billion worth of the latest military equipment into it in less than a decade.

Besides, in Africa this time round—in distinction to Khrushchev's practice—the Russians are supporting only governments and national liberation movements legitimized through recognition by the Organization of African Unity. And they are adhering to the OAU principle of accepting existing boundaries: they apparently counselled Ethiopia (even before American warnings to this effect) not to carry its victorious rollback of the Somalis over established borders. At least formally they dissociated themselves from the two Shaba invasions as well.

The USA, Western Europe and some uneasy African and Arab states don't accept the Soviet Union's bland assessment of its activities in the Third World. Henry Kissinger in particular decries the "adverse geopolitical momentum" of recent years, with the slide of an arc from Vietnam to Ethiopia into the Soviet orbit—or at least out of the American orbit. He contends that the USA must reverse the world perception of post-Vietnam American decline, demonstrate resolve, and shore up the next likely Soviet targets of opportunity—Turkey, Pakistan, Saudi Arabia, Zaire and possibly Egypt. The USA must restore the credibility of its security guarantees to friend and foe alike before the Soviet Union goes too far and a showdown occurs at a more disadvantageous stage in the global balance—with higher and more hazardous stakes.

In Kissinger's world view the basic Soviet urge to expansion is "implacable". The lesson of the past—ever since Ivan the Terrible vetoed conquering Siberia until the Cossacks presented him with a risk-free *fait accompli*—is that Russia restrains herself only when faced with countervailing power. Stalin pulled the Red Army back from postwar Iran only when he saw that Truman drew the line there. Khrushchev turned his

Cuba-bound ships around only when it came to a test of strength with Kennedy. And Brezhnev and his successors, even more than Khrushchev, display a disquieting reliance on military force to the exclusion of other persuaders as instruments of influence abroad.

This emphasis was already apparent in Khrushchev's 1956 invasion of the Soviet Union's errant Hungarian ally. It became even more conspicuous in Brezhnev's 1968 invasion of the domestically experimenting but still non-errant Czechoslovak ally, his 1979/80 invasion of the former buffer state of Afghanistan, and his early 1980s threat to invade Poland to end that ally's experiment in pluralism. It is manifested too in the USSR's utter discounting of Japan, that economic giant but military dwarf.

It was not always thus. In the twenties and thirties the new Soviet ideas spoke more eloquently to outsiders than did Soviet guns. Indeed, the weakness of Russian arms was taken by some as a special sign of grace. The USSR was a beacon to admirers in the West for its radical vision of social equality, of constructivist art, of the omnicompetent, unalienated man.

For idealists with the Renaissance, Reformation and Enlightenment in their blood, however, the price of utopia—the Hitler-Stalin Pact and the Gulag Archipelago—turned out to be too high. They were shocked into abhorrence of the Soviet political model. Galician Jew and chief Soviet intelligence head for Europe Walter Krivitsky committed suicide in the late thirties. George Orwell wrote *Nineteen Eighty-Four* and *Animal Farm*. Arthur Koestler, almost uniquely among those whose god failed, did not content himself with rewriting *Darkness at Noon* for the rest of his life, but went on restlessly to explore the nature of creativity and the origins of the Khazar Jews. Czech Old Bolshevik Arnosht Kolman resigned his party membership of half a century and left the Soviet Union for exile at the age of eighty-four after the Soviet invasion of Czechoslovakia.

The Swedes, not without some residual envy of their more chiliastic brother descendants of the Viking/Varangians, went on to perfect social democracy and modern furniture. The British fellow-travellers, with a few celebrated exceptions, renewed their appreciation of the dull but decent liberal virtues of legal process and individual rights. Only the French and Italian Communists clung to their conceit that their cultured, non-peasant, non-Tatar implementation of utopia would be different. Leninism no longer had much intellectual appeal abroad.

After World War II, the USSR presented a new economic attraction, however, as its steady state-planned growth rate outstripped America's cyclical capitalist growth rate. Looking at the contrast, Khrushchev could still expect to close the diminishing gap and overtake the West. But then this promise too faded, as capitalist Japan easily outclassed the USSR, and the increasingly complex Soviet economy itself slowed to a crawl.

Even the Communist grail of fairer distribution lost its lustre, as old-fashioned privilege raised its head inside the Soviet Union—and social welfare spread inside Western Europe. The Soviet Union ended up with a ratio between its richest 5 per cent and its poorest 5 per cent that was close to 6:1 in the mid-sixties; Sweden ended up with a far more equitable 3:1 ratio. And even in unequal, class-lingering, economic tailspinning Britain (with only a 5:1 semidecile ratio) there was no stampede from the bustling unemployment queues of Shepherd's Bush to the sleepy immigration desk of the Kensington Soviet Embassy.

The peaceable Soviet allure lasted longest of all in the Third World. In the early years of post-World War II decolonization, Marxist perceptions (and Russian freedom from any foreign imperial past, except in her own borderlands) gave Moscow an edge in understanding and communicating with the Third World. Leninist anti-colonialism, Soviet success in centrally planned industrialization (especially in Central Asia), Marxist sensitivity to issues of "economic imperialism" that lingered on after independence, and Soviet championing of economic and social equality above the West's often hollow political equality—all these addressed the desires of new Asian and African nations. And a dialectical concept of change and evolution often led the USSR, in contrast to the USA, to a tolerance of Third World reluctance to be drawn into East-West competition. In the 1950s Soviet aid was less tied to military or political (or often even developmental) strings than was American aid. Soviet technicians spread abroad to build the Aswan Dam that the USA had refused Egypt, to erect cement mills for India and a giant sports stadium for Indonesia. Khrushchev fully expected the Soviet Union to win over the Third World in economic and ideological competition. For all his abstract threats to obliterate England and Norway with a few nuclear rockets, Khrushchev confined his military aid in his one real war opportunity in Africa to a parsimonious sixteen transport planes for Patrice Lumumba in the Congo.

Khrushchev's successors were more sceptical about the readiness of African and Asian nations to ally themselves with the Soviet Union. They confined new aid to countries with policies compatible with the Soviet Union's, or with naval bases to offer Russia's expanding fleet. For reasons of prestige and ideology they continued Khrushchev's huge subsidies to Communist-ruled Cuba, but they declined to make a similar open-ended commitment to funding Marxist Salvador Allende's Chile.

By the mid-seventies, Soviet economic aid to developing lands was running at only a fifth of America's even as a percentage of GNP. (The amount soared in 1978, almost to the American level of four or five billion dollars, with the bulk of this Soviet aid going to Vietnam and Cuba. This jump appeared to be exceptional rather than representative of a new generous trend, however. Furthermore, Soviet credit terms remained hard and bound to the recipients' purchase of expensive and often inferior Soviet plant.)

At the same time as Soviet disenchantment with the Third World grew, both the Third World and the West became more sophisticated. Many Africans and Asians themselves became disillusioned with the miserliness of Russian aid and with the discovery that Slavic aid administrators could be just as racially arrogant as the old Western imperialists. Many Third World nations found that their natural economic connections were with the avid world traders of the West rather than with the autarchic Soviet Union—and that the capital investments and technical, agricultural and managerial expertise they needed to advance beyond the most rudimentary development was more readily available from the West than from the USSR.

The greater sophistication in the West also relaxed the original insistence on explicit Western political alignment among aid recipients. The amount of Western aid increased to a magnitude far exceeding Soviet development aid, and the West came to recognize at least rhetorically a rich-poor North-South gap that the comparatively wealthy Soviet Union has to this day never acknowledged. The Third World retained its suspicions of the West, but it also acquired comparable suspicions of the USSR.

By the 1980s the cumulative effect of these trends left the Soviet development model of centrally enforced peasant savings looking less relevant to many industrial neophytes than the phenomenal growth and prosperity of such mixed economies as Taiwan's, South Korea's and Brazil's.

And this in turn left a Soviet Union desirous of extending its influence in the Third World, as in the First and Second Worlds, largely dependent on the bite of its guns. It was a curious military dead end for the heirs of that revolutionary nineteenth-century prophet of underlying economic relationships and causation.

Western doves deplore the blinkered Soviet focus on military might in foreign affairs as much as Henry Kissinger does. But they argue that it is silly and dangerous for the West to inflate every contest in Timbuktu to a fundamental test of superpower manhood. In this world view the West risks mankind's survival if it exaggerates Soviet ambitions and power, and its own response.

The purest doves among Vietnam-recoil revisionists go much further than this in exonerating the Soviet Union: They find no foreign-policy flaw in Soviet actions in Africa or Afghanistan today, or in Stalin's actions in the early post-World War II years; they attribute the Cold War and continuing Soviet-American tension largely to American hubris. Mainstream doves however—although they fault the USA for pulling back on the Nixon-Kissinger promises in trade and for pressing détente too far in demanding Soviet domestic human rights as well as foreign policy transformations—still impute a drive for aggrandizement to the Soviet Union. They do not anticipate any end to the adversary relationship between East and West, but they advocate a controlled adversary relationship in which the West acknowledges and reinforces the moderate rather than the intransigent inclination within the Soviet leadership.

The softliners argue that the Kremlin has demonstrated its seriousness about détente not only in the obvious way of establishing strategic ceilings and permanent channels of consultation to limit superpower conflicts. It has also curbed its revolutionary instincts several times in order to avoid war and promote détente, and it has paid a high cost for détente within its own society and the world Communist movement.

Soviet restraint has been exhibited most dramatically in Chinese, Middle-Eastern, and Western European policies. Soviet unwillingness to risk ideologically exhilarating but nationally debilitating wars led to major ruptures with China and Egypt. And Soviet restraint in exploiting Western economic weakness was conspicuous after the inauguration of détente.

In 1957/58 the Chinese cheered the launching of sputnik, lectured the Russians that the East wind prevailed over the West wind—and pressed the Soviet Union to threaten paper-tiger America with nuclear bombs to win back the Quemoy and Matsu islands for China from Taiwan. A nuclear holocaust would raze imperialism, the Central Committee's journal *Red Flag* cheerfully assured the Russians, but millions of (presumably Chinese) socialists would survive and rebuild a better world "on the debris of a dead civilization". With horror, *Pravda* characterized the Chinese position as a "declaration that, for the sake of the achievement of a specific political goal, it is possible to sacrifice half mankind". The alarmed Russians subsequently reneged on their promise to deliver a sample A-bomb to China and informed the Chinese that the nuclear bomb's lethality knows no class distinctions. Other ideological and territorial disputes flared up as well, and the "eternal Soviet-Chinese friendship" came to an end after eight years.

A similar dispute precipitated the Soviet-Egyptian falling out a decade later. When it became involved in the Middle East for the first time in the wake of the British and French retreat from the region in the 1950s, Russia selected the leading Arab nation, Egypt, as the centrepiece of its regional policy. It supplied Egypt with extensive military and economic aid and some 20,000 Soviet military personnel to train the Egyptian army and help patrol the Suez canal. It was rewarded by the gratitude of the Arabs and, eventually, use of the splendid naval facilities at Alexandria.

As it became the Arabs' main weapons supplier the Soviet Union found it profitable to keep the cauldron boiling, even to the extent of fanning Arab militancy in the 1967 war, some evidence indicated. The greater the tension, the greater the Arab dependence on Soviet arms and the greater the Soviet penetration of the region. /

But a few years after the Middle East became a major arena of East-West confrontation Leonid Ilyich Brezhnev and Richard Milhous Nixon inaugurated their détente. Egypt yearned to test its new military strength against Israel one more time; Brezhnev demurred, not wanting to jeopardize détente, and declined to give Egypt all the arms it asked for. When the Egyptians launched their war anyway, in 1973, the Soviet Union did replace those weapons lost in the war but refused to go beyond that. And at this point—after a mutual alert that brought the superpowers closer to the brink of nuclear conflict than at any other time since the Cuban missile crisis—the Soviet Union co-operated with the US in imposing a truce on the warring client states.

Western hawks argue that this superpower imposition of a truce was one-sided, against the Israeli forces that would otherwise have decimated the surrounded Third Egyptian Army. Doves, however, find it more significant that the Soviet Union had to accept a total break with Egypt, expulsion of all Soviet military personnel from Egypt, closure of the Alexandria harbour to the Soviet Mediterranean fleet—and, eventually, an Egyptian-Israeli settlement that excluded the USSR altogether. They find it significant too that in recent years the Soviet Union has not given all-out support to the Arab rejection front following the American-sponsored Israeli-Egyptian settlement—and it has strained relations with Syria rather than rearm this client to the extent Syria wishes.

Immediately following the 1973 Middle East flareup came one more example of Soviet caution. During the West's economic nadir of oil crisis, recession, unemployment, and breakdown of the Bretton Woods monetary system—along with what seemed a revolutionary situation in Portugal—the Soviet Union did not try to exploit the Western weakness. It neither engineered a leftist coup in Portugal, nor did it repeat Khrushchev's earlier triumphant proclamation of a new stage in the "deepening general crisis" of capitalism.

Besides the cost of foreign restraint, the Russians have had to pay a high domestic and intra-Communist cost for détente. They have surrendered the popular notion of Americans and West Germans as implacable enemies, thus erasing one of the strongest justifications for social mobilization and consumer deferment. They have begun allowing emigration—an act they consider treasonous—of certain segments of Soviet citizens for the first time in Soviet history. They have, however irascibly, helped perpetuate dissidence by ceasing to expel Western journalists after every meeting with dissenters, by ending the jamming of foreign radio (until the 1980 Polish strike), by signing a Helsinki agreement that endorsed human rights—and by not killing or incarcerating Sakharov. They have, however reluctantly, permitted the breaching of the Russians' centuries-old obsession with secrecy. (The famous incident in which military officers on the Soviet SALT team privately reproached American negotiators for revealing [CIA] figures of Soviet military forces to the *Soviet* civilian negotiators is only the wryest expression of this deep anxiety.)

The Soviet Union has also paid for détente in the phenomenon of "Eurocommunism", with the Italian and Spanish (though no longer French) Communist Parties ostentatiously criticizing Soviet gaoling of dissidents and even Soviet "imperialism", discarding the hallowed "dictatorship of the proletariat", and endorsing the heresy of tolerating opposing political parties.

Moreover, the USSR has gained relatively little from détente beyond whatever basic enhancement of nuclear security and predictability it shares with the West. The Soviet Union did get key Western investment and technology for its oil and petrochemical industries, but the expected amount of Western long-term credits has not materialized. Détente legitimized, in the Helsinki Agreement, a permanent Western meddling in Soviet internal affairs on human-rights issues. The full American-Chinese normalization of 1979 was not blocked. The fear of a new surge of American technology into mobile missiles, just as the Soviet Union was catching up with the American lead in multiple warheads, far from being allayed, has been aggravated. The confusion of an American foreign policy that is split between President and Congress (and often enough between the contradictory views of a single administration) has not been clarified.

Besides, continue the doves, the tide of history is not as favourable to the Russians as an isolated look at the period 1975–80 might indicate. To Kremlin geopoliticians, the "loss" of China and Egypt must loom far larger than the "gain" of Ethiopia, South Yemen, Indochina and Afghanistan. And the newest potential "loss" of Poland to a heretical domestic pluralism —along with the dangerous long-term appeal of this example to other East Europeans, Lithuanians, and western Ukrainians, and the inhibitions on any Soviet military disciplining of Poland, given the Red Army's Afghan quagmire—must seem even more unwelcome.

Then, too, Soviet strategists must worry about the backlash effect of the USSR's assertiveness of the late seventies and early eighties in provoking the very "encirclement" the Russians have nightmares about.

Japan, after decades of steering a meticulous "equidistant" foreign policy between China and Russia, finally tired of the endless Soviet hectoring and the USSR's naval buildup on her northern doorstep. In 1978, Japan for the first time declared the Soviet Union to be her major threat, and signed a peace and friendship treaty with China opposing "hegemonism" (i.e. the extension of Soviet influence) in Asia. In 1980, following increased Soviet military use of Vietnamese air and sea ports and Soviet establishment of a divisional headquarters and expansion of naval tonnage in the four disputed Southern Kurils, Japan increased its military budget slightly closer to 1 per cent of GNP, and for the first time since World War II began building a public consensus for fleshing out the minimal Japanese forces. In the end, the Soviet hard line towards Japan succeeded only in diverting some of that country's efficient production into arms—and much of its enormous knowhow and energy from Siberian to Chinese industrialization.

In Northeast Asia, North Korea too has moved closer to China. And in Asia as a whole, the cost of Vietnam's exclusive Soviet alliance and military clashes with China and Thailand has been such a mistrust of the Soviet Union that the Russians' hopeful early seventies' feelers about an (anti-Chinese) Asian collective security system have long since been dropped. Even the tentative rapprochement between Vietnam and an Association of Southeast Asian Nations that is innately suspicious of China was scotched by Vietnam's 1980 invasion of Thai border areas.

In Africa, the large-scale Soviet-Cuban intervention in Angola and Ethiopia upset a number of centrist as well as conservative nations. The Sudan, Guinea, Ghana, Nigeria, Somalia, Equatorial Guinea and the Central African Republic have all retracted their once close political and military ties with the Soviet Union. Nigeria's Lieutenant-General Olusegun Obasanjo met with the applause of twenty-nine other African heads of state at an Organization of African Unity meeting in 1978 when he advised the Russians "and their friends" not to "overstay their welcome" in Africa. And even Angola began slipping away from its Soviet-Cuban dependence in the eighties.

The nonaligned movement, which happened to fall under Cuban chairmanship at the end of the seventies and beginning of the eighties, has been ambiguous. The (pre-Afghanistan) 1979 Havana summit displayed an anti-West radicalization in blaming the capitalist economies for underdevelopment more caustically than ever before. Yet the summit also condemned (Soviet) hegemony and rejected Cuba's contention that the USSR is the "natural ally" of the nonaligned. And after the Soviet invasion of Afghanistan the nonaligned nations voted overwhelmingly in the UN to condemn the Soviet occupation and, after 156 exhausting ballots, even to deny Cuba election to the Security Council.

Finally, in the USA, the Soviet Union's first use of its own troops in three decades to overthrow the government of a buffer state profoundly altered American perceptions in a hard-line direction. It ended the post-Vietnam retraction of US foreign commitments. It helped elect a hard-line Ronald Reagan president. It cast Senate ratification of SALT-2 into limbo. It underminded the assumption that there is more security in arms control than in yet another arms race.

Détente, if not dead, is at least moribund. The superpowers are embarked on a new—this time truly global—competition, with the old restraints broken, the new limits not yet clear, in the technologically most volatile decade of the nuclear age. Today, we are left with a greater risk of nuclear war than ever before, from the uncertainties of technology, silo vulnerability, intensified superpower confrontation, paranoia, pride, and hubris.

Personally, I'm more scared of a Soviet than of an American Dr Strangelove. But in an era of first-strike overkill, with current arsenals sufficiently well stocked to destroy every city in the world seven times over, I'm most scared of holocaust through mutual bungling. Either way, it would be a wasteful end to our three-and-a-half million year experiment in the galaxy. I'd hate to see the Baikal seals vindicated in their pessimistic reversion to the watery depths.

05.45 Il'ka

Moved by my apocalyptic ruminations I recite Robert Frost's mordant verse to Tanya and Grandmother:

> Some say the world will end in fire,
> Some say in ice.
> From what I've tasted of desire
> I hold with those who favour fire.
> But if it had to perish twice,
> I think I know enough of hate
> To say that for destruction ice
> Is also great
> And would suffice.

"Fire" and "ice" translate easily enough, but somehow the idea doesn't get across. Tanya looks resistant. Grandmother looks accommodating but puzzled. Breakdown in communication. May the hotline do better. I head for the restaurant car.

The cook cum maitre d. cum bouncer doesn't notice my arrival in time to perform his usual sleight of hand in arranging a magnificently vacant table for me alone where I won't mix with the natives. I quickly slip into a chair at a table already occupied by two young men.

It's an absurd duel, since I'm mixing with Grandmother and Tanya and Nina twenty-four hours a day anyway, but orders are orders. It's only because I'm a leftover foreigner—the eight others on our train have all been neatly packaged in their own hermetic compartments—that this anomaly has crept in. And the restaurant car chief is determined not to let the anomaly foul his nest, whatever the cause. He hurries over to remedy his momentary oversight and press me to accept a better table. Smugly, I take advantage of the inertia that for once is on my side: he won't use force to displace me, and he can't gracefully move the two original window-seat occupants of the table. I stay put, and so do my companions.

Instantly I regret my one-upmanship. The two lads are sailors in mufti. The one is too sloshed to believe he is talking to a foreigner and keeps challenging my identity in a voice that carries throughout the dining car. His more sober buddy becomes more and more miserable as our non-conversation proceeds. Recruits are forbidden to talk to foreigners while they are in the service, and I know it, and if they had had their uniforms on I would never have put them on the spot like this.

I didn't mind pressing a Murmansk fishing-boat captain in the Arctic home of the Northern fleet about his pelagic expeditions. I took a certain glee, in fact, in disregarding the pretence that we were casual friends enjoying a potluck banquet together aboard his ship and shouldn't spoil the occasion by talking shop. For the most part the captain gave all the right answers: no, his ratings didn't get bored, because they had a library and athletic competitions on the ship; no, he didn't mind at all being away from home ten months a year in icy, stormy waters. But when I asked him if his sons would follow in his footsteps, his spontaneous answer sounded as if he would do everything in his power to protect them from such a career. A bit callously, perhaps, I figured that the captain had chosen the life of one of the Soviet elite, with its political demands as well as its social perquisites; even if he would later have to answer for his slip to the KGB watchdogs, I didn't feel very sorry for him.

But these beardless boys—they're as far from being part of the elite as they could be. They probably joined the navy only to avoid the ennui of the army. I feel protective toward them. I don't ask how many missiles they have on board their ship, how good their hydrophones are, how cramped their bunks are, or what the propaganda officer has told them about the horrors of Japan. I don't ask them how conscripts survive on only three roubles a month, or if they've ever got bombed on boot polish spread on bread, as Far East soldiers reportedly do. I try to anticipate where the conversation is heading and prevent the tipsy one from blurting out anything that might be considered secret. I consume my borscht and mineral water as fast as possible, call the waiter to tot up my bill on his half-metre-long abacus, and leave the table.

Did those two pals volunteer for the navy, I wonder, after viewing that heroic, larger-than-life, technicolor film epic of adventure and superhuman survival against incredible odds (whose name I have mercifully forgotten) that I saw shortly after my arrival in Moscow? The movie became a box-office hit as soon as word leaked out that it had joined the obligatory modern *seins nus* vogue—and also had the chutzpah to depict newlyweds as moving into a Moscow apartment of their own immediately after their marriage. The phenomenal apartment and the glimpse of bare breast were there all right (the latter, it turned out, in a chaste shower scene, with the girl's mother rather than her lover in the background). But the main point of the film, I discovered, was glorification of the navy. It was the neglected service's answer to all those endless World War II "tankist" movies—and a lure to forthcoming army conscripts to join the glamorous navy instead. It was, no doubt, one of Admiral S. G. Gorshkov's greatest victories over the army.

Blessings on Russia, though. Her sloppy Slavic soul may save her yet. A colleague in Moscow during the flowering of détente was driving home on the night of 26 May 1972, just after the signing of SALT-1 by Nixon and Brezhnev. Two pedestrians hailed her—private rides "on the left" are an important means of transportation in taxi-short Moscow—and as she pulled over to the kerb she realized that the two men were wearing navy uniforms. She let them know right away that she was an American correspondent so they could get out and hail a substitute car if they wished. On this euphoric evening they didn't mind, however, and she ended up taking them home to their apartments at the far ends of Moscow. As they came to the second man's street, the bonhomie of the occasion inspired the officer to invite her up for a late snack. No, his wife wouldn't mind; he would wake her up and they could all celebrate together. Over the zakuski my colleague confessed that she couldn't tell one epaulet from another and was curious about the rank of her new friend. "Kapitan," he replied. "Kapitan of what?" she inquired. "Kapitan of a nuclear submarine," he elaborated, and jovially invited her to come visit again sometime soon.

And my friend Petya, my hopelessly romantic Petya, who is prevented from freezing every winter only by the solicitude of chums who keep verifying that he is actually wearing his donated coat. Dreamy, absent-minded, oblivious Petya, who thought that when the draft finally caught up with him he would escape by mutilating an arm prior to induction or by emigrating to Israel at the last minute. By one means or another—none of them as desperate as his original scenarios—he managed to slip unscathed through three conscription periods and several KGB interrogations about his armyless lifestyle before the authorities finally scheduled a showdown with him that augured either training camp or gaol. Petya presented himself at the police station at the appointed hour. It was the end of a long day at the end of a long week. Russia lacks the Prussian discipline of an East Germany. The responsible officer was tired and bored and wanted to go off to the bathhouse without setting in motion yet another interminable chain of paperwork. With lassitude worthy of an Oblomov he waved Petya out of his office and out of his life. Petya departed, convinced more than ever that God takes care of drunks, little children, and the Petyas of this world.

Alyosha wasn't as lucky. He was the one who had all the angles figured, who could somehow always wangle the hard-currency coupons to buy a Japanese tape recorder, or a doctor's stamp certifying that the collective-farm diet was doing unspeakable things to his liver and that he therefore should be released from the potato-picking brigade before it was fatal. He too escaped his first three draft periods still roaming Moscow in his genuine Levis. But the fourth time—even though he entered a hospital (where he got a ground-floor bed that enabled him to sneak out of the window at night and be back before the nurses made their rounds the next morning)—he finally got snared in the dragnet.

The night before the door of the military bus snapped irrevocably shut on his carefree student days was one of those gloomy-exuberant occasions, like some wake in which mourners are exhilarated by their loss of sleep and the determination that the departed would prefer them to go on living. Alyosha debated with himself and everyone else whether he should leave his beard to the last possible second and the mercy of army barbers, or whether he should shave it off himself eight hours earlier but do a decent job of it. He considered what clothes it would be best to wear to his induction, since he figured he'd never see them again. He wondered how he would survive with only wretched balalaika music around, since the army bans even seven-stringed guitars as Western and decadent. Wise friends who were already veterans counselled him to avoid assignment to East Germany, where he would be confined to barracks all the time, and above all never to disclose that he knew a Western language, lest he be trapped underground with monitoring earphones for the next two years, and not stand a ghost of a chance at travel outside the Soviet Union for five years after that.

At one end of the table Alyosha's girlfriend fretted that there wasn't enough food for everyone. At the other end of the table a survivor of the camps asked, over and over again, how God can exist when there's so much evil in the world; a husband and wife of Alyosha's generation assured him, over and over again, that God sends evil to test us. Through it all Alyosha concentrated on bracing himself to face putrid latrines and lice and no baths for two years, and the very thought of it sent him off to the shower at 2 a.m. in the middle of the party.

As it developed, Alyosha successfully evaded both East Germany and the windowless eavesdropping bunkers. But he didn't evade the augmentation (by 60 per cent in the 1970s) of Soviet troops on the Chinese border. He's a few hundred miles from here now, having had the couple of books he took with him stolen, having been beaten up by drunk NCOs to prove that he's no better than they are just because he's an intellectual. But at least he has the solace of facing a real enemy. He would have no heart for bayonet drills against the lands of rock 'n roll and good movies. Virtually the only political thought in his head is fear of the yellow peril and reimposition of the Tatar yoke.

07.05   Petrovsky Zavod

We all pile out of the train, not to purchase gooseberries or cedar cones this time, but to exercise lazy muscles and to gaze at the monument to the exiled Decembrists. It's a straightforward memorial with eight portrait cameos, not one of those shiny-faces-to-the-future jobs. To be sure, it's framed by vaguely Corinthian gilded pilasters; a twentieth-century Lenin, hand in pocket, towers anachronistically over the lot; and the Decembrists are wearing starched collars, coats, and other items of noble dress rather than their chains. But one has the feeling of seeing their faces as they were at some point, at least, and not a neutered, beatified version of them. One can imagine these men as the vague but ardent liberalizers who opposed military colonies and petty tyrants, favoured canals, constitutionalism, and annexation of Serbia, and failed miserably at insurrection.

The text embedded in the memorial, alas, is an uncharacteristic bit of bombast from Herzen praising "these heroes made of pure steel from head to toe, warring champions who consciously came out of manifest ruin to wake the young generation to a new life." Curiously, the tablet does not quote the famous poem of encouragement to the hundred-odd convicted Decembrists that Pushkin entrusted to the Siberia-bound wives:

> Deep in the Siberian mine,
> Keep your patience proud;
> The bitter toil shall not be lost,
> The rebel thought unbowed.
> . . . .
> The heavy-hanging chains will fall,
> The walls will crumble at a word;
> And Freedom greet you in the light,
> And Brothers give you back the sword.

I had hoped for a different monument, or at least an additional monument, one to the women. Petrovsky Zavod, after all, was where villagers nicknamed the lane some of the wives lived on "Ladies' Street". This was where those frightened and bone-weary and stubborn women eventually landed when they followed their husbands to the unknown wilderness a century and a half ago. These were the women who made Nikolai Nekrasov shout "Enough!" and burst into tears as Maria Volkonskaya's son read her diary aloud to the poet in 1871. These were the "Russian Women" then fixed in amber in Nekrasov's poem—the ones Eugenia Ginzburg summoned up as she involuntarily retraced their route in her prison train in 1939.

The wives who abandoned their Petersburg balls and coquettish intrigues and titles—and children—for an unimaginable primitive life in the taiga were young, only a few years older than Nina, when they made their extraordinary decision. They were unused to hardship or even to work. They hardly knew what they were committing themselves to, or if they would find the interior reserves of toughness to acquit their momentary resolve. But still they went ahead with this caesura in their lives—out of duty and idealism, nineteenth-century romantics said, out of apolitical conventionalism, some scathing twentieth-century feminists say.

"Hey," I ask Nina, "would you do that? Would you follow your husband to the end of the earth if he got sent there to do hard labour?"

"Of course," answers Tanya for her daughter, "if it was a capitalist court that sentenced him." Nina nods assent, but her gesture comes out as much a shrug as a nod. Grandmother shakes her head definitively. "I wouldn't!" she pronounces. "I'd live my own life." But it's Grandmother who scrutinizes the cameos to find out which one was the husband of the Duchess Trubetskaya.

Yekaterina Trubetskaya was the first wife to make the journey. At the beginning it was something of a lark; she travelled in style, in a cabin on a sledge drawn by six horses. The cabin had full furnishings, including, of course, an icon. The horses were changed every 40 kilometres; the sledge itself never stopped except for the rotation of the team, according to Nekrasov's account. It took Trubetskaya twenty days and nights to reach Tyumen', ten days and nights to reach the Yenisei River, close to ten more days and nights to reach Irkutsk. There she came to a halt (in Nekrasov's somewhat truncated version), blocked by the local governor on orders from above. For six months she cooled her heels in that muddy, bumptious town while the governor frantically pressed St Petersburg for instructions on how to deal with this highly irregular situation.

In reply the enraged Nicholas I personally issued the instructions:

1. Convicts and hoodlums were to consider Trubetskaya and other Decembrist wives as their equals; the women would receive no legal protection from insults, assaults, or violence from such riffraff. 2. Any children born in exile would inherit no family titles, but would become local peasants. 3. The women could take none of their former riches or money to Siberia. 4. The decision to proceed eastward from Irkutsk would cancel the women's right to own those serfs who had accompanied them thus far. 5. They could never return to Russia without the express permission of the tsar.

Trubetskaya signed her assent to the conditions—contemptuously, the romantics believed, turning society's rejection of her into her rejection of a backward society. Her husband's conspiracy was the first modern revolt in Russia, the first attempt to change the system rather than the despot. The surviving Decembrists and to some extent their consorts were conscious of this distinction and proud of their martyr's role.

The Irkutsk governor tried one last ploy. He would permit Trubetskaya to go the remaining 1,000 versts on foot, with the next chained and roped prisoner convoy. She called his bluff. He finally granted her the horses to proceed.

On arriving at her final destination Trubetskaya had to sign yet another document. She would not, she pledged, seek any meetings with her husband outside the two allotted one-hour sessions each week; speak French with him; give him money, papers, ink, pencils, or take any letters, papers or notes from him; send or receive any letters except through the local commandant; keep any money except that consigned to the commandant for her restricted expenses; nor stray from the village without permission.

Trubetskaya found a chimneyless log cabin with mica windows to rent from an irascible landlady. The twenty-year-old Maria Volkonskaya—whose angry cursing of the government would inspire a special report by an awed Siberian police agent—arrived shortly thereafter and joined Trubetskaya in the tiny cabin.

Like Trubetskaya, Volkonskaya would tame this wilderness with moral certitude and with civilization. She brought a clavichord with her by sledge and carriage the 6,000 versts from Moscow. She subscribed to magazines and newspapers, including foreign periodicals. And she was the one who fell at her husband's feet on being reunited with him on 8 February 1827. In her diary she recorded: "I threw myself on to my knees in front of him and kissed first his shackles, then my husband himself. I gave him a portrait of his father and mother and my own with the baby in my arms and thought: 'At last I am in the promised land.'"

The fourteen Decembrist women who came to Siberia were at first awakened at five each morning by the rattle of chains as the prisoners were led through the village on their way to the tsar's silver mines. (The chains were worn continually, except for church services and weekly baths.) The women rose, built the wood fire, and prepared food for all the Decembrists. With forethought, Trubetskaya had brought a cookbook with her, and another Decembrist's French commoner wife, who had had to learn such things in girlhood, taught the noblewomen how to manage their fires and pots. Often enough the wives could afford only bread and kvass for themselves, but they tried to feed soup and kasha, at least, to their men.

On the two days when visits were allowed, the women gave the meals directly to their husbands. On other days they gave the food to the guards, then sat on a large boulder in front of the prison's only window to catch glimpses of their husbands and exchange a few shouted words with them.

It must be admitted there was much poetry in our life [wrote the Frenchwoman who had left the comforts of even lower-class Paris so far behind her]. It's true, even though there were many deprivations, all kind of work and trouble. . . . Everything was common, sorrows and joys; everything was shared. We sympathized with each other in everything. We were all bound together by close friendships.

For Volkonskaya, the daughter of a famous general in the War of 1812, the life in Siberia brought another revelation: "I was among the people who belonged to the dregs of mankind. Nevertheless, they treated us with great respect. . . . How much gratitude and loyalty there were in these people who had been presented to me as some sort of monsters!"

By 1830 a new prison would be built for the exclusive occupancy of the Decembrists and their wives and (according to one account) any children who did better than the twenty-two buried in babyhood and survived. By 1840 the Decembrists would be released from hard labour and scatter to various villages to begin the modern study of Siberia's exotic jumble of flora, fauna, races, and languages. By 1856, thirty years after their original sentencing, the Decembrists would be amnestied, though not pardoned. Mikhail Volkonsky, the son of Maria and her beloved Sergei, would carry the new tsar's manifesto to this effect to the Decembrists in Siberia, outracing in his haste even the famed Peking-Petersburg couriers.

14.26   Chita

If Nekrasov wept on hearing of the treatment of the clavichord-transporting, newspaper-subscribing Volkonskaya, what would he have done on hearing of the treatment of Stalin's political prisoners in the infamous Chita taiga? Or of the treatment of the Mandelstams?

By the time Nadezhda Mandelstam came to Chita the worst was over. Stalin had died. His last secret police chief Beria had just been liquidated. The pain of uncertainty about Osip Mandelstam's fate had been replaced by anguish over his death. Nadezhda Mandelstam, by leading a nomadic life after her rescue by the textile workers of Strunino, had stayed one step ahead of the political police. The Education Ministry had reinstated her to a teaching post in Chita as a grudging token of her emergence out of danger.

Had she ever found her husband alive again in those terrible years, Nadezhda Mandelstam would most assuredly not have kissed his shackles. She no longer hoped for any promised land. She hoped only that she would live long enough to outlast the nightmare and again give the world "M.'s" great poetry that she had tenaciously memorized or hidden. With a bitterness that Volkonskaya never dreamed of, Nadezhda Mandelstam advised others to tell lies and scream.

"Should one lie? May one lie? Is it all right to lie in order to save someone?" Nadezhda Mandelstam asked in her memoirs. Her answer was an unashamed yes:

We were brought up from childhood to believe that lies and hyprocrisy are universal. I would certainly not have survived in our terrible times without lying. I have lied all my life: to my students, colleagues and even the good friends I didn't quite trust (this was true of most of them).

In similar vein Mandelstam asked

whether it is right to scream when you are being beaten and trampled underfoot. Isn't it better to face one's tormentors in a stance of satanic pride, answering them with contemptuous silence? I decided that it is better to scream. This pitiful sound, which sometimes, goodness knows how, reaches into the remotest prison cell, is a concentrated expression of the last vestige of human dignity. It is a man's way of leaving a trace, of telling people how he lived and died. By his screams he asserts his right to live, sends a message to the outside world demanding help and calling for resistance. If nothing else is left, one must scream.

And then she concluded, in the ultimate curse that a woman can utter: "All I can say . . . is: do not bring children into this unspeakable world."

20.18 Priiskovaya

Again, I stay awake long after the rest of the carriage has dozed off, this time to feel the presence of Nerchinsk, on a siding to the north, and the Onon River, in a valley to the south. It is the Nerchinsk Treaty of 1689 that the Chinese hail as the last fair treaty between Russia and China. It is the later treaties, more favourable to the Russians, that the Russians hail as the definers of the present-day Sino-Soviet border.

It must be said that the Russians tried their best at Nerchinsk. The host Russian negotiator positioned himself for the talks on a yellow damask chair behind a gilded writing table. Next to him—since the Chinese were such devotees of European clocks—stood a carved grandfather clock that must have made its own harrowing journey here by cart and sledge. The tsar's envoy provided no seats at all for the Chinese (Manchus, actually, since this was the Ch'ing dynasty), who had to devise rough benches for themselves if they were not to sit on the floor.

Despite the psychological warfare, the Manchus bested the Russians in the treaty that was eventually drawn up in Chinese, Russian, Manchu, Mongolian and Latin. The tsar had to abandon his settlements on the Amur and Zeya Rivers for the next two centuries. So pleased was the Manchu emperor with this first treaty China had ever made with a foreign power that he rewarded his Portuguese and French Jesuit interpreters with an edict of toleration for Christianity in China.

An even earlier Russian humiliation is commemorated by the nearby Onon River, the reputed birthplace of Genghis Khan. This prescient proponent of military advantage through technological superiority and blitzkrieg mobility led 129,000 warriors (out of a total Mongol population of no more than two and a half million) to conquer Eurasia. With the iron stirrup and the compound bow his nomads could shoot as they rode, and overwhelm peasant foot soldiers. They lived up well to the khan's reported creed: "Man's highest joy is in victory: to conquer one's enemies, to pursue them, to deprive them of their possessions, to make their beloved weep, to ride on their horses, and to embrace their wives and daughters."

This kind of victory Genghis Khan wreaked in China, Korea, Tibet, Samarkand, Bokhara, Afghanistan, Persia, Mesopotamia, Georgia, Armenia, Russia, Poland, Bohemia, and Hungary. In a sense, Russia would never recover.

In this desolate place that was once the centre of the world not a soul boards or leaves our train. In the next compartment the caged canary that belongs to a teenager from Kamchatka is jolted awake by the unnatural silence. He utters a reflexive *fioritura*, then lapses embarrassedly back into sleep.

CHAPTER VI
SATURDAY THE LEADERS

Kto kogo?
The traditional question in Soviet politics,
"Who (is on top of, or is knifing) whom?"

There was or there wasn't . . .
Czech version of "Once upon a time . . ."

09.10 *Erofei Pavlovich*

WE HAVE HEADED north, skirting the hump of Manchuria. By now we are
farther east than Peking, Shanghai, and all the major Chinese ports except
Dairen. But ahead of us we still have all of the Soviet Far East—the last and
largest of the three regions that constitute Siberia.

From here on the Trans-Siberian hugs the Chinese frontier, fifty miles to
the right of us, along the Amur (in Chinese, Black Dragon) River. It's the
last of Siberia's giant rivers, longer than the Yenisei, longer than the Lena,
second only to the Ob in Russia, surpassed by only six other rivers anywhere
in the world. In summer it is navigable over 1,800 miles. During the six-
month winter it is closed to all but horse or truck traffic.

For four centuries this river has been the meeting point—and clashing
point—of Russia and Asia. The Russians evacuated the Amur Basin with
the 1689 Treaty of Nerchinsk, and for almost two centuries thereafter it was
left to the Manchus to colonize this region, with forts, naval patrols, and
postal services. Then in the mid-nineteenth century the Cossacks came
back, floated down the Amur on barges and, quite in violation of the Treaty
of Nerchinsk, built stockades on the river's northern bank all the way to
present-day Khabarovsk. As usual, it was an ambitious Siberian viceroy who
took matters into his own hands, then persuaded the tsar to back him up.
The result was the 1858 Treaty of Aigun, assigning everything north of the
middle course of the Amur to Russia. China rejected the treaty the following
year, but with Russia, Britain and France all carving up the melon with
modern firearms, China had little choice. The Treaty of Aigun was recon-
firmed two years later in the Treaty of Peking.

More peaceably, the nineteenth-century Amur achieved some fame as the
passageway for the largest mirror in the world. This looking-glass was

purchased at the Paris Exposition of 1878, shipped half-way round the world, then put on a made-to-order barge to be hauled up the Amur and Shilka to Nerchinsk. There the astonished American journalist George Kennan found it in the 1880s in a nouveau riche mansion in deepest Siberia, along with parquet floors, silk curtains, stained-glass windows, chandeliers, Oriental rugs, satin furniture and marble statues.

Today the Amur and its tributary the Ussuri once again form the friction edge of Russia and Asia. Islands along the shifting river course are in constant dispute. China refuses to accept the Amur as the proper frontier at all. And in 1969, the occasional skirmishes along the rivers exploded into a battalion-sized battle on the Ussuri Damansky Island that some military attachés feared could be the start of war along the world's longest shared land border.

Our first town in the Soviet Far East is named after Erofei Pavlovich Khabarov, that tsarist epitome of rapacious capitalist greed who completed the conquest of Siberia for the Russians. It is a curious appellation for Soviet cartographers to cling to. Back in the Urals, Yekaterinburg has long since been expurgated to Sverdlovsk; in front of us on the track Tsarevich ("Crown Prince") has long since been purified to Svobodny ("Free")—someone's jest, perhaps, for the prison camp that was installed in that town after the Whites deserted it.

Erofei Pavlovich, however, lives on, lauding the man who gloated, after one clash with the natives, "With God's help we burned them, we knocked them on the head, and counting big and little, we killed 661." In this single profitable incident Khabarov's men also captured 243 women and girls and 237 horses.

Initially, the newcomers had been welcomed by the indigenous tribes, but the Cossacks' plunder of the inhabitants' furs, grain, livestock, and women quickly altered the reception. Ataman Khabarov and his band, returning the favours of the thirteenth- and fourteenth-century Tatar raiders of Russia, tortured and killed hostages without compunction in Genghis Khan's home territory in the seventeenth century. Two hundred years later descendants of the victims would still tell their offspring tales of the Russian roasting of Dahur and Ducher children.

Even by the generous standards of Muscovy the barbarity was excessive. Tsar Alexei I called Khabarov back to Moscow for discipline. When Khabarov demonstrated the riches he was winning for the crown, however, the tsar relented. Instead of fining, or flaying, or exiling Khabarov, Alexei I promoted and lionized him, and sent him back to Siberia (though not to the Amur) as a superintendent. The Amur tribes appealed for protection to the Manchus and Chinese, whose cannon- and musket-equipped army eventually routed the relatively few Russians—and culminated in the Nerchinsk Treaty.

I question Tanya about the anomaly. Wouldn't the Erofei Pavlovichites like a new, less tainted name?

The complaint is not unfamiliar; Tanya knows the proper answer. Those stories about Khabarov's cruelty were a lot of slander, it seems. There may have been a few incidents between the white men and the tribes. But the white men didn't mean to murder. They just wanted gold and furs. It's true that Khabarov was summoned back to Moscow for investigation, but he was cleared by a jury. There is a statue to him in the centre of Khabarovsk today, and there wouldn't be a statue if he had been a bad person.

So Erofei Pavlovich it is. And Erofei Pavlovich it remains.

As we leave the town, the landscape quickly turns desolate. Pine trees whose shallow roots have lost their grip in the permafrost sprawl aslant more upright trunks in what the Russians call a "drunken forest". Tracked vehicles that go through here and tear off the moss cover leave a scar that will not heal for a century in this inhospitable climate.

How deep down one has to go in this locale to reach the real permafrost—I don't know. Since this is a region of "discontinuous" permafrost, it could be close to the surface in one spot and totally absent in another. You can't tell just by looking.

Sometimes it's hard to tell even by digging, as the hapless Abbé Chappe d'Auteroche discovered in the eighteenth century. In Tobol'sk this omnivorous scientific observer determined to investigate the reports that "during the whole summer, the ground at Tobolsky was never thawed more than a few feet below the surface".

He set himself no easy task. In his own words:

I frequently endeavoured to get the ground digged: the difficulty of having labourers in a country where all are slaves, made me resolve to apply to the governor: he was so kind as to give me up a dozen criminals, who were chained and condemned to labour at the public works, like the galley-slaves with us. I had the ground digged by them ten feet deep and found it not frozen. I had intended going still deeper, but having increased the pay of these unfortunate wretches, which was only one half-penny English a day, they sent for large quantities of brandy, made the guard drunk, and escaped while they were asleep. I found their irons in the woods a few days after, but the governor not having thought proper to trust me with any more criminals, I was obliged to give up the work. They had already gone four feet deeper without finding the earth frozen. I then thrust my sword in it (for I travelled in a lay habit) up to the hilt with the utmost ease.

The indefatigable Chappe drew both scientific and reportorial conclusions from this fiasco:

It is very certain therefore, that the ground at Tobolsky thaws entirely, since the thaw prevails as far as sixteen feet deep. This experiment altered the idea I had conceived of the climate of Tobolsky, and made me still more cautious of advancing facts from tradition and hearsay; for I am persuaded the numerous mistakes found in the writings of some travellers, proceed rather from their credulity, than from their want of truth.

If only Chappe could have travelled a few hundred miles north of where we are now, he would have found all the permafrost he could have wished for. The permafrost centre of the world is at Yakutsk, capital of the Yakut Autonomous Republic. In Yakutsk windows are triple-paned instead of double-paned. The standard footwear half the year round consists of the reindeer mukluks that stay warm and soft in temperatures that crack leather or rubber. Children up to the age of ten are excused from school when the thermometer reaches −49 degrees F, though their older brothers and sisters are expected to persevere with their studies regardless.

In Yakutsk, buildings are of necessity elevated on pylons, so as not to melt the foundation earth into a bog. And the Obruchev Institute of Permafrost Studies conducts what is probably the world's leading scientific exploration of this mysterious "sphinx of the North", with its "pingoes" and "alases" and other arcane phenomena known only to an elite brotherhood of Siberians, Alaskans and Canadians.

Outside the institute stands a splendid specimen of a mammoth, preserved perfectly over the millennia in Yakutia's 300–400-metre-thick permafrost. He is stuffed rather than live, but if some ambitious Soviet biologists are successful, he and his kind will yet give birth to a revived posterity. Some deep-frozen cells are to be implanted in a female elephant, in hopes of somehow reproducing a mammoth calf.

When I visited the Obruchev Institute on one of the more successful Foreign Ministry trips one March, spring was just bringing a heat wave of −4 degrees F. Everyone celebrated the balmy weather by going cross-country skiing. Workmen hacking clear blue ice out of the Lena River near the heavy duty truck road across the river's twelve-mile width were coatless and gloveless. The "human habitation fog" that enshrouds the city at colder temperatures had lifted, and sunlight formed haloes of tiny frost crystals in the air. Snow squeaked underfoot. The reindeer races and wrestling matches would soon begin; the falcons and eagles would return; the snowdrops, bluebells, and marguerites would come with a rush.

Surely nowhere in the world is spring more longed for than in Russia. The spring sun, still pale, softens the edge of once rigid ice. The trickles commence, then grow to rivulets. Icicles accelerate their percussive drip onto crusted snow. Birches shrug off their softer snow, then give voice to a new kind of creak, less brittle, more supple. Squirrels stretch their limbs, emerge from their holes, and leave tufts of fur behind on jagged twigs. The freshets swell to streams; the streams grow eddies and whirlpools. The earth emits its first faint pungence. Steaming manure, radiating a moat of bare earth, distances itself from the surrounding whiteness. Trucks and sledges no longer dare to cross the rivers, and drizzles turn thoroughfares into morasses of mud. Only the most compulsive fisherman or loner still cradles his vodka in his pocket and goes to drop one last line through the ice. The faithful bless their Easter cakes and coloured eggs and pray and chant till dawn. The nightingale sings ecstatically. The river roars into life, gouging icebergs out of its frozen roof and hurling them downstream in a cacophony.

It was no wonder that a process so fraught with hope and resurrection became the metaphor for all of post-Stalin Russia. Ilya Ehrenburg, the Jewish writer who somehow survived Stalin's purges, christened the new period "the thaw" in a novel of that title, and the thaw it became. After the seemingly permanent winter of Stalin the country was ready for spring.

Within weeks of the March 1953 funeral the broadest amnesty in Soviet history, before or since, was declared. Within three months the last agent of Stalin's purges, the Georgian Lavrenti Beria, was arrested; when his trial and execution were announced in December, he was publicly charged with having killed innocent security, law-enforcement and judicial officials. Pensions were granted to the families of these purge victims, and their children were again admitted to universities.

All this was predictable; in the sudden vacuum after the tyrant's death the new leadership felt compelled to solicit the support of the crucial security forces, armed forces, and Leningrad and other Communist Party cadres that had been especially ravaged by Stalin's terror. What was unpredictable, however, was the zeal for more sweeping "de-Stalinization" on the part of Nikita Sergeevich Khrushchev, the protégé of Stalin who had himself risen to prominence on the corpses of the purged.

Khrushchev revealed himself on 24 February 1956; shortly before midnight he summoned the Soviet Twentieth Party Congress delegates (but none of the foreign Communist guests) to hear an unscheduled four-hour speech about Stalin's atrocities.

Stalin began abusing his power, Khrushchev told his deathly-still audience, when he started terrorizing the Communist Party in 1934–35 (but not, by implication, when he terrorized peasants and engineers in the earlier collectivization and "saboteurs" trials). In 1937–38 Stalin had 70 per cent of his own party's Central Committee shot and killed, sometimes after confessions extracted by torture. He had 1,108 out of 1,966 delegates to the previous Party Congress arrested on false charges of counter-revolutionary crimes. He had the commander of the Ukraine Military District, the Commander-in-Chief in the Far East, the Commander-in-Chief Land Forces, and two other leading commanders executed in the same period, on the eve of war. He wilfully ignored reports of a German attack—then when the attack came panicked and simply vanished for several days. In mid-war he had entire Soviet nationalities deported to Kazakhstan and Siberia. Even after the war, in 1948, Stalin had the top Leningrad party leadership killed on trumped-up charges. And there was every indication that Stalin was preparing a new purge on the basis of the imaginary "doctors' plot" when he finally died. In his years in office Stalin had supervised the terror. He had surrounded himself with a "personality cult". He had made himself into a "godhead".

Khrushchev had not known the extent of the "deformations" at the time. Shocked by their discovery, the new government would now make restitution. (Subsequently, if a story that circulated in Moscow is to be believed, Khrushchev obliquely admitted a greater familiarity with the purges. "Where were you when all these things were going on?" someone allegedly asked Khrushchev in an anonymous note as he lectured a party gathering on Stalin's crimes. Khrushchev read the challenge aloud, demanded to know who had written it—and when a pregnant silence ensued, remarked, "Well, that's where I was.")

Only later would some of the details seep out about Russia's twentieth-century Ivan the Terrible. In between the amusements of playing billiards, criticizing new gramophone records with such notations as "good" or "rubbish" on their jackets, and hand-tending his roses, apple trees, hothouse lemon trees and watermelons, Stalin enjoyed humiliating his entourage. He would slip tomatoes or cakes onto chairs Politburo members were to sit on. On a whim he would order Khrushchev, "Nikita, dance for us!" and Nikita would oblige. He would telephone his ministers at 2 or 3 a.m., then not listen to them and hang up in mid-conversation. He several times called Molotov, Voroshilov, and Mikoyan English spies, not as any prelude to their purge, apparently, but just to give them a scare.

Among other casual cruelties Stalin threw a lighted cigarette in his wife's face (on the night she committed suicide). One New Year's Eve, for lack of candles, he rolled pieces of paper on to the fingers of his personal secretary and burned them, and the secretary simply had to endure the pain. Neither he nor anyone else invited to a banquet by Stalin ever knew whether he would finish the night with a drunken ride home or a sobering ride to Lubyanka.

Stalin personally signed hundreds of death warrant lists, with multiple names on each list. He sometimes sanctioned sentences in advance of trials; he sometimes gave orders about what specific tortures should be visited on prisoners. Quotas were assigned for arrests, as for every other undertaking, and had to be met; if the original victim didn't happen to be at home when the time came to apprehend him, then the next-door neighbour would be arrested so the numbers came out right. As the investigators boasted, "Give us a man, and we'll make a case."

Besides the categories mentioned in Khrushchev's secret speech, those liquidated by Stalin included leading economists, trade union officials, judges, writers, artists, the country's most eminent Tibetan scholar, one of its most eminent linguists, historians, musicians, aerodynamics and rocket specialists, 221 out of the nation's top 295 military commanders, 85 Yugoslav, 120 Italian, and hundreds of other foreign Communist leaders who made fatal pilgrimages to Moscow. At the war's end three million returning Soviet prisoners of war were also dispatched to forced-labour camps; most expired there.

In all, a staggering twenty million Soviet citizens are estimated by sober Western and Soviet analysts to have died at Stalin's hand—a figure not surpassed by the Soviet military and civilian dead in World War II. Soviet demographic pyramids still show huge gaps from the purge and war, not only in the unborn, but also in the 12 per cent deficit of men to women that will finally be evened out only in the twenty-first century.

As for the nationalities that Stalin uprooted, their fate was best indicated in the account of a militia colonel who participated in the roundup of a Caucasus Chechen village and later described the operation to a friend of Roy Medvedev's:

It was towards the end of July in 1943. . . . Each of us was to put on the uniform of an army commander and take up position with a military unit close to the village that had been assigned to him. We were to get on sociable terms with the inhabitants of the village, ingratiating ourselves through gifts and flattery, and were to develop close relations with influential people in the village, showing conspicuous respect for their customs and way of life; in short to become their friends. . . . During the half year that we officers were to live among them, we were expected to study them closely and secretly to compile precise lists of all inhabitants, family by family, including the names of absent villagers and their present whereabouts. We were also to make preparations for a gala celebration of the next Red Army Day, to which all the men of the village would be invited. We would tell them that on this day the great services of the Chechen people in the struggle against the German aggressors would receive recognition, awards and certificates would be presented from the High Command, etc. . . . They all gathered for the ceremony and elected a presidum which included the totally unsuspecting chairmen of the local soviets, NKVD district heads, and all the local elite; an honorary presidium was also elected, composed of the entire Politburo with Comrade Stalin at the head. . . . The speeches began, then the presentations and statements by those who had fought in the war. . . .

At exactly 10.00 a.m. I rose and took a sealed envelope from the side-pocket of my tunic. I broke the wax seals, announced that I was about to read out a decree of the Presidium of the Supreme Soviet of the USSR, and then did so. My stunned audience was told that the Chechens and Ingush had betrayed the Motherland during the war, had given aid to the fascists, etc., and were therefore subject to deportation.

"It is useless to resist or attempt to escape," I added, "the club building is surrounded . . ."

Indescribable pandemonium broke out in the hall. People hurled themselves at the doors and windows but came up against machine guns. During the ceremonies the army unit had surrounded the building with a solid cordon several rows deep. And imagine, there was no real resistance, even though all those present were wearing their ceremonial dress, daggers and all. We disarmed them with no difficulty and led them in small groups under reinforced guard to the nearest railway station in Dzaudzhikau . . . where special trains with freight cars fitted out for the transport of prisoners were already waiting.

And while we were dealing with the men, others rounded up the unprotected women and children and took them away. They too were loaded on to freight cars but at a different station, and sent, one trainload after another, to Kazakhstan.

Even without all the subsequent details, Khrushchev's Twentieth Party Congress speech was a bombshell. Although the speech was secret, rumours about it spread immediately. Pro-Stalin riots with anti-Russian overtones broke out in Tbilisi in March. Polish workers' riots with anti-Russian overtones erupted in Poznan in June. Hungarians turned out their Kremlin-appointed government and withdrew from the Warsaw Pact in October—and were restored to the Soviet fold only by the bloody intervention of the Red Army. At just about the same time, the Poles resurrected Wladyslaw Gomulka, a national Communist imprisoned in the Stalinist era, installed him as First Secretary, and somehow persuaded the Soviet Union not to invade Poland while still accepting dismissal of the Russian Marshal K. R. Rokossovsky as Polish Defence Minister.

Khrushchev managed to survive all the explosions and, after a pause, to proceed further with de-Stalinization.

In distancing himself from the terror Khrushchev was steering the Kremlin power struggle to his own advantage, isolating Stalin's closest henchmen (like the "English spies" Molotov and Voroshilov). Yet he was also exhibiting what seemed to be genuine revulsion at his mentor's lethal caprices. Khrushchev's style and policies differed radically from his predecessor's.

He and his colleagues dismantled the worst of Stalin's apparatus of both systematic and arbitrary terror. They released nearly ten million political prisoners. They abolished some two-thirds of the labour camps. They improved living and working conditions in the camps that remained—so much so that veteran convicts still remember it as a golden age of real wages for work and semi-decent food that prisoners could actually buy. They dissolved the dread MVD (political police, formerly NKVD) Special Board that had tried and sentenced political prisoners outside the court system in the purges. They again subordinated the secret police to the party and formally reduced it to an investigative arm, whose findings would henceforth have to be turned over to prosecutors and courts. They set up a special commission to investigate the suspicious circumstances of the 1934 assassination of Politburo member and potential rival to Stalin, S. M. Kirov—the incident that triggered the purges. (Later the political climate would change, and the commission would never issue its report.) The succession leaders also parcelled out the MVD economic empire to various normal industrial ministries. They posthumously "rehabilitated" the purged generals and, ironically, some of the most unreconstructed purged Stalinists before the rehabilitations petered out. They vowed to restore "Leninist norms" to party life.

In the new atmosphere law also made something of a comeback. The criminal code was reformed, and criminal law reverted from federal to republican competence. Stalin's "Terror Decree" of 1934—depriving those accused of terrorism of the rights of counsel, appeal, and even presence at their own trials—was annulled. So was the 1937 amendment under which persons accused of "diversion" and "wrecking" received indictments only twenty-four hours before their non-appealable trials. The 1940 decree that made it a crime to leave a job was repealed. The notorious Stalinist guilt by analogy (under which acts that were not specifically illegal could still be punished under laws against vaguely "similar" offences) was retracted. Punishments were generally made less draconian (except for economic crimes, which could now invoke the death penalty).

To be sure, Khrushchev maintained a peasant suspicion of law and clever lawyers—clever in the old pejorative sense of sly Western inventions as contrasted to Russian simplicity. Khrushchev introduced a catchall "parasites" decree under which "persons avoiding socially useful labour and leading an antisocial, parasitic life" could be sentenced. And under Khrushchev, as under Brezhnev, the general trend toward greater "socialist legality" and predictability would be interrupted not only to silence political and religious dissidents, but also to mount periodic anti-crime campaigns with scant regard for due process—and, often enough, to show favouritism to party officials even in non-political cases.

For most Soviet citizens these exceptions to legality in the new era didn't matter, however. What was important was that people who avoided the political taboos could finally count on not having their private lives meddled in excessively by party and state. They could even throw an occasional deserved insult at the neighbourhood informer, and not go to gaol for it.

More broadly, the populist Khrushchev replaced Stalin's grim thesis of intensified class conflict in Soviet society with the notion of the "state of the entire people" and the "party of the entire people". He insisted that the leaders could rely on the new socialist society. "The young must be trusted," he announced. The scientific and technical specialists must be treated with "consideration" and respect. The masses must be "drawn in" to the policy implementing process. "The lordly and bureaucratic attitude toward the village . . . among some Communists" must stop, and peasants must at last be given a decent income. "Trust of the masses" became a favourite refrain.

In line with his convictions, this son of a peasant and grandson of an illiterate serf enlisted a wider circle of elite experts, party members and ordinary citizens to participate in affairs of state.

In contrast to the secretive, exclusivist policymaking of Stalin, Khrushchev invited non-party specialists to join in Central Committee meetings. The Communist Party and government opened a dialogue with mathematicians, cyberneticists, scientists, sociologists, resuscitated criminologists, undogmatic economists, and students of American management and optimization models. Expert advice was solicited, not only on the new law code, but also on nuclear power plants, fertilizer, educational reform, science. Some party proposals are said to have been substantially altered in the process.

Khrushchev also broke with Stalin's custom by publishing proceedings of Central Committee plenums. He increased the frequency of presidium sessions, congresses, and other party meetings. He greatly expanded party membership from seven million in 1956 to eleven million in 1964, with a special emphasis on recruiting Communists from the under-represented non-elite workers and the almost totally unrepresented non-elite peasants. He sextupled enrolment in the party's adult political education programme from six million (with 85 per cent party members) in 1957/58 to 36 million (with 78 per cent non-party members) in 1964.

To "draw in" more people to political activity Khrushchev offered an alliance to grass-roots party members against middle-level party and government bureaucrats. He prodded the primary party organizations, the *aktivs*, to criticize poor performance by the middle (though not the top) ranks. He shrank officials' discretionary power. He proposed rotation in office for all party executives (except the "indispensable" ones). He tried, unsuccessfully, to reduce the size of the party secretariat. He recruited fresh technocrats for many of the inner 2–4 per cent of paid party posts and promoted these outsiders above the apparatchiks trained in party schools. At the same time he reduced the traditional organizational and ideological emphasis of the party professionals and devoted more than half of their training hours to economics.

Khrushchev tried to bring government ministries down to earth as well. He decamped the Agriculture Ministry from the capital to the Mikhailovskoe Model State Farm 100 kilometres outside of Moscow virtually overnight, and he required all of the ministry's officials to put in non-deskwork time digging potatoes or shovelling manure. (1,700 out of the 2,200 staff members resigned.)

Relentlessly, Khrushchev pressed ahead with his changes. He established production committees in factories to give workers a share in economic management, and he urged factory union committees to protect workers against any illegal dismissals, overtime work, or improper pay. He expanded the competence of local soviets (the councils or legislatures, which before had generally only approved whatever the Communist Party proposed), and he prodded both trade unions and soviets to "wrangle really hard" with officials and protest any misuse of power.

("The socialist state apparatus serves the people and is accountable to them," declared the 1961 party programme. "It is the duty of the Soviet people . . . not to tolerate any abuses but to fight them.")

In society at large Khrushchev pursued an energetic policy of egalitarianism in incomes and education. He continued to pay premium salaries to managers in heavy industry—up to ten times the wages of a skilled worker. But he gave collective farmers assured cash incomes (even as he expropriated their private plots and livestock). He weighted university admission heavily against the intelligentsia and quasi-intelligentsia and required work experience for all entrants. He made vocational apprenticeship compulsory for all secondary school pupils one day a week.

At the same time Khrushchev increasingly gave the rising urban middle class the one-family apartments, bathtubs, refrigerators, leather shoes and bridal gowns they had formerly been denied. Involuntarily, through lack of suppression, he also gave young people black-market tapered trousers and "rock on the ribs"—rock 'n roll recorded from Western radio on used vertebrae X-rays.

Beyond Khrushchev's various specific measures lay a grand scheme. He envisioned a fundamental shift of public functions away from government to the management of mass organizations and volunteers. He gave the responsibilities of the state sports organization to the non-governmental Union of Sports Unions and Organizations. He expected other "social organizations" eventually to take over "management of theatres and concert halls, clubs, libraries, and other state-controlled cultural establishments". He ordered the writers to police themselves instead of depending on the party to maintain their ideological purity.

He also handed over much local justice to lay "comrades' courts"—and much rehabilitation of criminals to citizens' collectiveness. He wanted the trade unions to handle most prosecutions of criminals. He granted "social assemblies" in villages, factories, and apartment houses the right to exile "parasites" to remote parts of the country for up to five years. He invented the *druzhina* of citizens' police auxiliaries who not infrequently enforced socialist morality by such means as beating up Easter celebrants.

All Khrushchev's innovations presupposed an eventual withering away of the state but hardly of the party, the real wielder of governing power. On the contrary, Khrushchev's ardour for social transformation presumed even more direct intervention by the party and especially by its First Secretary in administrative and economic routine. His wildly unrealistic production goals required constant goading—and led to wholesale dismissals of party functionaries when they went unfulfilled. Khrushchev himself traversed the length and breadth of the country meddling compulsively, scolding peasants for leaving land fallow, nagging everyone to grow corn, firing directors of institutes he took a dislike to.

In artistic and intellectual fields, Khrushchev's activist personal style first broadened, then narrowed, the limits of the permissible. In literature, the post-Stalin thaw was at its most dramatic. Habitual social relations could change only sluggishly, however energetic Khrushchev's assault on them. Painting could break out of its socialist realist clichés only after artists had the time to acquaint themselves with a more modern vocabulary. But the quicksilver word of individual authors and thinkers could react to the new climate immediately.

A few cautious experiments, a poem here, a novella there, and the freeze of fear and suspicion was broken. Young poets and writers discovered that they were no longer alone, that they could trust one another. As "sons" of the Stalinists they even found allies against their "fathers" in the few "grandfathers" (like Pasternak) who had survived and still retained the old intellectual integrity. In a tropism that Dostoevsky and Chekhov would have understood, they sought not "freedom," but "truth". Their truth was *istina*, pure, unadulterated, uncompromising, painful truth, as opposed to *pravda*, the directed, adulterated, and often enough betrayed "truth" shaped and moulded to some further socialist end.

The inhalers of spring became delirious. Hypocrisy and evasions and informing on others were relics of the past. Anything was possible—or almost anything, other than Pasternak's *Dr Zhivago*.

In the early 1960s some 14,000 people filled Moscow's Luzhniki Stadium to hear Andrei Voznesensky, Bella Akhmadulina, and Boris Slutsky recite their odes to the new era. Students crowded around the new Mayakovsky statue almost every evening for impromptu poetry readings and free-wheeling debates about art and literature. A hundred thousand subscribers ordered Voznesensky's *The Triangular Pear* two months before its publication, and all the other hopefuls had to be turned away. Readers snapped up new editions of Akhmatova and Tsvetaeva (though still not the Jew Mandelstam) at black market prices. Foreign tourists brought their forbidden culture and chewing gum to Moscow and Leningrad. An American touring company brought *Porgy and Bess* to the Moscow stage. Two lively new theatres opened in the capital, the Sovremennik and the Taganka. The censors became, for them, almost wantonly tolerant.

Chansonnier Bulat Okudzhava sang songs of the Odessa underworld and bittersweet fancies of his own, and wrote, incredibly, not about the heroism of war, but about its fear and chaos and dehumanization. Vasily Aksyonov, the son of Eugenia Ginzburg, put slang into print. Voznesensky described the little, forgotten man and even some real down-and-outs. Evgeni Evtushenko dared to speak aloud of the massacre of Jews—Jews, not Ukrainians—at Babi Yar in 1941. Shostakovich, a "grandfather" by generation if not by the political recantations he made, dared to give "Babi Yar" a symphonic setting. And Evtushenko further badgered "The Heirs of Stalin" with a poem of that title (in *Pravda* of all places) warning men at the tyrant's grave to

> double,
> and triple the soldiers on guard by this slab,
> lest Stalin rise again
> and, with Stalin,
>
> the past.

Literature of guilt on the German model enjoyed a vogue—and exposed the guilt of the passive observer as well as the guilt of the false accuser. One young novelist wrote sympathetically about the Vlasov soldiers who bought their release from German POW camps by taking up arms against the Soviet Union. And after his aide read the manuscript aloud to him during a Black Sea vacation Khrushchev personally approved publication of a simply written novella, *One Day in the Life of Ivan Denisovich*, by an obscure provincial teacher named Alexander Solzhenitsyn.

Evtushenko and other Young Turks, having won election to the board of the Moscow branch of the Writers' Union, opened an investigation of Stalinist repressions of authors with the intent of rehabilitating and avenging their dead colleagues. As a first step they got one of the most unsavoury denouncers expelled from the Union.

Historians joined in the liberalizing trend by campaigning in specialized journals for more accurate history—even about such taboo subjects as Lenin's non-revolutionary, reformist rivals. Educator and Marxist Roy Medvedev, whose own father had been liquidated, began collecting first-person accounts by other purge victims to write his remarkable study of the terror, *Let History Judge.* The journal *Questions of History of the CPSU* (Communist Party of the Soviet Union) concluded that Stalin really had known of the suffering of the peasants in the first stage of collectivization— and declared that socialist democracy "should" include freedom, equality, government by the people, freedom of the press, and the right to form associations and unions.

Still, the spirited poets and historians were the exception. Moscow's literary coruscations were echoed in Tbilisi, but hardly anywhere else in the country, not even in Leningrad. And even in the capital, in that segment of the population that should have been the most enthusiastic about the new literary trends—the students—widespread indifference to the new writers coexisted with adulation of them. Those 14,000 might cheer and stamp their favourites at Luzhniki Stadium, but at the same time some foreign exchange students at Moscow State University could find few fans of the new authors among their classmates.

The more characteristic reaction to the intellectual ferment, perhaps, was disorientation. Khrushchev's attack on Stalin, along with the welter of new ideas, upset millions who had worshipped Stalin as the infallible leader and war hero, millions who were comfortable only with a clear orthodoxy of right and wrong. Even many honest intellectuals whose relatives or friends had been purge victims found it impossible to believe that Stalin could have killed not only the thousands that Khrushchev spoke about, but millions. Even those imprisoned in the purge, some of them, while cursing their gaolers had written paeans to Stalin. And the urban peasant proletariat that had itself escaped collectivization was even less prepared to think ill of its idol.

The steppe is harsh. Suffering is man's lot, with or without Stalin. The generous Russian credulity and tolerance of pain, the centuries-long habit of ignoring the alien stratosphere of political cause and effect, the decades-long defence mechanism of not exploring one's own thinking, lest something treasonous be unearthed—all these were shattered by Khrushchev.

The boy Vladimir Bukovsky, who in 1953 thought the world could not possibly go on without Stalin, resolved his trauma by becoming an implacable dissident. Numerous older people resolved their turmoil by converting it into anger at the presumptuous and undisciplined youths who disparaged the sacrifices of their elders. They wrote scathing remarks in comment books at the rare shows of semi-modern art that now appeared. They approved when snowploughs driven by plainclothesmen broke up one Mayakovsky Statue poetry reading.

And one Soviet army lieutenant observed by American author Patricia Blake demonstrated that the new generation too could look back with nostalgia. He marched up on stage in the discussion period after a public poetry reading and announced that he hadn't understood anything that evening except that the verse was depressing. Why didn't the poets write about happy, uplifting subjects like the Red Army, the lieutenant demanded—and added that if they didn't, the army would make them.

Within a few years the intellectual anarchy got too much even for the irrepressible Khrushchev. Some of the old guard, to demonstrate how far out of hand things had gotten, arranged for the First Secretary to visit an exhibition of non-representational art at Moscow Manege Hall in December 1962. The ploy worked to perfection. The outraged Khrushchev expostulated, "Such pictures were not painted by the hand of man but by the tail of a donkey!" Or worse, by "pederasts". The intellectual spring was over.

Three months later Khrushchev issued a marathon 15,000-word damnation of formalism and abstractionism as anti-Communist. He deplored and denied the generation gap. He ordered a return to such ideals as the Internationale in music and the Civil War tearjerker "How My Mother Saw Me Off to the War" in poetry. The hacks came back with a vengeance. Evtushenko and his pals were dropped from the Moscow board of the Union of Writers. The infamous denouncer whom they had drummed out of the union was readmitted. The public poetry readings were stopped. The resurgent Stalinist critics roundly condemned "rotten, overpraised, unrealistic, smelly writings". Tikhon Khrennikov, who as Composers' Union First Secretary had led the 1948 assault on Shostakovich's "formalism and decadence", kept a firm grip on musicians and dug in such a secure position for himself that he would still be around as Union First Secretary to lead the attack on Shostakovich's posthumous memoirs when they appeared in the West in 1979. An anti-Semitic wave was loosed that within a decade would drive even many assimilated Jews to emigration or attempted emigration.

In retrospect it is clear that Khrushchev's sometimes brilliant and sometimes disastrous improvisations added up to no philosophy of liberalization. His burst of temper at the Manege and his impatience with experimental literature outside the narrow confines of de-Stalinization amply illustrated this. So did his war on private plots, and his closing of half the churches that still remained open. Khrushchev was striving to mould not autonomous citizens' rights, but responsive citizens' duties. He was instigating "initiative", but he never intended that initiative be carried to the forbidden extreme of "spontaneity". Determination of political, economic, social and cultural goals—and even means—remained the prerogative of the top party leadership. But the masses' previous passive obedience to command was now to be transformed into voluntary and even enthusiastic compliance.

Marxism-Leninism handily explained the landowners' exploitation of peasants and the tsarist-Cossack-foreign capitalist exploitation of miners that Khrushchev had seen as a young man. He was a gut believer in the entire Soviet ideology—the last full believer ever to rule the USSR, perhaps—and he took the congruence of leaders' and citizens' interests to be self-evident. Shop-floor initiatives would not undermine but would fulfil the party's directives. Elite consultations—at least with the technical specialists, if not with the egghead lawyers and aesthetes—would not dilute the party's decision-making authority but establish it on a sound scientific basis. Together the party, the intellectual elites and the masses would develop the economy, shape the new Soviet man who would be equally competent at desk, shop and plough—and attain that future communist stage of society that Marx and Lenin had dreamed of. This happy state could arrive, Khrushchev projected, by the 1980s.

At times his criterion for full communism sounded to Western ears suspiciously like an accumulation equal to US per capita production, but this would be an oversimplification of Khrushchev's ideal of effecting a real social transformation. In his grand twenty-year party programme unveiled in 1961 (and never rescinded thereafter, though it has faded into invisibility) Khrushchev envisaged for his country not only adequate housing, the world's shortest workday and workweek, and more meat and butter than America had, but also free rent, utilities, public transport, factory and school lunches, and no income tax—and as good food, education and culture in the countryside as in the city.

In the end Khrushchev fell not because of his failure to produce this communist cornucopia, nor yet because of his humiliations in Cuba and China, not because of his erratic mix of belligerence and peaceful coexistence in relations with the West, nor even because of the ideological erosion that resulted from his permissive years. The biggest grudge Khrushchev's Presidium and Central Committee peers bore him, it seemed, centred on the chaos he created within the party. His 1960–61 (non-lethal) purge of most regional first secretaries and his massive 1962 reorganization that split the party apparat into separate agricultural and industrial hierarchies was the last straw after his wilful improvisation and his constant anti-bureaucratic incitement, his "subjectivism" and his "hare-brained schemes". In mid-October 1964, the vacationing Khrushchev was abruptly summoned back to Moscow from his Black Sea dacha and unanimously dismissed as First Secretary by the Central Committee.

After Stalin died Muscovites had wept uncontrollably. So painful was the loss, so eerie the unknown future without their father, teacher and friend, that even the daily bickering and sometime pitched battles among neighbours had ceased for a time. Silent, gloomy masses had poured into downtown Moscow for the three days that the uniformed, bemedalled body was on display. They had surged back and forth aimlessly, elementally, irrationally, trampling hundreds, perhaps thousands, of their own number to death.

Might some similar display follow the deposition of Khrushchev, the leader who had actively courted the masses? Khrushchev's usurpers worried about the possibility, according to Roy and Zhores Medvedev, and put the KGB (as the secret police was by then called) on alert. To their surprise, they needn't have bothered. No one demonstrated. No one wept. No one cared.

In my time in Moscow, more than a decade later, I never heard a good word about Khrushchev either. Puzzled by the vacuum I tried time and again to elicit some appreciation of this extraordinary individual. I never succeeded. The humanist intellectuals, who had him to thank for stripping away the dogma of the past, despised this grinning kopeck-pincher and blamed him for his latter-day crackdown on the arts. The professional politicians, who had him to thank for being able to sleep in their beds without straining to hear which floor the middle-of-the-night elevator would stop at, found him a troublemaker. The collective farmers, who had him to thank for staunching Stalin's bleeding of the peasantry, considered him a robber of their private plots. The urban proletariat, which scorned his proffered alliance against the entrenched bureaucracy, thought him a buffoon who consorted with milkmaids and melon growers. The man in the street, who had him to thank for restoring trust and decency among friends, detested this "corn hick".

Khrushchev's iconoclasm, it seemed, mocked the Siberian boys who had died with Stalin's name on their lips at Stalingrad. It offended the millions who mourned Stalin's death, those hundreds who were themselves trodden to death in that final posthumous bloodletting at Stalin's funeral. It belittled a giant whose medieval personal tyranny had itself demonstrated the greatness of the unruly Russians. Stalin was no contemptible, rational, folksy leader who had tamed them or could have tamed them. Stalin was the audacious, cunning autocrat whose very arbitrariness radiated his irresistible power and proved his fitness to be absolute master of the steppe. Stalin was the one who demonstrated the holy Russian capacity for innocent suffering, for trusting, enduring, forgiving, surviving.

Khrushchev stole more than their tsar from the Russians when he toppled Stalin from his pedestal. He stole from them as well their myth of themselves. Many would never forgive him for wrenching away their figleaf of ignorance and awe.

Leonid Ilyich Brezhnev brought a restoration—not of Stalinism, but of normality as defined by the party apparatus. He continued to hold frequent meetings of the Politburo, as the inner-circle Presidium was again called; and he gave more weight to these collective deliberations than his predecessor had. He imitated neither the personal autocracy of Stalin nor the hyperactive "subjectivism" of Khrushchev. Despite all the titles and laurels visited on him during his almost two decades in office—General Secretary,

Chairman of the Presidium of the Supreme Soviet, Marshal of the Soviet Union, Commander-in-Chief of the armed forces, Chairman of the Defence Council, the only person appearing ahead of alphabetical order in Politburo listings, seven-time Order of Lenin winner, three-time Hero of the Soviet Union, two-time Order of the October Revolution winner, Hero of Socialist Labour, Karl Marx Gold Medalist, International Lenin Prize winner, Arms of Honour holder (complete with personal sabre), Order of Victory winner, statue model in his own lifetime, compulsively quoted author, and, in the ultimate accolade, *vozhd* ("leader" or "Fuehrer", a name previously bestowed on Stalin alone)—Brezhnev remained only *primus inter pares*. He presided over a consensus.

Brezhnev's deference to his colleagues was at its most conspicuous in his cadre appointments. Here he followed a policy so stable as to approach stagnation. He did not install his own patronage tail in the party-secretary hierarchy as Khrushchev and Stalin before him had done. The one exception came in Brezhnev's old stamping ground of the Ukraine, where a challenge to Brezhnev's and the consensus's ascendancy apparently did arise, and was contained. Even this reshuffle was limited, though. And in the rest of the country First Party Secretaries were not fired; they just died or grew ill and retired—and when they did, their deputies routinely moved up to replace them. Seats on the Central Committee, the roughly 300-man recruitment pool for the Politburo, became virtually ex officio positions for the most important regional party secretaries and other party and state officials.

The Politburo's average age, which started at an already respectable sixty-one at Brezhnev's accession in 1964, simply crept up with every passing year (at a rate slowed by the occasional death and replacement of the deceased by someone marginally younger), to reach seventy by 1980. And the broader leadership—the Politburo candidates, the Central Committee Secretariat, the Central Committee itself, the top fifty military commanders, and the Presidium of the Council of Ministers (the government)—averaged only about five years younger. The Soviet gerontocracy came to surpass even the Japanese gerontocracy in seniority.

In many respects the new oligarchy continued Khrushchev's opening to the functional elites and the masses. Khrushchev's enthusiasm for social engineering and a diminished state may have been abandoned, and his erratic policy swings and idiosyncratic crusades against fallow ground, private plots and surviving churches may have been dropped. But Khrushchev's mobilization of specialists and the public into political and social participation was regularized. In some areas this meant expanding consultations with party outsiders. In other areas it meant pulling back from Khrushchev's excesses. In all cases, to avoid any misunderstanding, it meant reaffirming the authority of the middle-level as well as the top party hierarchy.

Khrushchev's assertion that the party and masses were not in conflict was preserved; Stalin's paranoid view of a society constantly at war with itself was not to be revived. But Khrushchev's populist appeal to low-level public opinion in the party and in the masses over the heads of the bureaucrats was abandoned. Calls to reinvigorate local party *aktivs* in relation to the party's inner 3 per cent of professional apparatchiks were supplanted by calls for "iron discipline" among party members. Khrushchev was rapped over the knuckles for substituting the "state of the entire people" for the "dictatorship of the proletariat" and the "party of the entire people" for the party's "political leadership of the working class, of the working people, and of the entire Soviet people".

"Trust in cadres" quickly replaced "trust of the masses" as the catchphrase, and "self-regulation" of officials without any grass-roots "anarchy, disorder, and lack of discipline" became the norm. Criticisms of individual malfeasance continued to appear in newspapers periodically, but they lost the whistleblowing character of Khrushchev's time and took on more the appearance of reprimands sanctioned from above as a disciplinary (or scapegoat) action.

Khrushchev's previewed withering away of the state as non-political social self-regulation increased, was replaced by an expectation of "strengthening of the state" and of political organization of society, as well as of the party's (rather than society's) ideological moulding of the new Soviet man. Adult education of non-party members in party schools duly dropped from 78 per cent to 38 per cent of the total, from 36 million to 20 million persons, in the decade following Khrushchev's fall.

The new leaders also chided Khrushchev for having turned legislative organs (soviets) into executive organs (usurping the party's role). They took back from the soviets and again gave to middle-level party committees the tasks of local industrial expediting and co-ordinating, and the incorporation of local housing, roads, and other infrastructure into the decreed Five-Year Plans. After 1971 they granted party *aktivs* in ministries, research institutes and some other institutions the formal authority to supervise state officials in their organizations. They had the Central Committee apparat resume a strong supervisory role in ministry headquarters. And when they finally wrote the new constitution in 1977 to replace the Stalin constitution, they stressed the party's leading role in all spheres of Soviet life.

In intra-party affairs the Brezhnev team also rebuked Khrushchev for downplaying political considerations in party recruitment through overemphasis on the extent of Soviet homogeneity and consensus. Shortly after Khrushchev's overthrow, they purged most of the "diploma specialists" recruited directly into party posts from 1962 to 1964, and they restored the prerequisite of party training for acceptance into and promotion within the party apparatus. They brought Central Committee meetings back into the family by once again excluding outside experts. They ceased publishing

Central Committee plenum transcripts and printed even the main Central Committee speeches only rarely.

The Central Committee itself, having fulfilled its purpose in confirming Khrushchev's ejection, was again clearly subordinated to the Politburo, with Central Committee plenums gathering no more than four or five days a year—well down from Khrushchev's apogee of thirty-one plenum days from 1956 to 1958. By virtue of their guaranteed tenure, however, the ex officio Central Committee members who were regional party secretaries did accrue more power relative to the centre in the governance of their own regions— and in the kingmaking that would decide Brezhnev's succession.

Along with the party's bureaucratic authority, the new oligarchy also resurrected Stalin's reputation to some extent. After all, it hardly shored up legitimacy to have both of the top leaders of the past four decades (and five-sixths of the Soviet Union's entire history) turned into pariahs. Khrushchev became the unperson. It was Stalin who was half revived.

Despite an initial scare (one that helped propel Sakharov into open dissent), full Stalinism was never reinstated. The planned mass production of Stalin portraits and busts for the ninetieth anniversary of the dictator's birth in 1969 was called off at the last minute (possibly because of China's kiss of death in championing Stalin); the "special science session" in honour of Stalin at the Institute of Marxism-Leninism was cancelled; and the publication of a new volume of Stalin's collected works never materialized.

Nonetheless, the reproaches of Stalin's "violations of Leninist principles of collective leadership" and "permitting unjustified mass repressions against prominent state, political and military leaders of the Soviet Union" were now offset by praises for Stalin's struggle to build socialism in one country, and his leadership of Russian victory over the fascists. His industrialization and collectivization were good; so was the expanded recovery of Russia's western borderlands. He was again hailed as an "outstanding theoretician" and organizer.

A plaque soon appeared over the grave abutting the Kremlin wall to which Stalin's mummy had been relegated when Khrushchev banished it from Lenin's mausoleum in 1961. Then in 1970 a bust replaced the plaque. In the same year a hagiographic novel about Stalin (which drew rave reviews from the Chinese) went too far and was censured by a Central Committee resolution. But by 1976 the new edition of the official party history dropped even the evasive phrase "personality cult" in discussing Stalin. In 1978 red carnations and yellow tulips appeared on the grave on the anniversary of Stalin's death.

On the centennial of Iosip Vissarionovich Dzhugashvili's birth, in 1979— even if he didn't rate any public ceremony or get back into the school curriculum for anything more than a perfunctory nod—Stalin did make a comeback on to the pages of the 15-million circulation Soviet Desk

Calendar. There he was elevated from his usual identification as only "a leading figure" of the party to "one of the distinguished figures of the CPSU, the Soviet state and the international Communist and workers' movement".

Rehabilitations of purge victims, which had already decelerated sharply in Khrushchev's last years, slowed even more, and finally ground to a halt under Brezhnev. And those victims who made it into the *Soviet Historical Encyclopedia* after 1967 were listed vaguely and impersonally as having been "illegally repressed". Stalin's name was no longer tarred with the repression.

The Brezhnev leadership's partial restoration of Stalin's reputation and full restoration of routine party supremacy did not mean a concomitant retreat from Khrushchev's experiment in consulting non-party scientists and scholars. The politicians might again exclude the outsiders from Central Committee meetings; they might personally despise these "romantics", as a few intellectuals with high access have testified. But the politicians needed help in order to run their increasingly complex economy and society. Given the importance of economic growth in justifying their rule, they needed to harness technology to the workbench. They needed to know what might motivate workers to boost sinking productivity. They needed to have a more nuanced concept of a West that now was interlocked partner as well as adversary.

Some evidence suggests that the Brezhnev Politburo in fact delegated more judgments to specialists than did Khrushchev. In the natural sciences they finally dropped Lysenkoism altogether, and initially they downplayed dogma in favour of empirical policy- and production-orientated research.

For a while, in fact, computers and mathematical analysis seemed the wave of the future. Stress on a "scientific" approach and "realism" in decision-making—in explicit contrast to Khrushchev's "wishful thinking, boasting and empty words" but also in implicit contrast to the old Communist normative meaning of "scientific"—led to a conscious effort to pay more attention to specialists' analyses before making political decisions.

In the soft sciences, "concrete sociological investigation" by new scientific commissions attached to party committees and bureaus enjoyed a vogue. Opinion polls were undertaken as a practical administrative tool. The infant criminology continued to develop (though investigations had to stop well short of prison gates). Various educational schools contended in public. Institutes for the study of international affairs in general and the West in particular were set up, with USA and Canada Institute Director Georgy Arbatov ranking as a candidate member of the Central Committee and an occasional interlocutor of Brezhnev. A certain amount of managerial discretion was introduced with the economic liberalization and increased pay incentives of 1965.

Law—which Stalin had branded a remnant of the capitalist past and which Khrushchev had hoped to supplant by a system of amateur justice—actually regained prestige under Brezhnev. It settled in as something that will disappear under the full communism of the future, when social morality has been internalized—but something that is essential in the interim.

The major work of rewriting the criminal code had already been carried out under Khrushchev, but now jurists—whose number began to expand—were called on to complete the family law reform that Khrushchev had blocked. In 1965, in addition, the worst kangaroo-court aspects of Khrushchev's anti-parasite laws were revoked: Khrushchev's "social assemblies" were dissolved; parasite cases were turned over to the courts in Moscow and Leningrad and to local soviets elsewhere; exile (apart from revocation of permits to live in Moscow or Leningrad) was rescinded as a community penalty.

In the early Brezhnev years legal scholars again raised some of the civil rights reform issues of the late fifties. Public proposals for the new constitution, justice and, most astoundingly, party reform, included: separation of powers; the right of appeal of official injustice to the courts; the presumption of innocence in trials; an adversary relationship between defence counsel and prosecution; a requirement that guilt be established in ways other than confession; impartiality of judges and their insulation from "public passion" as well as from political and personal "meddling"; objective press reporting of trials, with opinions of investigators and prosecutors labelled as such; election and recall of all officials by popular vote; freedom of press, association, and travel and other political rights for all; abolition of prearranged lists of speakers and rehearsed speeches and encouragement of spontaneous debate from the floor at party meetings; abandonment of "democratic centralism" and its compulsory obedience by all members once a decision has been made at the top; and broadening of policy discussions beyond the narrow circle of responsible officials to include "constructive" public criticism from "loyal opposition".

Most of these proposals were stillborn, however, and a new feature of arbitrary justice was even added in 1966, as cases of "hooliganism" were removed from court jurisdiction to the administrative authority of local police. With this change police could impose fines or, after a perfunctory hearing with a judge, put "hooligans" in the cooler for what soon became a standard fifteen days. In the same year, too, vaguely defined rumour-mongering was made a crime. And in the next year the Supreme Court Vice-President who had supported renewal of procedural reform was replaced by a man who had been Deputy Chairman of the KGB.

In the end, the right of court appeal against official injustice and some upgrading of individual rights in civil and, especially, criminal trials were incorporated into the constitution that emerged in 1977. But other civil rights were not. In its overall philosophy the constitution explicitly sub-ordinates individual rights and interests to the "interests of the state" and "interests of society". And in the long perspective—despite the increased autonomy of jurists in the post-Stalin era—Soviet lawyers today probably still have less professional leeway than their predecessors in tsarist times, some Western legal scholars suggest.

Political science fared less well than law under Brezhnev. Under Khrush-chev it had won a tentative autonomy from legal studies. And as late as January 1965, *Pravda* was still advocating that it be a separate discipline. As the new leaders settled in, however, such talk faded away. The Soviet Association of Political Science retained its formal existence and even hosted a world convention of political scientists in Moscow in the late seventies. Ultimately, however, the prospect of academic investigation of the shadowy process of decision-making within official organs proved too sensitive. Political science was again subsumed under law departments at the universities.

The discipline of history exhibited acute ambivalence. The permitted scope of inquiry certainly contracted from the early sixties—when *Pravda* could propose exploring Stalin's crimes back to the October Revolution, and nearly two thousand historians, "scientific workers", university instruc-tors and activists could exchange differing views on the Stalinist period. Under Brezhnev, the history of the party, of Stalin, and of the Great Patriotic War again became subject to fixed ideological interpretations, and revisionists who ignored the canons were duly pilloried. Official warnings were issued against disorientating youth by teaching history through mistakes and shortcomings rather than through great deeds. The manipulated truth of *pravda* won out over the pure truth of *istina*.

Nonetheless, pre-Bolshevik history could be treated with greater objec-tivity under Brezhnev than previously. And some historians even found ways to make professionally sound neutral studies of revolutionary topics, at least in specialized publications. Western historians sensed a new feeling of group identity and pride among Soviet historians, not excluding conserva-tive historians. Some Western historians and political scientists, after combing the literature, concluded that under Brezhnev history as a whole was freer and wider ranging than it had been under Khrushchev, both in documentation and argumentation.

The field of sociology at first flourished under Brezhnev, then languished. Typically, literary critic and amateur sociologist Alexander Yanov, who in 1966 could get an exposé of conditions on Smolensk collective farms published because of support going up all the way to the Politburo, found such patronage evaporated in later years. Nine-tenths of the articles he submitted for publication were rejected, and the disillusioned Yanov eventually emigrated to the West. His professional colleagues at the adventurous new Institute for Concrete Sociology were not exiled, but were dispersed to more inert Soviet institutions by the early seventies. Public opinion polls were restricted both in the range of questions and in their subsequent publication. Sociology was reduced to little more than an adjunct of industrial stimulation.

In the arts, the hopes of the humanist intellectuals for the Brezhnev era were dashed within a year. In the first few months after Khrushchev was deposed in October 1964 there was a conspicuous absence of political arrests. Half of the two hundred imprisoned Baptists were released early, and the press published criticism of the severity with which Khrushchev's anti-religious drive had been conducted. Crimean Tatar delegations were actually received and listened to by high-ranking officials in Moscow.

In June of 1965 arrests were resumed, however, with seven dissenters gaoled in Leningrad, then twenty-five in the Ukraine in August and September. An official campaign to vilify Solzhenitsyn in public and private lectures was launched. Writers Andrei Sinyavsky and Yury Daniel were arrested for publishing pseudonymous satires (*Moscow Speaking* and *The Trial Begins*) in the West. This time some of the writers' friends broke the virtual taboo on appeals abroad, and also organized the first annual Constitution Day demonstration (demanding adherence to the rights guaranteed in the USSR's basic law) in Pushkin Square on 5 December.

With these developments some of the disillusioned intelligentsia irrevocably forsook faith in reform to embrace martyrdom instead. The coordinated dissident movement was born.

As late as 1974, the long blocked first postwar edition of Mandelstam could be printed (though in a minuscule edition of 15,000, with most of it earmarked for foreign sales). An *istina* novel about the 1930s military purge could still get the Lenin Prize (possibly because the protagonists were established officers and not just Ivan Denisoviches). And light fiction—whodunits, sci fi or romances—could get a bit livelier. But the overall climate was best defined by the benchmark Sinyavsky–Daniel conviction in 1966, on the innovative juridical grounds that authors are guilty of the negative views expressed by their fictional characters. In vain did the defendant novelists counter that Raskolnikov's ruminations, say, hardly represented Dostoevsky's convictions. Such reasoning elicited only a triumphant court rebuke of the novelists for their delusions of grandeur in equating themselves with the classic masters.

Under Khrushchev there had been one prominent writer's trial: Leningrad poet Joseph Brodsky was sentenced to hard labour in the Arctic for "parasitism", then released early (a year after Khrushchev's fall) and expelled from the Soviet Union after a wave of international indignation. And of course individual poets and novelists got gaoled or harassed in the provinces in the Khrushchev era without anyone's hearing of their existence

in Moscow and Leningrad. But the dissident movement hadn't yet co-
alesced; the truth-seekers were still hoping to carry out their soul-searching
openly and legally. Now, with the chain reaction to the Sinyavsky–Daniel
conviction, the circulation of transcripts of the trial, the appearance of the
periodic *Chronicle of Current Events*, and the new linkage between dissidents and Western reporters, dissent became institutionalized in its own
quirky way. A network of mathematicians, scientists, writers, Crimean
Tatars, Jews, Ukrainians, and lay Orthodox believers began to engage in
what Reddaway calls "open alliance-building".

The party and KGB apparat sought to suppress this institution, while still
(in the run-up period to détente) avoiding arrests of those figures who were
well enough known to trigger wide publicity in the West. In 1966 elastic new
legislation outlawing circulation of "fabrications known to be false and
which defame the Soviet state and social system" was passed. In the same
year, 170 Baptists were arrested, or rearrested. In the first two months of
1967 the young *Chronicle* editors and fifty other dissidents in Moscow,
Leningrad, and the Ukraine were arrested.

When these moves gleaned more publicity in the West than Soviet
authorities had anticipated, there was another lull. But in 1968 a rein-
vigorated and strengthened KGB moved again. Intimidation was applied
successfully to perhaps 750 out of the thousand signers of various petitions.
The remainder were deprived of Communist Party membership, fired from
jobs, or (in two prominent cases) committed to psychiatric hospitals.
Solzhenitsyn was expelled, senior *Chronicle* editor Pyotr Yakir gaoled and
broken.

For non-dissident literature the *coup de grâce* was the Etkind affair. In
1968 Efim Etkind, Professor of Philology for twenty years at the Herzen
Pedagogical Institute in Leningrad and senior member of the Leningrad
Writers' Union, was unexpectedly called in to his publishers about an
anthology of Russian verse translations he had edited. The collection had
already made it through the several months and twelve layers of censorship,
and had emerged with flying colours. It had already been printed, and the
25,000 copies had been distributed to outlets. At this point some anonymous
person "high up" suddenly sniffed out one offensive sentence. In a foreword
Etkind explained how it came about in the 1940s and early 1950s—for the
first time in Russian history—that so many eminent poets became professional translators. In this period, he indicated in his one infamous sentence,
"Russian poets were deprived of the possibility of expressing themselves to
the full in original writing and spoke to the reader in the language of Goethe,
Orbeliani, Shakespeare and Hugo." That was all. Khrushchev had indicated
as much about Stalinist times himself.

In 1968, however, it was no longer the era of Khrushchev. It was the era of
the resurgent Nikolai Vasilievich Lesyuchevsky, General Director of the

"Soviet Writer" publishing house that was bringing out the anthology. Lesyuchevsky travelled from Moscow to Leningrad personally to set in motion the *prorabotka* (public criticism session, with emphasis on humiliation of the target). Lesyuchevsky was a master at this kind of thing. He had won his way to the top of the most prestigious Soviet publishing organization by long years of service in denouncing whatever writers the party wished denounced. On his word poet Boris Kornilov was arrested and shot in 1938. On his testimony poet Nikolai Zabolotsky was arrested and spent eight years in the camps before being rehabilitated and dying a natural death.

Now Lesyuchevsky accused Etkind of "slandering the Soviet system . . . driving a wedge between the Party and the writers". He demanded, "When were poets not allowed to talk freely? When were they forced into translation? Your sentence is an ignorant lie . . . a lying piece of slander."

A month later the obligatory *prorabotka* took place, and set the tone for literature in the Brezhnev era. The rector of Etkind's institute accused Etkind of prevaricating when he wrote that the *dolnik*—a form of verse with feet of two and three syllables—first appeared in Russian verse in Mayakovsky's translations from Heine; on the contrary, shouted the rector, "Mayakovsky's poetry was born of the Revolution!" Besides, Etkind had criminally overestimated Pasternak's squalid, sordid and unfaithful translations of Shakespeare.

The head of the Department of Soviet Literature was less harsh; in her opinion Etkind's sentence was only a "blunder" that crept in because Etkind had his nose buried in books and was too "apolitical". The kindly head of the Department of French Language agreed, and thought the error could be traced to Etkind's "neglecting the raising of his ideological and theoretical level".

The big gun of the *prorabotka*, however, the head of the institute's Department of Party History, was not content to treat Etkind's rash sentence as simple negligence. Etkind, he charged, had "stung to the quick every Soviet man or woman", had dispensed with Marxist analysis, had failed "to see the upsurge of the whole of Soviet literature caused by the Great October Revolution". Etkind had ignored Lenin's teaching "that to play at democracy is to clear the way for counter-revolution". Etkind had dared to say that " 'In the Soviet Union the level of translation rose even higher than in Germany, the land of translation.' Could Etkind be talking about the Germany of the thirties? The Germany where progressive poets were consigned to the flames? The Germany of Hitlerite fascism?"

Obviously, Etkind's pro-fascist sentence could not survive. In the end the 25,000 copies of the anthology were withdrawn for revision; the new version expunged a handful of the poets altogether and downgraded Pasternak from a "great lyric poet" of "absolutely individual lyricism" to an "important lyric poet" of "lyricism". Dozens of editors lost their jobs over the affair. Some four hundred people, by Etkind's count, spent an average two and a half hours each dealing with Etkind's one heretical sentence.

The Etkind affair inaugurated a general crackdown in literature. Its severity can be gauged by one more victim—philologist Viktor Levin. Levin, who had managed to keep his party membership despite his opposition to the theories of Stalin's favoured linguist, N. Y. Marr, back in the thirties and forties, was suddenly expelled from the party in the early seventies—precisely because of his opposition to Marr thirty years before. The astounded Levin pointed out that the Communist Party and Stalin himself had reversed positions in 1949 and adopted Levin's views of linguistics. And this impertinence prompted the party officials who were expelling him to chastise him for setting himself against the party and "boasting" that he had been right in advance of the party.

In 1969/70, for reasons that can only be guessed at—the Sino-Soviet border clashes, perhaps, or the frightening Czechoslovak attempt to evolve "socialism with a human face" and dissolve "democratic centralism" into grassroots spontaneity, or the need to reinforce ideological moorings of the Soviet intelligentsia against the onslaught of Western ideas that would accompany impending détente—the chill spread from literature and the arts to the hard sciences as well. The Central Committee opened an anti-revisionist campaign in research institutes, placing more stringent political demands on scientists at every stage, controlling university admission and the granting of higher degrees, and imposing periodic ideological "shrinkages". Party organizations were given the "right of control" at educational and scientific institutions, and exercised this right by giving a more severe ideological screening to scientific research proposals. The term "scientific decision-making" retreated perceptibly from an empirical emphasis toward the old political meaning that the party best knows what is historically scientific.

Within the instrumental range set by the party, a certain meritocracy, autonomy and prestige of scientists did persist. But non-dissident scientists I came into contact with were much more impressed by the constraints than by the franchises of the late Brezhnev era.

As for mass political and social participation, this persisted in its more manageable forms and faded in its more random forms in the Brezhnev era. Four thousand amendments were offered in public discussions about the draft constitution, with more than two and a half million letters on the topic coming to *Izvestia* alone. The *druzhina* vigilantes continued to expand, though without Khrushchev's fanfare. Ombudsman-like People's Control organizations were set up, on the pattern of older organizations with differing names, with representatives elected biennially in workplaces and apartment houses; their numbers grew to 10 million activists. Comrades' courts were revived in 1977. Some 4 million deputies and non-deputies became involved in the work of local soviets.

Party membership also kept on growing, though not quite as fast as it had under Khrushchev. The 11 million Communists of Khrushchev's later years reached 17 million, or 9.3 per cent of the adult population, at the end of the Brezhnev era—with an impressively high 44 per cent of all males over thirty with a secondary education, and an impressively low 2.5 per cent of all women, holding party cards.

Subbotniks, "voluntary" Saturdays of spring gardening in parks or chipping away embedded ice from streets, continued to be popular with the leadership, if not always with the volunteers. Electoral campaigns—not to promote alternative candidates, of course, but to mobilize citizens to go to the polls to cast their yes votes—became more and more of a bargaining process. Those canvassers who arranged to have precinct roads paved or apartment elevators fixed would get a 99.9 per cent turnout to their credit. Those aspiring Communist activists who failed to provide such services would get a less favourable turnout, and blight their own chances of party advancement. Cities prudently began allocating repair teams to intensive pre-election duty and even distributing some scarce goods to voters at polling stations on election day.

In the new climate, real grass-roots initiatives sometimes worked and sometimes didn't. One Russian friend, appalled by what he saw in a Moscow mental hospital—no rugs on the floor to soften falls, doors falling off the mixed men's and women's toilet—wrote a letter of complaint to the Soviet Ministry of Health. A few months later he received a reply saying that the Moscow City Council had closed that section of the hospital pending repairs. Another Russian friend, horrified by what she saw in old people's homes— overcrowding, low-paid nurses charged with up to a hundred patients each, no dignity whatsoever for the elderly—wrote a letter of complaint to a Moscow newspaper. A reporter was assigned to the story—and the result was a complete whitewash.

Still, this friend looked on the bright side. She was grateful that she didn't suffer any reprisals—the more usual fate of do-gooders, it seems.

One less fortunate do-gooder, a non-drinking, blue-ribbon Archangel'sk tractor driver named Popov—learned the hard way not to cross what an ex-lawyer from the Soviet Justice Ministry calls the kleptocracy. According to émigré lawyer Konstantin Simis, Comrade Popov began writing complaints to the Communist Party and newspapers about the "company store" run by a local VIP, the wife of the director of the district timber-processing mill. "A portion of each worker's monthly salary was paid by the workers to the factory director and his subordinates in return for goods retailed to them at excessively high prices," Simis wrote in the autumn 1977 issue of *Survey*;

"customers at the cafeteria received little more than half of what they had paid for, and any inhabitant of the settlement would work for free in the [mill director] Romanovs' orchard or garden whenever requested to do so." Since the Romanov outlet was the only store and cafeteria in the settlement, the system was effective.

Unfortunately for tractor driver Popov, the Romanovs had adequately insured their operation with the "required protection to the powers-that-be of the district (in the form of building materials, provisions, vodka, and money)". When Popov, despite warnings, continued filing his complaints, he was fired (in violation of the Labour Code) and expelled from party membership "for discrediting honest Party members". He was then convicted for slander and spent five months in gaol before his daughter in Moscow got the sentence repealed by the Supreme Court of the Russian republic. When Popov returned to Archangel'sk, he was threatened with a new suit until he finally took the hint, sold his house, and left the district. Popov's case, lawyer Simis asserts, is "absolutely typical" of a widespread system of bribes, kickbacks and virtually total immunity of ranking local Communist Party members from prosecution.

However discouraging the record on whistleblowing, 600,000 Soviet citizens a year have enough hope in the process to write their comments, gripes or suggestions to one newspaper alone, *Komsomolskaya Pravda*—so many that the paper has to assign 10 "creative workers" and 20 to 25 "technical workers" to process its mail. Similarly, some 1,500 readers write to *Izvestia* each day; and local newspapers pride themselves on following up on correspondence. And when *Journalist* ran an article explaining away some UFO sighting as atmospheric chemical phenomena, it was inundated with letters from readers claiming UFO sightings of their own.

In policies affecting consumers, the Brezhnev team continued making more meat and washing machines and television sets available. It even made that one brave, abortive, attempt (1970–75) to expand light-industry faster than heavy-industry production. More successfully, it removed many restrictions on private housebuilding and for the first time consigned part of the growing automobile output to general private sales.

More broadly, the Brezhnev leadership eased the pressures on ordinary citizens by abandoning Khrushchev's drive for social transformation. It eliminated Khrushchev's frantic campaigns to fulfil outrageously unrealistic production targets. After 1969, though, it did bear down on workers and peasants to increase productivity. And as it retreated from the 1965 flirtation with economic reform it also retreated from differential pay incentives back toward more moral exhortation. This move may have appealed to lower grade workers, but at the same time it limited workers' capacity for consumer accumulation.

In the countryside, however much it prodded peasants to increase their collective productivity, the regime still gave farmers back their private plots and livestock. It effectively completed rural electrification, which reached 74 per cent of farms in 1965, 98 per cent in 1971. It also, for the first time, gave pensions and internal passports to collective farmers. The rising peasant pay, along with lower-paid workers' wage increases, continued moving income distribution in an egalitarian direction, from a 4.4 top-to-bottom decile ratio in 1956 to 3.7 in 1964, and 3.2 in 1970.

In education, some Brezhnev measures were less egalitarian, some more egalitarian than Khrushchev's. The campaign for universal secondary education made the biggest difference in the countryside schools and thus promoted greater equality. At the age extremes, however, kindergarten and university enrolment again moved in a somewhat more elitist direction, the former because of the expansion in urban child facilities, the latter because of a return to more exacting academic standards for higher education. Brezhnev's relaxation of Khrushchev's strictures on string-pulling in university admissions also favoured children of the existing elite once more.

The question for the Brezhnev succession must then be: do the changes of the last decades add up to a channelling of the Soviet Communist Party's old totalitarian thrust into a new pragmatic one? Or, in the formulation of some Western scholars, is an embryonic pluralism developing in Russia?

Western behaviourists who in the 1960s and early 1970s challenged the lingering but senescent "totalitarian" school of analysis suggested as much. Or at least they carried their cynicism about how much free will really is involved in Western democracies' politics over to their view of Soviet politics. There is little difference between political systems, was the implication; men are always buffeted by forces they can't control and barely understand, and we are deceiving ourselves if we think Western pluralists are freer than Soviet subjects.

As Western political scientists explored this new thesis, some shifted the emphasis in a more positive direction for the Soviet Union. Political processes are broadly comparable in all systems, they contended; it won't do just to dismiss Soviet democratic forms as sham. Rational proto-interest groups have indeed developed in the USSR, and their articulation of middle-level demands constitutes one of the most striking phenomena of the new Soviet Union. The "attentive public" does have some political influence in Western democracies; the "attentive public" does have some political influence in the Soviet Union.

Innovative researchers took to counting the frequency of key words in speeches to establish a spectrum of Kremlin soft- and hardliners, or to extrapolating variations in hospital beds into differential local initiatives.

Some of the resulting analysis was mechanistic and sterile; some of it was ingenious and stimulating. Some of it only confirmed common sense; some of it yielded startling new insights.

Among the most eloquent of the new scholars is Jerry Hough of Duke University, who asserts that while the Soviet system remains authoritarian, Brezhnev represented no counter-revolution of the clerks. The Brezhnev administration, he contends, was conservative only in style, not in substance; public political participation continued to expand even after Khrushchev's fall (and could even compare favourably with apathetic rates of direct community participation in Western democracies); Brezhnev was actually more lenient on dissent than Khrushchev, but wider publicity in the West made him seem more repressive; educated elites had more say in the Brezhnev than in the Khrushchev era, both in policy and in their own areas of research, and they exchanged a wider range of opinions; the Brezhnev party leadership limited its directing role of intellectuals essentially to mediation of conflicts between specialized interests; functional elites can still espouse incremental change (and thus manifest "institutional pluralism") as long as they do so in specialized journals, without throwing down a challenge to the leading role of the party.

The reasoning behind this tentative liberalizing interpretation is simple: a complex modern economy and society require a certain amount of depoliticization, tolerance, autonomy, flexibility, and feedback if they are not to become dysfunctional. Predictability impels legality. A sophisticated economy necessitates creative innovation. Industrial efficiency mandates non-ideological pragmatism. An overloaded centralized system can be relieved only by some devolution of authority. These needs show the direction the Soviet Union is moving in—the direction of incipient pluralism.

Sceptics scoff at such theorizing. They inquire rhetorically if the technocrats or the mobilized masses of the Third Reich, for all their political "participation", liberalized Hitler's regime or lent any pluralism to it. They do not equate instrumental feedback with a real sharing of the political definition of alternatives and choice of priorities. They do not equate rational decision-making, or the delegation of decisions that the party deems routine to a specialist meritocracy, or even greater openness in expert advice to the oligarchs, with any dilution of the party's monopoly on power. They do not see any political impact by the public in the ritual displays of policy approval, or even in the various safety valves for citizens' complaints. They do not believe that tabulations of local administrative politics yield much insight into national politics. They mistrust the new empiricists' disregard of historical context, their discounting of behind-the-scenes coercion and "kleptocracy". They cannot discern any real flesh and blood in the revisionists' few concrete examples of Soviet interviewees' assurances that such-and-such finance professor's "advice" is "often accepted" by budgetary commissions, or that a certain criminologist spends as much time on local soviet legal affairs as on academic work.

The doubters regard the statistics of millions of opportunistic party members, or thousands of proposals for constitutional amendments that in the end produce no substantive change, as poor guides to the quality of political participation—especially when the "drawing in" of ever more people into public affairs is accompanied by pointed calls for increased "discipline" and subordination of individual to state interests. Instead, they gauge the quality of participation by the Soviet urban public's political apathy and cynicism, the peasants' studied apoliticism, and party steering of the various institutions for popular participation.

Thus, for example, the ombudsman People's Control Committees are charged less with the official task of ferreting out official malfeasance than with their unofficial task of insuring that party directives are fulfilled by restaurant, factory or ministry. The committees are themselves headed by ranking party officials who time and again bury reports—such as the one about high atmospheric radioactivity in Moscow—that would reflect adversely on the party's own stewardship. The 9.5 million elected shop-floor activists often enough don't even know that they have been named as "scouts", according to one émigré who was chief of the satirical section of a local Moscow newspaper and drew much of his material from People's Control lore. And the hapless scouts who do acknowledge their selection, if they report such deficiencies as delays in unloading consignments of raw materials (as in one Moscow ventilation works) can end up doing the unloading themselves. In such cases "participation" amounts to little more than unpaid labour.

Much the same point could be made about the ineffectiveness of the legislative soviets. Membership in them confers considerable prestige and access to better consumer goods (as well as free busrides, at least in Georgia). But with their high turnover, amateur status and brief life (a few days a year for the Supreme Soviet, six times a year at most for local soviets) they do not have the organizational muscle to develop much of their formal legislative or representational role; they are totally dependent on the staff work and tutelage of the party. Not surprisingly, there is no record of any soviet ever having turned down a government proposal.

As for the dissidents, the revisionists among American political scientists are no doubt justified in recoiling from the common Western magnification of dissent in the Soviet Union. But they overcompensate in arguing that Brezhnev was tough only with those who sought to go outside the system and was more permissive than Khrushchev with those intellectual innovators who did conform politically. When this borderline is defined unilaterally and arbitrarily by the party, such a distinction evades rather than answers any question of increased latitude or legality.

In fact, one could profitably turn the distinction around and say that the crime of the human-rights dissidents is precisely that they claim to be a legitimate part of the political process within the system. They are not politically apathetic, as they are supposed to be. They agitate for observance of existing Soviet law, or possibly for evolution in present practices. Solzhenitsyn, the would-be emigrants, and a few others have, of course, propounded solutions outside the present political system. But the democratic mainstream of dissent—including Sakharov, the Helsinki Agreement monitoring committees, the mental hospital fact-finders, and the handicapped founders of a would-be Action Group for the Defence of the Rights of Invalids who suffer arrest and assault by KGB heavies—has been directing its efforts at working within the present Soviet system. And this presumption to pluralism is precisely what the oligarchy will not tolerate. The fact that no known defendant charged with political or religious offence has ever been acquitted by a Soviet court shows just how resistant the Soviet polity remains to any fermentation of diversity, or establishment of impartial justice.

To some extent the Western scholarly feuding over "participation" in the Soviet Union is probably semantic—a dispute about whether the glass is half empty or half full. Power is not an all-or-nothing affair. Virtually everyone agrees there is some upward pressure even on absolute rulers. Virtually everyone agrees that local Communist Party apparatchiks perform a vital economic and social function of co-ordinating and reconciling conflicting demands, and that they persuade far more than they coerce. But these axioms hardly answer the questions of where initiative originates, when it gets stifled, and what "pluralism", embryonic or full, really means.

In the murky world of Soviet politics—where outsiders have few clues as to who decides what, how or when—no one but the future principals will be able to prove a thesis of greater post-Brezhnev pluralism right or wrong. For now the best that onlookers can manage is a very crude perception of who those principals might be. And for now, just about the only clearly discernible facts are that it will probably take the usual five years after Brezhnev's departure for the real leader to emerge from the succession skirmishing—and that the new leader will probably jump an entire generation.

This much demography decrees. The septuagenarian party chief Brezhnev and his septuagenarian ideological and organizational chiefs, his retirement-age incumbents of the sixty top party and government posts, and his entrenched retirement-age administrators of virtually every Soviet ministry and institute and union—these are all being replaced in the succession's wholesale reshuffle by men in their fifties. (This phenomenon is less marked in the less ossified military than in other professions, and less true in all hierarchies in youthful Siberia. But these are the conspicuous exceptions to the general gerontocracy.)

Brezhnev and his cohort began their careers as the precocious beneficiaries of the Great Purge and the Great Patriotic War. Brezhnev became head of propaganda in the Ukraine's most important industrial *oblast'* at age thirty-two, Red Army political commissar and lieutenant-colonel at thirty-four. His fellow Politburo member and quarter-century-long Foreign Minister, Andrei Gromyko, became head of the ministry's North American desk at thirty, ambassador to the United States at thirty-four. Politburo member and Premier Alexei Kosygin became Commissar of Light Industry at thirty-five. Politburo member and Defence Minister Dmitri Ustinov became People's Commissar of Armaments at thirty-three. They all shot up fast—and they held their high posts over four decades. Their ten-years younger colleagues were cannon fodder in the war or, if they survived, never got a chance to finish a higher education in the urgency of postwar reconstruction. Their twenty-years younger colleagues were frozen on their entire careers—until now—in third-echelon positions. So sharp is the cleft that political scientist Seweryn Bialer considers the post-Brezhnev succession to be only the second major turnover of leaders in Soviet history. The first was in the 1930s, when the original revolutionaries were killed off.

The life history of the new fifty-year-olds is very different from that of Brezhnev's generation. They were born in the late twenties or early thirties. They did not suffer Stalin's collectivization and starvation and purge as adults. They were too young to have fought in World War II or (probably) to have experienced the horror of war directly. They were shocked by the revelations of Stalin's murders. They have seen the Soviet Union grow from postwar devastation to a mighty superpower in their own lifetime, and they bask in this glory.

They are far better educated than the Brezhnev generation (in technical and engineering subjects, of course, not in humanist studies); they are the first Soviet generation whose education was uninterrupted. They are more sophisticated than their predecessors. They are probably much more confident. Yet they have had far less responsibility in their jobs than Brezhnev's colleagues had at a comparable age. And they have had no more exposure to foreign countries than the Brezhnev team had when it acceded to power.

The new leaders, in fact, are probably even more provincial than the Brezhnev neophytes were, given their very lack of promotion and the stagnation that left them in their same regional sinecures during Brezhnev's almost two decades in power. They have grown accustomed to the Brezhnev consensus style—and they have risen as high as they have today by becoming bland and faceless parts of that consensus during the party's long meticulous sifting out of nonconformists. They may now be especially eager to assert themselves, however, after having had their own advancement blocked for so long.

Brezhnev's successors don't want or expect any return to Stalinist terror, but they take the closed Soviet system for granted in all of its present aspects, from central planning to ideological rectitude to KGB disciplining of wrong-thinkers. They share the self-centredness of any huge continental country and its lack of curiosity about the outside world. They presumably accept the rational necessity of nuclear détente for survival, but they may not have the same trauma about nuclear war as a Brezhnev who personally lived through total conventional war in the Ukraine. Moreover, they presumably doubt the advantages of a sub-nuclear détente that has neither prevented full normalization of Chinese–American relations nor enabled the USSR to catch up with Western industrial technology.

Significantly, they have at their disposal—for the first time for any in-coming Kremlin leadership—a military machine that not only includes the world's mightiest army but also challenges the American superpower in everything from intercontinental nuclear missiles to Eurostrategic weapons to air and sea projection in Southwest Asia.

During the half decade of the post-Brezhnev transition there will certainly be strong pressures for tougher foreign and domestic policies, at first within the incremental consensus that Brezhnev built, later even outside it.

To be sure, a kind of liberalism of confusion could conceivably arise in a period of no clear master and no clear ideological line. But during the succession manoeuvring (if post-Stalin history is any guide) it is much more likely that candidates for the top leadership post will be imprinted by the pressures for discipline. It is difficult for politicians to outbid rivals with moderation—and Brezhnev's skilful avoidance of grooming any heir apparent ensures a flurry of fast, competitive bidding in his wake.

The party secretary of Leningrad, who is always (rather unjustly) sus-pected of Westward inclinations, could hardly afford to be accused of liberalism. Nor could the party secretary of the Ukraine, with its nationalist yearnings, afford to seem revisionist. Nor could the Moscow party secre-tary—who has seen his security cadres humiliated by dissidents who go right on meeting Western journalists and issuing treasonous slanders—be eager to open the floodgates of spontaneous complaint. Nor would the military, with its hard-line predilections and its customary gain in political influence during power struggles, be a likely advocate of sharing out power among a wider elite.

Furthermore, with no recent terror of Stalinist dimensions from which to recoil, there is nothing like the incentive for "de-Stalinization" that Khrushchev seized on in his fifties' defence of the party security and mili-tary hierarchy against further capricious liquidation. Indeed, today Stalin is less a whipping boy for liberalizers than a potential rallying symbol for centralizers and Russia-firsters. The Georgian Stalin might seem an illogical personification of Russite chauvinism, but personification he is, for millions. He is without peer in drawing the admiration of Slavs in the political and cultural hierarchies for his defiance of the West. Time has blurred the neo-Stalinists' sixties' embarrassment through the Chinese embrace of their idol (and through Stalin's daughter's defection to the West). Stalin, however dormant he may have been in the last years of the Brezhnev era, could in the eighties again acquire the aura that pragmatism and consensus have never won.

Stalin, after all, led the Soviet Union to an impossible victory over the enemy. Stalin was not wishy-washy. Stalin had no dissidents. Stalin didn't give the favoured intelligentsia trips abroad. Stalin didn't let the privileged Jews up and leave Russia. Stalin didn't let East European ingrates eat and dress and play better than Russians. Stalin didn't permit any anarchy of bewildering choices.

This common image of Stalin has no counterweight. The decentralizers or pragmatists (or whatever would-be liberalizers might choose to call themselves) no more have a symbol than they have an agreed non-pejorative name. Their abstract call for greater efficiency may sound sensible to a few bureaucrats and managers. But it inspires neither aspirants for the world's most powerful job nor their presumed proletarian constituents.

Might the pragmatists have more appeal, though, in the calmer period after the succession struggle is decided? Might the old rigidities then seem irrelevant to the sociological complexities and economic sophistication and better education of the late eighties? Or, to put it another way, might a good tsar emerge out of the manoeuvrings whose hand would finally be free to perform the twentieth-century equivalent of liberating the serfs?

Different observers answer these crucial questions differently.

Hough is the most hopeful in expecting that the new leaders in the Kremlin will want the stability and predictability of more "institutional pluralism". In Moscow Roy Medvedev too would like to see a move towards what he terms socialist democracy—though he sounds less convinced of the probability of such a development with every passing year. From his vantage point in the West, publicist Yanov also hopes for (but doesn't quite credit) an evolution of elite liberalism.

The CIA—while dismissing any coherent institutional pluralism as unlikely, given the fragmentation of views within each one of the institutions —postulates a dangerous instability arising from national separatism, from recurring political crisis, or from cumulative structural crises. It speculates further that there could well be a Russite fundamentalist response to such instability.

Glasgow University economist Alec Nove also supports the minimal-evolution theory in stressing the unique lack of impact of societal pressures on Russian government ever since Ivan the Terrible sacked Novgorod and the tsars ruled unchallenged by any independent cities, strong guilds, aristocracy or merchant class. It's much more likely, Nove concludes, that the Russian–Soviet "hypertrophy of the state" will prove stable and enduring.

In line with this conservative view, *Le Monde* correspondent Michel Tatu suspects that today's lower cadres and tomorrow's top leaders are even more dogmatic and suspicious of détente than their elders. Similarly, Yugoslav Milovan Djilas thinks (as he told the *Los Angeles Times*) "that the Soviet system cannot change itself", that there is no "possibility of successful revolution or reform", that "it will continue to live as it is until there is a great catastrophe or rot". Gorky resident Sakharov agrees; in a communication to the *Washington Post* after his expulsion from Moscow he declared: "Our totalitarian society . . . is extraordinarily inert. It can rot and petrify for years without any attempt at change."

From the perspective of a Djilas or a Sakharov, then, it would seem visionary indeed to perceive incipient pluralism in the Soviet Union when the very centralized Communist Party still has totalitarian pretensions in its direction of the command economy, ideological purity and social values; when the party keeps an iron grip on all key administrative, industrial, political, social and cultural appointments through the *nomenklatura* list (as the Russian tsars have done ever since Peter the Great established the equivalent "table of ranks"); when the 3 per cent of career party activists exercises comprehensive guidance both of the party and of society; and when party command flows from the Politburo down, with "democratic centralism" forbidding the challenge of contrary opinions.

It would take a real dreamer to conjure up a Soviet Ralph Nader, or even an anti-nuclear power rally in this nation with the worst nuclear accident record in the world and the greatest number of nuclear plants with the least shielding closest to urban centres. It would take an incurable romantic to imagine some grass-roots civil rights movement (or Supreme Court decision) that would overturn ingrained racial habits—or, certainly, any student anti-war movement that would edge the USSR out of Afghanistan.

And yet a question mark must always remain. So much depends on the personality of the individual—now unknown—who will ultimately inherit the leadership that, in the end, Bialer sensibly concludes that no predictions can be made.

At any rate, all the speculation about the future *kto kogo*—who will be Moscow's nominative actor, who the accusative object—leaves my Moscow friends cold. There's one thing only that they're sure of, both dissidents and non-dissidents: they are *kogo* and never *kto*. Their daily frustrations and encounters with obscurantism make them utterly cynical about mass "political participation" and even about increased political consultation of the elites. The rate of change seems glacial to them, the level of intermediate articulation of interests well below that of the intelligentsia in tsarist Russia. They are glad that the party and KGB leave them alone more in their homes (though they still unplug the telephone if conversation takes a sensitive turn). But they don't entertain much hope that their children or even their grandchildren will be able to live more honest and satisfying lives intellectually and spiritually. And it doesn't even occur to them to ask if their grandchildren will lead more satisfying lives politically.

When I showed a Hough article on incipient pluralism to one very non-dissident scientist whose institute is among those the party turns to for empirical help, he thought the notion so bizarre that he could hardly discuss it. He is the one who tells me he never knows how or why decisions are made even about internal affairs in his own institute; he is the one who counsels me to read *Nineteen Eighty-Four* to see what Russia is really like.

As for the man in the street, none of the intellectuals expects any demand at all for a greater political voice from this quarter. Any popular aspiration for greater dignity and a say in one's own fate is too easily diverted into anti-Semitism, xenophobia, or the potato-line substitute of demanding equal discomfort for those stuck-up eggheads with reformist fantasies. The *gegemon* is satisfied with bread and the security of no confusion of competing ideas. He revered Stalin for lowering prices. The rest is indifference and *meshchanstvo*.

More caustically, logician Alexander Zinoviev concludes in *The Yawning Heights* that even Khrushchev's relaxation of intellectual life led not to freer thinking or to broader initiative, but only to a "Period of Perplexity". Corruption, bureaucratism, and official arrogance proved not to be an imposition, but the natural state of affairs. A dab of fictitious power proved to be enough flattery for the masses to ally themselves with the authorities against anyone with troubling new ideas.

It was in this period [wrote Zinoviev], that it became clear that the ideological monolithism of Ibanskian society was an organic phenomenon which could develop even in the absence of constraint. In the Boss's epoch the authorities feared that if the reins were slackened then Ibanism would crumble. They themselves did not believe in its all-conquering strength nor in its youth. They themselves believed it to be the product of oppression and enforcement from outside, since historically it had indeed been imported into Ibansk. The Period of Perplexity revealed that Ibanism would have survived even without oppression and that it would have prospered even without any imports from abroad. For Ibanism is the organic product of this society.

*

Once upon a time—back in that linden-fragrant summer of 1968—I would have dismissed Zinoviev's savage exaggerations out of hand. My change of heart came with a 2.30 a.m. phone call on August 21. "The Russians have invaded; don't call me back," Vladimir said without identifying himself, and hung up. And then I heard the Soviet AN-12s flying in low to land at Ruzyne airport.

Like every other Praguer, I walked downtown in a daze to witness the unthinkable. There they were, alien tanks with white stripes painted on them to distinguish them from their Czech twins, incongruously leaving tread tracks on the cobblestones in front of the baroque façades.

The Czechs were angry, incredulous—and peaceful, except for some initial stone throwing and burning of five tanks. The Czechoslovak government, fearing a bloodbath like Budapest's in 1956, ordered its citizens not to fight. And the Czechs and Slovaks, who had suddenly come to trust their government in the past seven months, obeyed. Instead of battling with the invaders, the Czechs argued with them, in Russian.

It was crazy, they explained to the Soviet gunners. The Czechoslovaks were the only Eastern Europeans who still—until the invasion—liked the Russians. Their search for a compassionate "socialism with a human face" was intended to benefit Russians as well as Czechoslovaks, by example.

One youth bared his chest to the nozzle of a tank gun. One veteran of World War II went up to a Soviet guard, compelled him to shake hands, then demanded to know why he was doing this to brothers, friends, and war comrades. Everyone chalked his emotions on walls. "Ivan go home." "The Russian circus is in town again." "Lenin, wake up, Brezhnev has run amok." "USSR", with s's drawn like the Nazi SS insignia. "You have technology, but you have no heart." "Soviet people, where are your conscience and honour?" "What do you tell your mother about the dead?" "To the strong the weak are always guilty. [Nineteenth-century Russian fabulist I. A.] Krylov." "Speak the truth, guard the truth, wish the truth to everyone." [Jan Hus, no attribution necessary except the chalice symbol of the pre-Luther Bohemian Protestants.]

In that weird week in which the shanghaied Czechoslovak leaders were held in Moscow half as prisoners, half as negotiators, the only government in Czechoslovakia was the clandestine radio. It commanded instant obedience. When the radio said, remove street signs so the invaders can't find addresses, teenagers ripped off these signs—and in hand lettering renamed every avenue and alley after reform party leader Alexander Dubcek or President Ludvik Svoboda, whose double-entendre name conveniently meant freedom. When the radio said, stall the radio jamming equipment that is being rushed to Prague, railroad workers dismantled some track and parked dead locomotives in the way of the freight train carrying the equipment.

Peasants, when asked the way to Prague or Pilsen by *tankisti*, sent the tanks down the wrong roads. Czechoslovakia's notorious secret police, who in the 1950s had administered the most violent Stalinist purge of any in Eastern Europe, protected reformers. And the Prague workers hosted and hid the Extraordinary Fourteenth Czechoslovak Communist Party Congress that was summoned at the spur of the moment under the noses of the occupying forces. Some 1,219 congress delegates unanimously re-elected the kidnapped First Secretary Dubcek and a clear pro-reform Presidium, and demanded the withdrawal of foreign troops.

The Tolstoyan–Gandhian passive resistance was heroic. And it was futile, except in preventing the Soviet murder of at least one Czech leader (the Jew Frantisek Kriegel) on the pattern of the murder of Hungary's Imre Nagy a decade earlier. Some twenty-two Soviet divisions, to be reduced to five after "normalization", took up posting in Czechoslovakia. Prague's experiment with the quixotic notion that men are rational and decent—and that a one-party state can evolve towards decency—came to an end.

"Yes, this circle is yellow," one Brno magazine captioned a red square on its first post-invasion cover, conceding the return of lies. Vladimir emigrated, and would write the best book on *The Intellectual Origins of the Prague Spring* (Vladimir Kusin, Cambridge, 1971). It was a history book, not a book on current affairs. The Prague spring had proved to be no match for the Russian winter.

While it lasted, the Czechoslovak experiment was one of the most remarkable demonstrations of citizens' political involvement I have ever witnessed, in Russia, America, or anywhere else. A few writers, philosophers, social scientists and party functionaries appealed to their countrymen to redress the murders and persecutions of the nation's Stalinist years. And their countrymen responded. It was a kind of self-fulfilling idealism; intellectuals with no tangible power somehow created out of raw conscience an atmosphere in which a few quirks of history could move the Czechoslovaks from atomization to a sudden reassertion of the nation's integrity.

In the process the memory of the West's Munich betrayal and of the Czechoslovaks' own Nazi and Stalinist collaboration ceased to be paralyser and became catharsis. The silent acquiescence of the past was shocked into eloquent redemption of that past. The least excitable and most pragmatic of the Slavs began to act, in the face of overwhelming odds, as if a man is ultimately responsible for his own fate—even if he lives in a police state, even if his is a tiny nation compressed between behemoths. And they did this with modesty, without self-pity, with humour as well as passion. It was a rare wedding of the moral and political that for a few euphoric months turned the Czech genius for moderation away from indecision and mediocrity to a steady resolution.

It was a time, Czechs told each other, when Schweik met Hus.

The converging of the martyr Hus with the Good Soldier Schweik—the World War I bumbler who cheerfully subverted his Habsburg masters by literal obedience to every command—was hardly predestined. The Communist Party that brought about the confluence had been almost more papist than pope Stalin. It had had no qualms only fifteen years earlier about executing some 300 political deviants, sentencing 80,000 to 100,000 persons to the Jachymov uranium mines and other labour camps (and letting up to 10,000 of them die there), and torturing, firing, or dispossessing unknown numbers of Catholic priests, small shop owners, tailors with two employees, and farmers who made home brew with their grain rather than surrender it to the state. The party had continued its show trials even after Stalin's death. It had had to be prodded by Khrushchev before it made even slight gestures toward de-Stalinization. It was the Communist Party with the least claim to legitimacy in all of Eastern Europe, the one that far from replacing any quasi-fascist regime or industrializing a backward economy, had bankrupted Central Europe's one humane democracy and advanced industrial state.

Yet it was this same party that in 1968 finally responded to the crisis of its own creating with imaginative, radical measures that among other things sharply reduced the party's own power and privileges. It was factional manoeuvring within this constipated party that eventually opened up the entire political system.

Alexander Dubcek—the compromise new party First Secretary whom the various disgruntled factions agreed on in January because he was indistinct and had the fewest enemies—had himself risen to power within the old party apparatus. His one personal issue seemed to be Slovak nationalism, potentially more of a "conservative" than a "progressive" force, in the reformers' cautionary lexicon. By all logic he and the rest of the takeover generation then in their forties should have chosen the less risky course of self-perpetuation, whatever the cost to Czechoslovak society. Especially when Dubcek's predecessor Antonin Novotny and the entrenched old guard fought the new party leadership in February and March, the most likely reaction for the still shaky coalition would have been to reduce reforms to the lowest common denominator acceptable to all party factions.

The predictable did not happen, however. On the contrary, the scope of reform was broadened as the new leadership appealed for support to the lower party organs and—to a certain extent—to the public. When the press and the public then responded with demands to be told the truth about the past, the leaders acceded. Some closet liberals within the party declared themselves. Enough momentum built up to make it opportune for a number of the old party hardliners to jump on to the reform bandwagon.

The evolution was unique among ruling Communist Parties. For all his de-Stalinization and populism, even Khrushchev would have been alarmed by such grass-roots improvisation. He had, after all, kept his secret de-Stalinization speech within the party. And when he saw intellectuals' acclaim for Evtushenko's "The Heirs of Stalin" and Solzhenitsyn's *One Day*, he quickly called a halt to the poetry readings and the publication of prison camp literature.

In Czechoslovakia, however, the situation was quite different. The relations between the creative intelligentsia and the party were at the same time more independent and more intimate. It was the humanist intellectuals, not the hacks, who were by now the moving spirits in the Writers' Union. In bitter fighting they had already wrested enough autonomy from the party to "rehabilitate" Franz Kafka in 1963, to write wide-ranging anti-dogmatic feuilletons thereafter, and to condemn the corruption of power and call for limits on censorship at the Fourth Writers' Congress in 1967. At the same time many of the most fervent liberalizers among intellectuals were still Communist idealists, and when the party began to lean toward reform, they could strengthen the tilt from within.

In their own non-party way Prague students also reinforced the liberal trend. Starting with a good-natured protest against a dormitory power failure one night back in the Novotny days ("We want light," they had chanted) they had gone on to demand the issuing of numbered identity badges to police after thirteen of the protesters were seriously beaten in the demonstration. And when the officers in the Communist youth organization refused to push their demands, the students left the official organization en masse and founded rival groups.

Improbably, the writers and students were also joined in their 1968 agitation for more freedom by the journalists—members of a profession that had previously been more noted for political pliability than for investigative zeal. Reporters started to solicit the life stories of former political prisoners. And the accounts they heard fired their anger and determination to winkle out those who had made the prisons possible.

As one correspondent from the first newspaper to publish eyewitness details about prison brutality described the genesis:

A colleague of mine got the name of a colonel in the Free Czech forces during the war who had been imprisoned [in the Stalinist period] and called him up to ask for a story from him. At first the colonel said no. My colleague assured him he wouldn't mention his name, but nothing would happen to him anyway—nothing could happen as long as everyone spoke out. So he consented, and this article was published in our paper. It was a shock, the first time a war hero had told about being beaten, about things that nobody thought possible, conditions just like in Nazi concentration camps. He gave the names of prison guards who had beaten him.

The next day one of the guards appeared in our office and made a row.

My colleague is a Communist whom I didn't like very much, but he was heroic against the guard. He won all my respect. Suddenly he got furious about the whole thing and began looking for any prisoners he could find. Then hundreds of them came to the paper telling their own stories. They undressed and showed the marks left on their bodies, and they cried when they remembered what they'd gone through.

Soon all the papers began writing about the abuses, and the letters started pouring in. Some said, it's not possible that these things happened in our country, under socialism. So to prove it we asked more people to tell their stories.

Television cameramen went to gaols to confront persons named as torturers and ask for their version of events. The key role of Soviet "advisers" in the Czechoslovak Ministry of the Interior in the early 1950s was hinted at. The first two indictments for murder were prepared against warders. Nervous breakdowns suddenly assumed a high incidence among prison personnel.

In mid-March, Radio Prague announced that listeners could call in questions any time between 8 a.m. and 4 p.m. for answers by experts, scholars, or politicians. Armed with these questions, rash young men in the studios began phoning government and party offices, not excluding the infamous Interior Ministry, to corner discomfited officials on live microphones.

Direct audience participation in radio and television discussion programmes soared. Announcers began apologizing for the unwieldy number of speakers on round-tables, explaining that normally only half of those invited appeared, but that now everybody was turning up.

At the same time Communist Party officials began holding open meetings to answer citizens' blunt questions. Where were these officials when all this illegal repression was going on? (Behind bars, some of them.) What was the party doing now to insure that there would be no further abuse of power? Would freedom of speech, assembly, and movement be guaranteed? Would censorship be abolished? Would there be a constitutional court? Did Jan Masaryk really jump from that Foreign Ministry window in 1948, or was he pushed? (Actually, this question was still too delicate for public meetings, but it did surface very early in the press.)

The meetings lasted for three hours, five hours, seven hours, to standing room only. One gathering was so mobbed that the iron entrance gates to the area were knocked down, and the audience passed the hat to finance a replacement. Overflow spectators who couldn't squeeze into the halls or parks listened to proceedings on radio. Some 90 per cent of the adult population of the country heard the biggest rally at Fucik Park, one rough survey suggested optimistically.

Prague's thirty-eight superb repertory, mime, and music theatres couldn't match the drama on the streets and played to empty houses. Even one sure-fire British rock combo imported by Pragokoncert incredibly lost money.

In the new climate the two vestigial Czech political parties other than the Communists enjoyed a surge of new members as soon as the Communist Party lifted their permitted ceilings. People who were dissatisfied with all of the existing parties formed a proto-political Club of Committed Non-party Members and listened to public pleas for real opposition. Even those who had been victims of political persecution in the past formed themselves into an association they named K-231 after the number of the political-crimes statute.

One veterans' meeting which for the first time admitted soldiers who had fought on the western as well as the eastern front opened with a minute's silence to honour unperson Thomas Masaryk, founder and president of an independent, democratic Czechoslovakia—then went on to call for the resignation of the current president. (Novotny had lingered on in this government post after yielding his party post.) The Anti-Fascist Union, Moravian air clubs, the Union of Czechoslovak Lawyers, the Women's Union—every conceivable organization—began to dabble in politics. New organizations sprang up—the Farmers' Union, the combined church and lay Cause of Conciliar Renewal, the Union of Circus and Stage Performers, associations of engineers, of managers. Existing organizations voted out old officials and wrote reform programmes for themselves. The Union of Consumers' Co-operatives lobbied for restoration of its pre-Communist role in handling retail trade and representing consumer interests.

Workers demanded the recall of the Novotny-backed chief of the trade union organization—and got it. On the local level they agitated for new trade union delegates and a more representative balance of non-party and party representatives—and got them. They formed some new industrial unions outside the official framework. They began negotiating seriously about wages and backed their demands with occasional wildcat strikes.

One Slovak friend of mine instigated a new election of union leaders in his plant local, was himself voted into office, and shortly used his new position to trace a co-worker who had simply vanished one day. The man, it turned out, had stepped in to defend a woman who was being truncheoned by police during a peaceful demonstration and had himself been arrested. Eugen was not able to secure the man's immediate release, but he did get the union to support the man's family in the interim, despite reprisals.

(Eugen was also the one who took the passport that suddenly came to virtually anyone for the asking in 1968, and fulfilled his lifelong dream of travelling to America and the Pacific Ocean. So enraptured was he on first beholding this distant sea that he stood on a California beach just gazing at it for an hour. His reverie was broken by a policeman's tap on his shoulder; a distant passer-by had found his motionlessness suspicious and called the police to prevent the obviously intended suicide. The policeman, relieved that no suicide was in prospect and surprised that Eugen came from Czechoslovakia, quickly shifted roles and inquired if Eugen could afford steak every day in a Communist country. He, a simple American policeman, could afford such a diet. Eugen didn't doubt such affluence, but nothing would do but the policeman had to take him home and personally feed him a steak. A very tasty steak, Eugen related.)

As the final showdown with Novotny approached at the end of March, students conducted street campaigns for their preferred presidential candidate. And when their favourite was not selected, they converged on Central Committee headquarters at midnight to ask Dubcek why the Russian-decorated Svoboda had been chosen instead. Dubcek came to the door and explained why.

There seemed to be no end to the innovations. The police were in fact issued numbered badges. The Greek Catholic church again won its autonomy from the Orthodox church. Ordinary people stopped using the habitual we/they compartments in referring to alien officials. Kiosks began selling postcards of Thomas Masaryk. The procuracy undertook a serious investigation of the death of Thomas's son, Jan. The novelists and poets, having successfully boycotted the Writers' Union's old newspaper that the party had confiscated and turned into a Culture Ministry propaganda sheet, founded a new independent weekly. With a circulation of 300,000 and a readership of at least a million *Literarni listy* quickly became the voice of the progressives.

The party hierarchy began giving such detailed information and so few orders to its bewildered primary aktivs that considerable chaos resulted. The party relinquished its monopoly on appointments to *nomenklatura*-listed positions. It installed a reformer as rector of the Higher Party School. The Central Committee suddenly allowed detailed public reportage of its sometimes acrimonious debates. It approved a reform "Action Programme" that presaged a separation of legislative, executive, and judicial functions, and of judges from prosecution and police. It was a programme that would evolve within a few months to include protection of minority opinions within the party and abandonment of Lenin's hallowed democratic centralism.

The National Front (composed of the Communist Party, the two atrophied Czech "bourgeois" parties, two even more atrophied Slovak parties, and a host of non-party organizations) was reactivated. The National Assembly elected new officers by secret (and very split) ballot, and began acting like a real parliament. The government began acting like a real government and not just an amplifier for the party. The old Ministers of Justice and the Interior were sacked, as were the Procurator General and the Chairman of the Supreme Court. The new Interior Minister—a person who had resigned as Deputy Minister in 1950 to protest the terror, and had himself been imprisoned and tortured for his scruples—began to tame the secret police. The new economic planners charted a market-mechanism revamping of the economy.

Milos nonchalantly collected bold signatures of both Czech and foreign visitors on an apartment door, sure that this permanent record of Western contacts could not again harm him. Josef finally hammered the last shingle onto his country cottage and moved family and dog to it for the rest of the summer. Karel finally managed to wangle the arcane parts he needed to render his 1927 Lancia roadworthy again and be reinstated in the club of classic cars. Radoslav finally managed to find for his jazz combo a compatible eighteen-year-old bassist who did not have a family, therefore did not need to moonlight all the time to make ends meet, therefore could make the number of rehearsals that Radoslav insisted on. Jiri tore himself away from Czechoslovakia long enough to visit kibbutzim in Israel—and would race back to Czechoslovakia, enraged and heartbroken, as soon as someone translated the news of the Soviet invasion to him.

Vladimir, who back in 1957 had been expelled from the Communist Party and fired from his university lecture post after requesting intra-party discussion of Khrushchev's secret speech, began dreaming of becoming a journalist and leaving the translation job he had finally taken (after two years of manual labour) as the only work available for an excommunicate. And Vladimir and practically every other Czech came to assume that the phones were no longer bugged, or to ignore it if they were.

In the Slavia café on the Vltava that had been the nineteenth-century nationalist hangout, Praguers sipped Turkish coffee for hours, devoured the newspapers provided for the clientele, and vociferously debated politics— even in the presence of strangers at the same table. "The gorillas are still around," one fifty-five-year-old warned me apprehensively at the Slavia. But his younger countrymen didn't believe him and plunged ahead as if the gorillas had already been vanquished.

By May Day the traditional parade was a flower-bedecked love-in. Dubcek was obliged to sign endless autographs like some film or football star. A few banners that might have been composed by Schweik ("Long live the USSR—but at its own expense") appeared among the marchers. Old uniforms from First Republic organizations like the Boy Scouts and the Sokol sports club again appeared in public.

One of the best reflections of the atmosphere was the "New Wave" of films that swept Prague. Most of them had been filmed before the Prague Spring actually blossomed. But with their wry boy-doesn't-quite-get-girl, or girl-wishes-boy-hadn't-gotten-her-after-all themes, or pioneering feminism, or peasant adjustments to the occupation of a farmhouse by an urban string quartet, they epitomized the mood of the Prague Spring. *Fireman's Ball, Closely Observed Trains, Loves of a Blonde, Intimate Lighting, The Shop on*

High Street—they all shared the diffidence and that offhand compulsion to decency that marked Dubcek and the era.

There was a constant undercurrent of wonder and delight. Czechs woke up every morning feeling vaguely pleased, then remembering why: the once vanished sense of possibility had been restored. Fatalism and resignation were superseded by guarded enthusiasm. The old adage that "he who does not steal, steals from his family" yielded to the tentative hypothesis that maybe honesty is more useful.

"You might as well be an optimist," Zdenka explained; "otherwise you'd kill yourself."

"It's our last chance," Emil said, "to make up for 1938 [when the Czechs didn't fight the German occupation] and 1948 [when the Czechs didn't resist the Communist coup]." He had a premonition that 1968 might be no more successful, but on balance it seemed better to try than not to try.

One random housewife interviewed on television agreed. "Life is so short that we barely have time to get warm," she said, quoting an old proverb. "It's so short that one gets few chances to help decide the history of mankind by his own voice, his own actions. We are at such a crossroads now, when the voices of everybody may help a little bit.

"Let us speak now and help decide this history so that our children will not be ashamed of us."

In summer 1968 Novotny was removed from the Central Committee and suspended from the Communist Party pending investigation into his role in the political trials of the past. The rehabilitation law and abolition of censorship were promulgated. State compensation was set at up to 20,000 crowns ($3,000 or £1,250) per year for each victim of injustice, with administrative as well as judicial injustice covered. Those officials responsible for the victimization were to be investigated and, after due process, dismissed. The Foreign Ministry reinstated some diplomats who had earlier been purged. The Education Ministry re-employed 295 teachers and 11 professors. The Philosophical Faculty of Charles University rehabilitated some 25 professors. The preliminary report on comprehensive rehabilitation approved by the Central Committee pointed out the "duty" of party members not to carry out illegal party commands.

Public opinion polls that no longer required advance party approval either of the questions or of the answers ("public opinion from above", as the progressives dryly referred to it) showed overwhelming approval for the fledgling pluralism, or "many concepts", as the questionnaire called this phenomenon. And when Soviet pressure on Czechoslovakia to disavow its "counter-revolution" mounted, this pressure only served to strengthen the Czechoslovaks' conviction that they were on the right path. Even the Union of Czechoslovak-Soviet Friendship gave full backing to the party leadership.

The political process unrolled by fits and starts, with much resistance and inertia on the part of the party bureaucrats, especially in the beginning. Novotny and the old guard tried to rally the unskilled industrial proletariat to their side by playing on philistinism and pointing out the risks of unemployment and greater pay differentials under the planned economic reform. For a time this looked like succeeding. But students fanned out to factories to expound the advantages of freedom and truth for all. Various intellectuals went back to reason with fellow workers in construction crews they themselves had been banished to in the dark days. ("Pass me a brick, Doctor," the Prague foreman at what was nicknamed "Scholars" Bridge allegedly ordered one day in the 1950s, and was felled by the shower of bricks that hit him from all the Ph.Ds labouring under him.)

Gradually the centuries-old Czech democratic egalitarianism asserted itself over the Russian-style egalitarianism of envious levelling down. This, after all, was the land where Hus had preached respect for all men in the sight of God. He had required every Christian to read the Scriptures himself, and the Czechs early became a literate people. Peasants had access to Charles University, and they might even (like Hus, the son of a peasant) rise to become rector of the university. The future Pope Pius II, no friend of the Hussites, marvelled at the time, "Any Hussite woman, no matter who, knows the Holy Scriptures better than many cardinals in Rome." The Bohemian tradition of untutored village authors began with Peter Chelcicky, a fifteenth-century mystic pacifist who influenced Tolstoy.

Even after Hus was burned at the stake and his Czech noble followers were wiped out, and early educational reformer Comenius was forced to flee the country, the brotherhood of poet and peasant did not die. On the contrary, in the absence of a native nobility, there was little class gap among the Czechs. When linguists and writers forged a cultural and political renaissance out of the peasant Czech language in the nineteenth century the common people felt themselves part of the awakening. They donated their few coins to build a national theatre—and when the building burned down shortly after it was completed, they pitched in again to rebuild it. And when their nationalism finally led to independence in 1918 the masses revered their philosopher-president (and son of a peasant coachman), Thomas Masaryk.

As they thought it over, then, Czechoslovakia's 1968 workers concluded they had more in common with the reformer intellectuals than with the philistine apparatchiks. They did not have enough dormant anti-Semitism to be turned against the progressives by this kind of diversion. And they, unlike Soviet workers, decided that their intellectuals were campaigning for a bigger pie for all rather than a bigger slice for themselves.

Typically, Ostrava miners invited Prague's gadfly philosopher Ivan Svitak to lecture to them—and gave him much more applause than they gave the party functionaries. Typically, in the middle of a sleepless night a fortnight before the Soviet invasion, Dubcek would unselfconsciously consort with Slovak railwaymen coming off the late shift, and discuss the situation with them in their canteen.

Still, even as late as July, it was touch and go within the Czechoslovak Communist Party hierarchy. The reform leaders insisted on reinstating legality by legal means. They maintained that democratization must be accomplished democratically, with scrupulous regard for everyone's procedural rights. They rejected a reverse purge, even one that went no further than firing the reactionaries from party positions without party elections. Thus it was only after the mid-summer district and regional nominating conferences for the Fourteenth Party Congress that the progressives knew for certain they had won more than 80 per cent of the seats at the forthcoming congress.

This comfortable majority reassured the Czechoslovak reformers—and alarmed the Russians. The Soviet Union again warned the Czechoslovaks to halt their "counter-revolution"—and advertised their concern by conducting Warsaw Pact manoeuvres in Czechoslovakia and postponing the departure of their troops.

In the ensuing war of nerves the Prague leadership calculated that the Soviet demands were negotiable. 1968 was not 1956. The cautious Brezhnev was not the impulsive Khrushchev. The Soviet Union was seeking détente with the West and would not jeopardize this by a repetition of the invasion of Hungary. And the Soviet Union had already shown its understanding of more subtle means than tanks in dealing with the restive Poles.

Moreover, the Czechoslovaks were being punctilious in not repeating the two Hungarian mistakes of displacing the Communist Party and withdrawing from the Warsaw Pact. They were eschewing any overture to West Germany that could be misinterpreted. They bore no animosity toward the Russians as the Hungarians and Poles did, and therefore saw no reason for the Russians to be worried about their defection.

Besides, the Czechoslovak party leaders and especially Dubcek—a convinced Communist, son of a convinced Communist who had sold all his belongings and emigrated to the Soviet Union to help build the promised land after the revolution—genuinely believed that the Czechoslovak experiment would benefit the Soviet Union. The Czech economic reform, which was similar to the abortive Soviet market socialism of 1965 but more far-reaching, would lift both the Czechoslovak and Soviet economies out of the doldrums. Moral restitution for Stalinist crimes would quicken humanity and conscience in both countries. Tolerance of a diversity of views—this would come more slowly in the Soviet Union, to be sure, but it would come—would release that creative innovation so essential for any society. "Socialism with a human face," recapturing Marxist idealism, would be an antidote to the regimentation of the East as well as to the alienation of the

West. Far from weakening Communist Party leadership, the Czech reforms would popularize and strengthen it.

Prague's gloss went unappreciated in Moscow. The Soviet Union, with the co-signature of other Warsaw Pact members, issued an ultimatum. The Czechoslovak party reassured the Russians, clarified misunderstandings (as it still viewed them), and stood by its liberalization. And for the first time Dubcek—who before this had relied on quiet conciliation with the Russians—appealed openly to his nation's public to support him in the skirmishing with the Soviet Union.

It was an exhilarating time. With no demon figure, with no charismatic leader or mesmeric monism, the Czechs and Slovaks still rallied as they had rallied only once before in this century, when Masaryk won their independence in the aftermath of World War I.

"We're with you; be with us" became the quiet slogan of public trust in Dubcek and the Communist Party. Petitions of encouragement to the Czechoslovak leadership were signed in institutes, in villages, on makeshift tables at "Hyde Park" in downtown Prague, where amateur orators argued man's moral and political responsibility. One million out of Czechoslovakia's fourteen million signed one reform manifesto alone, the famous "Two Thousand Words"; another million signed equivalent statements. The original "Two Thousand Words" appeared in *Literarni listy* on a Thursday; by Saturday afternoon the trade-union newspaper *Prace* had received letters from 14,000 readers, with all but four approving the manifesto. For the first time whole collectives of workers in factories publicly backed the Prague Spring, and delegations from large plants in Prague visited newspaper offices personally to present their petitions. In many factories workers began putting in extra shifts and contributing their overtime wages to a Fund for the Republic that someone suddenly proposed. Families with little enough for themselves donated old jewellery and watches to a voluntary gold collection. Three million dollars was amassed.

In Sastin in western Slovakia Catholic pilgrims to St Mary's celebrated a mass for Communist First Secretary Dubcek. In Martin, the old centre of Slovak nationalism, the townspeople waited for the Czech President Svoboda to come out of meetings in order to touch his arm or clothes, as one might a saint. In Prague, one frail elderly woman went to the Hradcany Castle Spanish Hall during a Central Committee debate to give a carnation to the National Assembly Chairman and a rose to Dubcek.

In all of my conversations I never met anyone who opposed the Prague Spring. Everyone I talked to, whether burly CKD labourer, masseuse, seventy-eight-year-old French tutor, South Moravian sawmill worker, almost blind Slovak potter, old woman in rubber-soled shoes peddling flowers in a Prague restaurant, tobacconist, fruit stand operator or tram driver, shared the common pride and resolve.

In the Czechoslovak media in this period the Soviet adversary was not castigated; the Soviet Union was in fact mentioned as rarely as possible. *Literarni listy* caricatured anonymous tanks, however, in a way that reportedly incensed the Russians even more than the weekly's insouciantly reformist prose. The cartoon gallery included playful tanks and useful tanks, soaring tanks suspended from telephone wires like some monorail, and obverse earthbound tanks whose spars upheld electric wires, tanks utterly shorn of menace or dignity. In every frame the daisies, by some stroke of floral ingenuity, or more often by sheer innocence, always managed to prevail over the armour.

Armed with these cartoons, students packed the Old Town Square, where the last Czech nobility had been executed under the Gothic town hall tower, to sing Hussite hymns. Here the medieval caravans had converged from east and west to trade their slaves, furs, and metals. Here in the Romanesque beer cellars town and gown had clashed. Here in the spired Tyn church Jan Hus had once preached his heresy. A stone's throw away Rabbi Löw had evoked his golem, Mozart had conducted the premiere of *Don Giovanni* in the Tyl Theatre, Kafka had sensed terror in the crooked alleyways, Schweik had dyed the coats of favoured mongrels and gorged them on brandy to boost their morale (and fetch pedigree prices).

When Prague's cosmopolitan Charles IV was inheriting the Holy Roman Empire and founding the fourth oldest university in Europe, the Tatars were ravaging Russia. When Prague was acquiring its Renaissance loggia and Reformation fascination with the individual, Ivan the Terrible was founding his personal *oprichnina* terror squads. When Bohemian burghers were erecting their disciplined baroque townhouses on ancient Romanesque foundations, Peter the Great was turning a Baltic swamp into the Italianate jewel of St Petersburg—and having his son tortured to death, various wives imprisoned in nunneries, and one cast-off wife's rather unsuccessful lover broken on the wheel. When Thomas Masaryk was running a model democracy, Stalin was butchering more of his own subjects than Czechoslovakia's entire population.

The hymn-singing students in the Old Town Square, being Czech, didn't fully believe that the pen is mightier than the sword that summer of 1968. But, being Czech, they chose to act as if it were, with Prague's stone palimpsest of history as their witness.

"We thought," Josefa reminisced after the Soviet invasion, "that we would free Russians as well as ourselves. We didn't realize: the Russians don't want to be freed."

13.00 Bam

I head for the dining car again, and this time obligingly sit at a vacant table. I draw the line at policing myself, however. Three times in a row incoming Russians triumphantly spot the empty chairs at my table and seat themselves. Three times the waiter orders them to another table or back into the waiting line. All leave obediently, even the cripple who is moved to a seat crammed on top of so many kitchen supplies that he can't get his legs under the table. I have the crystal bread goblet, the cut phlox, and the passing scenery to myself.

A wave of pessimism engulfs me. If no one resists the petty tyrants, who then will resist the grand tyrants? The Russians' endurance and adaptability are superhuman. They are awesome. They are admirable. They make for superb novels that within a few decades of the Russians' taking up this new art form become world classics. They make for ice hockey teams that within a few years of the Russians' taking up this sport become the monotonous world champions—perennially seconded (and in one fairytale year actually bested) only by the dogged, tiny, non-Arctic, temperate, improbable Czechoslovaks. But the Russian forgiveness and tolerance of suffering have also made the Russians endure and perpetuate the scourges of an Ivan the Terrible and a Stalin. Like Nadezhda Mandelstam, I wish that just once, instead of patiently adapting, the Russians would scream.

I take out my frustration by ordering the Baikal Lake speciality of omul fish that I see listed (with a price filled in, meaning it should be available) on the signed menu. The waiter is astonished, and when I point it out gazes wonderingly at the carbon smudged name. "Somebody must have put it there as a jest," he decides. I settle for greasy solyanka.

Our train makes an unscheduled stop here at Bam, and several railroad workmen swing on board to hitch a short ride to Skovorodino. They are bluff, loud, self-contained. They joke among themselves and—apart from scanning the passengers for any pretty girls—pay no attention to the effete intruders who are only momentarily passing through their Siberia. They are building the Eastern end of the "project of the century"; a spur of track goes north from here 75 miles to Tynda to link up with the BAM Railroad, then continues north another hundred miles to Neryungri.

When it was inaugurated in 1975, this "Little BAM" spur was one of the special triumphs of this whole extraordinary line. It is short in distance, but it cuts through the Stanovoy Range that is the north-south watershed. Its seven-tenths-of-a-mile-long tunnel under the Stanovoy crest is the world's first tunnel ever completed in permafrost. In addition, Little BAM required the construction of 58 bridges and 180 other unidentified "structures" in the permafrost.

I have chatted with other BAM workers like these men (no thanks to the Soviet press officers, of course, who besides arranging special mid-week holidays for labourers on the sites we visited, quickly herded us back onto our quarantine bus every time we managed to discover the exceptional

non-holidayed worker and converse for a few minutes before being discovered). The riveters and assembly-men we did meet complained good-
naturedly about the poor housing, and especially about the dearth of fresh
vegetables and fruits; these, apparently, were the treasonous words the
authorities were so anxious to shield us from. But the workers also talked
with considerable animation about their life in Siberia. The work is
strenuous. It's cold. But with their own hands they are transforming this
virgin forest. They are proud of their accomplishments.

Many won't last out the three years of their contracts, and will forfeit their
pay incentives. Some will stick out only the three years, then turn their
savings into a car back in their native Moldavia or Dagestan. But others will
stay on to become permanent Siberians, hunting and fishing on weekends,
wolfing down those slivers of raw frozen fish and vodka at the slightest
excuse for a celebration, shucking off the excessive constraints of the more
bureaucratized civilization west of the Urals.

The adventure and heroism and macho of Siberia are all part of the official
propaganda, of course. *Pravda* ritually praises the heroic sacrifice of its
idealized Arctic and Siberian workers. A state medal "For the Construction
of the Baikal-Amur Mainline"—one that, unlike most Soviet awards, may
be inherited—was instituted in the late 1970s.

But outside of Moscow there is a lot less cynicism about this kind of thing
than a Western city dweller (and convert to the virtues of zero growth) might
assume. Especially in such a slow-growth country, economic development
still has a strong aura of romance. The engineer who guides a hovering
helicopter to top an impossible bridge in boggy, seismic permafrost feels a
sense of accomplishment. The truck operator who removes two hundred
tons of a coal mountain at one go feels the thrill of raw power. The party
secretary who manages to browbeat his suppliers into sending the pre-fab
housing sections in time to keep his workforce from living in tents (and
probably vanishing) knows he is fulfilling an essential task. The Voroshi-
lovgrad designer who puts together the world's first 8,000-horsepower gas
turbine engine for the demanding BAM route is proud of his feat. And when
these feelings are reinforced by incomes that prove both a man's worth and
his rise in the living scale (in vacations and motorboats if not in meat,
vegetables and ballet), so much the better.

The American Pioneers knew very well this kind of pride in the 1870s. The
Soviet subway and power-plant builders—and the poets who paeaned
factory whistles and the first electric light bulbs—knew this same pride in the
twenties and thirties. The Russian patriots knew it as they finally beat back
the Germans against overwhelming odds in the Forties. Today's domestica-
tion of Siberia may yet join Russian patriotism as the popular legitimation of
the regime.

13.29   *Skovorodino*

Since we have a fifteen-minute stop here, Nina and I go to buy ice cream. Others, uttering the magic words "exact change", cut in at the head of our line. But we are in no rush. It's pleasant just to stand upright on solid ground for a few moments.

I tell Nina about some California junior high schoolers I met who had studied a year of Russian and were touring the Soviet Union. They were having a lark discovering that they really could be understood, could buy shashlik when they got hungry and figure out the way back to meeting places after getting lost in unpredictable buses. They revelled most of all, perhaps, in just being away from home. The hotel room I interviewed them in was an anthropological treasure trove of old bottles and cups, Intourist brochures, paperbacks, matryoshka dolls, dirty, unmatched socks, shirts, and general debris on a scale I would have thought would have taken an American teenager at least a month to accumulate in his own bedroom at home.

The California laid-back faculty guide maintained discipline in those areas that really mattered—no hard liquor, no black-market roubles—and for the rest let the kids behave as they pleased. It worked well. Only once had there been any trouble; their departure was delayed from one city because of a missing room key. In that case the teacher simply had all the kids dump their suitcases out in the hotel lobby until the vagrant hunk of metal declared itself with a clunk.

The kids liked Moscow's ornate marble subways ("just like a bank," observed one boy). They liked the glasses at "gassy water" vending machines—you slosh in a bit of water upside down to wash them, then you drink and replace them over the nozzle. They didn't much like the identical distance between the identical trees on the road into Moscow from the airport. Nor did they like the constant reprimands they got from Russian strangers, to sit up straight, or take their feet off the seat in front of them at the movies, or cut their hair (the boys) because they "looked like girls".

But most of all they were puzzled. Where had the Russians hidden their own teenagers away? There were no hamburger joints, no jeans shops, no California subculture hangouts. The outside doors of the cafés were locked at night, and you apparently had to be some Komsomol hotshot to get inside. When they met young Russians and Ukrainians for discussions arranged by their Soviet hosts, their counterparts were always six or seven years older than they were. And there weren't even very many kids to be seen on the streets.

So where do all the teenagers hide out? I ask Nina. How come the Californians couldn't find any? She guesses they were at home studying— but that couldn't have been the case, since it was the end of summer. Then maybe they were away at summer camp? But since school was beginning the next day, this doesn't seem likely either. We never do figure out where the kids could have disappeared to, or where the Americans should have gone to meet their cohort.

Nina herself has never got to know any students from other countries. The Komsomol, which she has just joined, organizes trips to East Germany or Czechoslovakia sometimes, but those generally go from Moscow or Kiev. Her Komsomol chapter has never gone anywhere.

Perhaps Nina is well off. What little I've heard about those Komsomol trips to Eastern Europe has been disastrous. Alyosha went on one Soviet-Polish friendship visit on which a couple of the Poles' suitcases got stolen on the train. Some of the Komsomol student leaders, it turned out, had made the heist, so the whole thing was hushed up, the thieves were never punished, the Poles never got their things back—and a crushed Alyosha never got anywhere with the glamorous Polish girls. And Vadim—who on a trip to East Germany stayed in his room winning money at cards instead of attending the obligatory meetings for solidarity with Vietnamese and oppressed Africans—got grounded for his frivolity, and was barred from visiting any fraternal country again for several years thereafter.

I inquire if Nina had fun in the Pioneers she has just graduated from and what she liked best. Her favourite activities were folkdances and parades, and sometimes marching and standing guard like real soldiers at an eternal flame to the war dead.

Nina didn't have especially high grades, so would not have been steered to election as a Pioneer chairman. But I'm sure she faithfully wore her red neckerchief all the time, and did her share of the routine tattling on misbehaving schoolmates for their re-education. She probably thought that the Pioneer leaders themselves decided which students to single out for scolding rather than getting their directions from teachers. She no doubt found the public shaming of bedwetters at camp completely normal.

When she gets a little older Nina would like to be a Komsomol volunteer on the BAM Railroad if they are still building it. Tanya encourages this, remembering rather dreamily her own Komsomol days breaking-in the Kazakhstan virgin lands. Nina isn't keen about facing the swarms of gnats or having her hair freeze to the pillow from her own breath in tents, but she thinks she could cope with the vicissitudes. She's seem the BAM patches that some of the older Komsomol members wear on their jackets, and she's heard some of the songs they sing with their guitars about the railroad, and it sounds exciting.

14.05   Never

Siberia's one long-distance paved road (other than the *trakt* alongside our railroad) begins here. The road heads directly north, intersects the BAM mainline at Tynda, crosses the Stanovoy range, then presses on through

Neryungri, Aldan, Yakutsk, Oymyakon, and Elgen, to curl down at last over the Kolyma Mountains to Magadan on the Sea of Okhotsk.

Along it tough truck drivers convoy food, hay, and petrol from here 2,000 miles to the northeast, then return through the blizzards with precious gold from the Soviet Klondike. In summer the road bakes in Riviera heat. In the eight months of winter at Oymyakon it traverses the coldest spot on earth. In the January average of −58 degrees F tyres split, engines freeze, and forged steel becomes brittle; trucks are usually left running overnight.

The wilderness along this road is rapidly being tamed. Neryungri, on the other side of BAM, didn't exist in 1975. But by the early eighties it had a population of some 20,000 bursting out of its sooty wooden houses and was on its way to becoming the centre of the biggest "territorial industrial complex" east of Baikal. Its base of industry is a prodigious seam of 430 million tons of coal packed into six square miles, with six billion tons of iron ore and perhaps 13 trillion cubic metres of gas nearby, and rich non-ferrous ores farther away.

I never made it to Neryungri on my Yakutsk trip. We were scheduled to go there, but a blizzard prevented even our hardy Yak plane from flying in. The nearest I got was Aldan, on the first visit to this gold mining centre permitted to American journalists. Since the Yakut Gold Mining Trust officials we met around the inevitable green baize-covered table declined to answer all questions about their operation—their yearly output, methods of refining, transport, or effectiveness of a river dredge we were shown that was idle while waiting for repair—we were mystified as to why we had been taken there at all.

The best we could do was to get our very gold-toothed mining engineer host to tell us a very chaste tale about the discovery of gold in Aldan in 1923. A Yakut prospector named Mikhail Tarabukhin, it seems, found a stream that yielded a huge 15 to 20 grams of gold per pan. At just about this time the Moscow government, having finally won the civil war and smelling gold in the area, outfitted a search expedition of its own. The expedition happened upon Tarabukhin as he was washing his pan in his tent, and the selfless Tarabukhin immediately donated his stake to the government, receiving two government orders in return.

Toothy gold smile and end of yarn—except for the important addition that Aldan District's 70,000 inhabitants now have 833 automobiles and 3,000 motorboats, and half the population now watches television programmes relayed by satellite. No vulgar shootouts, no claim jumping, no skeletons of labour-camp miners, and no mention that the Yakuts—the second largest Siberian nationality, with a highly developed culture of their own—fought the Bolshevik Russians tooth and nail in the civil war. No mention either, of course, that long after the civil war Yakuts resisted forced de-nomadization and the collectivization of their reindeer herds with massive slaughter of the animals. To this day the herds have still not recovered their 1929 pre-collectivization levels.

We did learn that in the two generations since the Bolsheviks broke up the Yakuts' traditional clan hierarchy, the Yakuts have gained a much higher standard of health, literacy and general education, and that in 1956 Yakutsk acquired a university which automatically accepts any native Siberian student with a passing C average. The Yakuts' share in the new industrial jobs of the 1980s is still very small in proportion to the immigrant Slavs. But it is growing, and it is already greater than that of any other native Siberians.

Not surprisingly, our Yakutia trip did not take us farther east on the Never–Yakutia–Kolyma road, where the ghosts of the past are at their most violent. To Russians the name Kolyma is as sinister as the name Auschwitz.

Kolyma was not a single camp, but a complex of at least 120 major camps—including Oymyakon, Elgen (the Yakut word for "dead") and the Magadan headquarters—that constituted the NKVD's Far Northern Construction Trust Dalstroy. Poet and terror-researcher Robert Conquest estimates, conservatively, that three million prisoners died in Stalinist times in Kolyma alone. Only one out of fifty, or possibly a hundred, survived. From 1937 until Stalin's death, as one camp commandant stated openly, the major aim of the camps was less to mine gold than to kill off the prisoners. Twenty—or at most thirty—days in the gold mines, working twelve to sixteen hours a day on starvation rations, sufficed. The average cost of one kilogram of gold was one human life.

Eugenia Ginzburg was one of the few to survive Kolyma.

Like all the other prisoners, Ginzburg entered this hellhole at the seaport of Magadan. The Never–Magadan road was not yet constructed—prisoners would build it from scratch—and there would not have been enough trucks to transport the millions of convicts even if there had been a road.

Unlike many other Kolyma prisoners, Ginzburg at least had a few weeks in the Vladivostok transit camp to recover from the debilitation of her month-long Trans-Siberian rail trip before setting out on this, her first sea voyage. Her recuperation did not prevent her from becoming ill and losing consciousness for two days on the boat, but it did prevent her from dying altogether. Others were not so fortunate.

Ginzburg's passage with 6–9,000 other prisoners in the hold of the Dutch-built SS *Dzhurma* was relatively uneventful. Routinely, she and her sister political prisoners were initially robbed of their bread and their few bundles by the animal-like, tattooed women criminals packed in with them. Perhaps uniquely, however, one of their own number so hypnotized the criminals with her own hard swearing and forceful personality that the criminals returned the bread and rags.

No men criminals were turned loose on Ginzburg's load of women prisoners to rape them, as happened with other boatloads. No prisoner that

Ginzburg was aware of was thrown to the sharks on her voyage. None was boiled alive (as some were a fortnight later when a fire broke out on the ship Ginzburg's former Yaroslavl cellmate travelled on). None was hosed with seawater and then left to freeze, as happened repeatedly on other prison transports.

So calm was the passage, in fact, that the captain and crew could enjoy a Saturday-night foxtrot, presumably in the company of specially selected women prisoners whose reward was a real meal, a real shower, and real bed sheets for the first, and last, time in years. (This presumption must be drawn from the accounts of other survivors of the Middle Passage; Ginzburg could hear the foxtrot music in the sick ward but could not see the company involved.)

As a final grace, when the SS *Dzhurma* arrived in Magadan, the bay had not yet frozen, and the prisoners could disembark on land instead of having to drag themselves across the ice to the accompaniment of the waltzes and marches of the welcoming Dalstroy prisoner orchestra on the beach. The ill Ginzburg was in fact carried ashore (as were the dead) and left lying on the shore all night.

Although she arrived after the change that turned Kolyma into a death camp—prisoners were now made to wear canvas instead of felt boots, rations were reduced, daily work hours were raised from four or six hours in winter and ten hours in summer to twelve daily hours officially and sixteen hours in reality—Ginzburg was again lucky in Kolyma. A doctor, fascinated perhaps by the professional challenge of resuscitating such a near corpse, kept her in the infirmary and fed her decent food for a luxurious two months. And once on the mend, she got to earn white bread and sugar by embroidering a cushion for one of the (non-political prisoner) nurses, reading "Sweet dreams Grisha, Sonya loves you".

After the hospital Ginzburg went on the regular labour regime—hacking frozen ground with picks and spades in a −40 degrees wind—and within two weeks she was again on her last legs. But again fortune smiled on her. A criminal trusty stole a wool jacket an incoming prisoner had just given Ginzburg. And since this trusty, "unlike many of her kind, was a high-principled taker of bribes", she paid Ginzburg back by giving her a month washing floors with warm water in the warm guest house—where she could once more earn white bread, sugar, and kasha with fat, this time by doing laundry on the side.

An additional week's work in the canteen built Ginzburg up sufficiently for her to survive the next moves—out of Magadan to the much worse camp of Elgen, then out of Elgen to the much worse virgin taiga. At Kilometre Seven Ginzburg was put to work sawing down trees on low rations, with constantly wet, frostbitten feet. But she found cranberries in the snow left over from the previous year. She lived in a hut rather than a tent. The criminals who were quartered with the politicals stole the politicals' foot-cloths, but did not steal their wood, did not break their bones, did not axe them to death, as frequently happened elsewhere in Kolyma.

Ginzburg never got sent to Mygla, the punishment camp for Elgen, nor to Izvestkovaya, the punishment camp for Mygla. She was never reduced to eating several-days-old horse carcass, machine grease or moss. She never grew hunger crazed, never turned into an animal, growling and rooting around in the garbage on all fours. And, as a woman, she never got sent to the gold mines. The nearest she got to this "human slag" was when she ladled soup in the canteen for the returning miners. Even her own experience had not prepared her for the sight:

> The weird creatures that passed before me, muffled in rags and bits of sacking, with black, frostbitten cheeks and noses covered with running sores, with bleeding, toothless gums. Had they issued from primeval night, or from the sick fantasy of a Goya? I was paralysed by horror.

Kolyma is another subject I don't raise with Tanya. She wouldn't admit to any knowledge of the horror. Or if I cited specific names and camps she might eventually concede that there were camps in the past—but she would assert that they no longer exist and have no relevance to post-Stalin Russia. This argument I have heard from Intourist guides, and most of them probably believe it, for a variety of reasons.

It's true, of course, that today's bustling Siberia is a raw, new society that hardly glances at the past. Neryungri wasn't even a gleam in a planner's eye a decade ago. Most of Siberia's very young population wasn't even born at the time of the NKVD forced labour empire. And those few camps that remain here—their presence is attested to by dissident reports of such incidents as the 1980 death of the eighty-four-year-old Seventh Day Adventist leader in the Tabuga strict regime camp in Yakutia—count for less and less with every passing year in the dynamic, pioneering, industrializing Siberia.

Or do they?

Even discounting the dissenters who are exiled here, Yakutia and Kolyma—and Chita—still contain hundreds of thousands of former prisoners who were released in Khrushchev's amnesties but never formally rehabilitated. These freedmen continue to eke out their lives in Siberia, afraid to go back to their families in Russia (if in fact their families still exist) because they are broken men. These men too are today's Siberians. And Alexander Galich's songs about the Kolyma transport are still sung where Moscow and Leningrad students gather—and still bring a frisson of fear.

The repressed, unexorcized past always lies latent in a land where the secret police stays intact, and willed and unwilled ignorance of that past provides little resistance to its repetition. In Vladimov's metaphor, the camps' guard dogs that now roam this taiga as semi-wolves await recall to duty.

High Stalinism is unlikely to return; surely history visits an Ivan the Terrible on a single nation no more than twice. But until Kolyma is faced, the chill of Kolyma lingers on.

"Once the machine of destruction is in being, it is outside the power of man to control it," warns Nadezhda Mandelstam. "Even when it is only idling, as today, it continues to function in essentially the same manner as before. At any moment, after lying dormant for a time, it could start up again at full speed."

She continues:

> The experience we have had is the only thing that can give immunity—like a vaccine or inoculation. . . .
>
> The trouble is that we continue to hide our experience—it cannot be tapped without making a certain effort, but people have neither the patience nor the curiosity. Best of all would be if we could gradually accumulate powers of resistance to the use of brute force, until the machine ground to a halt and began to rust. But this would be a very long process for people like us with no language, no standards, no light to guide us. All we have is our craven fear.

14.30   Kerak River

Grandmother and Tanya play "Sixty-six", arguing hotly over the cards. Tanya accuses Grandmother of cheating, and Grandmother protests vociferously. They offer to teach me how to play, but I consider it the better part of valour to stay out of family quarrels. I settle down instead with an Anthony Powell novel I have brought along. ("Oh," says Grandmother when I explain that it's part of a twelve-volume English cycle, "just like Sherlock Holmes or Nick Carter.")

At the other end of the corridor four braided six-year-olds who have become best friends on this journey tuck their dolls into bed on one of the tip-up seats. Then, with effervescent giggles at the unsteadiness of the train, the girls practise ballet steps at the corridor barre.

CHAPTER VII
SUNDAY THE SUSPENSE

A. You write a poem out of a certain knowledge which overcomes the odds.
Q. The odds of what? Of accident? Confusion?
A. Both. All kinds. Your basic mistrust of yourself . . . A poem is the closest possible interplay between ethics and aesthetics.

Interview with Joseph Brodsky

And a long road, a long road, a long road . . .

Song by Bulat Okudzhava

0.37 *Belogorsk*

OUR LAST DAY dawns behind dramatic pink and purple clouds. The mountains, permafrost and drunken forest have all vanished. We are on a friendly plain of haystacks and sunflowers. Instead of the split rails and crude frontier cabins of the Siberian hinterland we see picket fences and houses with fretwork window frames. It could be the outskirts of Moscow all over again—minus the onion domes, of course.

As we pull into the train station I rouse myself sufficiently to join other early birds on the platform. Unfortunately, only one kiosk is open, and there is no breakfast bread to be had. The possible purchases are tinned fish and boiled eggs, and the latter are all sold out before I get to the head of the line. I return to my bunk empty-handed.

Grandmother has awakened enough to commiserate with me over my fruitless expedition. She tries to doze off again, since she supposes she won't get much sleep overnight in the Khabarovsk train station. But for once oblivion eludes her. After a month in the Ukraine and a week on the Trans-Siberian she is eager to reach her own home and bed. The few butterflies in her stomach won't let her drift into unconsciousness again.

We pass scattered barley and buckwheat fields that are heavy and golden, awaiting harvest. The lone reapers we see, though, ignore the grain to gather in the last hay, pitching it onto wagons with three-pronged forks and wooden rakes.

The dark clouds converge, and rain spatters our dusty window, rolling off at a thirty-degree angle that registers the languor of the train. It lasts no more than a quarter of an hour before the sun breaks through again and paints a pastel rainbow. It's a good omen for Grandmother's homecoming.

Tanya wakes, and we pool our leftovers for our last breakfast together. She too regrets my failure to find any fresh bread, but we have enough saved from the day before to make a meal. The conductress, spruced up in a fancy lace blouse, filigree earrings, and platform shoes, brings our tea from the samovar and collects the linen. She glances disapprovingly at the still sleeping Nina, and Tanya prods her daughter awake to surrender her sheets and blanket.

Tanya and Grandmother once more enjoin me to "improve myself", to sugar my tea and eat more bread. Otherwise, how will any of the fellows look at me in Khabarovsk? They acknowledge that the younger generation nowadays wants to look "French-style"; the younger generation is certainly different. But in Russia, where everyone eats bread for the first course, bread for the second course, and bread for the third course, how can anyone look French-style? Besides, Russian men like their women well filled out— and yes, Russian women like their men well filled out too.

In the corridor the waiter who won't forget his native mother goes by with his final messplates of mashed potato. He doesn't waste a glance on our compartment.

05.55 Arkhara

Here we are recompensed for Belogorsk's lack of fresh bread. The speciality of Arkhara, we discover, is corn on the cob—a delicacy I've seen nowhere else in all the Russias. "Do you have it in America too?" Nina asks, and I wax nostalgic about August meals in my Pennsylvania childhood, with suppers of the freshest possible corn ("If you trip on the way to the pot, it's too late"), vine-ripened tomatoes and huge tree-ripened peaches with skins that peel themselves.

Arkhara corn doesn't quite match Pennsylvania corn, despite Khrushchev's best efforts. But on the seventh day of the Trans-Siberian it is nonpareil, especially when joined by hot piroshki meat dumplings and little red plums, and consumed under the watchful eye of a silver-sprayed Lenin. There's nothing like it.

One fellow passenger, I notice, ignores the corn altogether. He sprints out of the station and returns triumphantly before the fifteen-minute intermission ends, with two bottles of vodka tucked under his arm. In a half-hearted attempt to curb drunkenness, restaurant cars do not sell vodka, nor do station kiosks. But this is small deterrent to those who are fleet of foot, skilled at sniffing out liquor stores quickly in strange cities, and adept at jumping lines. My fellow traveller (an old and honoured word in Russian, used in its literal sense) no doubt brought enough supplies for the first six days, but not for the seventh. He joins the other dawdlers in swinging onto the moving train as we pull out of the station with our customary slow acceleration.

08.48   Obluch'e

We leave the plain and come into a region of hills. They are fairly steep, but they are evenly forested and look soft rather than rugged to the eye. Here, Grandmother informs me, flies, mosquitoes and gnats are especially vicious.

The station sign at Obluch'e is in Yiddish as well as Cyrillic; we have just entered that curious experiment of the Birobidzhan Jewish Autonomous Region. Back in the days when the British had mixed feelings about setting up a Jewish homeland in Palestine, Stalin established this Jewish National District (in 1928), then advanced it to an autonomous region (in 1934).

The experiment hasn't worked very well. Neither the urban Jews of Moscow and Bukhara, nor the rural Jews of the Caucasus wished to move half-way around the globe. And any number of Gentiles viewed the dispatching of Jews to the wilds of Siberia as punishment rather than promise. One of Nadezhda Mandelstam's ill-wishers—a secret policeman with literary pretensions who moved into her apartment after Osip Mandelstam's arrest—summed up popular attitudes when he swore daily, before evicting her from her own home altogether, "These bitches [Nadezhda Mandelstam and her mother] should be sent to Birobidzhan."

So few Jews actually came to Birobidzhan that they constitute less than 7 per cent of the region's population today. Only 0.5 per cent of all Soviet Jews live here. But still the party secretary of Birobidzhan is ostentatiously Jewish in nationality, if not in religion. And Birobidzhan's crowning glory is a Yiddish national theatre that was founded in 1977, some thirty years after Moscow's Jewish State Theatre was suppressed. This new Birobidzhan Yiddish Musical Chamber Theatre has been allowed to play in Moscow since 1978 (as has Moscow's Jewish Dramatic Ensemble, founded in 1962, but kept off the Moscow stage for a decade and a half for alleged lack of audience interest). So successful are both theatres artistically that tickets to their performances of Sholem Aleichem and contemporary playwrights are said to fetch $100 "on the left".

Birobidzhan's other cultural attractions are less scintillating. The Yiddish newspaper does little more than translate two pages from the local Russian paper. The Yiddish monthly (sent out here from Moscow) runs more to Soviet than to Jewish themes. Birobidzhan Radio confines its Yiddish broadcasting to news bulletins. Neither radio nor television carries programmes in Yiddish (or even in Russian) on Jewish topics. And only a little over two dozen books have been published in Yiddish in the entire period since 1959.

It's a far cry from the early Bolshevik days. It's a far cry even from the rich community life of the *Fiddler on the Roof* shtetl and the renowned Vilnius Talmudic Academy of tsarist times.

09.59   *Izvestkovaya*

Again we see peasants scything grass on the railroad verge. They might be harvesting for private fodder. Or—since this is an area of state rather than collective farms, and family livestock is discouraged on state farms—the muzhiks may simply be fulfilling the campaign in this grain-short year to harvest every blade of grass for the state, wherever it may grow.

We pass more barley meadows, then more birches, those quintessential symbols of village Russia. I visualize Egor, the hero of Vasily Shukshin's novella and movie *Snowball Berry Red*, apostrophizing his beloved trees, tying his citified necktie around the whitest and most graceful birch, hanging his hat on a neighbouring stump, then stepping back to admire this "natty couple".

"Ah, my beauties, standing here all by yourselves at the edge of the field. Well, have you got what you were waiting for? You've finally turned green . . ." He caressed one of the trees. "What pretty dresses! Oh, my little brides, what beautiful clothes you've put on—but you stand here saying nothing. You could have shouted and called me, but all you did was get dressed up and stand there. But now I've finally seen you. You're all beautiful. I must go back to my ploughing now. But I'll be right near by, and I'll visit you again sometime."

Egor, like all of Shukshin's characters, was a drifter, half from the turmoil of Soviet history, half from his own nature. He never settled down, even after collectivization ended, war ceased, and the population stopped its restless migrations. Russia was still being torn painfully from its rightful rural roots, and Egor's muzhik soul was being torn with it, never knowing whether he was peasant or proletarian, thief or philanthropist, debaucher or committed lover, boaster or shy introvert.

Egor, like all of Shukshin's characters, sought the freedom of *volya* and not *svoboda*—a distinction that is as great as that between the differing words for truth. The effete *svoboda* can sometimes have overtones of an almost Western liberal concept of freedom, including elements of reciprocity and individual purpose, fulfilment and discipline. The centuries-old peasant *volya* (meaning primarily "will") is more akin to an explosion of sudden, total escape from intolerable reality. One finds *volya* in vodka, in the bathhouse, in a burst of anger, in irrationality, in abandoning responsibility, in Stenka Razin's doomed but gratifying seventeenth-century serf revolt, in fairytales, violence, miracles, banditry, anarchy, anti-Western Slavophilism, in contemplating the purity of birch trees. Anything less means becoming an "ass-kisser", Egor decides as he quits his cushy job as chauffeur to the collective farm chairman on his first day, and curses himself for apologizing to the chairman as he does so.

Egor gets offended when friends say that cognac smells like bedbugs instead of at least saying that bedbugs smell like cognac. He swears at the moon for shining too brightly and preventing his sleep after Lyuba won't let him into her bed on the first night. He mourns the memory of his mother's cow that a neighbour murdered with a pitchfork because it ate some of the neighbour's hay. He tries to go straight after he gets out of a corrective labour camp, but his old gang of thieves murder him for his betrayal, in a birch copse.

While he lives, Egor (inimitably acted in the film by Shukshin himself) has the most glorious non sequitur arguments in contemporary Soviet cinema. And the dismal orgy he gets the waiter Mikhailych to set up with the only available women in the regional capital is a classic:

"Why is everybody so sad?!" said Egor loudly and cheerfully, as he proceeded to the head of the table. He paused, gazing at them all attentively.

"Yes," he said, the words tumbling out of him. "Tonight we'll tear out our sorrow by its tail! Pour the drinks!". . .

"Spring . . ." he went on. "Soon the little flowers will begin to bloom. The birch trees will turn green." Egor suddenly choked up completely and had to stop. . . .

Egor got genuinely angry at himself. And then the words began to pour out of him, loud and angry, as though a crowd of hecklers were standing in front of him. "You all took me for a fool, didn't you? Three hundred roubles, and I just threw it to the wind! But what if it just so happens that I love everybody today? I feel tender and loving today, like the most . . . like a cow that has just calved! . . . But don't misunderstand me—I'm not stupid and I'm not a fool. And if anyone thinks he can do what he wants with me just because I'm tenderhearted—he'll get a surprise from me. Dear people! Let's love one another!" Egor was almost shouting now and beating himself on the chest. "Well, why are we rustling around here like spiders in a jar? Do you know how easily they die?! I don't understand you . . ." . . .

Egor [began] organizing the debauchers into a choir.

"We'll start up the melody," he said, pulling at the bald man, "and you all over here, as soon as I wave my hand, you start singing 'bom-bom.' Okay, start:

"Those evening bells . . . Those evening bells . . ."

Egor waved his hand, but the "bom-bom" group didn't respond.

"What's the matter with you?! I told you, as soon as I wave, you go 'bom-bom.'". . .

"Those evening bells . . . Those evening bells . . ."

"Bom . . . bom . . . bom." The bells in the tower rang helter-skelter and all off key, spoiling everything. . . .

"You don't even know how to sing 'bom-bom!'" Mikhailych chided them all. "What's so hard about that?"

"Yeah, it came out off key . . ."

"That was Kirill's fault . . . He started too soon."

"Who started too soon?" said Kirill, insulted. "I certainly know you can't hurry that up. Because a bell—first you have to swing it.". . .

"It seems like we didn't deserve to be yelled at—because maybe I don't even know how to sing. How am I going to sing like some canary, if I wasn't even born with a good voice?"

Egor, disgruntled, was reclining on the couch when Mikhailych walked in.

"I'm really sorry, Georgii, that we didn't do it right—with the bells."

Egor was silent for a minute, then asked peevishly:

"And how come they were all so ugly?"

Mikhailych was completely dismayed.

"Well, look Georgii—all the good-looking ones are married, with families. I only got the single ones—like you told me."

Grandmother and Tanya saw *Snowball Berry Red* at the movie theatre twice and cried both times. Nina sat through it once and thought it was boring.

10.17   Birakan

The day hovers between sun and thunderstorm, and we are treated to another rainbow—a double one this time. An especially good omen for Grandmother's homecoming.

And for Russia's? Where does the future lie for this sprawling, incoherent, proud, suspicious country that like Egor is so afraid of playing the fool? With the double rainbow or the storm? With the rainbow, if one believes the propagandists. With the storm, if one believes Lermontov.

At heart the question of Russia's future is as unanswerable as the question an Armenian boy in Tbilisi asked me: Are Americans a happy people? Or the wistful-sceptical one a Russian posed in Leningrad: Is there real freedom in America? Yes and no, Aram. Yes and no, Kolya. Yes and no, both and neither, Russia.

My own image of the Soviet future, I suppose, is humdrum. There will be crises, I'm sure—in agriculture, on the Afghan borders, in the next Eastern European country to grow restive under Soviet constraints. But I rather expect that these crises will trigger a retreat to the old verities rather than a leap to innovation—and that in the absence of any prolonged, disruptive war (or any short nuclear cataclysm) the old verities will let Russia muddle through. The Soviet system, no less than the Russian people, has an enormous capacity to absorb punishment.

I don't believe the new leaders will be so stupid as to resist all change until the pressure cooker explodes. But on the other hand I don't believe they will surrender any more of their own power than absolutely necessary. Over the long run I expect a lurching relaxation—at a snail's pace.

The Georgians and Lithuanians and Estonians—and the late 1980s' 55 million Muslims—will no doubt become bolder, and mount a soccer riot or two that will be quelled by paratroops. Consumers will have better housing and a few more cars, but little meat—and they might even stage a few more isolated demonstrations about shortages at Novocherkassk or the Volga River. The odd Siberian manager will go beyond chafing at irregular deliveries to lobby for more leeway in setting his own product mix and maybe even prices. Various dissident philosophers, historians, novelists and other parasites will continue to be exported to Siberia or to the West. And for all its anti-Western phobia Russia will continue to hold a Eurocentric view of the world and measure itself against the West.

The man in the street—the neglected elderly, the overworked wife, the truck driver who gets shaken down by the police and has no recourse—will continue to be subject to petty tyrants. And they will continue to support the Soviet Union's generous military assistance to the Hungarians, or Czechs, or Afghans, or Poles, or whoever needs it next. The Times-Square marquee in downtown Moscow will continue to cajole in moving lights, "Parents! Teach your children how to use the elevator!" The diminishing number of veterans will continue to put on their chestful of medals every May 9th victory anniversary. Families will continue to have Sunday shashlik cookouts in the woods. Crafty Cheliabinsk mothers-in-law will continue to denounce divorced Moscow sons-in-law to the KGB for their contacts with foreigners in order to prise away the sons' Moscow apartments.

Most Russians will continue to be studiously apolitical and simply ignore rules wherever possible rather than try to change them. The *nomenklaturists* will continue to replicate themselves successfully. The brilliant mathematicians, chess players, violinists, ballet dancers and physicists will continue to be drafted into the Communist Party—and a number of them will continue to hide their membership from their friends as long as possible.

The party probably won't find any new rationale that can recreate the old utopian zeal for the new socialist man, romantic industrialization, and the deified Stalin. High school textbooks will continue instead to stress patriotism and—despite stagnant living standards—the legitimation of rising living standards. The party will continue to be torn between its avowed totalistic, transformational goals (which justify police-state mobilization today and jam tomorrow) and its quotidien function of mediating between bureaucracies (which doesn't justify police-state jam tomorrow).

But Russia will probably be rather more successful than the West in curbing unrealistic material and psychic expectations. It will probably be more successful than the West (though not Japan) in providing the connective tissue of friendships and belonging. The rulers will command ample coercive and manipulative means to reinforce men's mental lethargy and defences against uncomfortable truth. They will find sufficient social cement in traditional awe of authority, the habits of power and paternalism, cynicism, suspicion, generosity, naïveté, *meshchanstvo*, the stability of private lives, and pride in Russian uniqueness and might.

And through it all the time bomb of a new arms race in the hairtrigger 1980s will put Soviet as well as Western as well as Third World survival at greater risk than ever before in history.

This is my vision of the Soviet future.

But who knows? Who could have predicted that the massive Russian army would melt away in desertions in World War I? Or that Lenin would be able to restore the national unity he had so masterfully shattered? Or that the borderland Stalin (like the borderland Alexander the Great, and Napoleon, and Hitler) would subdue the heartland? Or that the Soviet army which had been decapitated by Stalin and humiliated by tiny Finland, would stand and finally repel the Wehrmacht that had conquered France in six weeks? Who could have foretold the murderous genius of Stalin or the impetuosity of Khrushchev or the consensus of Brezhnev? Who would have guessed that Andrei Sinyavsky, a product of the Komsomol, the right university, and Moscow's elite academic ghetto, would turn into satirist Abram Tertz? Or that Tertz, sequestered in the Gulag, would seize inspiration from his compulsory lumbering to write one highly original exploration of Pushkin, another of Gogol, and a third book of ethereal musings that would invent its own form? Who knows what Shukshin's Egor will do next?

I'm sobered by the warning a new Russian acquaintance once gave me at an overcrowded communal table in someone else's apartment: "There's a lot you won't understand here as a foreigner." He shook his head ever so slightly and added, "But there's a lot I don't understand as a Russian either." He began singing, softly, one of those bitter-comforting songs from the Siberian camps he had been in. Several friends at the table joined in, softly.

He and Eugenia Ginzburg and those few others who survived the camps—how did they do it? How did they endure, and how did they keep their humanity while enduring? Here too there must be some clue to the future of Russia.

Of course, they met with some especially benign external factors: Not catching typhus. Not getting sent to the goldmines. Getting sent instead to a virtual resort like Ivan Denisovich's camp, where the prisoners could eat with spoons they had surreptitiously cast from aluminium wire and could work at bricklaying instead of quarrying stone, in −17 degrees temperatures rather than −50 degrees. Or, in the worst camps, escaping "general assignment" in the tundra and taiga and landing instead the less terminal jobs of baker, dishwasher, medic, engineer, locksmith, translator, tailor, barber, glassblower, accordion player, gravedigger. Getting a little medical attention, and the little rest it afforded, each time one verged on death. And, ultimately, being released by Khrushchev—in Ginzburg's case, after eighteen years in the Gulag.

As Ginzburg remembers it:

During the eighteen years of our ordeal, many times I found myself face to face with death, but it was an experience I never got used to. Each time, I felt the same frozen horror and made the same frantic efforts to escape. Each time, my indestructibly healthy body found some miraculous way of preserving the flicker of life from extinction. What is more, each time something intervened, something at first sight accidental, but which was really a manifestation of that Supreme Good which, in spite of everything, rules the world.

Time and again the "interventions" were manifested in mutual help of fellow prisoners.

In Magadan, a deaf German dishwasher protected Ginzburg against rape by the chief cook—at the certain cost of his own life-saving job indoors. In Yaroslavl, when Ginzburg became apathetic and threatened to turn into one of the walking dead, her cellmate nagged her not to give up but to drag herself to afternoon exercise. At Kilometre Seven a real doctor suddenly appeared, one who had been arrested a year after Ginzburg and, most wonderfully, had seen her son alive and well in Leningrad just before his own arrest; he ended Ginzburg's constant exhaustion and hunger by getting her transferred to medical work in the children's home. And in all the camps, Ginzburg observed, prisoners who could see guided by the hand those who were struck with night blindness.

Not everyone accepted the necessity of mutual help. A good number sought their survival at the expense of their fellows, or at the cost of their own degradation. They stole weaker convicts' bread and their less ragged underclothes. They informed on other convicts' contraband homemade tools in return for soft jobs in the kitchen. They maimed themselves sufficiently to be declared (in the less inhumane camps) unfit for heavy labour.

And they, along with the generous and the merely decent, relied heavily on individual ingenuity.

Ivan Denisovich fashioned a hacksaw from a piece of metal and hid it through the searches. Later he could use the saw to repair boots, and trade this service for a bit of bread, maybe even an end piece. Vladimir Bukovsky's fellow convicts contrived to plant an excessive number of lice in the penalty isolator, thus rendering it unusable, at least for the few days it took to disinfect the box. And Bukovsky himself, when he landed at the Swiss airport on his expulsion from the Soviet Union, still had the mattress cover with banned penknife, razor blades, crude awl and ball-point pens, that he had clutched in reflex action as he was hauled without explanation out of his cell in 1976. Bukovsky sorely regretted that he had not managed to leave his treasures behind; they were, he calculated, worth enough bribes for hot gruel to equal three weeks of a man's life.

And what else? What else was strong enough to sustain the survivors in their months and years of hell?

Bukovsky lived on pure rage. He would come out of prison each time furious at the Soviet "regime of utter scum", caustic about former confederates who had abandoned the struggle, were leading normal family lives, and "smelt of diapers".

L., Osip Mandelstam's friend at the Vladivostok transit camp, lived on stubbornness. In Nadezhda Mandelstam's description, he "went around the camp with clenched teeth, stubbornly repeating to himself: 'I can see everything and know everything, but even this is not enough to kill me.' He was single-mindedly bent on one thing: not to allow himself to be destroyed, but to survive despite all the odds." And Nadezhda Mandelstam adds, "I know this feeling very well myself, because I too have lived like that for almost thirty years, with clenched teeth." In Mandelstam's clenched teeth was her husband's lifework that she was determined to deliver to the world, lest the poetry be annihilated with the poet.

Today, in the 1980s, would-be Jewish emigrant Ida Nudel endures by vehemently denouncing the void. She is ostracized by the villagers in her Siberian place of exile; "even children who touched and petted my dog were later questioned by the police," she relates on a tape smuggled to Israel. She has to ward off night-time attacks by some of the sixty knife-wielding ex-cons she shares a hut with—"men who behave like apes," she says. She is discouraged. But she insists on a purpose:

I am weak, as every human being is. I cry, but not as an expression of weakness or sorrow. . . . This meaninglessness is the principal reason for my suffering. Only the knowledge that I helped Jewish people leave the Soviet Union gives me strength and satisfaction.

Some of Ginzburg's sister convicts in Magadan endured by a faith that also denounced the void—or, more accurately, stayed aloof from the void. These devout, semi-literate peasant women refused to commit the sin of working at Easter. They sang hymns as they were punished by having to stand barefoot in ice-covered forest pools the whole day—and, the awed Ginzburg records, they never became ill from the exposure.

And Ivan Denisovich Shukhov, Solzhenitsyn's Everyman, he survived by remaining inconspicuous and inert and living one day at a time. At night

> Shukhov went to sleep fully content. He'd had many strokes of luck that day: they hadn't put him in the cells; they hadn't sent his squad to the settlement; he'd pinched a bowl of kasha at dinner; the team-leader had fixed the rates well; he'd built a wall and enjoyed doing it; he'd smuggled that bit of hacksaw-blade through; he'd earned something from Tsezar in the evening; he'd bought that tobacco. And he hadn't fallen ill. He'd got over it.
>
> A day without a dark cloud. Almost a happy day.

And Eugenia Ginzburg? For her, survival lay in a kind of elemental wonder at each one of those almost happy days. Even in the wasteland of Kilometre Seven she could savour reading and rereading the single miraculously available book. ("The gods lived on Mount Olympus; they drank nectar and ate ambrosia.") And she could detach herself and view her eighteen years in the Gulag almost as an outsider: "During those years I experienced many conflicting feelings, but the dominant one was that of amazement. . . . Perhaps it was this very amazement which helped to keep me alive. I was not only a victim, but an observer also."

Some of her companions did succumb to torpor. But

> By far the greater number actively clung to life. We still took pleasure in the fugitive mists of morning, the violet sunsets that blazed over us as we returned from the quarry, the proximity of ocean-going ships which we felt by some sixth sense—and in poetry, which we still repeated to one another at night. . . . I felt instinctively that as long as I could be stirred to emotion by the sea breeze, by the brilliance of the stars, and by poetry, I would still be alive, however much my legs might tremble and my back bend under the load of burning stones. It was by preserving all these treasures in our minds that we should resist the onslaught of the horrors around us.

I have lived with Eugenia Ginzburg for seven days now, thinking her thoughts, tasting her thirst, listening to her poetry. And I wonder—how well would our little compartment of women have done in her place? How successfully would we have resisted the onslaught of horrors?

Grandmother, with her peasant shrewdness, I would give the best chance. Tanya, I suspect, would not have made it; she would not have found enough interior compassion on the one hand or ruthlessness on the other. Nina—I can hardly judge; she's still a cipher, even to herself.

And myself? Blessedly, barring Armageddon, I'll never be forced to answer that question.

The kilometre signs rush past, recording the distance from Moscow: 8,478, 8,479, 8,480. I toss a conundrum into the air: What will Russia be like in another generation?

Grandmother murmurs, "God grant that things don't get worse." Nina, our only link to posterity, stays silent. Tanya predicts authoritatively, *Vsyo budyet normal'no*—everything will be normal.

It's a pregnant word in Russian. For Tolstoy normality was a curse. ("Ivan Ilyich's life had been most simple and most ordinary and therefore most terrible.") For Nadezhda Mandelstam normality was, after Stalin, an impossibility. ("The only excuse for the behaviour of Soviet people, whether in big or small matters, is that they are mentally sick. Everybody is sick—some more so, because . . . they are born that way, and others to a lesser degree because their psychosis is only acquired. But that anybody could be normal is quite out of the question.")

In today's vernacular "normal" has acquired positive and often even superlative connotations. How are you making out with your thesis, or your cactus growing husbandry, or getting your child into the right school? "Everything's normal." How are the latest cosmonauts doing in space? "Everything's normal." Are you out of your downer? "Everything's normal." After war and famine and dislocation and terror Tanya is expressing the height of optimism when she asserts that in another generation, as now, "everything will be normal."

Oh, I hope so, Tanya! How much I hope so! In this country, on this railroad, normality is indeed the romantic dream.

I think of my last conversation with my schoolteacher friend Volodya in Moscow. He demurred at first from my pessimism about Russia. "What you say is all correct," he began slowly. "It's right logically and rationally. But something is missing. It doesn't have the emotional side: the personal ties, how people take care of each other. That's the important thing. That's what sustains us. That's how we survive.

"Dostoevsky wrote about that. When he travelled in Europe he was shocked by the emotional wilderness there. In Russia, even when he was sentenced to forced labour—especially in prison, in fact—he felt these ties.

"Here people help you live, even in the most difficult times. In a land where law protects men, where the administration is compassionate, where there are no 'floating corks' vulnerable to the whim of authority, this mutual help isn't so necessary. But here it is a central part of life. When Russians leave and emigrate to the US they are homesick for these everyday celebrations of friendship.

"You know the proverb, 'Don't have a hundred roubles; have a hundred friends.' Friends take care of you; they feed you. Even when they have little themselves they give it all away to you, like a dear little mother. This humanity was strongest during Stalin's terror. But it remains true today, among all classes of people.

"The Soviet leaders aren't bad people. They're not fascists. That's where my hope lies. They are Russians too. They know the feeling of love of friends."

Volodya fell silent. The silence grew and gnawed at his words. When he spoke again it was with a different voice. "No. I'm not optimistic either. Maybe in a hundred years—a hundred years!—something will change." He paused again, then added, "I'm tired. I'm very tired."

Outside the Trans-Siberian the lambent northern sun breaks through clouds and suffuses the surrounding woods and houses. Thin birch trunks dissolve in dapples of light. The late afternoon rays reach far under our wheels, and our shadow leaps wide of the train itself. Farmers drive horse-carts home and fetch cows for milking. Villagers sit on benches in front of their picket fences to gossip and soak up the day's, perhaps the summer's, final radiance.

Tanya announces abruptly, "We don't believe in God here." It's a bit of my education about her country that she wants to pin down before we part company. Grandmother seconds Tanya's declaration with the Soviet axiom that the cosmonauts found no God in space. For both of them science in its rigid nineteenth-century materialist sense disproves religion once and for all. The ambiguities of relativity and quantum physics have not yet crumbled that philosophical world for them.

"Do you believe in God?" Tanya continues. She asks out of politeness. But on this train, in this bloodied Siberia, it comes out more as a challenge than a question. When I answer, it is in Ginzburg's words: Yes. In spite of everything.

Tanya, dredging up her long-ago schooling in the abstruse subject of scientific atheism, probes further, "One God or three? That's the difference between Christians and Jews."

"One God." I ignore the Christian-Jewish dichotomies. "But not as a person. Principle, rather, and Love."

I wait for Tanya's dismissal, but it is Grandmother who responds. "Ah," she says lightly, "God as Spirit . . . Perhaps." The canny Soviet peasant hasn't totally written off God after all.

Our theological discussion ends, and Tanya starts singing, in her powerful Russian soprano—arias from *Tosca, Madame Butterfly*, and *Pique Dame*, "I Could Have Danced All Night", "Summertime". Music is like medicine, she comments, strong medicine. Whenever she feels disturbed or upset, she sings, and the bad feeling just melts away. Her favourite music is sad, romantic, languid.

I contribute one Russian folksong I learned from a record, and Tanya informs me, not unkindly, that the song is so passé that her circle refers to it as "coming from the sarcophagus". It portrays a shy village courting, while Tanya's folk melodies tend more to laud the brave Komsomol youth who dies in battle with White Guards in the Ukraine.

Presently the old woman in the next compartment can stand our vocalizing no longer and complains that the noise is bothering the baby in her compartment. "Hmph!" snorts Grandmother, dismissing the busybody, "it doesn't bother the baby at all; it just bothers her! When the baby cries, she probably tells the mama it's bothering us!"

We do become quiet, though, our joint repertoire exhausted. Tanya marches off to the dining car. The limpid dusk wanes, then mellows into twilight.

Five, six minutes pass, and in the darkness Grandmother begins to recite poetry, that lifeblood for her as for Eugenia Ginzburg. Her poems portray homesick lads who dream of their mothers and girlfriends. One of the boys is among alien people who are not from his village; another is at war. The lyrics are sentimental, Grandmother's voice ardent:

> Just wait for me and I'll return.
> But wait, oh, wait with all your might . . .
> Wait when your heart is saddened by
> The pouring rains, the sallow light.
> Wait when the wind heaps up the snow,
> Wait when the air is dry and hot.
> Wait when the rest no longer wait
> For those whom they too soon forgot.

Nina strokes her grandmother's arm.

In mid-strophe our door is flung open. Tanya flips the electric switch on, floodlighting the compartment. Grandmother mutters, "She spoiled the atmosphere," and stops reciting. Oblivious to the shock she has administered, Tanya doles out the candies she has brought back from the restaurant car and relates her vicissitudes in procuring them. We drink our last tea together; all three women drop sugar into my glass, and I no longer protest. We joke that already we are observing the old Russian custom of sitting tranquilly with friends just before a leavetaking.

"You know," Tanya remarks in a valedictory, "this is the first time I ever met a foreigner personally. I thought it would be complicated. But we found out we had the same interests. We have much in common—literature, music and so forth. Instead of finding complications, we grew closer together." She wishes us all happiness and peace in the world. She doesn't invite me to visit her home. Grandmother sheathes herself in a far-off silence.

We weep a few tears and hug each other.

"And this vast expanse is Russia," Dr Zhivago once mused, "famed far and wide, martyred, stubborn, extravagant, crazy, irresponsible, adored, Russia with her eternally splendid, and disastrous, and unpredictable adventures."

A harsh, betrayed, and still promised land. An alien, and yet a familiar, land.

SELECT BIBLIOGRAPHY

This book is not intended for specialists, and I have not wanted to burden it with footnotes. Basically, statistics on economic size and growth rates have been drawn from the annual CIA Handbook of Economic Statistics; other economic statistics from official Soviet sources; population figures from the 1979 census; meat consumption from US Department of Agriculture figures; other agricultural statistics from Karl-Eugen Wädekind's research reports for Radio Liberty; standard of living figures from the 1975 NATO report (with updating) and income distribution from Peter Wiles's book. Military statistics are taken primarily from the International Institute of Strategic Studies' *The Military Balance* and *Strategic Survey*, 1980 editions, with updating. Harmon Tupper's labour of love, *To the Great Ocean*, was invaluable for everything about the Trans-Siberian railroad itself. Among periodicals' material, *Problems of Communism*, Radio Liberty research reports, *Soviet Studies* and *Survey* have been indispensable.

Books

Adams, Jan S., *Citizen Inspectors in the Soviet Union: the People's Control Committee*. New York, Praeger, 1977.

Adomeit, Hannes, and Robert Boardman, *Foreign Policy Making in Communist Countries*. Westmead, Saxon House, 1979.

Akhmatova, Anna, *Selected Poems*, ed. Walter Arndt. Ann Arbor, Ardis, 1976.

Alliluyeva, Svetlana, *Twenty Letters to a Friend*, trans. Priscilla Johnson. London, Hutchinson, 1967.

Amnesty International (Trans), *A Chronicle of Current Events*, No. 54. London, 1980.

Amnesty International Report, *Prisoners of Conscience in the USSR*. First edition, London, 1975; second edition, London, 1980.

Atkinson, Dorothy, et al., eds, *Women in Russia*. Stanford, Stanford University Press, 1977.

Atlantic Council's Working Group on the Soviet Maritime Challenge, *The Soviet Merchant Marine: Economic and Strategic Challenge to the West*. Boulder, Westview, 1979.

Azrael, Jeremy R., ed., *Soviet Nationality Policies and Practices*. New York, Praeger, 1978.

Barghoorn, Frederick C., *Politics USSR*. Second edition, Boston, Little, Brown, 1972.

Beeson, Trevor, *Discretion and Valour*. Glasgow, Collins, 1974.

Bennigsen, Alexandre, and S. Enders Wimbush, *Muslim National Communism in the Soviet Union*. Chicago, University of Chicago Press, 1979.

Berlin, Isaiah, *Russian Thinkers*. London, Hogarth Press, 1977, New York, Viking, 1978.

Bettelheim, Bruno, *Surviving and Other Essays*. New York, Knopf, London, Thames & Hudson, 1979.

Bialer, Seweryn, *Stalin's Successors: Leadership, Stability and Change in the Soviet Union*. New York, Cambridge University Press 1980.

Billington, James H., *The Icon and the Axe*. London, Weidenfeld, 1966, New York, Vintage, 1970.

Blake, Patricia, and Max Hayward, eds, *Half-way to the Moon*. London, Weidenfeld, 1964, Garden City, Anchor, 1965.

Bloch, Sidney, and Peter Reddaway, *Russia's Political Hospitals: the Abuse of Psychiatry in the Soviet Union*. London, Victor Gollancz, 1977.

Bociurkiw, Bohdan, and John W. Strong, eds, *Religion and Atheism in the USSR and Eastern Europe*. London, Macmillan, 1975.

Boorstin, Daniel, *The Americans, the National Experience*. New York, Vintage, 1965.

Breslauer, George W., *Five Images of the Soviet Future: a Critical Review and Synthesis*. Berkeley, University of California, 1978.

Brodsky, Joseph, *Selected Poems*. Harmondsworth, Penguin, 1973.

Brown, Archie, and Michael Kaser, eds, *The Soviet Union since the Fall of Khrushchev*. London, Macmillan, 1975.

Bukovsky, Vladimir, *To Build a Castle—my Life as a Dissenter*. London, André Deutsch, 1978, New York, Viking, 1979.

Carlton, David, and Carlo Schaerf, *Arms Control and Technological Innovation*. London, Croom Helm, 1977.

Carrère d'Encausse, Hélène, *Decline of an Empire: the Soviet Union Republics in Revolt*. New York, Newsweek, 1980.

Center for Strategic and International Studies, Georgetown University, *Nationalities and Nationalism in the USSR: a Soviet Dilemma*. Washington, 1977.

Chappe d'Auteroche, *Russia Observed*. New York, Arno Press and the New York Times, 1970 from *A Journey into Siberia,* London, 1770.

Churchward, L. G., *The Soviet Intelligentsia*. London, Routledge & Kegan Paul, 1973.

Cline, Ray S., et al., *Main Trends in World Power*. Washington, CSIS, Georgetown University, 1978.

Cocks, Paul, et al., eds, *The Dynamics of Soviet Politics*. Cambridge, Harvard University Press, 1976.

Coffey, J. I., *Arms Control and European Security*. London, Chatto & Windus, 1977.

Cohen, Stephen, F., Alexander Rabinowitch, and Robert Sharlet, *The Soviet Union Since Stalin*. Bloomington, Indiana University Press, 1980.

Collins, John M., *American and Soviet Military Trends since the Cuban Missile Crisis*. Washington, CSIS, Georgetown University, 1978.

——, *US-Soviet Military Balance*. New York, McGraw-Hill, 1980.

Connor, Walter D., *Socialism, Politics and Equality*. New York, Columbia University Press, 1979.

Conolly, Violet, *Siberia Today and Tomorrow*. London, Collins, 1975.

Conquest, Robert, *The Great Terror*. London, Macmillan, 1968.

——, *Kolyma, the Arctic Death Camps*. London, Macmillan, New York, Viking, 1978.

Cox, Terence, *Rural Sociology in the Soviet Union*. London, Hurst, 1979.

Des Pres, Terrence, *The Survivor*. New York, Oxford, 1976.

Dostoevsky, Fyodor, *Memoirs from the House of the Dead*, trans. Jessie Coulson. London, Oxford University Press, 1965.

Douglass, Joseph, Jr., and Amoretta Hoeber, *Soviet Strategy for Nuclear War*. Stanford, Stanford University, 1979.

Dunham, Vera S., *In Stalin's Time*. Cambridge, Cambridge University Press, 1976.

Edmonds, Robin, *Soviet Foreign Policy 1962–1973*. London, Oxford University Press, 1975.

Erickson, John, and E. J. Feuchtwanger, eds, *Soviet Military Power and Performance*. London, Macmillan, 1979.

Etkind, Efim, *Notes of a Non-Conspirator*, trans. Peter France. Oxford, Oxford University Press, 1977.

Fainsod, Merle, *How Russia is Ruled*. Cambridge, Mass. Harvard University Press, 1963 revised edition. London, Oxford University Press, 1963.

Feifer, George, *Russia Close-Up*. London, Jonathan Cape, 1973.

Feldbrugge, F. J. M., *Samizdat and Political Dissent in the Soviet Union*. Leyden, A. W. Sijthoff, 1975.

Field, Mark G., ed., *Social Consequences of Modernization in Communist Societies*. Baltimore, Johns Hopkins, 1976.

Florinsky, Michael T., *Russia, a History and an Interpretation* (2 volumes). New York, Macmillan, 1947, 1953.

Frankland, Mark, *Khrushchev*. Harmondsworth, Penguin, 1966, New York, Stein and Day, 1969.

Freedman, Lawrence, *The Evolution of Nuclear Strategy*. London, International Institute for Strategic Studies, 1981.

Friedgut, Theodore, *Political Participation in the USSR*. Princeton, Princeton University Press, 1979.

Frost, Robert, *The Poetry of Robert Frost*, ed. Edward Connery Lathem. New York, Holt, Rinehart and Winston, 1969, and London, Jonathan Cape, 1971.

Gehlen, Michael P., *The Communist Party of the Soviet Union*. Bloomington, Indiana University Press, 1969.

Gessen, A., *Vo Glubine Sibirskikh Rud . . .* Moscow, Detskaya Literatura, 1965.

Ginsburgs, George, and Alvin Z. Rubinstein, *Soviet Foreign Policy toward Western Europe*. New York, Praeger, 1978.

Ginzburg, Eugenia Semyonovna, *Journey into the Whirlwind*, trans. Paul Stevenson and Max Hayward. New York, Harcourt, Brace & World, London, Collins and Harvill, 1967.

—— (Jewgenia Ginsburg), *Gratwanderung*, trans. Nina Schawina. Munich, Piper, 1980.

Goldman, Marshall I., *Environmental Pollution in the Soviet Union*. Cambridge, MIT, 1972.

Gompert, David, et al., *Nuclear Weapons and World Politics*. New York, McGraw-Hill, 1977.

Griffith, William E., ed., *The Soviet Empire: Expansion and Détente*. Lexington, Lexington, 1976.

——, *The Enigma of Soviet Petroleum—Half Empty or Half Full*. London, George Allen & Unwin, 1980.

Hasek, Jaroslav, *The Good Soldier Svejk*, trans. Cecil Parrott. London, Heinemann, 1973, Harmondsworth, Penguin, 1974, New York, Thomas Y. Crowell, 1974.

Herspring, Dale R., and Ivan Volgyes, eds, *Civil-Military Relations in Communist Systems*. Boulder, Westview, 1978.

Hingley, Ronald, *The Russian Mind*. New York, Charles Scribner's Sons, 1977, London, Bodley Head, 1978.

Hodnett, Grey, *Leadership in the Soviet National Republics, a Quantitative Study of Recruitment Policy*. Oakville, Ontario, Mosaic, 1978.

Hough, Jerry F., *The Soviet Union and Social Science Theory*. Cambridge, Harvard, 1977.

——, *Soviet Leadership in Transition*. Washington, Brookings, 1980.

——, and Merle Fainsod, *How the Soviet Union Is Governed*. Cambridge, Harvard, 1979.

Institute for the Study of Conflict, *The Soviet Empire: Pressures and Strains*. London, 1980.

International Institute for Strategic Studies, *The Military Balance, 1980/81*. London, 1980.

——, *Strategic Survey, 1979*. London, 1980.

Joint Economic Committee, US Congress, *The Soviet Economy in a Time of Change*, vols. 1 and 2. Washington, US Government Printing Office, 1979.

Juviler, Peter H., *Revolutionary Law and Order*. New York, Free Press, 1976.

Kahan, Arcadius, and Blair A. Ruble, eds, *Industrial Labor in the USSR*. Elmsford, NY, Pergamon, 1979.

Kaiser, Robert G., *Russia: the People and the Power*. New York, Atheneum, 1976, London, Secker & Warburg, 1977.

Katz, Zev, et al., *Handbook of Major Soviet Nationalities*. New York, Free Press, 1975.

Kennan, George F., *Russia and the West under Lenin and Stalin*. New York, Mentor, 1960, London, Hutchinson, 1961.

Khrushchev, Nikita S., *Khrushchev Remembers: The Last Testament*, ed. and trans.

Strobe Talbott. London, André Deutsch, 1971, Boston, Little, Brown, 1974.

Kirk, Grayson, and Nils H. Wessell, *The Soviet Threat: Myths and Realities*. New York, Praeger, 1978.

Kohler, Phyllis Penn, ed. and trans., *Custine's Eternal Russia*. Coral Gables, University of Miami, 1976.

Kopelev, Lev, *To Be Preserved Forever*, trans. Anthony Austin. New York, Lippincott, 1977.

Kusin, Vladimir, *The Intellectual Origins of the Prague Spring*. Cambridge, Cambridge University Press, 1971.

——, *From Dubcek to Charter 77*. Edinburgh, Q, 1978.

LaFeber, Walter, *America, Russia and the Cold War 1945–1975*. New York, John Wiley and Sons, 1976.

Lane, David, and Felicity O'Dell, *The Soviet Industrial Worker: Social Class, Education and Control*. Oxford, Martin Robertson, New York, St Martin's, 1978.

London, Kurt L., ed., *The Soviet Impact on World Politics*. New York, Hawthorn, 1974.

Mandelstam, Nadezhda, *Hope Against Hope*, trans. Max Hayward. New York, Atheneum, and London, Harvill Press, 1970.

——, *Hope Abandoned*, trans. Max Hayward. New York, Atheneum, and London, Harvill Press, 1974.

Mastny, Vojtech, *Russia's Road to the Cold War*. New York, Columbia University Press, 1979.

Mazour, Anatole G., *Women in Exile: Wives of the Decembrists*. Tallahassee, The Diplomatic Press, 1975.

McAuley, Alastair, *Economic Welfare in the Soviet Union*. Madison, University of Wisconsin Press, 1979.

Mac gwire, Michael, ed., *Soviet Naval Developments*. New York, Praeger, 1973.

Medvedev, Roy A., *Let History Judge*, trans. Colleen Taylor. London, Macmillan, 1972, New York, Vintage, 1973.

——, *On Socialist Democracy*, trans. Ellen de Kadt. New York, Knopf, 1975.

——, *On Stalin and Stalinism*, trans. Ellen de Kadt. Oxford, Oxford University Press, 1979.

—— and Zhores A. Medvedev, *Khrushchev, the Years in Power*, trans. Andrew R. Durkin. New York, Columbia University, 1976, London, Oxford University Press, 1977.

Medvedev, Zhores A., *The Rise and Fall of T. D. Lysenko,* trans. Michael Lerner. New York and London, Columbia University Press, 1969.

Morton, Henry W., and Rudolf L. Tokes, eds, *Soviet Politics and Society in the 1970s*. New York, Free Press, London, Collier Macmillan, 1974.

Murphy, Paul J., ed., *Naval Power in Soviet Policy*. Washington, US Air Force, 1978.

NATO Directorate of Economic Affairs, *Economic Aspects of Life in the USSR Colloquium*. Brussels, 1975.

Nekrich, Alexandr, *The Punished Peoples*, trans. George Saunders. New York, Norton, 1978.

Newhouse, John, *Cold Dawn*. New York, Holt, Rinehart & Winston, 1973.

Nove, Alec, *An Economic History of the USSR*. London, Allen Lane, 1969.

——, *The Soviet Economy*. New York, Praeger, 1972.

——, *Political Economy and Soviet Socialism*. London, George Allen & Unwin, 1979.

——, and J. A. Newth, *The Soviet Middle East: a Model for Development*. London, Allen & Unwin, 1967.

Pasternak, Boris, *Doctor Zhivago*, trans. Max Hayward and Manya Harari. New York, Pantheon, London, Collins and Harvill, 1958.

Pipes, Richard, *Russia under the Old Regime*. London, Weidenfeld, New York, Charles Scribner's Sons, 1974.

Plyushch, Leonid, *History's Carnival*. London, Collins, 1980.

Proffer, Carl and Ellendea, eds, *The Ardis Anthology of Recent Russian Literature*. Ann Arbor, Ardis, 1976.

R.U.S.I. and Brassey's Defence Yearbook, 1977/78. London, Brassey's, 1977.

Rakowska-Harmstone, Teresa, ed., *Perspectives for Change in Communist Societies*. Boulder, Westview, 1979.

Reddaway, Peter, ed., *Uncensored Russia*. London, Jonathan Cape, 1972.

Riasanovsky, Nicholas V., *A History of Russia*. London and New York, Oxford University Press, 1969.

Rigby, T. H., *Communist Party Membership in the USSR 1917–1967*. Princeton, Princeton University, 1968.

——, A. H. Brown and P. B. Reddaway, eds, *Authority, Power and Policy in the USSR: Essays Dedicated to Leonard Schapiro*. London, Macmillan, 1980.

Ryavec, Karl W., ed., *Soviet Society and the Communist Party*. Amherst, University of Massachusetts, 1978.

Sakharov, Andrei D., *Sakharov Speaks*. New York, Vintage, London, Collins and Harvill, 1974.

Schapiro, Leonard, *The Communist Party of the Soviet Union*. New York, Random House, London, Eyre & Spottiswoode, 1960.

Shalamov, Varlam, *Kolyma Tales*. New York, W. W. Norton, 1980.

Shukshin, Valery, *Snowball Berry Red and Other Stories*, ed. Donald M. Fiene. Ann Arbor, Ardis, 1979.

Simes, Dimitri, and associates, *Soviet Succession: Leadership in Transition*. Beverly Hills/London, Sage, 1978.

Simmonds, George W., ed., *Nationalism in the USSR and Eastern Europe in the Era of Brezhnev & Kosygin*. Detroit, University of Detroit, 1977.

Simon, Gerhard, *Church, State and Opposition in the USSR*, trans. Kathleen Matchett. London, C. Hurst, 1974.

Skilling, H. Gordon, *Czechoslovakia's Interrupted Revolution*. Princeton, Princeton University, 1976.

—— and Franklyn Griffiths, *Interest Groups in Soviet Politics*. Princeton, Princeton University, 1971.

Skirdo, M. P., *The People, the Army, the Commander*. Moscow, 1970, Washington, US Air Force, undated.

Smith, Hedrick, *The Russians*. New York, Quadrangle, London, Times Books, 1976.

Sokolovskiy, V. D., *Soviet Military Strategy*. New York, Crane Russak, London, Macdonald & Janes, 1975.

Solzhenitsyn, Alexander. *The Gulag Archipelago*, vols. 1, 2 (trans. Thomas P. Whitney) and 3 (trans. H. T. Willetts).New York, Harper and Row, and London, Collins and Harvill, 1973, 1975 and 1978.

——, *One Day in the Life of Ivan Denisovich*, trans. Ralph Parker. London, Victor Gollancz, 1963.

—— et al., *From Under the Rubble*, trans. Michael Scammell et al. Boston, Little, Brown, 1975, London, Collins and Harvill, 1976.

Stockholm International Peace Research Institute, *Tactical Nuclear Weapons: European Perspectives*. London, Taylor & Francis, 1978.

——, *World Armaments and Disarmament Yearbook 1980*. London, Taylor & Francis, 1980.

Strong, John W., ed., *The Soviet Union under Brezhnev and Kosygin*. New York and London, Van Nostrand, 1971.

Szamuely, Tibor, *The Russian Tradition*. London, Secker & Warburg, 1974.

Talbott, Strobe, *Endgame: the Inside Story of SALT II*. New York, Harper, 1979.

Tatu, Michel, *Power in the Kremlin*, trans. Helen Katel. London, Collins, 1969.

Tokes, Rudolf L., ed., *Dissent in the USSR*. Baltimore, Johns Hopkins, 1975.

Tolstoy, Leo, *The Complete Works of Count Tolstoy*, vol. XXII, trans. and ed. Leo Wiener. London, J. M. Dent & Co., 1904.

——, *Resurrection*, trans. Rosemary Edmonds, Harmondsworth, Penguin, 1966.

Trifonov, Yury, *The Long Good-Bye*, trans. Helen P. Burlingame and Ellendea Proffer. New York, Ardis, Harper and Row, 1978.

Tupper, Harmon, *To the Great Ocean, Siberia and the Trans-Siberian Railway*. Boston, Little, Brown, London, Secker & Warburg, 1965.

US Central Intelligence Agency, *Prospects for Soviet Oil Production*. Washington 1977.

——, *The Soviet Economy in 1978–1979 and Prospects for 1980*. Washington, 1980.

——, *The World Oil Market in the Years Ahead*. Washington, 1979.

US Department of Defense, *Annual Report (Secretary of Defense) Fiscal Year 1981*. Washington, 1980.

——, *Military Posture (Chairman of the Joint Chiefs of Staff) for Fiscal Year 1981*. Washington, 1980.

——, *Program for Research, Development, and Acquisition, Fiscal Year 1981 (Under Secretary of Defense Research and Engineering)*. Washington, 1980.

US Office of Technology Assessment, *The Effects of Nuclear War*. Washington, 1979.

USSR Academy of Sciences, *Atlas Baikala*. Irkutsk, Limnology Institute, 1969.

Ulam, Adam, *Expansion and Coexistence*. London, Secker & Warburg, 1968.

Van der Post, Laurens, *Journey into Russia*. Harmondsworth, Penguin, 1965.

Vigor, P. H., *The Soviet View of War, Peace and Neutrality*. London, Routledge & Kegan Paul, 1975.

Vladimov, Georgi, *Faithful Ruslan*, trans. Michael Glenny. New York, Simon and Schuster, 1978, London, Cape, 1979.

Weeks, Albert L., *The Troubled Détente*. New York, New York University 1976.

Werth, Alexander, *Russia at War 1941–1945*. London, Pan, 1965, New York, Discus, 1970.

Whetten, Lawrence, ed., *The Future of Soviet Military Power*. New York, Crane, Russak, 1976, London, Macdonald & Janes, 1977.

——, ed., *The Political Implications of Soviet Military Power*. New York, Crane, Russak, London, Macdonald & Janes, 1977.

Wiles, Peter, *Distribution of Income: East and West*. Amsterdam, North-Holland, 1974.

Willrich, Mason, and John B. Rhinelander, *SALT: the Moscow Agreements and Beyond*. New York, Free Press, London, Collier Macmillan, 1974.

Yanov, Alexander, *The Russian New Right: Right-Wing Ideologies in the Contemporary USSR*. Berkeley, University of California, 1978.

Yanowitch, Murray, ed., *Soviet Work Attitudes: the Issue of Participation in Management*. White Plains, NY, M. E. Sharpe, 1979.

Yarmolinsky, Avrahm, ed., *An Anthology of Russian Verse 1812–1960*. Garden City, Doubleday Anchor, 1960.

Yergin, Daniel, *Shattered Peace*. Boston, Houghton Mifflin, 1977, London, André Deutsch, 1978.

Zinoviev, Alexander, *The Yawning Heights*, trans. Gordon Clough. London, Bodley Head, New York, Random House, 1978.

Periodicals and Occasional Papers

Ball, Desmond, *The Future of the Strategic Balance*, Reference Paper No. 16 of Strategic and Defence Studies Centre, Australian National University, Canberra, undated.

Berlin, Isaiah, "Conversations with Akhmatova and Pasternak," *New York Review of Books*, 20 November 1980.

Bush, Keith, "Soviet Economic Growth: Past, Present, and Projected", *Survey*, Spring 1977/78.

Coles, Robert, "Victims of Soviet Psychiatry: A Report from Honolulu", *New York Review of Books*, 27 October 1977.

Garthoff, Raymond, "Mutual Deterrence and Strategic Arms Limitation in Soviet Policy", *International Security*, Summer 1978.

Hoffmann, Stanley, "Reflections on the Present Danger", *New York Review of Books*, 6 March 1980.

Lifshitz-Losev, Lev, "What It Means To Be Censored", *New York Review of Books*, 29 June 1978.

Nekrich, Alexandr, "Inside the Leviathan", *New York Review of Books*, 14 April 1977.

Novikov, Jouri, "Kronzeuge gegen den KGB", *Stern*, 22 and 29 March, 6, 13, 20 and 27 April 1978.

Pond, Elizabeth, "Deterring Nuclear War", *The Christian Science Monitor*, 26, 27, 28 and 29 August 1980.

Reich, Walter, "Grigorenko Gets a Second Opinion", *New York Times Magazine*, 13 May 1979.

Shapley, Deborah, "Technology Creep and the Arms Race", *Science*, 22 and 29 September and 20 October 1978.

Simes, Dimitri, "The Death of Détente?", *International Security*, Summer 1980.

Sinyavsky, Andrei, "Interview: Solzhenitsyn and Russian Nationalism", *New York Review of Books*, 22 November 1979.

Sivard, Ruth Leger, *World Military and Social Expenditures 1980*. Leesburg, Virginia, WMSE Publications, 1980.

Sonnenfeldt, Helmut, and William Hyland, *Soviet Perspectives on Security*, International Institute of Strategic Studies Adelphi Paper No. 150

US Foreign Broadcast Information Service, *Analysis Report, President Brezhnev's and the Soviet Union's Changing Security Policy*, 25 May 1979, FB 79-10009.

Wren, Christopher, "Russia in Entropy", *Harper's*, June 1978.

INDEX

Murmansk

Baltic Sea

(R.S.F.S.R.)Russian
Soviet Federated
Socialist Republic

Tallin
Estonia

Lithuania

Archangel'sk

Leningrad

Latvia

Byelorussia

Yaroslavl

Kiev   Moscow

Mendelyeevo

Moldavia

Gorky

Perm

Ukraine

Mordovia

Volga

WES

Sverdlovsk

Black Sea

CAUCASUS MTS.

Volgograd

Tyumen

URAL

Dagestan

Ishi

Georgia
Tbilisi

Kazakhstan

Armenia

CENTRAL ASIA

Aral Sea

Azerbaijan

Caspian Sea

Uzbekistan

Turkmenistan

Kirgizist

IRAN

Tadzhikistan

AFGHANISTAN

500 mile